The Original Compromise

The Original Compromise

What the Constitution's Framers Were Really Thinking

DAVID BRIAN ROBERTSON

OXFORD
UNIVERSITY PRESS

OXFORD
UNIVERSITY PRESS

Oxford University Press is a department of the University of Oxford.
It furthers the University's objective of excellence in research,
scholarship, and education by publishing worldwide.

Oxford   New York
Auckland   Cape Town   Dar es Salaam   Hong Kong   Karachi
Kuala Lumpur   Madrid   Melbourne   Mexico City   Nairobi
New Delhi   Shanghai   Taipei   Toronto

With offices in
Argentina   Austria   Brazil   Chile   Czech Republic   France   Greece
Guatemala   Hungary   Italy   Japan   Poland   Portugal   Singapore
South Korea   Switzerland   Thailand   Turkey   Ukraine   Vietnam

Oxford is a registered trade mark of Oxford University Press in the UK and certain other countries.

Published in the United States of America by Oxford University Press
198 Madison Avenue, New York, NY 10016

Library of Congress Cataloging-in-Publication Data
Robertson, David Brian, 1951–
The original compromise : what the Constitution's framers were really thinking / David Brian Robertson.
p.   cm.
Includes bibliographical references and index.
ISBN 978-0-19-979629-8
1. Political science—United States—History—18th century. 2. United States—Politics and government—Philosophy.
3. United States—Politics and government—1783–1789. 4. United States. Constitutional Convention (1787)
5. Constitutional history—United States. I. Title.
JA84.U5R54   2012
320.473—dc23   2012017136

1 3 5 7 9 8 6 4 2
Printed in the United States of America
on acid-free paper

To my friends and colleagues in the Politics and History Section of the American Political Science Association

CONTENTS

ACKNOWLEDGMENTS

The idea behind this book always was straightforward to me. No book is devoted exclusively to explaining the collective reasoning of the U.S. Constitution's framers during the deliberations they conducted under the veil of secrecy during the Philadelphia Convention of 1787. Yet these frank sessions are well documented. I was determined to help people understand the logic of the Constitution as the framers themselves constructed it. But doing so required more time—and much more help—than I imagined.

Sarah Hoff carefully slogged through an early, very long version of this manuscript, and she provided countless valuable comments as she did so. Three anonymous reviewers also read the long version and helped me see the many weaknesses of this initial approach. R. B. Bernstein read a nearly final draft of the manuscript, and he went above and beyond with exceptionally extensive, thoughtful, and constructive comments. David Siemers, an extraordinary reviewer, provided many sobering points about the same version, challenged me to improve it, and then provided another far-reaching set of comments when I did. Sidney Milkis meticulously worked through the manuscript and reminded me to keep focused on what the framers wanted and what they achieved. I deeply appreciate his wise and wonderful comments. Ilkka Janhunen also provided comments on the nearly final draft. I took each one very seriously, and each one helped me make the final book stronger. David McBride, my editor at Oxford, did a wonderful, patient job nurturing this book along and making sure that I had all the help I could get from reviewers. David knows that I needed it all, and I am deeply indebted to him. I also am indebted to those who put in so much effort to develop and produce this book for Oxford, including Caelyn Cobb, Natalie Johnson, Michele Bowman, Venkat Raghavan Srinivasa Raghavan, Cherie Hackelberg, and Woody Gilmartin.

I dedicate this book to the many friends in the Politics and History section of the American Political Science Association, too many to mention except for a few leaders: Jim Morone, Sid Milkis, Ira Katznelson, Suzanne Mettler, Margaret Weir, Richard Bensel, Elizabeth Sanders, Rick Valelly, Robert Lieberman, Eileen McDonagh, Gretchen Ritter, and Bat Sparrow. I hope they see their great influence in these pages. They have helped me in many ways that I more fully appreciate each day.

Thanks much to my graduate students in seminars in American Political Development and in Political Economy, and undergraduates in several classes who have taught me so much about the Constitution. Bruce Hanebrink contributed very helpful background research. I thank other scholars of the founding, notably Richard K. Matthews and Christopher Collier, who have given me valuable encouragement in efforts to analyze the Constitutional Convention. Thanks also goes to my University of Missouri-St. Louis colleagues. I want to single out Terry Jones, who as longtime dean of our college, and as a recently (somewhat reluctant) department chair, has done much more than he knows to support my writing, and especially this book. He deserves credit for many scholars' accomplishments. I also thank David Kimball, Bob Bliss, Dennis Judd, Lana Stein, Brady Baybeck, Lana Vierdag, and Raphael Hopkins for making my research and everything else at the University of Missouri-St. Louis so great for my work. Jane Allen helped me find my way through a vast project. Past assistance from the University of Missouri Research Board and the Institute for Political History, and a conversation with Linda Kowalcky at the beginning of my Constitution research, greatly helped to get my work on the Constitutional Convention off to a good start. Thanks to Don Critchlow and Pat Powers, who have nurtured the *Journal of Policy History*; my involvement with the journal has been priceless for my historical knowledge and understanding. As in my last two books, I deliberately ended this book with the word "idealism," because I am determined to repay all the help and support I've received by keeping that notion alive.

This book simply would not exist without two people. My son Bryan constantly inspires me. My wife Cathie is a patient, frank, decisive, and kind companion. She supports my continuing effort to think, teach, and write my way through all the questions I need to try to answer. She makes me a better scholar and a far better person.

PRINCIPAL SPEAKERS AT THE CONVENTION

Gunning Bedford Jr., Delaware
David Brearly, Maryland
Pierce Butler, South Carolina
Daniel Carroll, Maryland
John Dickinson, Delaware
Oliver Ellsworth, Connecticut
Elbridge Gerry, Massachusetts
Nathaniel Gorham, Massachusetts
Benjamin Franklin, Pennsylvania
Alexander Hamilton, New York
William Samuel Johnson, Connecticut
Rufus King, Massachusetts
John Langdon, New Hampshire
William Livingston, New Jersey

James Madison, Virginia
Luther Martin, Maryland
George Mason, Virginia
Gouverneur Morris, Pennsylvania
William Paterson, New Jersey
Charles Pinckney, South Carolina
General (Charles Cotesworth)
    Pinckney, South Carolina
Edmund J. Randolph, Virginia
George Read, Delaware
John Rutledge, South Carolina
Roger Sherman, Connecticut
Hugh Williamson, North Carolina
James Wilson, Pennsylvania

Other Delegates Who Contributed to the Debates

Abraham Baldwin, Georgia
William Blount, North Carolina
Jacob Broom, Delaware
George Clymer, Pennsylvania
William R. Davie, North Carolina
Jonathan Dayton, New Jersey
Thomas Fitzsimons, Pennsylvania
William Houstoun, Georgia
Daniel of St. Thomas Jenifer, Maryland
John Lansing Jr., New York

James McClurg, Virginia
James McHenry, Maryland
John F. Mercer, Maryland
William Pierce, Georgia
Richard D. Spaight, North Carolina
Caleb Strong, Massachusetts
George Washington, Virginia
    (Convention President)
George Wythe, Virginia

ABBREVIATIONS

JCC   *Journals of the Continental Congress, 1774–1789*, ed. Worthington C. Ford et al., 34 vols. (Washington, DC: Government Printing Office, 1904–1937). Also online at http://memory.loc.gov/ammem/amlaw/lwjc.html.

PJM   *The Papers of James Madison*, ed. William T. Hutchinson et al., 17 vols. (Chicago: University of Chicago Press and Charlottesville: University of Virginia Press, 1962–1991).

RFC   *The Records of the Federal Convention of 1787*, ed. Max Farrand, 4 vols. (New Haven: Yale University Press, 1937). Also online at http://memory.loc.gov/ammem/amlaw/lwfr.html.

RFC   1987 Supplement James L. Hutson, *Supplement to Max Farrand's The Records of the Federal Convention of 1787* (New Haven, CT: Yale University Press, 1987).

The Original Compromise

‖ 1 ‖

Introduction

The founders of their nation fascinate Americans, but their Constitution created a government that often mystifies them. What is the logic behind it? What were the Constitution's framers trying to accomplish in 1787? Why did they create the United States Congress, the presidency, the courts, and the federal system the way they did? How did they expect these parts to work together? These questions are vital now. We cannot understand today's United States without understanding the thinking behind the Constitution.

The Constitution shapes American life today. The Constitution still provides the framework for the way the U.S. government makes laws, defends the nation, and provides for Americans' prosperity. The U.S. House of Representatives and the Senate still must agree completely whenever they make a law. States with large populations, like New York, still have far more seats in the House of Representatives than small states like Delaware; in the Senate, however, each state is represented by two senators no matter how small or large its population. The president, at the head of a separate and independent executive branch, still wields the power to veto Congress's bills, to appoint important officials with the Senate's consent, and to command the nation's military. Judges on U.S. courts are still appointed to the bench under the original rules, and the U.S. judicial branch is still very independent of the other branches. The states still control a wide range of policies that directly affect all Americans, such as policy toward crime and punishment, marriage and family, and business and labor. The Constitution still orchestrates the rhythms of American politics, with Congressional elections every two years, presidential elections every four, and an Electoral College that chooses the president even if his opponent wins the popular vote.

As I studied the founding, I discovered that there is no book that explains the framers' *reasoning* during the meeting that produced this durable Constitution. This book addresses the unfilled need for a narrative of the Constitutional Convention's logic that is accurate, understandable, and drawn primarily from the actual records of the Convention itself.

I show that conflict and negotiation drove the making of the Constitution and explain its logic. Huge political differences, not just philosophical disagreements, divided the delegates. To bridge these divisions, the framers applied their formidable political skills to work through the choices a new government required. *Political* reasoning accounts for the design of the Constitution—and it required bargaining, deliberate ambiguity, evasion, and at times the surrender of dearly held objectives. The framers built their Constitution with the bricks and mortar of political compromise.

In this chapter, I describe the framers' aspirations for the Constitution, the importance of compromise in making the Constitution possible, and the need for a narrative that explains the way these aspirations and compromises produced the final Constitution. I describe the way I used political analysis and the framers' own records to account for the way the framers understood their own work, and the Constitution that Americans inherit today.

The Framers' Aspirations

What were the framers really thinking? The Constitution's framers aspired to build a stronger and republican national government. The framers' core principles were effective government and a government based on the consent of the people. It would have been hard *either* to build a stronger national government, or to build a *republican* national government. But it was infinitely more challenging to achieve *both* these goals at the same time. They aimed to build self-government on a grand scale. The task was made even harder because the framers disagreed about the way to make this government safe for their vital state, local, factional, and personal interests. The delegates to the Constitutional Convention, in short, had set a nearly impossible task for themselves. Only their formidable talents for political compromise made it possible for them to write a Constitution that narrowly won national approval after a bitter, closely contested fight for ratification in the states.

A Stronger National Government

During the 1780s, many American leaders hammered away at the need for a more effective national government for the United States. The Revolution had forged a sense of national purpose across the colonies, but just as Americans turned to nation-building after the war ended, the sense of common purpose seemed to fade.[1] A committee of the Confederation Congress in 1782 reported that, for the United States to "become respectable, it must be by means of . . . more energy in" its national government.[2] In 1783, George Washington urged Americans to strengthen their national government. In a public circular, he encouraged his fellow citizens "to forget their local prejudices and policies, to make those mutual concessions which are requisite to the general prosperity, and in some instances, to sacrifice their individual advantages to the interest of the Community." It was essential, wrote Washington, "that there should be lodged somewhere, a Supreme Power to regulate and govern the general concerns of the Confederated Republic." In a nation so free and prosperous, "who will grudge to yield a very little of his property to support the common interest of Society, and insure the protection of Government?"[3]

Young, energetic leaders like James Madison and Alexander Hamilton committed themselves to strengthening the national government. In preparation for the Convention, Madison wrote that the sovereign power of government must serve the "public good and private rights" of the *whole* society.[4] He believed that the inability of the Confederation government to manage commerce was holding back the nation's prosperity and damaging its future by making it difficult to pursue its comparative economic advantages. He complained that the decentralization of so much power to the states was undermining the nation's interests.[5] Madison told the delegates at the Constitutional Convention that he would "shrink from nothing which should be found essential to such a form of Government as would provide the safety, liberty and happiness of the Community."[6] Madison's friend, Thomas Jefferson, frustrated by the states' unwillingness to fund the national Confederation government and support a navy, wrote in 1786, "The states must see the rod; perhaps it must be felt by some one of them."[7]

To strengthen the Confederation's commercial powers, several states sent delegates to a meeting in Annapolis, Maryland, in 1786. Madison, Hamilton, and five other men who attended later served as delegates to the Constitutional Convention. The Annapolis meeting reported "that the power of regulating trade is of such comprehensive extent, and will enter so far into the general System of the federal government," that it could require other changes in the political system. They called for a Convention of all the states in Philadelphia on May 14, 1787, "to devise such further provisions as shall appear to them necessary to render the constitution of the Federal Government adequate to the exigencies of the Union."[8]

A Republican National Government

The framers also aspired to make their government truly republican—that is, a government whose authority was based on the consent of the people themselves. Republicanism provided the guiding principles for any American government reform in these years after the Revolution.[9] As George Mason insisted at the Constitutional Convention, despite their differences, the American people agreed that any government of the United States had to be republican.[10]

Key leaders of the Convention, including Mason, Madison, and Roger Sherman, were dedicated and unyielding republicans. Madison emphasized that the problems of the Confederation threatened *both* the national interest *and* republicanism.[11]

Republican government required the consent of the governed. Any government could be legitimate only when based on the authority of the people. Key government officials, such as legislators, had to be agents of the people.[12] In John Adams's words, the people's legislative representatives should "think, feel, reason, and act like them."[13] In 1776, Congress asked the colonies to construct governments with "all the powers of government exerted, under the authority of the people of the colonies."[14] During the Revolution, the American people seemed to seize power from the British, hurriedly build new republican governing institutions, "and began to govern themselves directly."[15] State legislatures, with at least one house popularly elected, "now became . . . sovereign embodiments of the people with a responsibility to promote a unitary public interest that was to be clearly distinguishable from the many private interests of society."[16]

These republican ideals required the separation of governing institutions. In an absolute monarchy, the king could make laws, implement laws, interpret the meaning of the laws, and arbitrarily punish those who disagreed. Such abuse of power could be prevented by the separation of the legislative, executive, and judicial powers.[17] Before the Convention, most suggestions for reforming the Confederation government included proposals to add a new, separate executive and judiciary.[18]

Republican ideals guided the delegates in their desire for a more effective national government. The delegates were themselves accomplished and gifted republican leaders. Most had helped to build republican polities in their own states and had constructed vigorous political coalitions to make them work.[19] Connecticut instructed its delegates to consider changes in the national government that were consistent "with the general principles of Republican Government."[20]

From Aspiration to Compromise

The Constitution depended on political compromise because the two aspirations of republicanism and national government power were hard to reconcile, and because they were tangled up in a variety of conflicting regional, state, and personal interests. Even in theory, it seemed almost impossible to reconcile republicanism with a durable, effective, and "energetic" national government. Conventional wisdom was that the people could govern themselves only in small-scale polities. Most delegates admired British government, but they viewed it as too strong, overbearing, corrupt, and divorced from the public will. On the other hand, the new American state republics seemed *too* democratic, too quick to respond to the fleeting popular passions of the moment, and too unstable.

Popularly elected state legislatures dominated government, and these state legislatures often passed laws that were popular with voters and that dealt with issues such as paper money, relief from debts, and trade restrictions. But these laws threatened the sound money, unshakable property rights, and predictable contracts that the framers believed were essential for a robust market economy.

As political scientist James Morone pointed out, the framers insisted on popular consent and government based on the people, but they did not want a government that was *too* democratic. Too much democracy imperiled the pursuit of national interests. They wanted a national government based on popular consent, but in which that consent was controlled and filtered by institutions that could check democratic passions and administer the nation effectively.[21] Elbridge Gerry, a delegate from Massachusetts, expressed this sentiment at the start of the Convention. Gerry confessed that he had "been too republican heretofore: he was still however republican, but had been taught by experience the danger of the leveling spirit," that is, the willingness of state governments to pander to voters with unsound currency, credit, trade, and other policies.[22] Madison, in the heat of a debate over representation in the Senate, warned that the Convention was "now digesting a plan which in its operation would decide forever the fate of Republican Government," and that "we ought not only to provide every guard to liberty that its preservation could require, but be equally careful to supply the defects which our own experience had particularly pointed out."[23]

To balance republicanism with government effectiveness, the framers had to compromise. Abraham Baldwin, a Georgia delegate, put the problem succinctly: "It appears to be agreed that the government we should adopt ought to be energetic and formidable, yet I would guard against the danger of becoming too formidable."[24] On the one hand, they had to avoid government so enervated and unstable that it could not further national goals. On the other, they had to avoid a government so powerful that it would rule by fiat. No two delegates who spoke seemed to have exactly the same idea about the best way to achieve this balance, or about how much the system should tilt toward republicanism or toward more national effectiveness. Several harbored the conventional view that no effective national government over so large a territory could ever be truly republican.

The framers compromised by making institutions more independent of each other, and more capable of checking one another, than any delegate had proposed at the start of the Convention. In effect, they resolved the collision of republicanism and effectiveness by distancing the people from most of the levers of government. The people ruled by controlling a switch—by electing members of the House of Representatives—that could sometimes start the machinery of government. But once the machinery started, it would distill the people's immediate passions through, as Madison termed it, a series of "successive filtrations" via institutions beyond immediate popular control.

Conflicting interests in the Convention made the aspiration to build an effective, republican national government much more complicated. United by fear for the nation's future, animosity to some of the states' policies, and hopes for improving national governance, these delegates disagreed among themselves about the policies a new national government should produce. More effective national government meant different things to different delegates. New England wanted a more effective government to secure trade agreements and restrict foreign competition. The South wanted free trade for its crops and a guarantee that the new government would not interfere with slavery. Georgia and South Carolina wanted to continue the slave trade. Farmers in smaller states surrounding New York wanted to prevent that state from using its harbor in a way that exploited them.[25] A growing western population wanted a government that could protect settlers against Indians and American trade on the Mississippi River. Every state had a stake in a national government that could more effectively implement some tasks—but such a government also could harm any state and unfairly advantage some states at the expense of others. Their agreement on general principles helped moderate these differences, but the records of the Constitutional Convention show that these differences divided the delegates from beginning to end.

With aspirations and interests so intertwined, the framers had to negotiate almost every important feature of the Constitution. Their republican political skills enabled them to work through compromise after compromise on Congress, the president, the courts, national authority, state powers, economic management, slavery, and national defense. The resulting Constitution—this original compromise—has proved remarkably durable and authoritative. It has anchored the national government through spectacular economic growth, social changes, and expansions of democracy and rights that were inconceivable in 1787. It is easy to forget that politicians produced this remarkable document—talented, often idealistic politicians, but politicians nonetheless.

The Records of the Constitutional Convention

There is no narrative of these negotiations, as important as they are for understanding the United States. The best records of the framers' deliberations are the documents they wrote during the Convention. These documents chronicle its three-and-a-half arduous months of intense debates. They reveal the frank discussions held in secrecy, and they show how frustrating stalemates, political give and take, and reluctant bargains shaped the Constitution. James Madison, representing Virginia, kept a comprehensive record of the confidential deliberations of the Convention, attending each session and sitting at the front center, a "favorable position for hearing all that passed." Madison meticulously noted each discussion, motion, and vote, and he carefully wrote out these notes after the delegates adjourned for the day. His task was easier because he was familiar "with the style and the train of observation and reasoning" of "the principal speakers," most of whom had served with Madison in the Confederation Congress.[26] Madison's notes provide us with the most complete and accurate available record of the delegates' remarks. The Library of Congress published Madison's Convention notes and other papers four years after his death in 1836. Other delegates also took valuable notes, including John Lansing of New York, James McHenry of Maryland, and Rufus King of Massachusetts.[27] These notes, however, are still limited. They are not a word-for-word record of each session, and they include little information about the delegates' discussions off the floor of the Convention.[28]

Max Farrand collected most of these Convention records and published them in three volumes in 1911. Farrand's *Records* include the sketchy official journal of the Convention, Madison's notes, and other delegates' records and letters. In 1987, James H. Huston, a historian at the Library of Congress, added a fourth volume that included many manuscripts that became available after 1911. Together, these four volumes of Farrand's *Records* include about 1,600 pages of delegates' records between May 15, 1787, the date initially set for the Convention to meet, and September 17, when the Convention officially ended.

Although Farrand's *Records* provide the primary source for understanding the reasoning behind the Constitution, it is practically impossible to follow the framers' logic simply by reading these volumes. First and most important, Farrand organized the records chronologically, not by topic. He arranged the notes as the debates happened, day-by-day. But the delegates did not reason through the provisions of the Constitution chronologically, completing one section before moving to the next. Instead, they constructed the Constitution piecemeal, talking about an issue for part of a day, often putting it aside and moving on to some different topic, returning to the issue days or even weeks later. The delegates' decisions about critical issues like the presidency are scattered throughout Farrand's *Records*, making it extraordinarily difficult to find and understand the delegates' thinking on most issues while their reasoning evolved. Second, because the topics are scattered throughout Farrand's *Records*, their arrangement makes it very difficult to understand the sequence of compromise and collective choice. Agreements about the apportionment of seats in the House of Representatives in July changed perceptions about power in Congress and affected choices about all the other government institutions thereafter. Third, Farrand's *Records* provide little or no context about the delegates' strategies, interests, and circumstances. The delegates were experts in the Confederation's problems, and did not have to explain to one another the problems of Shays's Rebellion, the slave trade, paper currency, debt relief, or foreign threats. The debates are sprinkled with disconnected references to these problems. For that reason, it is very difficult for those who read Farrand's *Records* today to appreciate fully the information the delegates took for granted when, for example, they used Rhode Island as the prime example of a state government gone wrong. Finally, the records are notes of eighteenth-century debates, so that their wording, spelling, and phrasing make it even more challenging for modern readers to understand. Small wonder that many people turn to other sources to understand what the framers were thinking.

Accounts Written after the Convention

After the Convention ended, many of the Convention delegates explained and justified the Constitution as they battled for ratification in their own states. This rancorous struggle was most closely contested in Massachusetts, Virginia, and New York. *The Federalist* is a compilation of newspaper articles written between October 1787 and March 1788 to persuade New Yorkers to support the ratification of the Constitution. Written under the pseudonym "Publius" by two Convention delegates, Alexander Hamilton and James Madison (along with John Jay, who was not chosen as a delegate to the Convention), the articles argued the need for the Constitution, and defended each of the Constitution's provisions in eighty-five topical essays.[29] These essays were primarily written for a New York audience; they had a limited circulation inside and outside that state.[30]

The Federalist became the most widely read account of the ideas behind the Constitution. As historian Bernard Bailyn wrote, "Generations of people—scholars and politicians alike—believed *The Federalist* to be the finest explanation of the principles that underlie the American government and the most accurate analysis of the intentions of those who designed it."[31] *The Federalist* is treated with reverence, and often used as an authoritative account of the framers' reasoning.[32] As early as 1789, in the first months of the first Congress, a member of the House of Representatives cited *The Federalist* as an authoritative source of rules for removing appointed national officers.[33] Thomas Jefferson cited the papers as "evidence of the general opinion of those who framed and those who accepted the Constitution of the U. States on questions as to its genuine meaning."[34] Two centuries later, President Ronald Reagan's Domestic Policy Council cited one of James Madison's *Federalist* essays, rather than the 1787 Constitution itself, as the authority for its claim that national government power had grown far beyond the framers' intent.[35] In 2011, conservative political commentator Glenn Beck published a popularized version of *The Federalist* because "they offer us a guide to understanding the Founders' core constitutional principles."[36] Supreme Court justices in recent years increasingly have cited *Federalist* essays as, in Justice Scalia's words, "indicative of the original understanding of the Constitution."[37] Both liberal and conservative Justices have used *The Federalist* to establish the credibility of their arguments because, in the words of law professor Melvyn Durschlag, drawing on the words of the "Framers generally and *The Federalist* . . . particularly is the secular equivalent to citing the Bible. It is an appeal to a higher and more revered authority."[38]

But most Constitutional scholars know that *The Federalist* does not provide a *reliable* record of the arguments of the fifty-five delegates who participated in the Constitutional Convention.[39] Hamilton, Madison, and Jay wrote these polemical essays to persuade New Yorkers to support ratification, not to provide a full or accurate record of the actual reasoning behind each written provision of the Constitution.[40] The rule of secrecy in Philadelphia allowed the delegates to be much more candid about their goals, interests, anger, and fears than the authors of polemical essays meant to calmly persuade citizens that the Constitution was reasonable.

The Federalist gives the impression that the Constitution resulted from a relatively coherent, rational set of ideas, instead of a series of the excruciating political negotiations that is plain throughout Farrand's *Records*. In *Federalist* 2, John Jay (who had not participated in the Constitutional Convention) wrote that the delegates, motivated only by "love for their country," had recommended a Constitution "produced by their joint and very unanimous councils."[41] Farrand's *Records* proves that this portrait Convention unanimity is false. Sharp conflicts of interest filled the Convention from beginning to end and drove it to the brink of collapse in July. Angry delegates from New York and Maryland left the meeting early, and three delegates who stayed refused to sign the final Constitution.[42] Two of these delegates, George Mason and Elbridge Gerry, joined the Anti-Federalists in the fight against ratification.

While *The Federalist* essays help illuminate the Constitution, in important ways they gloss over, evade, or even distort the delegates' actual reasoning as revealed in the Convention records. Slavery offers a very important example. *The Federalist* barely touches on the issue of slavery.[43] But the delegates' passionate conflicts about slavery and their grudging compromises on that issue profoundly shaped Congress, the presidency, national government authority, and other provisions of the Constitution. Another important example deals with the Constitutional provision that "All Bills for raising Revenue shall originate in the House of Representatives." In *Federalist* 58, Madison described this provision as "the most complete and effectual weapon with which any constitution can arm the immediate representatives of the people."[44] But during the Convention, Madison said that he considered this provision worthless. As late as August 8, he made a proposal to delete it. Even George Washington thought it was useless, but voted for it simply to win later votes from its proponents.[45]

Although James Madison's *Federalist* essays suggest that the Constitution closely matched Madison's own ideas for the design of American national government, the final Constitution deeply disappointed him. Madison's plans at the start of the Convention differed greatly from the final product. He sought broader power for the national government throughout the Convention, insisting that the national government required the authority to veto state laws. The final Constitution restricted national government power much more than Madison wanted, and it gave state governments more authority than he thought safe. At the same time he was writing entirely positive *Federalist* essays for public consumption, Madison was writing private letters in which he intensely criticized several specific provisions of the Constitution, and expressed pessimism about its future.[46] Jefferson suggested that Madison's *Federalist* essays defended opinions with which Madison himself disagreed.[47] Madison's *Federalist* essays in fact incorporated many of the strongest, most idealistic arguments for a republican national constitution that he made during the Convention. In *The Federalist*, he wove these observations together into a case for a Constitution that fell short of his aspirations.

The Federalist, then, addresses "masterfully our permanent concerns with political power."[48] But the great virtues of *The Federalist* are not the same as an authentic analysis of the actual collective reasoning of the many delegates who together produced the Constitution. These shortcomings of *The Federalist* underscore the need for a more accurate account of the thinking behind the Constitution.

Historians have written excellent, engaging narratives of the Constitutional Convention, but have not written a systematic, analytical account of the reasoning behind the Constitution.[49] Several landmark studies of the founding period are devoted not to the Constitutional Convention alone, but instead to illustrating the themes that transcend Constitutional design, such as the brilliance of American democracy (championed by nineteenth-century historians), the Constitutional construction of economic privilege (advanced by "Progressive" historians like Charles Beard), or the evolution of civic republican ideals (put forward by Gordon Wood and Jack Rakove).[50]

Political scientists, notably Thornton Anderson and Calvin Jillson, have analyzed the Convention as a political event. These political scientists, however, focus on the Convention votes and do not provide a systematic, comprehensive analysis of the Convention's reasoning and compromises.[51] Rakove, John P. Roche, Forrest MacDonald, and David Hendrickson wrote about the Convention with the political realism required to understand it, but none provided an inclusive, systematic analysis of the political negotiations themselves.[52]

Analyzing the Constitutional Convention

This book addresses the need for an analytical account of the Constitutional Convention's logic that is accurate, understandable, organized by topic, and drawn directly from the actual records of the Convention itself. It reorganizes, distills, and synthesizes Farrand's *Records* into a series of chapters that examine each conceptual part of the puzzle of Constitution-making in 1787. The Constitutional Convention fundamentally was a *political* event: the delegates were political leaders engaged in writing rules for later politicians to use. In this process, the delegates integrated their ideas and their interests, engaged in collective political decision-making, advanced alternative strategies for building a republican national government, and made choices in a sequence that itself shaped the result.

Ideas and Interests

Many authors who have tried to explain the logic of the framers fall into one of two camps. First, many emphasize the ideas and the inherited experiences that the framers drew upon in writing the Constitution. Bernard Bailyn, Gordon Wood, Douglass Adair, and other prominent historians skillfully explained the impact of evolving American political beliefs rooted in republicanism, representative government, the protection of property, and political freedom. Political scientist Donald Lutz carefully documented the many sources of political ideas that influenced constitutional theory in the founding period.[53]

Second, other historians consider economic interests as the dominant driving force of the Convention. In the early 1900s, Charles A. Beard boldly claimed that the Constitution was "an economic document drawn with superb skill by men whose property interests were immediately at stake; as such it appealed directly and unerringly to identical interests in the country at large."[54] Many historians, such as Forrest McDonald, Robert E. Brown, and James Ferguson, have argued that the evidence does not support Beard's claim.[55] At the same time, many scholars have detailed more carefully the way that specific economic and political interests *did* affect the proceedings and the outcome. Economic historian Robert McGuire demonstrated that interests and votes were closely related at the Convention.[56]

We cannot enter the mind of any delegate to specify how he personally untangled ideas and interests when he spoke or voted during the Convention. One delegate's eloquent appeal to principle may have masked his driving ambition for his constituents or for national office. Another delegate's defense of slavery or state powers may have reflected his sincere belief in the ideas of faithfully representing his constituents and in the moral superiority of his state's social,

economic, and political order. McDonald showed that delegates worked to accommodate a variety of interests and ideas.[57] Jillson studied the Convention votes and
concluded that ideas and interests divided the delegates in different ways.[58] Rakove
described the Convention as both an intellectual and a political process, and he
concluded that the relative role of ideas and interests is "elusive."[59]

The Convention records show that the delegates took principled positions
that almost always served their political goals and interests. Madison, for example, shrewdly coupled theory and pragmatic politics in his arguments.[60]

Politics

Farrand's *Records* shows that the delegates were skilled in politics. They keenly
understood the political costs, benefits, and risks of specific decisions. They had
already engaged in collective political negotiations in state constitutional conventions, state legislatures, and the Confederation Congress. They conducted
the process for the Convention much the same as they had conducted the
process of making laws.[61] Together, these delegates had to engage in political
bargaining to formulate a single plan for a new government that would receive
substantial political support inside and outside the Convention. They had to
reach agreement on a blueprint in spite of the different ideals, priorities, interests, and experiences each one brought to the Convention.

The delegates showed exceptional political ingenuity in these negotiations.
Farrand's *Records* shows that they used all the political arts of compromise,
invention, and even evasion to arrive collectively at this new government plan.
They compromised on the contentious question of representation by devising
one legislative chamber based on population and another based on the states
as political units. They constructed a new kind of federalism, in which the national and state governments would share political authority. They also
invented the system of presidential electors and the vice presidency to deal
with the problem of presidential selection and replacement. They resolved
some intractable disputes simply by delaying implementation (the slave
trade), by using symbolic language (the House of Representatives' control of
money bills), and by writing ambiguous words and phrases to paper over differences about specific powers (with such deliberately imprecise phrases as
"general welfare" or "necessary and proper").

Political calculation, negotiation, and compromise inevitably shaped the document that evolved at the Convention. These processes played a more explicit
role as the weeks wore on. Understanding that the framers were politicians
engaged in the most important political fight of their lives does not diminish
them; I believe it ennobles them. By understanding the political obstacles to the
Constitution, we can better appreciate its enduring achievements. The framers,

for example, found a long-lasting solution to the dilemma of ensuring the peaceful transition of power from one national leader to a rival.

Studying the Convention offers the opportunity to understand real democracy as a profoundly human process. American history offers no better opportunity to examine this process.

Broad Nationalism and Narrow Nationalism

The delegates' policy strategies provide the intellectual bridge that connected their aspirations, their personal interests, and the circumstances that drove them to achieve the ambiguously stated goal of making "the federal Constitution adequate to the exigencies of Government & the preservation of the Union."[62] *Policy strategy* refers to a set of related premises about goals, expectations, assumptions, facts, and political tactics that political leaders combine to achieve a desired change in government outcomes.[63] At the Constitutional Convention, the delegates' policy strategies are found in statements of support and opposition for specific Constitutional provisions. Farrand's *Records* is filled with explicit inferences about public opinion, political necessity and impossibility, interests, tactics, and expectations about the likely effects of one provision or another.

Two conflicting policy strategies regularly produced disagreements at the Convention.[64] First, delegates such as Madison, Hamilton, James Wilson, and Gouverneur Morris took a position in favor of *broad* nationalism. In this view, the national government required strong and very extensive policy authority. The national government should exercise all the important powers of government, and the state governments' role should be reduced to a minimum. Madison was the most active supporter of broad nationalism. Madison and his allies framed the problem of American governance as the result of too much state government independence and power. The solution was a strong national republican government that could make national policy in all important areas. The Virginia Plan embodied these notions and aimed to set the agenda for the Convention.

A second, contrasting position emphasized *narrow* nationalism. This position, championed by such delegates as Roger Sherman and Oliver Ellsworth, sought to expand national authority in a narrow, limited way, and to protect as much of the existing policy authority of the state governments as possible. Supporters of narrow nationalism wanted a stronger national government, but they wanted a few specific new national powers, and not the broad, sweeping authority that Madison sought. These delegates emphasized that the states were functioning polities that already enjoyed the loyalty of their citizens. States had to be part of any plan for governing the nation. The most ardent supporters of narrow nationalism represented the small and economically vulnerable states between the large states of Virginia, Pennsylvania, and Massachusetts. Delegates from Connecticut, New Jersey, Delaware, and Maryland advanced the most effective opposition to broad nationalism and the Virginia Plan. Many of them collaborated on the New Jersey Plan, which aimed to reframe the agenda of the Convention and divert support for the Virginia Plan.

The advocates of broad and narrow nationalism clashed again and again over distinct issues throughout the Convention. Neither strategy decisively defeated the other. Indeed, a number of swing delegates voted with the broad nationalists on some issues and the narrow nationalists on others.

Most important, key Southern delegates initially behaved as *conditional* "broad nationalists"—that is, they supported Madison's plan for broad national authority on the condition that seats in the new Congress were apportioned on the basis of population, a formula that seemed to protect Southern interests. Once the Connecticut Compromise created a Senate that diluted Southern votes in Congress, delegates from South Carolina fought for narrow national powers and protections for state power. Important swings in the Convention, like the swing of Southern delegates away from broad national powers, followed from the sequence of decisions.

The Sequence of Constitutional Choice

The delegates engineered the Constitution piece by piece. They spent eighty-five working days debating and accepting specific provisions in the Constitution. This incremental decision-making process made later decisions contingent on earlier ones, and it made the Constitution increasingly complicated as the Convention unfolded.

At the Constitutional Convention, early choices influenced later choices. Delegates tended to accept most of their early commitments as settled when they decided other issues.[65] Most notably, the Connecticut Compromise in July changed the way the Convention played out. The delegates arduously arrived at an agreement that each state would have an equal number of votes in the Senate. Rather than reverse this commitment or abandon the Convention altogether, key delegates accepted it and moved on to other issues. But the Connecticut Compromise changed many views of national government institutions and authority.

The delegates resisted changing earlier votes because, with each succeeding day, they had sunk more and more time and effort into developing areas of agreement. George Mason, for example, opposed the elimination of a proposal for House control of the national budget because the change would "unhinge the compromise" on proportional representation.[66] They did not want to revisit earlier antagonisms they had overcome to make decisions. They also did not want to unravel these agreements—and risk wrecking the Convention—by pulling out one thread of the intricate fabric they were weaving. Furthermore, once the advocates of a policy strategy had won a point, they subsequently worked to consolidate that gain by nurturing a coalition of allies and fending off challenges to these advantageous decisions. (There were exceptions, notably the process for selecting the president.)[67]

Thus, the delegates made the Constitution through a sequence of political compromises, rather than through a deliberate, planned blueprint. The most important sequence of events that drove the development of the Constitution involved the clash between broad and narrow nationalism:

- Madison put forward the Virginia Plan to create a new national government based on the strategy of broad nationalism;
- opponents responded with proposals aimed at narrow nationalism;
- the adversaries of each strategy battled over representation until they compromised; and
- the consequences of this compromise affected subsequent compromises about national authority and institutional power.

The result was a Constitution that was acceptable to most of the remaining delegates, but that no delegate embraced wholeheartedly at the end.

What the Framers Produced

The unexpected sequence of Convention compromises increased the complexity of the proposed scheme of government. The final design was much more complicated than any delegates had expected when they arrived in Philadelphia.[68] As the delegates grew more uncertain about the way the Constitution would work in practice, several grew more cautious about ensuring that their vital interests would be protected. By mid-August, Oliver Ellsworth observed, "We grow more & more skeptical as we proceed."[69] They placed a priority on strengthening the defensive power of the institutions they believed would best protect their interests. Thus, the delegates from the large states sought to increase the power of the House of Representatives because its allocation of seats favored their interests, while the smaller, more economically vulnerable states favored Senate power because small states and large states had equal votes in the Senate. These disagreements spilled over in the struggle over presidential power and selection. Delegates also fought to protect state prerogatives in areas that the national government might endanger, such as state militias or slavery.[70]

Second, compromises helped produce a national government with more authority than the Confederation government, but at the same time a national government that was difficult to use. As the delegates armed their favorite institutions

with more independence and the power to fend off rival institutions, they gradually built a more cumbersome policy-making process. Within the national
Congress, the House and Senate would have equal law-making power and would
have to be brought to complete agreement on any legislation. The president
could veto the law, and even if the president approved it, the courts might assert
the power to rule that the law was invalid. Congress would declare war, but the
president would conduct it. The Constitution also created a government that
was "partly federal, partly national" in the words of Oliver Ellsworth (a "compound republic" according to James Madison), a system in which the state and
national governments would share power—and, they knew, could struggle with
each other to control public policy. In June, for example, Sherman worried, "It
would seem that we are erecting a Kingdom at war with itself," when delegates
debated a rule that prohibited members of the U.S. House of Representatives
from serving in state offices.[71] Truly, it was a government in which ambition
counteracted ambition, as Madison described it in *Federalist* Number 51. But
this result was not the product of abstract, detached reasoning among the delegates, as Madison's essay can imply. Rather, Madison was rationalizing the result
of collective, incremental political reasoning.

The Plan

To analyze the Convention's logic, I began by closely examining Farrand's
Records. I disentangled debates on separate substantive issues and reorganized
all the records into eleven separate conceptual categories: the delegates; the
problems; the necessary remedies; representation in Congress; the House and
Senate; the presidency; the courts; national authority and federalism; slavery;
national defense; and amendments and ratification. For example, in chapter
four, I drew on speeches about the problem of controlling republican politics
made on thirty-four different days of the Convention, between May 31 and September 15, and organized them into a narrative about the problems of majority
rule. I then wove all the records of the Convention debates into a preliminary
250,000-word draft of the political logic that played out in each area. This long
draft quoted every substantive claim made at the Convention. Finally, I condensed this long draft down into much shorter chapters.

To make the framers' discussions easier to understand and appreciate, I frequently reorganized the sequence of comments during any day's debate on a particular issue. I changed the words taken from Farrand's *Records* as little as necessary
to make them easily readable; thus, I left numerals and familiar symbols ("&"),
which serve as reminders that you are reading the framers' own accounts. I transformed most words (except in the text of the final Constitution) to modern

American English spelling, spelled out contractions, and corrected misspellings. Several delegates, and especially Madison, dwelled on the experiences of other federations, past and present. To ensure the flow of argument, I condensed these references to other contemporary and historical nations, but did not include long discourses on the workings of foreign confederations. I also condensed quarrels about representation of the states in the Articles of Confederation. I rarely report the actual tally of the vote on a Constitutional provision, because I want readers to focus on the reasoning behind the choices rather than a box score of votes. I dropped a very few minor disagreements, such as the discussions of whether the United States could define piracies and felonies committed on the high seas (August 17) and whether to speed up the ratification process (August 31).

I have organized this book so that it roughly parallels the organization of *The Federalist*. The first part, "The Illness and the Cure," discusses the political and economic problems that the delegates thought they were confronting (topics discussed in *The Federalist* Numbers 1–22). This part also explains their general approach to solutions, the more specific proposals put forward by the Virginia delegation, and the objections to the Virginia Plan by the authors of the New Jersey Plan. The second part, "The Politics of Building Government Institutions," discusses the way the delegates constructed Congress (*The Federalist* Numbers 52–66), the president (*The Federalist* Numbers 67–77), and the courts (*The Federalist* Numbers 78–83). The third part, "The Politics of Government Power" deals with federalism and the powers of the national government (*The Federalist* Numbers 23–51).[72] Chapters 7 through 17 conclude with a brief discussion of the path of American government developments after 1787.

This book presents each element of the Constitution as the framers themselves understood it, and as part of a larger political struggle to answer the challenging, divisive questions that were necessary to address in order to build a government. It begins by allowing the framers to describe in their own words the crisis they believed they faced.

PART ONE

THE ILLNESS AND THE CURE

‖ 2 ‖

The Setting

State governments sent prominent political leaders to represent them at the Constitutional Convention. Many of these delegates had thrived in the vibrant political life of America in the 1780s. They agreed that the nation faced an urgent crisis. The bankrupt Confederation Congress could hardly act, much less cope effectively with daunting problems of national defense, internal insurrection, economic hardship, and commercial disarray. But the delegates viewed the crisis in different ways because they brought diverse aspirations, experiences, and interests to the Convention. Some aimed to build a much stronger, more centralized American state, while others presumed that the existing Confederation could be repaired with some additional institutions and policy authority. The delegates' interests were bound up in these aspirations, and they came into conflict because each region and state had its different hopes and needs for a reconstituted national government. For almost four months, they battled over their different priorities and different visions of the nation's present and future.

Who Were the Delegates?

Fifty-five men attended the Constitutional Convention at one time or another. As a group, they were among the world's most experienced and skilled republican politicians. Nearly all had been elected to their state's legislature. One-fourth of these delegates had served in other important state offices. Two were governors of their states, and two others had served as governors in the past. Others served as state attorney general, speaker of the lower house, or a judge of the state supreme court. More than half had represented their states in the Confederation Congress. James Madison described the group as "in general . . . the best contribution of talents the States could make for the occasion."[1] The two dozen most important delegates—those who attended most sessions, spoke most often, and made the most proposals—were virtually full-time political leaders. These included elder statesmen, such as the 81-year-old Benjamin Franklin of

Pennsylvania, 66-year-old Roger Sherman of Connecticut, and 61-year-old George Mason of Virginia. Half of the Convention delegates were younger men, in their 30s and 40s. Virginia's James Madison was only 36 years old. New York's Alexander Hamilton was only 30.

As few as two dozen delegates played a decisive role in developing the Constitution. The large Virginia delegation, which included Madison, Mason, George Washington, and Governor Edmund Randolph, was particularly influential. Days before the scheduled opening of the Convention, Virginia's delegates were carefully planning their strategy, meeting regularly for two to three hours a day.[2] Along with Franklin, Pennsylvania sent James Wilson and Gouverneur Morris, usually Madison's allies. Massachusetts sent Nathaniel Gorham, a key swing delegate, the maverick Elbridge Gerry, and Rufus King, soon another Madison ally. Alexander Hamilton spoke for New York even after two colleagues from his state abandoned the Convention midway through. Connecticut sent an unusually unified and effective delegation, headed by Roger Sherman, along with his protégé, Oliver Ellsworth, and his law teacher, William Samuel Johnson. South Carolina sent a strong-willed delegation headed by former governor John Rutledge, along with Pierce Butler, General Charles Cotesworth Pinckney (hereafter, General Pinckney), and his younger cousin, 29-year-old Charles Pinckney (hereafter, Charles Pinckney). Other state delegations were not as strong but included influential personalities. Delaware sent George Read and John Dickinson (an eminent national leader as well as a former president of both Delaware and Pennsylvania); New Jersey sent former state Attorney General William Paterson; North Carolina sent Hugh Williamson; and the often-divided Maryland delegation sent Daniel Carroll and Attorney General Luther Martin.[3]

Madison played a singularly important role in designing the Constitution. Already an experienced politician and authority on American government, Madison had helped write Virginia's Constitution of 1776, served in the state's House of Delegates, and represented Virginia in the Continental Congress. Madison had an unusual gift for using abstract principles and logical arguments to advance his goals. Because he understood that the initial agenda for the Convention would powerfully shape the proceedings and results, Madison prepared more carefully for the Convention than any other delegate. He studied ancient and contemporary governments, developed notes diagnosing the problems of government in the United States, and built support for his own reform agenda in private letters to friends and key potential allies. His most important contribution was the Virginia Plan, a set of resolutions introduced at the beginning of the Convention. Madison spoke or entered motions 177 times during the Convention.[4]

Connecticut's Roger Sherman became Madison's most tenacious adversary on many issues. Sherman had served in a number of state and local public offices, and spent decades helping to construct the government in Connecticut. Sherman had helped draft both the Declaration of Independence and the Articles of Confederation. Other politicians recognized Sherman's skills and independence. One notable political leader in Connecticut expressed satisfaction with his state's delegation to the Constitutional Convention "except Sherman, who, I am told, is disposed to patch up the old scheme of Government." He warned that Sherman "is as cunning as the Devil, and if you attack him, you ought to know him well; he is not easily managed, but if he suspects you are trying to take him in, you may as well catch an Eel by the tail."[5] Another delegate observed that Sherman "is an able politician, and extremely artful in accomplishing any particular object;— it is remarked that he seldom fails."[6] Sherman spoke, made motions, or seconded motions 160 times during the Convention (despite a six-day absence in July). Sherman spoke in opposition to Madison more often than any other delegate, thirty-nine times in all. Often, he questioned the need for Madison's proposals, raised doubts about their likely results, and proposed alternatives. He and his Connecticut colleagues proposed politically pragmatic compromises for such contentious issues as representation in Congress, the slave trade, the authority of the House of Representatives, and the selection of the president.[7]

George Washington and Benjamin Franklin, the two leading citizens of the nation, also played critical roles. Washington's gravity, dignity, and quiet leadership helped keep the tone respectful and the process constructive. Franklin urged the delegates to remember the larger spirit of their aspirations, and to find ways to accommodate one another. The participation and signatures of both helped boost the authority of the final Constitution.[8] Washington's civility and Franklin's spirit of compromise also were essential for weathering the Convention's political storms.

The Central Role of Politics

Madison, Sherman, and other Convention leaders were skilled practitioners of the political arts. They had mastered the tools of legislative politics in their state legislatures and in the Confederation Congress, and used these tools to build majorities or to cut away at support for their opponents' positions. To achieve their goals, they used logic, emotional appeals, moral claims, and arguments for political expediency. They developed proposals shrewdly written to win over other delegates. They negotiated over specific provisions. The most difficult decisions at the Convention—on representation in Congress, on slavery and trade, and on the presidency—resulted from such political compromises.

During the Convention, political collisions were routine. But while the politics of the Convention were very similar to legislative politics, they were much more challenging because of the stakes involved. The delegates were making up the rules about the way future national laws would be made, enforced, and interpreted. In a national government, a majority could do much more damage than the harm currently done by the feckless Confederation Congress and the state governments. A national army, a treaty helping one region and hurting another, taxes, or spending power could enrich some states and wreak havoc in others. In August, for example, Gerry argued that the new U.S. Congress "could not be trusted with" the power of taxing exports because "It might ruin the Country. It might be exercised partially, raising one and depressing another part of it."[9] The smaller, more economically vulnerable states, such as Delaware, New Jersey, and Connecticut, were especially wary of a stronger national government's power to harm them.

The delegates' conflicting interests and ideas surfaced immediately and haunted the proceedings. In the Convention's second week, Gunning Bedford of Delaware pointed out the states' different interests and economic rivalry.[10] Bedford later told the delegates that the Convention itself contained all the desires and passions that characterize politics in every political society, charging that the states' votes had been driven by interest and ambition.[11] Benjamin Franklin quickly gave up all hope that delegates would stop jousting over their regional and state interests.[12] Gerry "lamented that instead of coming here like a band of brothers, belonging to the same family, we seemed to have brought with us the spirit of political negotiators."[13] In the most contentious days of the Convention, George Washington acknowledged, "To please all is impossible, and to attempt it would be vain."[14]

As the Convention wore on, their debates increasingly exposed the delegates' deep political divisions, ambitions, and fears. As their political differences and the Constitution's provisions became clearer, so did the potential threat of any specific provision to any delegates' interests. As they built institutions that seemed to represent different interests, then, they insisted that the institution that was most favorable to their interests have the power to resist the others. Madison, interested in a strong national government, emphasized the need for presidential power and independence, while Sherman, who sought to protect state prerogatives, emphasized the need for a strong U.S. Senate. The principal motive to keep negotiating at all was the profound conviction that they could not afford to fail.

The National Crisis

By 1787, many Americans believed that the current American government could not endure much longer. For Washington "the situation of the general government, if it can be called a government, is shaken to its foundation, and liable to be overturned by every blast. In a word, it is at an end; and, unless a remedy is soon applied, anarchy and confusion will inevitably ensue."[15] Madison told the Convention that the Confederation "has disappointed every hope placed on it."[16] The Articles of Confederation, approved in 1781, established a Confederation Congress as virtually the only national governing institution. This Congress was nearly moribund by 1787. In the Confederation Congress, each state cast a single, equal vote. A few states or even a single state could often block the Congress from taking action. The Articles required an extraordinary majority of nine states to enact any major defense and financial policies, and required large majorities to do any business. As time went on, fewer and fewer delegates attended, making it difficult for Congress to even begin to get anything done. Madison wrote that "Congress are reduced to five or six States, and are not likely to do any thing during the term of the Convention."[17] There was no alternative to this failing national legislature, for the Confederation government had no executive branch and no courts.

The Confederation Congress had very limited powers. It could not impose taxes. Without a reliable source of revenue, the national government could not perform its basic functions. It could borrow money and request that the states provide it funds, but it could not force the states to pay these requisitions. By the summer of 1786, Congress was broke. It defaulted on the interest on its debts; the "King of France [was] unpaid, Creditors ruined, and Soldiers languishing."[18] Though a large majority of states supported efforts to allow the Confederation Congress to tax imports, individual states killed these proposals by denying them a unanimous vote. The national government could not provide effectively for the nation's defense. The powerful British navy still commanded the Atlantic Ocean, and the British retained a military presence in Canada and balked at abandoning forts on U.S. soil; Spain closed the Mississippi River to American trade; the Barbary pirates preyed on American merchant ships in the Mediterranean; and conflicts with Native Americans continued at the nation's western frontiers. Trade was especially vital to the country, but Congress could not reach a consensus on developing commercial ties to other nations. Wilson argued, "The true reason why Great Britain has not yet listened to a commercial treaty with us has been, because she had no confidence in the stability or efficacy of our Government."[19] A few days later, Wilson said that "the great fault of the existing Confederacy is its inactivity . . . The complaint has been that they have governed too little. To remedy this defect we were sent here."[20]

The states did most of the governing in the new nation, and their independent policies also contributed to the worsening problems.[21] Many had used their powers to restrict or tax imports, exports, or vessels from other nations or states. Each state had a different policy on trade. New York, for example, imposed the same taxes on both British goods and goods that came into the state from Connecticut and New Jersey. Farmers in these small middle states, along with

Delaware, felt increasingly vulnerable to the states of New York and Pennsylvania because New York City and Philadelphia ports were essential for shipping their crops. New Jersey demanded that Congress act to restrict New York's commercial discretion. Congress could only advise these states to retaliate.[22] Many delegates believed the states' independence and abuse of power were at the root cause of a national crisis. George Washington was convinced "that the primary cause of all our disorders lies in the different State Governments." Their jealously guarded sovereignty and parochialism were making "the situation of this great Country weak, inefficient and disgraceful."[23] Wilson told the Convention, "No sooner were the State Governments formed than their jealousy & ambition began to display themselves. Each endeavored to cut a slice from the common loaf, to add to its own morsel, till at length the confederation became frittered down to the impotent condition in which it now stands."[24]

Prominent Americans were appalled at the actions of individual states, which increasingly were acting as if they were independent, sovereign nations. Each had a militia, and nine states were developing navies. Each state printed as much currency as it pleased, borrowed money, and imposed a variety of taxes and laws. Rhode Island printed an especially large amount of paper money and established low interest rates by law. The state fined creditors who refused to accept its paper money as payment for debts. When merchants refused to accept the paper money because its value was so low, riots broke out and the state government simply eliminated the debts, outraging the creditors.[25] For most of the delegates, Rhode Island provided the chief example of unacceptable state government behavior.[26] In contrast to Rhode Island, Massachusetts imposed high taxes and enforced debts, allowing sheriffs to foreclose on financially strapped small farmers. A small army of outraged debtors, led by Revolutionary War veteran Daniel Shays, rebelled in western Massachusetts, seizing towns and burning courthouses. Shays's Rebellion seemed to foreshadow a future firestorm of anarchy across the nation.[27]

The Delegates' Differences

The delegates all generally agreed on the pressing need to strengthen the national government. But they found it very difficult to agree on exactly *how* to strengthen it. Their states shared common British traditions, laws, and language, yet economic and other differences made it seem impossible to arrive at a shared solution to the nation's governance problem. Though most Americans earned their livelihood by farming, agriculture differed profoundly from one end of the country to the other. The Southern states—Georgia, South and North Carolina, and Virginia—had the benefit of a long growing season and vast expanses of fertile soil. These states depended on growing huge quantities of tobacco, rice, and indigo to ship abroad, and they nurtured large plantations to grow these crops. Southern planters, in turn, depended on slaves to produce their crops. Farmers in states in the middle of the country, including Maryland, Pennsylvania, Delaware, New Jersey, and New York, had smaller farms and raised more diverse crops. In these middle states, iron manufacturing and other industries were beginning to develop, and New York and Philadelphia were becoming important commercial cities. New England's soil, terrain, and climate were much less hospitable for agriculture, forcing many people in the region to take up other occupations, such as whaling or cod fishing. Some New Englanders took up commerce, shipping goods among the colonies and between the colonies and their trading partners abroad. These activities, in turn, spurred the growth of shipbuilding and maritime insurance.[28]

The distinct economies of New England and the South had put them on a political collision course. The South heavily depended on exporting plantation crops, and its plantations depended on slave labor. Southern leaders wanted slave ownership protected, and they wanted to encourage as many foreign and domestic shippers as possible to compete to hold down the cost of sending Southern crops abroad. New England had little stake in slavery but an enormous stake in national policies that would favor New England's commercial shipping and fishing industries, even if that made commerce more expensive for other states. Southerners suspected that New England sought to boost trade at their region's expense. Conflict over trade on the Mississippi River hardened these regional rivalries. When Spain closed the river to Americans in 1784, it shut down a trade artery the South considered indispensable. While Southerners demanded national action to negotiate the river's reopening, Northern merchants, who depended on the Atlantic trade routes, became more willing to acquiesce to Spain's action. U.S. envoy John Jay, a New Yorker, proposed a commercial agreement in 1786 that conceded Spain's right to block the Mississippi for 25 years. For Southerners, the proposed treaty realized their worst fears about the North. The dispute paralyzed Congress.[29]

Thus the political conflicts in Philadelphia were far more complex than a simple clash of "large" versus "small" states. The division between Northern and Southern interests was fundamental. Hamilton believed that "[t]he only considerable distinction of interests lay between" states that had commercial shipping and those that did not, a difference that divided the large states of Massachusetts and Virginia.[30] Madison thought that the most important difference between states "resulted partly from climate, but principally from the effects of their having or not having slaves."[31] Pierce Butler "considered the interests" of the South and New England "to be as different as the interests of Russia and Turkey."[32]

The delegates recognized that other political rivalries divided the states within each of these regions. Charles Pinckney acknowledged five distinct regional interests: New England's fishing and commercial interests; New York's interest in free trade to maximize commercial traffic in New York City; New Jersey and Pennsylvania's interest in trading wheat and flour; Maryland and Virginia's interest in the tobacco trade; and South Carolina and Georgia's interest in the rice trade.[33] Each of these interests implied somewhat different national policies. Slavery split the nation, but the slave *trade* split the South. Georgia and South Carolina lacked enough slaves for their plantations and demanded that the slave trade continue, while Virginia and North Carolina, with a sufficient number of slaves, did not support slave imports. A halt to the slave trade would boost the value of Virginia and North Carolina slaves. Population constituted another political dividing line. Virginia was the wealthiest and most populous state; one of every six Americans lived in Virginia. Half the entire U.S. population lived in just four states: Virginia, Pennsylvania, Massachusetts, and North Carolina. Many believed that the Southern states would grow faster than the Northern states, and that areas to the southwest, like Kentucky and Tennessee, would solidify Southern dominance of the new nation.[34] It was clear that the new states in the West—the future Tennessee, Kentucky, and Ohio—would have different interests from the coastal states, and some delegates feared Western dominance of the coastal states. Access to land also divided the states. While Massachusetts, Pennsylvania, and the four Southern states enjoyed land in abundance, states that lacked large expanses of land resented them and demanded access. The states with smaller land areas and populations, then, had reason to feel that large states threatened to dominate them.

Connecticut, New Jersey, Delaware, and Maryland—smaller states wedged between the large states of Massachusetts and Virginia—had a special interest in a stronger national government, but also in protecting themselves from the larger states with more people and resources. Taxes imposed in the ports of Philadelphia and New York City drew off the profits of farmers in these states and enriched the states of Pennsylvania and New York. For these states, rules requiring equal representation in the Confederation Congress, large majorities to enact legislation, and unanimity for amendments to the Articles of Confederation all provided necessary political defenses against larger states with more economic resources.[35]

Any state, then, could find itself damaged by national government reform, depending on what powers were added to the national government and how the national government exercised them. If given the power to ban the slave trade, the national government could hurt South Carolina and Georgia, and if given the power to ban slavery altogether, it could wreck the foundation of Southern wealth. In the mid-1780s, over half of New York's state revenue came from taxes on goods imported into the United States. If the national government had the power to control import taxes and deny that power to the states, New York would lose the lion's share of its revenues and confront the need to raise other taxes—a combination of changes that might persuade New York to refuse to ratify the Constitution.[36] Connecticut could lose its authority to support religion. States with extensive public lands could sacrifice these economic and political assets.

New England stood to gain more than the South if the national government could more easily make commercial treaties with other nations. The South stood to gain more from a national treaty with Spain making it possible to ship goods down the Mississippi River to foreign ports. South Carolina, which had put off payment of debts it had run up during the Revolution, stood to gain more than any other state if the national government simply assumed responsibility for all the states' debts. Georgia faced threats from Spain and Native American tribes on its borders, and it stood to gain more than most states if the national government created an army. Any national commercial agreement with another nation could give special treatment to the products and industry of a particular state.

These conflicts already tore at the fabric of the newly independent nation. Newspapers were discussing the serious possibility that the nation would break up into three separate nations. On June 29, Madison warned the delegates that the breakup of the United States would create the same kinds of ceaseless warfare among governments that had plagued Europe:

> The same causes which have rendered the old world the Theatre of incessant wars, & have banished liberty from the face of it, would soon produce the same effects here. The weakness & jealousy of the small States would quickly introduce some regular military force against sudden danger from their powerful neighbors. The example would be followed by others, and would soon become universal. In time of actual war, great discretionary powers are constantly given to the Executive Magistrate. Constant apprehension of War, has the same tendency to render the head too large for the body. A standing military force, with an overgrown Executive will not long be safe companions to liberty. The means of defense against foreign danger, have been always the instruments of tyranny at home. . . . Throughout all Europe, the armies kept up under the pretext of defending, have enslaved the people. . . . These consequences . . . ought to be apprehended whether the States should run into a total separation from each other, or should enter into partial confederacies. Either event would be truly deplorable; & those who might be accessory to either, could never be forgiven by their Country, nor by themselves.[37]

Hamilton added that the parts of a fragmented United States would form alliances with European powers, "who will foment disturbances among ourselves, and make us parties to all their own quarrels."[38]

A Capsule History of the Convention

The Convention was scheduled to begin on Monday, May 14, 1787. But those delegates who arrived on time discovered to their frustration that there were not enough state delegations to begin the meeting. By Thursday of that week, delegates from only four states—Virginia, South Carolina, New York, and Pennsylvania—were present. Washington reported that this tardiness was "highly vexatious to those who are idly and expensively spending their own time here."[39] A week and a half later, Rufus King, alarmed by the continued absence of delegates from New England, urged them to hurry to Philadelphia. "Believe me," warned King, "it may prove most unfortunate if they do not attend within a few days."[40]

A sufficient number of delegations arrived to begin business on Friday, May 25 (see appendix 1 for a Convention chronology). Eleven state delegations had sufficient representation, or were about to have it. New Hampshire's delegates did not arrive until July. The Rhode Island legislature strongly supported paper money and generally opposed a stronger national government; it sent no delegates to the Convention.[41] Some prominent American leaders did not participate in the Convention, most notably John Adams (serving as the minister to Great Britain) and Thomas Jefferson (serving as minister to France). Other leading Americans declined to serve because they also opposed a much stronger national government; these included Samuel Chase of Maryland and Patrick Henry of Virginia, who "smelled a rat."[42] Their refusals portended some of the conflicts that would erupt at the Convention, as well as the harsh battle over ratification after the Convention. Both Chase and Henry were outspoken Anti-Federalists who opposed the Constitution.

These delegates agreed to conduct the *process* for designing the Constitution much the way they had made laws in Congress or state legislatures.[43] Like the Congress, the rules required strict secrecy to encourage frank discussion.[44] The rules specified that the Convention would vote by states (as in the Confederation Congress), rather than by delegates. Unlike the Confederation Congress, a simple majority vote would carry any issue, including the most contentious ones. Delegates would not share information about the proceedings with outsiders.[45] As in a legislature, they created special committees to deal with knotty problems, and to put together most polished drafts of their work. No one could be sure how long the deliberations would take. Mason feared they would stay "until July, if not later."

On Tuesday, May 29, Virginia Governor Edmund Randolph "opened the main business" by presenting Virginia's plan for reforming America's national government. The delegates began to discuss Virginia's fifteen resolutions, one by one, on May 30. Thereafter, the Convention generally met for six days a week, holding a total of eighty-five working sessions in all (it temporarily adjourned for nine days near the end of July, and for a few other days). The Convention debated the Virginia Plan as a "committee of the whole" into July.[46] On June 12 the Convention approved an amended version of the Virginia Plan. Three days later, William Paterson proposed an alternative plan drawn up by delegates from New Jersey, Connecticut, New York, Delaware, and Maryland. This New Jersey Plan proposed to keep the existing Confederation Congress and add a national executive, a national supreme court, and a few new national powers. The Convention rejected the New Jersey Plan on June 19 and then began to debate each of the Virginia resolutions again. The problem of representation in Congress, however, stymied the Convention.

On July 2, when many delegates felt they had reached an impasse, they turned over the problem of representation to a "grand" committee, that is, a special committee made up of one delegate from each state. The committee reported a compromise plan on July 5: each state would continue to have equal representation in the Senate, as in the Confederation Congress, but in the House of Representatives, each state would have a larger or smaller number of representatives depending on the number of people living in the state. After several days of heated debate, the delegates approved this compromise (here termed the "Connecticut" Compromise) on July 16. Over the next ten days, the delegates worked through the remaining Virginia resolutions. They turned their work over to a five-member Committee of Detail on July 26.[47] This committee, chosen by ballot, developed a more detailed draft of a Constitution and presented it on August 6. For the next month, the delegates debated each provision of the Committee of Detail draft, line by line, and sometimes word by word. The delegates turned over additional contentious issues to committees, including a dispute on slavery and trade, and another in the vexing problem of the presidency. The Convention approved a recommended solution to the slavery and trade dispute on August 29, and in early September it approved proposals for the presidency developed by a grand Committee on Postponed Matters. A final, five-member "Committee of Style" (again, chosen by ballot) put all these agreements into a nearly final draft of the Constitution in mid-September.[48]

On Monday, September 17, three and a half months after the Convention began, thirty-nine of the delegates signed the final Constitution and the meeting adjourned permanently. The Convention had worked for fifteen weeks, with a break in late July and early August. The Convention secretary recorded 569 separate roll call votes.

Participating in the Convention was unpleasant in many ways. The summer of 1787 was hot, humid, and often uncomfortable in Philadelphia. Disease was a constant worry for delegates.[49] Port cities like Philadelphia were gateways not only for commerce, but also for disease and filth. Yellow fever and typhoid imperiled the city's residents, especially in warmer weather. For Dickinson, these conditions intensified existing health problems.[50] Attending the Convention took delegates away from their families, and the expense of even modest accommodations mounted as weeks turned into months.[51] Small wonder that so many delegates came to Philadelphia late, or left early, or went away for a sustained period during the Convention. Hamilton attended sporadically and returned home to New York twice, and Gouverneur Morris of Pennsylvania was absent for most of June.[52] Some left angry, disgusted by the evolving compromises. John Lansing and Robert Yates of New York left for good in July, and Luther Martin of Maryland left in August. Those who did stay often were maddened by the Convention's endless political quarrels and the sluggish pace.[53]

Despite these problems, the intense sense of crisis motivated these prominent political leaders to keep to their task. George Mason wrote to his son that the difficulties of the Revolution and the creation of the states "were nothing compared to the great business now before us" which would influence "the happiness or misery of millions yet unborn."[54] When James Wilson "considered the amazing extent of country, the immense population which is to fill it, the influence which the Government we are to form will have, not only on the present generation of our people & their multiplied posterity, but on the whole Globe, he was lost in the magnitude of the object."[55] James Madison wrote: "The whole Community is big with expectation. And there can be no doubt but that the result will in some way or other have a powerful effect on our destiny."[56]

From Crisis to Reconstitution

The delegates believed that the nation's political crisis required them to reconstitute the nation's fundamental structure of governance. They understood that their many diverse interests, and their loyalty to their states, would make the task of overhauling the nation's government daunting. Virginia's Governor Edmund Randolph said that he viewed the crisis as the glue that would hold the Convention together: "When the salvation of the Republic was at stake, it would be treason to our trust, not to propose what we found necessary. He painted in strong colors, the imbecility of the existing confederacy, & the danger of delaying a substantial reform."[57]

|| 3 ||

The Remedy

The sense of crisis made it urgent to change the course of the United States. The delegates all were nationalists, in the sense that they agreed that the country required an effective national government, capable of mounting an effective military defense and nurturing the nation's prosperity. The Convention had a unique opportunity to overhaul the national government and persuade Americans to accept far-reaching changes. The delegates overcame two serious concerns: first, that the Convention lacked the authority to reconstitute the national government, and second, that Americans would not accept the proposals they produced.

Monarchy was the most common form of government in eighteenth-century Europe, but the delegates dismissed monarchy as an option for the United States. A more capable national government was acceptable only if it was based on republican principles: the people must exercise supreme authority over the government, and the representatives of the people make important public policy choices. Government's authority had to be derived from the people, majorities had to determine its actions, and its powers had to be separated. These open-ended principles guided—but could not decide for them—more specific choices about the way the national government should be designed.

Was It Necessary and Timely to Reconstruct the Nation's Government?

The Virginia delegates began the Convention debates with a forceful argument for a thorough overhaul of the national government. James Madison asserted that he would not be afraid to consider anything that would benefit the safety, freedom, and happiness of the nation.[1] George Washington privately wrote that all the delegates seemed to share this view.[2] For John Dickinson of Delaware, a highly respected delegate from the smallest state, "All agree that the confederation is defective" and "all agree that it ought to be amended."[3] As soon as Roger Sherman took his seat, he "admitted that the Confederation had not given sufficient power to Congress and that additional powers were necessary, particularly that of raising money which he said would involve many other powers."[4]

Many delegates also believed that there never would be a better moment to change the nation's path and create a more effective, durable national government. The United States was at a critical turning point, and political support for replacing the Articles of Confederation would never be stronger. When Edmund Randolph concluded his presentation of Virginia's plan for a new government, he exhorted the delegates "not to suffer the present opportunity of establishing general peace, harmony, happiness and liberty in the U.S. to pass away unimproved."[5] Randolph later warned that there are circumstances in which "the ordinary cautions must be dispensed with; and this is certainly one of them. . . . The present moment is favorable, and is probably the last that will offer."[6] Another delegate heard Randolph say, "We would be Traitors to our Country if we did not embrace this parting Angel."[7]

Other delegates amplified Randolph's conviction that this was the moment to rebuild the government. Alexander Hamilton bluntly insisted that the "crisis . . . which now marked our affairs, was too serious to permit any scruples whatever to prevail over" everyone's duty to "the public safety & happiness."[8] Hamilton asserted, "This was the critical moment for forming" a government that possessed "sufficient stability and strength to make us respectable abroad." It was miraculous that the delegates were engaged in "tranquil & free deliberations on the subject," but it "would be madness to trust to future miracles."[9] Charles Pinckney of South Carolina "was extremely anxious that something should be done, considering this as the last appeal to a regular experiment."[10] Despite his sharp criticism of the plans of the largest states, Delaware's Gunning Bedford admonished the delegates "that something should be immediately done. It will be better that a defective plan should be adopted, than that none should be recommended."[11]

But did the Convention have the authority to seize the moment and reconstruct the national government? On May 30, the delegates overwhelmingly voted for the proposition "that a national government ought to be established consisting of a supreme Legislative, Judiciary, and Executive," that is, a government fundamentally different from the Confederation. General Pinckney of South Carolina immediately questioned whether the Convention had the authority to take this necessary step, and Elbridge Gerry of Massachusetts shared his uncertainty.[12] These questions did not stop the delegates from continuing to build a new government plan.

Later, the smaller states raised these doubts as a tactic to try to stop Virginia's plans for the new government. William Paterson of New Jersey directly challenged the Convention's authority to propose far-reaching changes in the Confederation government. The Convention and the states, he argued, had agreed to a Convention only to reform the Articles; "the people of America were sharpsighted and not to be deceived," he claimed. Paterson invoked political pragmatism, arguing, "We have no power to go beyond the federal scheme, and if we had the people are not ripe for any other. We must follow the people; the people will not follow us." The delegates, he asserted, should return home and ask the states for more authority to revise the nation's government.[13] New York's John Lansing claimed that "New York would never have concurred in sending deputies to the convention, if she had supposed the deliberations were to turn on a consolidation of the States, and a National Government" (but Lansing admitted "that there was no certain criterion of the public mind on the subject").[14]

For the vast majority of the delegates, the nation's perilous situation overwhelmed such doubts about the Convention's authority. George Mason considered the existing system dissolved "by the appointment of this Convention to devise a better one."[15] Charles Pinckney "thought the Convention authorized to go any length in recommending, which they found necessary to remedy the evils which produced this Convention."[16] Pennsylvania's James Wilson "conceived himself authorized to *conclude nothing*, but to be at liberty to *propose any thing*."[17] Randolph, answering claims that voters had not authorized the creation of a national government, discounted the doubters' claims and argued that no state would have had the boldness to identify all the Confederation's weaknesses in a public statement.[18] Madison and Hamilton emphasized that the Confederation could not be repaired. "The States sent us here to provide for the exigencies of the Union," Hamilton pointed out. "To rely on & propose any plan not adequate to these exigencies, merely because it was not clearly within our powers, would be to sacrifice the means to the end."[19] In the end, despite their doubts about the Convention's warrant, General Pinckney and William Paterson both signed the Constitution.

Public Opinion and Constitutional Reform

The delegates knew that, if their final plan were unpopular with American citizens, the Constitution would be rejected and the moment for government reconstruction would be lost. George Mason observed, "If the Government is to be lasting, it must be founded in the confidence & affections of the people, and must be so constructed as to obtain these."[20] Hamilton believed the delegates had to persuade the people to embrace an adequate government: "We must devise a system on the Spot—It ought to be strong and nervous [that is, vigorous], *hoping* that the good Sense and principally the *Necessity of our Affairs* will reconcile the People to it."[21]

Delegates who did not like one provision or another naturally tried to argue that the public would reject the Constitution if the objectionable provision were included. Gerry was especially quick to raise this objection throughout the Convention. In June, he insisted that "it was necessary to consider what the people would approve," as all legislators do.[22] In August, Gerry observed, "We cannot be too circumspect in the formation of this System. It will be examined on all sides and with a very suspicious eye." Americans had revolted against the abuses of the British government, and Gerry said that this recent experience "will produce a critical attention to the opportunities afforded by the new system to like or greater abuses."[23] Delegates who opposed Virginia's plan employed these doubts tactically, questioning whether such far-reaching changes were politically practical. Paterson preferred more modest changes in the Confederation "because it accorded . . . with the sentiments of the people."[24] Lansing reminded the delegates that the states had rejected a proposal to tax imports only four years earlier, and asked if "so great a change" in public opinion could "have already taken place"? Trusting that the people would embrace a far-reaching overhaul of the government "would be trusting to too great an uncertainty."[25]

Delegates who wanted a strong national government challenged these assumptions about public opinion. Madison said, "No member of the Convention could say what the opinions of his Constituents were at this time," much less their opinions in the months after the Constitution became public. "The distinguished delegates who wrote it would give it more authority, as would the support of "all the most enlightened & respectable citizens. Should we fall short of the necessary & proper point, this influential class of citizens will be turned against the plan, and little support in opposition to them can be gained to it from the unreflecting multitude."[26] For Gouverneur Morris, Americans' opinions "were unknown. They could not be known. All that we can infer is that if the plan we recommend be reasonable & right; all who have reasonable minds and sound intentions will embrace it."[27] Mason tried to turn Lansing's argument against him, inferring that the alternative, simply "to augment the powers of Congress, never could be expected to succeed."[28] Wilson pointed out that the people were not demanding the reform of their state governments to solve the nation's problems, but instead expected relief from "the National Councils."[29]

Madison and his allies turned questions about the Convention's authority to their advantage, arguing that a worthy Constitution would win public support. When the Convention received the formal proposal for the Connecticut Compromise, Madison implored the delegates to write a Constitution "which would be espoused & supported by the enlightened and impartial part of America," because the "merits of the system alone can finally & effectually" win public support.

The people of states like Delaware and New Jersey would "acquiesce under an establishment founded on principles the justice of which they could not dispute" and which would protect them from the commercial interference of neighboring states.[30] In August, Wilson tried to enlarge the delegates' understanding of public opinion. Wilson said he was

> acting & responsible for the welfare of millions not immediately represented in this House. . . . [W]hat [would he] say to his constituents in case they should call upon him to tell them why he sacrificed his own Judgment in a case where they authorized him to exercise it? Were he to own to them that he sacrificed it in order to flatter their prejudices, he should dread the retort: did you suppose the people of Pennsylvania had not good sense enough to receive a good Government?[31]

Privately, Madison wrote to Thomas Jefferson, then in France, "that the public mind will now or in a very little time receive anything that promises stability to the public Councils & security to private rights, and that no regard ought to be had to local prejudices or temporary considerations."[32] When he wrote this letter, the Convention was putting the finishing touches on the Constitution. Only its adherence to republican principles enabled the delegates to take the critical step toward a stronger national government.

A Republican National Government

The American people—and the delegates themselves—would only accept a strong new national government if it were a *republican* government, with ultimate authority based squarely on the will of the people. All the states had built republican governments during the American Revolution.[33] While the delegates disputed whether the public would accept this or that provision, Mason advised the delegates to step back and reflect on the shared republican values that united the country. According to Madison's notes, Mason said that:

> Much has been said of the unsettled state of the mind of the people. He believed the mind of the people of America, as elsewhere, was unsettled as to some points; but settled as to others. In two points he was sure it was well settled. 1. in an attachment to Republican Government. 2. in an attachment to more than one branch in the Legislature. Their constitutions accord so generally in both these circumstances, that they seem almost to have been preconcerted. This must either have been a miracle, or have resulted from the genius of the people.[34]

In a letter to his son, Mason expressed his confidence that the delegates as a group valued republicanism as much as he did.[35] Roger Sherman declared, "Government is instituted for those who live under it. It ought therefore to be so constituted as not to be dangerous to their liberties."[36]

For Mason, republican governments derived their strength from "the love, the affection, the attachment of the citizens to their laws, to their freedom, and to their country. Every husbandman will be quickly converted into a soldier when he knows and feels that he is to fight not in defense of the rights of a particular family, or a prince, but for his own."[37] James Wilson observed that the widely respected French political philosopher Montesquieu favored "confederated Republics. I am for such a confederation if we can take for its basis liberty, and can ensure a vigorous execution of the Laws."[38] For Wilson, "A confederated republic joins the happiest kind of Government with the most certain security to liberty."[39]

Charles Pinckney argued at length that Americans' culture, habits, and economy required a republican government: "The people of the United States are perhaps the most singular of any we are acquainted with." They were divided by "fewer distinctions of fortune & less of rank" than the inhabitants of other nations. "Every freeman has a right to the same protection & security," and a small property holding "entitles them to the possession of all the honors and privileges the public can bestow," producing "a greater equality, than is to be found among the people of any other country." In a new nation like the United States,

> possessing immense tracts of uncultivated lands, where every temptation is offered to emigration & where industry must be rewarded with competency, there will be few poor, and few dependent—Every member of the Society almost, will enjoy an equal power of arriving at the supreme offices & consequently of directing the strength & sentiments of the whole Community. None will be excluded by birth, & few by fortune, from voting for proper persons to fill the offices of Government. . . . Our true situation appears to me to be this—a new extensive Country containing within itself the materials for forming a Government capable of extending to its citizens all the blessings of civil & religious liberty—capable of making them happy at home. This is the great end of Republican Establishments.

Pinckney blamed the national crisis on "the weakness & defects" of a moribund government, and not on the people themselves.[40]

The delegates rejected monarchy out of hand. The world's leading governments were monarchies in 1787, but Mason "hoped that nothing like a monarchy would ever be attempted in this Country. A hatred to its oppressions had carried the people through the late Revolution."[41] Wilson reflected that the size of the United States seemed to require a monarchy, but the nation's "manners are against a King and are purely republican."[42] Gerry said that "there were not 1/1000 part of our fellow citizens who were not against every approach towards Monarchy."[43] In the first week, even Dickinson, who frankly described limited monarchy as "*one* of the best Governments in the world," conceded that this form of government "was out of the question" for the United States because "[t]he spirit of the times—the state of our affairs, forbade the experiment, if it were desirable."[44] When James McClurg proposed an unlimited term for the national executive, Gouverneur Morris, who supported the idea, felt it necessary to make clear that he did so not to establish a monarch but to make republican government work better, "to establish such a Republican Government as would make the people happy and prevent a desire of change."[45]

Many of the delegates cited the British constitutional monarchy as the best government in the world, but they considered the British model unsuitable for American circumstances. For Wilson, an admirer of the British system, it "was inapplicable to the situation of this Country."[46] Hamilton also liked the British model, but he understood that it would be politically unwise to propose "any other form" than a republic without a king.[47] Charles Pinckney pointed out that the "peculiar excellence" of the British constitution could "not possibly be introduced into our System" because the United States lacked the landed nobility that balanced the commoners and the king in the British system. Instead of the king, the nobles, and the commoners, each of whom controlled one branch of British government, the United States had only commoners, making it impossible to form a government like Britain's, "consisting of three branches, two of which shall have nothing to represent."[48] (The Articles of Confederation prohibited the Confederation Congress from granting any title of nobility, and the Convention unanimously added this prohibition to the Constitution).[49]

The delegates also rejected democracy in its purest form, the direct participation of the people in governance. While some delegates used the term "democracy," they rejected the idea that the people should directly deliberate and make government decisions. When he introduced the Virginia Plan, Randolph identified "the democratic parts" of the state constitutions as the "chief danger" the nation faced. None of the state constitutions had "provided sufficient checks against the democracy."[50] In June, Hamilton observed that "The members most tenacious of republicanism were as loud as any in declaiming against the vices of democracy."[51]

Madison criticized direct democracy, and he distinguished it from the admirable democratic *form* of government he advocated at the Convention.[52] Direct democracy threatened both government effectiveness and Americans' liberty.

He believed in a democratic government, based on direct election of one legislative house, but the choices of which subsequently would be filtered by the
decisions of institutions that were not directly selected by the people: a second
legislative house, an executive, and a judiciary.[53]

John Dickinson believed that Britain's example taught Americans to nurture
a government attuned to their own nation's culture: "Experience must be our
only guide. Reason may mislead us." Reason had not produced the treasured
practice of trial by jury. "Accidents probably produced" the discoveries that
shaped the development of British government, "and experience has given a
sanction to them. This is then our guide."[54]

The Requirements and Ambiguities
of Republicanism

Republican principles placed three conditions on the new national government.
First, the people must be the ultimate source of government authority. Government action, the delegates believed, is legitimate only when made by institutions
controlled by the citizens. The delegates had to ensure that national policy-makers
would be accountable and responsive to the people.[55] Madison said, "The people
were in fact, the fountain of all power, and by resorting to them, all difficulties
were got over."[56] "In free Governments," said Benjamin Franklin, "the rulers are
the servants, and the people their superiors & sovereigns."[57] "Notwithstanding
the oppressions & injustice experienced among us from democracy," observed
Mason, "the genius of the people is in favor of it, and the genius of the people
must be consulted."[58] Mason believed that "you should draw the Representatives
immediately from the people. It should be so much so, that even the Diseases of
the people should be represented—if not, how are they to be cured?"[59]

Second, rule by the people implied *majority* rule—majorities should determine
government actions. Madison pointed out, "According to the Republican theory
indeed, Right & power being both vested in the majority, are held to be synony-
mous."[60] Wilson asserted, "The majority of people wherever found ought in all
questions to govern the minority," and added, "If the majority cannot be trusted, it
was a proof . . . that we were not fit for one Society."[61] Sherman argued that "to
require more than a majority to decide a question was always embarrassing as had
been experienced in cases requiring the votes of nine States in Congress."[62]

Third, republicanism required that government institutions with different
policy responsibilities must be kept separate. A strong national government needed
an executive leader and a national court—but a republican national government
required that these new bodies be kept independent enough to prevent any single
part of the government to control all its power. Separate institutions would have to

make the laws (a legislature), to enforce the laws (an executive), and settle disputes about the laws (a judiciary). The abuse of unified power had occurred in Europe over and over again. The republican state constitutions all separated government branches.[63] To further separate the power to make laws, most states had created *bicameral* legislatures, that is, legislatures with two chambers, sometimes distinguished as a larger house of representatives and a senate with fewer members than the house.

The delegates generally agreed that a republican national government required the same kinds of institutions. Pierce Butler observed that he had "opposed the grant of powers to Congress heretofore, because the whole power was vested in one body. The proposed distribution of the powers into different bodies changed the case, and would induce him to go great lengths."[64] Nathaniel Gorham wrote that all the delegates agreed on the separation of powers, and the delegates endorsed a national government consisting of "a supreme Legislative, Executive and Judiciary" early in the Convention.[65]

Madison reasoned, "If it be a fundamental principle of free Government that the Legislative, Executive & Judiciary powers should be *separately* exercised; it is equally so that they be *independently* exercised," and the delegates agreed in principle.[66] As Madison explained (and later elaborated in *The Federalist* Number 51), the independence of these institutions had to be guaranteed by more than mere written guidelines. Independence meant that the legislature, executive, and judiciary should have substantial powers that other branches could not remove, so that any branch could stop the efforts of ambitious leaders in other branches from encroaching on the authority of other branches and throwing the system out of balance. As Madison told the delegates,

> If a Constitutional discrimination of the departments on paper were a sufficient security to each against encroachments of the others, all further provisions would indeed be superfluous. But experience had taught us a distrust of that security; and that it is necessary to introduce such a balance of powers and interests, as will guarantee the provisions on paper. Instead therefore of contenting ourselves with laying down the Theory in the Constitution that each department ought to be separate & distinct, it was proposed to add a defensive power to each which should maintain the Theory in practice. In so doing we did not blend the departments together. We erected effectual barriers for keeping them separate.[67]

Gouverneur Morris argued that each branch had to have a stake in its own power and in stopping other branches from intruding on that power, so that "[v]ices as they exist, must be turned against each other."[68]

It was particularly important to keep Congress under control. Madison argued that abuses in the state legislatures proved the need for carefully limiting legislative power, particularly by strengthening the executive, because

> Experience had proved a tendency in our governments to throw all power into the Legislative vortex. The Executives of the States are in general little more than Cyphers; the legislatures omnipotent. If no effectual check be devised for restraining the instability & encroachments of the latter, a revolution of some kind or other would be inevitable. The preservation of Republican Government therefore required some expedient for the purpose.[69]

Because the legislature would have such power, Madison believed it was especially crucial to arm the other branches with political weapons to defend their powers.[70]

To keep the powerful national legislature in check, most delegates believed that it had to consist of two separate legislative houses. Wilson argued, "If the Legislative authority be not restrained, there can be neither liberty nor stability; and it can only be restrained by dividing it within itself, into distinct and independent branches. In a single house there is no check, but the inadequate one, of the virtue & good sense of those who compose it."[71] Bicameralism in a legislature was a "source of stability," Dickinson believed.[72] Even the champions of the New Jersey Plan, which retained the unicameral Confederation Congress and gave it additional power, conceded that bicameralism was an important check in a powerful legislature.[73] Roger Sherman "admitted two branches to be necessary in the State Legislatures, but saw no necessity for them in a Confederacy of States."[74] Still, the pragmatic Sherman agreed to a bicameral legislature to overcome the intractable dispute over representation in Congress. On May 31 and again after they rejected the New Jersey Plan, the Convention overwhelmingly approved a bicameral legislature, in which each house could propose and had to agree to new laws.[75]

But it is essential to point out that these general republican principles did *not* provide guidance for most of the *specific* decisions the delegates made in Philadelphia. Republicanism did not specify precisely *how* powers should be separated, checked, and balanced.[76] After all, republican governments in Rhode Island and other states were producing awful policies. Each of the state republics had implemented these basic principles in a different way, and none of the states offered a satisfactory example of how to separate powers and ensure that government would produce good results. Republicanism provided no guidance on the method for choosing officers of the government, judges, or the upper house of the legislature. Pennsylvania's 1776 Constitution was unusually democratic; Pennsylvania (as well as Vermont and Georgia) had a single house legislature.[77]

Republican values did not determine who would be eligible to vote, or to serve in office. They did not specify what powers the government should have, what powers any one branch should have, or how the independence of the branches would be guaranteed. They did not speak to the problem of ratifying the Constitution. Most important, they did not determine what, if any, powers the existing states should exercise in the new constitutional order. In other words, republicanism established some very general guidelines for the Constitution, but these principles could not resolve the conflicts that tormented the delegates as they confronted specific choices about government design. Other factors, such as ideas, interests, politics and individual visions for the new government, shaped these choices.

The Challenge of Reconstitution

All the delegates aspired to a more capable national government as a necessary remedy for the nation's crisis. Doubts about public opinion and their own authority did not deter them in the task of building this government. Their agreement on republicanism and rejection of monarchy gave them a basic foundation for moving forward. But the republican ideal created far more questions than it answered. Should new national authority be broad or narrow? Most important, how could the people ultimately control the government and still ensure that it would pursue policies that would be good for the nation?

4

Controlling Republican Politics

The Main Challenge

The delegates' dedication to republican principles, and their determination to build a strong national government, forced them to confront an agonizing dilemma. How could they build a national government responsive to "the people" and still guarantee that the government would pursue policies that would be good for the nation? For example, citizens could demand that government provide them with short-term relief for their debts, but short-term government debt relief could harm the nation's long-term prosperity. Politics was inevitable in republican government, and political skills are essential for making republican government work. Republican governments created politicians because they created elective offices, and elective offices inspired candidates to seek those offices. Republican politics required majority rule, and republican legislators used their negotiating skills to craft majorities. But the delegates' experience with the state legislatures proved that interests and factions could unite into a destructive majority, and abuse republican power to pursue policies that harmed liberty, property, prosperity, and stability. Dishonorable politicians regularly manipulated public opinion and abused their public trust. The kinds of politicians who caused so much turmoil in the states would also serve in the new national government, where their misconduct could cause far more damage. As Gouverneur Morris warned, the new national legislature could "ruin the Country" if it wanted, no matter how the delegates designed it.[1] This central problem of building a republican government that was safe and stable influenced all the choices that the Convention made.

The Central Role of Political Majorities in Republican Government

Politics are inseparable from republican government. Majorities rule in a republic. Assembling a majority in a legislature required a full toolbox of political skills: careful framing of issues, controlling the discussion agenda and the rules, using persuasion, bargaining over policy (including swapping a vote for one person's bill in return for his vote on a different bill), and artfully compromising. Robust political coalitions aimed at building majorities—called "parties" or "factions"— existed in every state. Delegates such as Robert Morris of Pennsylvania, George Read of Delaware, John Langdon of New Hampshire, and Edmund Randolph of Virginia were leaders of political factions in their states.[2]

But majority rule allowed a majority to use its power to advance its members' selfish interests at the expense of the nation. George Mason expressed this central problem succinctly: "He admitted that notwithstanding the superiority of the Republican form over every other, it had its evils. The chief ones, were the danger of the majority oppressing the minority, and the mischievous influence of demagogues."[3] Mason believed that "a majority when interested will oppress the minority."[4]

On June 6, James Madison explained how contending factions of citizens undermine democracy and create a fundamental dilemma in designing a republican government. These comments anticipate his analysis in *The Federalist* Number 10, one of the most famous of *Federalist* essays. Here, in the secrecy of the Convention, Madison could be much more explicit than he was in *The Federalist*:

> All civilized Societies would be divided into different Sects, Factions, & interests, as they happened to consist of rich & poor, debtors & creditors, the landed, the manufacturing, the commercial interests, the inhabitants of this district, or that district, the followers of this political leader or that political leader, the disciples of this religious sect or that religious sect. In all cases where a majority are united by a common interest or passion, the rights of the minority are in danger. What motives are to restrain them? A prudent regard to the maxim that honesty is the best policy is found by experience to be as little regarded by bodies of men as by individuals. Respect for character is always diminished in proportion to the number among whom the blame or praise is to be divided. Conscience, the only remaining tie, is known to be inadequate in individuals: In large numbers, little is to be expected from it. Besides, Religion itself may become a motive to persecution & oppression.
>
> These observations are verified by the Histories of every Country ancient & modern.... Why was America so justly apprehensive of Parliamentary injustice? Because Great Britain had a separate interest real or supposed, & if her authority had been admitted, could have pursued that interest at our expense. We have seen the mere distinction of color made in the most enlightened period of time, a ground of the most oppressive dominion ever exercised by man over man.

What has been the source of those unjust laws complained of among ourselves? Has it not been the real or supposed interest of the major number? Debtors have defrauded their creditors. The landed interest has borne hard on the mercantile interest. The Holders of one species of property have thrown a disproportion of taxes on the holders of another species.

The lesson we are to draw from the whole is that where a majority are united by a common sentiment and have an opportunity, the rights of the minor party become insecure. In a Republican Government the Majority if united have always an opportunity.[5]

Madison believed "the spirit of contention & faction," driven by the quest to build majorities, was "One of the greatest evils incident to Republican Government."[6] He repeated this conviction in *The Federalist* Number 10.

More ominously, the new national government would attract the kind of politicians who were pursuing wicked goals in the states. These rogues and demagogues would try to stir popular passions and build majorities for the bad public policies that dismayed the delegates and prompted the Constitutional Convention in the first place. Schemes to gain power (often termed "cabals" and "intrigues" at the Convention) would be common. Mob furor was inherent in human nature, warned Alexander Hamilton: "When a great object of Government is pursued, which seizes the popular passions, they spread like wild fire, and become irresistible."[7] "Notwithstanding the precautions taken in" designing Congress, concluded Mason, it still would be so much like the state legislatures "that it must be expected frequently to pass unjust and pernicious laws."[8]

Unfortunately, the American people had proved that they were vulnerable to such political manipulation. Few delegates matched Roger Sherman's dedication to republican values, but at the beginning of the Convention he emphasized that the people lack "information and are constantly liable to be misled."[9] For Elbridge Gerry, "The evils we experience flow from the excess of democracy. The people do not want virtue; but are the dupes of pretended patriots." The people of Massachusetts "are daily misled into the most baneful measures and opinions by the false reports circulated by designing men, and which no one on the spot can refute." He was still a republican, but now he was wary of the harm republican governments could do.[10]

To drive home the point, some delegates evoked a dark future in which those Americans with little or no property would become a majority of the population and threaten republican government. Gouverneur Morris envisioned a time "when this Country will abound with mechanics & manufacturers who will receive their bread from their employers. Will such men be the secure & faithful Guardians of liberty? Will they be the impregnable barrier against aristocracy?"

Children cannot vote because of their immaturity, and, Morris added, "the ignorant & the dependent can be as little trusted with the public interest."[11] John
Dickinson argued that the right to vote should be restricted to those with property to erect "a necessary defense against the dangerous influence of those mul-
titudes without property & without principle, with which our Country like all
others, will in time abound."[12] While "the people" were the foundation of republican government, ambitious politicians could mold popular emotions into
explosive force in support of their malevolent projects.

Malicious Politicians

Unprincipled politicians, then, posed the greatest threat to a new republican
government for the nation. These malicious individuals would combine routine
legislative skills with lies, manipulation, extortion, bribery, secret plots, and
other unscrupulous techniques to enlist support for their plans. The Convention's most experienced statesmen harbored unsentimental pessimism about
some of their fellow politicians. As early as June 2, Benjamin Franklin painted a
gloomy portrait of politics in the new government:

> Sir, there are two passions which have a powerful influence on the af-
> fairs of men. These are ambition and avarice; the love of power, and the
> love of money. Separately each of these has great force in prompting
> men to action; but when united in view of the same object, they have in
> many minds the most violent effects. Place before the eyes of such men
> a post of *honor* that shall at the same time be a place of *profit*, and they
> will move heaven and earth to obtain it. The vast number of such places
> it is that renders the British Government so tempestuous. The struggles
> for them are the true sources of all those factions which are perpetually
> dividing the Nation, distracting its councils, hurrying sometimes into
> fruitless & mischievous wars, and often compelling a submission to dis-
> honorable terms of peace.
>
> And of what kind are the men that will strive for this profitable pre-
> eminence, through all the bustle of cabal, the heat of contention, the
> infinite mutual abuse of parties, tearing to pieces the best of characters?
> It will not be the wise and moderate, the lovers of peace and good order,
> the men fittest for the trust. It will be the bold and the violent, the men
> of strong passions and indefatigable activity in their selfish pursuits.
> These will thrust themselves into your Government and be your rulers.
> And these too will be mistaken in the expected happiness of their situ-
> ation: For their vanquished competitors of the same spirit, and from

the same motives will perpetually be endeavoring to distress their administration, thwart their measures, and render them odious to the
people.[13]

Madison personally "had witnessed the zeal of men" who had public debts "to
get into the Legislatures for sinister purposes."[14] Gerry claimed that "the worst
men" were elected to the lower house of the Massachusetts legislature, stating,
"Men of indigence, ignorance & baseness, spare no pains however dirty to carry
their point against men who are superior to the artifices practiced."[15] Nathaniel
Gorham argued that legislatures should not appoint judges because such "Public
bodies feel no personal responsibility and give full play to intrigue & cabal."
Rhode Island illustrated "the insensibility to character produced by a participation of numbers, in dishonorable measures, and of the length to which a public
body may carry wickedness & cabal."[16]

No one was immune to the temptations of public office, warned Madison,
and "all men having power ought to be distrusted to a certain degree."[17] Institutions would develop their own political interests and try to dominate other
institutions. "The Legislature will continually seek to aggrandize & perpetuate themselves," warned Gouverneur Morris, and they "will seize those critical moments produced by war, invasion or convulsion for that purpose."[18]
Time and time again, the delegates predicted that politicians would game
any particular rule to gain political advantage. For example, if senators were
given long, six-year terms in office, Mason thought the senators "will probably settle themselves at the seat of Government [and] will pursue schemes
for their own aggrandizement."[19] Madison and others believed that the
House of Representatives' proposed power to "originate" tax and spending
legislation amounted to nothing because the Senate would scheme to shape
these bills anyway. For example, the Senate could reject bills sent to it by the
House of Representatives and force the House to accept its tax and spending
priorities.[20]

The process of choosing the nation's leader would create exceptional opportunities for political scheming. Madison warned that giving Congress the responsibility to elect the president would be a disaster, because "Public bodies are
always apt to be thrown into contentions, but into more violent ones by such
occasions than by any others."[21] Gerry warned that if Congress chose the president, there would be constant conniving for the job: "The Legislature & the candidates would bargain & play into one another's hands. Votes would be given by
the former under promises or expectations from the latter, of recompensing
them by services to members of the Legislature or to their friends."[22] These
worries about "the great evil of cabal" help to explain why the debates on the
election of the president dragged on for so long.[23]

Every public office in a republican government could be abused. As delegates spoke in favor of presidential power to check the legislature, Franklin suggested that "We seemed to have too much confidence" in individual leaders, but "Experience showed that caprice, the intrigues of favorites & mistresses" and so on were the individual abuses "most prevalent in monarchies."[24] Franklin said that in Pennsylvania, the governor's veto power "was constantly made use of to extort money. No good law whatever could be passed without a private bargain with him."[25] Gerry predicted that some judges would be corrupt.[26] When the delegates discussed a rule prohibiting Congress from trying to influence judges' salaries, Gouverneur Morris cautioned that shrewd legislators would find a way to evade such a rule: "Judges might resign, & then be re-appointed to increased salaries."[27]

The delegates spent more time debating the selection of government officials than in defining government authority or designing the inner workings of the government because they expected that U.S. Representatives, Senators, presidents and administrators would constantly pander to those upon whom they depended. Wilson evoked Montesquieu when he asserted that "an officer is the officer of those who appoint him."[28] Gouverneur Morris observed sardonically, "In Religion the Creature is apt to forget its Creator. That it is otherwise in political affairs." Noting the delegates' eager defense of their states, Morris added that the Constitutional Convention itself provided "an unhappy proof" that representatives and appointees would be beholden to those who selected them.[29] Madison and others regularly warned that Government officials would tailor public policy to satisfy those on whom they depended for their appointments, elections, or salaries, whether the people at large, or Congress, or the president.

The delegates expected bald corruption, such as patronage appointments and bribery. They understood that public officials could reward their friends with appointments to prestigious and lucrative government jobs. Given the power to make appointments, James Wilson believed, "The appointment to great offices ... was notorious, was most corruptly managed of any that had been committed to legislative bodies."[30] If the Congress selected the national judiciary, the result would be "Intrigue, partiality, and concealment."[31] When Madison proposed to prohibit members of Congress from holding other offices, King responded that "the idea of preventing intrigue and solicitation of offices was chimerical."[32] Madison and others routinely took the likelihood of bribery into account as they worked through institutional design.[33]

Unchecked, all this political scheming and chicanery could result in relentless turmoil, instability, and partisanship. Charles Pinckney voiced the common belief that "Ancient Republics fell of their own turbulency."[34] Republican legislatures, said Rufus King, were "utterly unfit" to grant pardons for crimes against the United States because "They are governed too much by the passions of the moment." In the wake of Shays's Rebellion, "In Massachusetts, one assembly would have hung all the insurgents in that State: the next was equally disposed to pardon them all."[35]

Could a Republican Government Control Republican Politics?

The delegates had to build a national government that would control the inevitable problems that some politicians caused in republican governments. Their fundamental challenge was to find a way to prevent the worst consequences of political ambition fueled by imperfectly informed and easily inflamed voters. They had to limit the effects of sinister politicians, and encourage politicians to use the government for the benefit of the nation. Dickinson hopefully observed, "If ancient republics have been found to flourish for a moment only & then vanish forever, it only proves that they were badly constituted; and that we ought to seek for every remedy for their diseases."[36]

No delegate took this problem more seriously than James Madison. He had experienced the way the grueling reality of day-to-day republican government had eroded the idealism of the Revolutionary years. "What we once thought the Calumny of the Enemies of Republican Government is undoubtedly true," Madison admitted.[37] In notes written before the Convention (and echoed later in *The Federalist* Number 51), Madison had written that the great necessity in designing a government "is such a modification of the Sovereignty as will render it sufficiently neutral between the different interests and factions, to control one part of the Society from invading the rights of another, and at the same time sufficiently controlled itself, from setting up an interest adverse to that of the whole Society."[38]

While republican theorists viewed the separation of powers as a defense against a dictatorial king, Madison argued that a separate Senate could guard against wicked politicians in the new national legislature. A discussion of the Senate in late June gave Madison the opportunity to explain his ideas about the design of republican political institutions, and the Senate's place in that plan. The Senate aimed

first to protect the people against their rulers; secondly to protect the people against the transient impressions into which they themselves might be led.

A people deliberating in a temperate moment, and with the experience of other nations before them, on the plan of Government most likely to secure their happiness, would first be aware, that those charged with the public happiness, might betray their trust. An obvious precaution against this danger would be to divide the trust between different bodies of men, who might watch & check each other. In this they would be governed by the same prudence which has prevailed in organizing the subordinate departments of Government where all business liable to abuses is made to pass through separate hands, the one being a check on the other.

It would next occur to such a people, that they themselves were liable to temporary errors, through want of information as to their true interest, and that men chosen for a short term, & employed but a small portion of that in public affairs, might err from the same cause. This reflection would naturally suggest that the Government be so constituted, as that one of its branches might have an opportunity of acquiring a competent knowledge of the public interests. Another reflection equally becoming a people on such an occasion would be that they themselves, as well as a numerous body of Representatives, were liable to err also, from fickleness and passion. A necessary fence against this danger would be to select a portion of enlightened citizens, whose limited number, and firmness might [r]easonably interpose against impetuous counsels. It ought finally to occur to a people deliberating on a Government for themselves, that as different interests necessarily result from the liberty meant to be secured, the major interest might under sudden impulses be tempted to commit injustice on the minority.

In all civilized Countries the people fall into different classes having a real or supposed difference of interests. . . . There will be particularly the distinction of rich & poor. It was true as had been observed by Mr. Pinckney we had not among us those hereditary distinctions, of rank which were a great source of the contests in the ancient Governments as well as the modern States of Europe, nor those extremes of wealth or poverty which characterize the latter. We cannot however be regarded even at this time, as one homogeneous mass, in which every thing that affects a part will affect in the same manner the whole.

In framing a system which we wish to last for ages, we should not lose sight of the changes which ages will produce. An increase of population will of necessity increase the proportion of those who will labor under all the hardships of life, & secretly sigh for a more equal distribution of its blessings. These may in time outnumber those who are placed above the feelings of indigence. According to the equal laws of suffrage, the power will slide into the hands of the former. No agrarian attempts have yet been made in this Country, but symptoms of a leveling spirit, as we have understood, have sufficiently appeared in a certain quarters to give notice of the future danger.

How is this danger to be guarded against on republican principles? How is the danger in all cases of interested coalitions to oppress the minority to be guarded against? Among other means by the establishment of a body in the Government sufficiently respectable for its wisdom & virtue, to aid on such emergencies, the preponderance of justice by throwing its weight into that scale.[39]

Madison told the delegates that the plan was to be critical for preserving liberty and for the ideal of republican government itself.[40] Elbridge Gerry would "not deny . . . that the majority will generally violate justice when they have an interest in so doing," but added that he did not see "any such temptation in this Country" because the "great body of lands yet to be parceled out & settled" would absorb these pressures for the foreseeable future.[41]

Hamilton echoed Madison, warning that "if we did not give to" republican government "due stability and wisdom, it would be disgraced & lost among ourselves, disgraced & lost to mankind for ever." While Hamilton did not himself "think favorably of Republican Government," he did advocate liberty. "It was certainly true that nothing like an equality of property existed," and he believed that "inequality would exist as long as liberty existed, and that it would unavoidably result from that very liberty itself. This inequality of property constituted the great & fundamental distinction in Society."[42]

Shrewdly, Madison turned arguments about the failures of republicanism into a forceful case for enlarging and strengthening the national government. Roger Sherman, said Madison,

had admitted that in a very small State, faction & oppression would prevail. It was to be inferred then that wherever these prevailed the State was too small. Had they not prevailed in the largest as well as the smallest, though less than in the smallest; and were we not thence admonished to enlarge the sphere as far as the nature of the Government would admit? This was the only defense against the inconveniences of democracy consistent with the democratic form of Government. . . . The only remedy is to enlarge the sphere, & thereby divide the community into so great a number of interests & parties, that in the first place a majority will not be likely at the same moment to have a common interest separate from that of the whole or of the minority; and in the second place, that in case they should have such an interest, they may not be apt to unite in the pursuit of it. It was incumbent on us then to try this remedy, and with that view to frame a republican system on such a scale & in such a form as will control all the evils which have been experienced.[43]

A larger "sphere"—that is, enlarged national responsibilities over a larger geographical area—would make it difficult to form malevolent majorities that posed the central threat to republicanism.[44] The majority coalitions in the national government would have to be much broader than the majority coalitions that formed in the states. These national majorities would inevitably be more diverse, and harder to sustain, than political coalitions in the states. In *The Federalist* Number 10, Madison employs this logic to justify a geographically extensive republic, on the grounds that a large territory will make it difficult to form an effective majority bent on invading citizens' rights.[45]

While political ambition was unavoidable, Madison and others believed they could design institutions in a way that harnessed this ambition to make republican government work for the common good. For example, the Convention rejected term limits for elected officials so that naturally ambitious office-seekers would feel more incentive to serve the people. Sherman believed that "[f]requent elections are necessary to preserve the good behavior of rulers. They also tend to give permanency to the Government, by preserving that good behavior, because it ensures their re-election."[46] Oliver Ellsworth thought the president "will be more likely to render himself worthy of [re-election] if he be rewardable with it. The most eminent characters also will be more willing to accept the trust under this condition, than if they foresee" that they will be forced to leave office at a fixed time.[47]

Some of the delegates expressed faith in politicians in general, arguing that many were sincere and dedicated to the nation's best interests. Madison himself said that it would be wrong to assume that a majority of the members of Congress would "lose their capacity for discharging, or be bribed to betray, their trust." The "integrity and fidelity of Congress" would be constrained by "their personal integrity & honor, the difficulty of acting in concert for purposes of corruption," and "the soundness of the remaining members."[48]

Wilson avidly defended republican politicians. He denied that "the ambition which aspired to Offices of dignity and trust" was "an ignoble or culpable one." It was counterproductive to consider public office disreputable, "or to withhold from it the prospect of those rewards, which might engage it in the career of public service."[49] Wilson celebrated the idealistic aspirations of young politicians when he asserted that it was wrong to stigmatize as venal "the laudable ambition" of rising in public service into "the honorable offices of the Government." This ambition was "most likely to be felt in the early & most incorrupt period of life, and . . . all wise and free Governments" have cherished, not checked, this ambition. "The members of the Legislature have perhaps the hardest & least profitable task of any who engage in the service of the state," said Wilson. "Ought this merit to be made a disqualification?"[50]

The Challenge of Republican Government

Politics was inevitable in republican government, and even if many or most politicians could be trusted with public power, some could not. The delegates confronted this problem over and over again as they worked through specific provisions of the Constitution. To deal with their doubts, the delegates placed a greater and greater burden on the separation of institutional powers. In republican theory before the 1780s, the separation of powers aimed to prevent abuses by a nation's leader. In the minds of the framers, the separation of powers came to be a remedy for the problems of republican legislatures as well. By separating powers, the delegates imagined they had a chance to limit the effects of these politicians, even if such persons tried to inflame voters' passions to achieve some corrupt purpose. Every choice about the rules became difficult as delegates imagined the political manipulation that any rule could set in motion.

The delegates did not have to start with a blank slate, however. They were politicians themselves, with the skills and experience to build majorities in the Constitutional Convention. James Madison already had begun to plan the way the new government could work, and to develop a strategy for guiding this plan through the Convention.

|| 5 ||

Broad Nationalism

The Politics of the Virginia Plan

James Madison brought to Philadelphia not only a far-reaching plan to overhaul American government, but also a carefully prepared strategy for winning the Convention over to this plan. Madison was a "broad" nationalist: he sought a national government with broad authority, including complete power over taxes, commerce, and the military, and the power to veto any state law. In this government, the national legislature, the most important policy-making body, would be separated into two houses in which each state would have a number of representatives proportional to its population. Madison's strategy included framing the problem in an advantageous way and building a coalition of six state delegations to support the plan. The Virginia Plan, overwhelmingly based on Madison's preparation, made fifteen proposals for government reform that became the basis for the initial negotiations over the Constitution.

Madison's Strategy for the Convention

In the half dozen years before the Constitutional Convention, Madison had emerged as one of the nation's brightest young political leaders, a friend and an ally of notables such as George Washington, Thomas Jefferson, and Alexander Hamilton. From the moment he arrived in Congress in 1780 as a young representative from Virginia, Madison had fought to increase the powers of the national government. He had played a leading role in the Annapolis Convention of 1786.[1] After the Constitutional Convention, he went on to serve in the U.S. House of Representatives, as U.S. Secretary of State, and as president. He helped build the Democratic-Republican Party. During his political career, he ran for elective office more times than did Bill Clinton, George W. Bush, or Barack Obama.

For a young, ambitious leader like Madison, the Constitutional Convention was the chance of a lifetime. A natural political strategist, the 36-year-old Madison already had mastered the arts of republican politics and legislation. He grasped that winning political battles in any republican assembly required extensive preparation in advance. By framing the nation's problems carefully, he hoped to guide other delegates to support the plan for government reform he favored. Madison sought to take advantage of the general view that this was the moment for fundamental change. He seemed to understand instinctively that by carefully arranging the Convention's initial agenda, he could focus the delegates' attention on specific choices in a specific sequence, thus shaping the delegates' reasoning. In correspondence with his friends and potential allies just before the Convention, he methodically developed proposals that could galvanize the delegates' discontent with the Confederation and turn that discontent into a consensus on fundamental change. He aimed to convince the delegates to lay aside their parochial concerns and focus on building a strong national government that could pursue the nation's interest.[2]

Madison's strategy involved eight steps.

1. *Command the Facts.* In the months before the meeting, Madison read everything about government available to him, including books Jefferson sent him from Europe. He studied past and present confederacies and republics, and wrote "Notes on Ancient and Modern Confederacies" to help lay out a more systematic record of the problems encountered by confederated governments like that of the United States. He also drafted "Vices of the Political System of the United States," his diagnosis of the political crisis in which the United States found itself. He wrote letters to friends and key potential allies to build more support for his diagnosis of the nation's problems and his ideas for a solution.[3]

2. *Arrive Early.* Madison arrived in Philadelphia on May 3, 1787, eleven days before the scheduled start of the Convention. He met with several of the Pennsylvania delegates, including Robert Morris, Gouverneur Morris, and James Wilson, to build support for his agenda. As they waited for the meeting to begin, Virginia's delegates, including Madison, Washington, Governor Edmund Randolph, and George Mason, met frequently and coalesced behind Madison's agenda.[4]

3. *Arrange for Advantageous Rules and a Friendly Umpire.* The Virginia and Pennsylvania delegates discussed the rules for the Convention in advance. Pennsylvania's delegates hoped that the states would vote according to their population size. The Virginia delegates "stifled" this rule, fearing that it would spark "fatal altercations" between large and small states. Virginia argued that the delegations should vote as equals, as they did in the Confederation Congress, because "it would be easier to prevail" on the small states "to give up their

equality for the sake of an effective Government" than "to disarm themselves of the right" of an equal vote from the start and "thereby throw themselves on the mercy of the large States."[5] But unlike the Confederation Congress, a simple majority in the Convention would carry *any* vote, including the key votes on representation and national authority. Madison and his fellow Virginia delegates, then, were gambling that equal state votes at the Convention would enable them to pass their agenda. The Convention's rules committee (chaired by Virginia delegate George Wythe) recommended and the Convention adopted Virginia's voting rules, as well as the rule of strict secrecy.[6] Madison also helped convince a reluctant George Washington to serve as a Virginia delegate, and the delegates naturally selected Washington as their presiding officer.

4. *Put Forward a Diagnosis that Infers Your Cure.* Madison blamed state governments' autonomy for as many national problems as possible. The states governments' selfish parochialism, and their power to pursue it regardless of the nation's interest, was the fundamental flaw of American government in 1787. Madison's "Vices of the Political System of the United States" blamed the failure of the Confederation's finances on "the number and independent authority of the States." States were violating foreign treaties, encroaching on national power, and on each other. State policy-makers provided politically expedient "base and selfish measures" for their own constituents, though these measures harmed citizens in other states.[7] In introducing the Virginia Plan, Edmund Randolph elaborated on these points. Madison reinforced these arguments several times during the Convention debates, most notably when he spoke against the New Jersey Plan on June 19.

5. *Draw Your Cure from Your Diagnosis.* Before the Convention, Madison proposed that "the national Government should be armed with positive and complete authority in all cases which require uniformity," including full taxing power, all commercial powers, and most military powers. He repeatedly battled to broaden one national power or another. He also insisted that it was absolutely necessary to authorize the national government to veto any state law.[8] In a rebuilt government dedicated to truly national interests, each state should have representation in the legislature according to the size of its population, unlike the Confederation Congress. Larger states like Virginia should have more representatives than small states like Delaware. Some delegates referred to this principle as "proportional representation," or representation in Congress based on each state's proportion of the national population.

6. *Build a Strong Political Coalition.* Madison aimed to build a coalition of six states. The coalition would depend, first, on the three largest states, Virginia, Pennsylvania, and Massachusetts. It also depended, second, on three Southern states that were expected to grow large in the near future: North Carolina, South Carolina, and Georgia. If Rhode Island sent no delegates, these six states would

constitute half the states at the Convention, and if they held together, they could block alternatives to his plan. Madison used the weeks before the Convention to line up support among these potential allies.

7. *Organize the Proposals in an Advantageous Sequence.* Madison believed that the Convention had to establish proportional representation in Congress before it took up the expansion of national power. This sequence of choices would cement together his six-state coalition. The three states with the largest population—Virginia, Massachusetts, and Pennsylvania—would support proportional representation because they immediately would have more power in the new national legislature than in the Confederation Congress. The three Southern states—Georgia, South Carolina, and North Carolina—were expected to grow rapidly, and could expect to gain power in the national legislature under proportional representation. Prior to the Convention, Madison wrote to Washington, "*A majority of the States, and those of greatest influence, will regard it as favorable to them*" (italics added).[9] He forecast that the smaller states would yield to the larger ones on this issue, and with more weight in Congress, these six states would agree to much more national government authority.

Establishing proportional representation first was essential because some of the Southerners supported broad nationalism with reservations. These *conditional* broad nationalists supported the Virginia Plan on the condition that the new national legislature had two houses, and that states had representation in both houses based on their proportion of the population. This formula offered greater influence for the South, and more protection for its slave economy. Pierce Butler observed that he had "opposed the grant of powers to Congress heretofore, because the whole power was vested in one body. The proposed distribution of the powers into different bodies changed the case, and would induce him to go great lengths" toward expanding national authority.[10]

Once the Convention had established that the larger states would have more influence in the new national legislature, their "*principal objections . . . to the necessary concessions of power*" would be mitigated, and his political coalition would approve the rest of Virginia's proposals for adding national power (italics added).[11] In other words, Madison believed that he could construct a durable six-state coalition that would win a commitment to proportional representation in Congress, and this early victory for proportional representation would allow the coalition to sweep the even more important priority—an extensive expansion of national power—into the final Constitution. During the debates in July, Madison specifically predicted that the failure of proportional representation in the Senate would cause the Convention to withhold "every effectual prerogative" of national authority.[12]

8. *Ensure that the State Governor Introduces the Plan.* Madison, a well-known advocate for stronger national powers, did not introduce the Virginia Plan at

the Constitutional Convention. Instead, that honor went to Virginia's governor, Edmund Randolph—Virginia's leading *state* official at the Convention. This choice not only solidified the Virginia delegation, but it also gave its recommendations more legitimacy in the eyes of the many other state officials at the meeting.

Virginia's Diagnosis

On May 29, after establishing the Convention's rules, Governor Randolph opened the Convention's deliberations with a wide-ranging indictment of the Confederation government. Randolph emphasized the gravity of the nation's crisis, "and the necessity of preventing the fulfillment of the prophecies of the American downfall."[13] Aware that some of the Convention delegates had helped bring the Articles of Confederation into being, Randolph

> professed a high respect for its authors, and considered them as having done all that patriots could do, in the then infancy of the science, of constitutions & of confederacies, when the inefficiency of requisitions was unknown; no commercial discord had arisen among any states; no rebellion had appeared as in Massachusetts; foreign debts had not become urgent; the havoc of paper money had not been foreseen; treaties had not been violated; and perhaps nothing better could be obtained from the jealousy of the states with regard to their sovereignty.[14]

But the Confederation government could not cope with such problems, Randolph charged. He cited five major failings, each rooted in the excessive power of the state governments.

First, "the Confederation produced no security against foreign invasion," the most fundamental responsibility of a national government. Congress could neither "prevent a war nor . . . support it by their own authority"; nor could it prevent the states from breaking treaties, or provoking a war with other nations. "The Imbecility of the Confederation is equally conspicuous when called upon to support a war," Randolph said. State militias were inadequate for the nation's defense.[15]

Second, the Confederation "government could not Check the quarrels between states, nor a rebellion in any," such as Shays's Rebellion in Massachusetts.[16] There existed "no provision to prevent the States [from] breaking out into war." The states could engage in cutthroat economic competition by lowering taxes on imported goods, luring trade at the expense of their neighbors.[17]

Third, the nation could gain "many advantages" under a reconstituted government "which were not attainable under the Confederation." These advantages included "a productive impost," that is, a tax on imported goods that could yield a steady revenue for the federal government, and a power to reduce trade barriers and counteract the hostile trade regulations of foreign countries.[18] James McHenry recorded Randolph's sought additional Congressional "power to prevent emissions of bills of credit," a power states were abusing, and the power to establish "great national works—the improvement of inland navigation—agriculture—manufactures—a freer intercourse among the citizens."[19]

Fourth, the "federal government could not defend itself against the encroachments from the states."[20] The states did not fulfill their responsibilities to the union, especially in supplying needed requisitions, because "[i]n every State assembly there has been a party opposed to federal measures."[21]

Fifth, the Confederation Congress "was not even paramount to the state constitutions" because the state legislatures, rather than the voting citizens, had approved the Articles of Confederation.[22] McHenry heard Randolph emphasize that most of the state constitutions were written during the early stages of the American Revolution, "and by persons *elected by the people* for that purpose." The Articles of Confederation were approved "long after this, and had [their] ratification not by any *special appointment* from the people, but from the several assemblies. No judge will say that the *confederation* is paramount to a State constitution."[23]

At the conclusion of his indictment of the current situation, Randolph "reviewed the danger of our situation and appealed to the sense of the best friends of the U.S.—the prospect of anarchy from the laxity of government everywhere."[24] According to McHenry, Randolph concluded that

> we see that the confederation is incompetent to any *one* object for which it was instituted. The framers of it [were] wise and great men; but human rights were the chief knowledge of the times when it was framed so far as they applied to oppose Great Britain. . . .
>
> Having pointed out its defects, let us not be afraid to view with a steady eye the perils with which we are surrounded. Look at the public countenance from New Hampshire to Georgia. Are we not on the eve of war, which is only prevented by the hopes from this Convention?
>
> Our chief danger arises from the democratic parts of our constitutions. It is a maxim which I hold incontrovertible, that the powers of government exercised by the people swallows up the other branches. None of the constitutions have provided sufficient checks against the democracy. The feeble Senate of Virginia is a phantom. Maryland has a more powerful senate, but the late distractions in that State, have discovered that it is not powerful enough. The check established in the

constitution of New York and Massachusetts is yet a stronger barrier against democracy, but they all seem insufficient.[25]

In light of the pervasive sense of crisis, even the most ardent defenders of state prerogatives had to concede that major change was necessary.

Virginia's Plan for a New National Government

Randolph's indictment of the Confederation's weaknesses closely followed Madison's own diagnosis of the vices of American government, and Randolph proposed a cure that closely followed Madison's prescription. The remedy, said Randolph, "must be the republican principle," and he explained each of Virginia's fifteen resolutions.[26] These resolutions were arranged in the sequence that Madison believed essential for success. They emphasized a much stronger national government, and they reduced state government autonomy.[27]

Virginia proposed, first, that "the articles of Confederation ought to be so corrected & enlarged as to accomplish the objects proposed by their institution; namely 'common defense, security of liberty and general welfare.'" All these purposes were written in the Articles of Confederation. By agreeing to this resolution, the delegates would go on the record as favoring in principle the expansion of national power to achieve goals already accepted as the basis of the current American national government. The delegates would begin by committing themselves to an "enlargement" of the Articles of Confederation to make the national government more capable of fulfilling its duties. There would be little disagreement about the need to take this step.

Second, "the rights of suffrage in the National Legislature ought to be proportioned to the Quotas of contribution, or to the number of free inhabitants." By approving this resolution, the delegates would be forced to take the next step in Madison's sequence, to go on record supporting representation in the legislature based on relative size of a state's population or its relative contribution to national revenue.

Third, "the National Legislature" (eventually termed "Congress") would "consist of two branches." Now, the delegates would agree to a two-house legislature, and, given approval of the previous resolution, representation in *each* would be based on relative size of a state's population or revenue.

Fourth, "the members of the first branch of the National Legislature" (eventually, the House of Representatives) "ought to be elected by the people of the several States" for a term of some specified number of years, to be determined. They would have to meet a minimum age requirement. Members of the House of Representatives would not be chosen by state governments, as was true in the Confederation Congress, but directly by voters, completely bypassing the state legislatures. These national legislators would "receive liberal stipends," reinforcing their independence from the state governments. Their loyalty would be focused on the nation because they would be "ineligible to any office established by a particular State, or under the authority of the United States" while they served in the legislature and for a time thereafter. They could not be reelected for a specified number of years after the expiration of their term, and their voters could force them out of office before the end of their term.

Fifth, the House of Representatives would choose "the members of the second branch of the National Legislature" (eventually, the Senate) "out of a proper number of persons nominated by the individual Legislatures." Again, there would be a minimum age requirement. The senators "would hold their offices for a term sufficient to ensure their independency" and "receive liberal stipends." Like the members of the House, they would "be ineligible to any office established by a particular State, or under the authority of the United States" while they served and for a time thereafter. The selection by the House ensured that the Senate also would be independent of the states.

Only after taking these first five steps did Virginia's agenda turn to the task of broadening national authority. The first five resolutions established representation based on population size, and once the Convention approved these measures, Madison hoped his six-state coalition would support a vast expansion of national power.

Sixth, the House of Representatives and the Senate could originate new laws, and the new national legislature would have the powers of the Confederation Congress as well as the very broad power "to legislate in all cases to which the separate States are incompetent, or in which the harmony of the United States may be interrupted by the exercise of individual Legislation." The new Congress would also have Madison's proposed power to veto "all laws passed by the several States, contravening in the opinion of the National Legislature the articles of Union." If any state failed "to fulfill its duty," the "force of the Union" could be brought against it.

Seventh, the new government would have a "National Executive" (eventually, the president). Congress would choose this leader for some fixed term of years. To protect a measure of independence, he would "receive a fixed compensation for the services," and Congress could not raise or lower this salary to try to manipulate him. The executive would serve a single term and could not be reelected. Most delegates agreed that the lack of an executive was a serious flaw in the Articles of Confederation.

Eighth, the national executive, together with "a convenient number of the National Judiciary," would have the power to review and veto acts passed by Congress. Congress would be able to override this veto with some large majority (left unspecified). This provision placed a check on Congress, an appealing feature for delegates who believed that the state legislatures had too much power and were too quick to bend to the voters.

Ninth, there would be a National Judiciary "to consist of one or more supreme tribunals" (eventually, the U.S. Supreme Court) and "inferior tribunals" with original jurisdiction in federal cases. Congress would select the national judges, who would serve for an unlimited term (holding office "during good behavior") and, to ensure their independence, receive a fixed salary that Congress could not raise or lower. The Supreme Court would hear appeals of lower court decisions and have jurisdiction in cases of piracy, foreign citizens, and other cases "which may involve the national peace and harmony." The delegates generally agreed that the lack of a national judiciary also was a flaw of the Articles of Confederation.

Tenth, new states could be brought into the union. Most of the delegates anticipated that the western parts of Virginia (now Kentucky) and North Carolina (now Tennessee), along with parts of the Northwest Territory (much of the Midwest), would seek to join the union as independent states. Thus, the Virginia Plan anticipated a government for a larger nation than the original thirteen states.

Eleventh, the new Constitution should guarantee "a Republican Government" to each state. This provision allowed the U.S. government to intervene militarily against insurrections, such as Shays's Rebellion, in the states.

Twelfth, the existing Congress would be phased out smoothly, and the national commitments made by the Confederation would be honored by the new government. This provision reassured the nation's creditors that the national government would repay its loans, facilitating the national and international acceptance of the reconstituted government.

Thirteenth, the new Constitution could be amended. The process of amendment could bypass Congress, so that national legislators could not block a change in their own powers. This provision permitted future adjustments, and potentially could diminish any dissatisfaction delegates might harbor when their work was done.

Fourteenth, members of Congress, the president, and the national judges "ought to be bound by oath to support the articles of Union" to constrain their ability to violate the Constitution. This provision added a motive for national officials to focus on the interests of the entire nation.

Fifteenth, when the Convention completed its work, its recommended changes would be sent to the Confederation Congress for its "approbation" and submitted to "an assembly or assemblies of Representatives, recommended by the several Legislatures to be expressly chosen by the people, to consider & decide thereon." Neither Congress, nor the state legislatures, would ratify the Constitution. Instead, special state ratifying bodies, chosen by voters, would ratify it. Madison believed it was crucial to bypass the state governments to ratify the Constitution, because these governments would have strong incentives to block the loss of their powers to a new national government.

From Agenda to Battleground

Madison could not have hoped for a start to the Convention more favorable to his plans. The rules, the presiding officer, and most important, the agenda, all worked in his favor. Once Governor Randolph put the plan before the delegates, they examined it, in part, as stewards of the interests of their states. The role of these states in the new system became a key rallying point for Madison's opponents.

‖ 6 ‖

Narrow Nationalism

The Virginia Plan's Opponents

The Virginia Plan posed a severe political threat to the smaller states excluded from James Madison's coalition of large and Southern states. Many of the leading delegates from these states supported a much narrower form of nationalism than Madison. Each of these smaller states had an equal vote in the existing Confederation Congress. This equal vote gave them leverage against larger states enacting laws that would harm them. The Virginia Plan would create a more powerful national government in which they the smaller states would have less influence. Virginia's proposed new government could run roughshod over the smaller states.

Soon after Randolph proposed the Virginia Plan, leading delegates from these vulnerable states, such as Connecticut's Roger Sherman, began to articulate an alternative "narrow" nationalism and to mount a defense of the states' authority. These narrow nationalists delayed Madison's agenda, put its supporters on the defensive, and built a political coalition to protect the states' influence. By the third week of the Convention, they had developed an alternative agenda—the New Jersey Plan—that aimed to protect most of the state governments' existing prerogatives. The authors of the New Jersey Plan failed to substitute their agenda for Virginia's. But their challenge shaped the Convention's negotiations and compromises.

The Virginia Plan's Threat

Virginia's proposals posed a clear threat to the smaller and medium-sized states between Massachusetts and Virginia—that is, the states left out of Madison's coalition of large and Southern states. If representation in the legislature were based on the size of a state's population, smaller states easily could be outvoted on critical national issues, allowing the large and Southern states to enact laws harmful to the other states. Moreover, every state would lose power if the national government took over the authority to tax, to regulate commerce, and to veto any state law. New York could no longer tax imports—a critical source of New York State's revenues and independence. New Jersey and Connecticut could no longer prevent large states with ports from colluding in Congress to pass laws that increased costs for their citizens. A grant of economic authority so broad, then, in combination with reduced influence in Congress, posed a substantial threat to the vital interests of New York, New Jersey, Connecticut, Delaware, and Maryland. Delaware's delegates warned each other about the intentions of the larger states even before the Convention began.[1]

The frank words of some of Madison's allies undoubtedly intensified the apprehensions of the delegates from these states. Gouverneur Morris insisted that ultimate government authority, or sovereignty, could not be divided between the states and the National government.[2] Clearly, if the United States created a true national government, the states would surrender all their authority to the nation. After more than a month of frustrating debate, Morris attacked state governments more bluntly. According to Madison, he spun out a nightmare scenario if the larger states agreed to the Virginia Plan and the small states refused:

> This Country must be united. If persuasion does not unite it, the sword will. [Morris] begged that this consideration might have its due weight. The scenes of horror attending civil commotion can not be described, and the conclusion of them will be worse than the term of their continuance. The stronger party will then make traitors of the weaker; and the Gallows & Halter will finish the work of the sword. How far foreign powers would be ready to take part in the confusions he would not say. Threats that they will be invited have it seems been thrown out. He drew a melancholy picture of foreign intrusions . . . State attachments, and State importance have been the bane of this Country. We cannot annihilate; but we may perhaps take out the teeth of the serpents.[3]

Two days later, Morris observed, "It had been one of our greatest misfortunes that the great objects of the nation had been sacrificed constantly to local views." The states took advantage of the Revolution to extort from the large states an equal vote in the Confederation Congress, and they now demanded to keep that equal vote. But the urgency of the Revolution had passed, and "the large States are at liberty now to consider what is right, rather than what may be expedient. . . . What if all the Charters & Constitutions of the States were thrown into the fire, and all their demagogues into the ocean? What would it be to the happiness of America?"[4]

Alexander Hamilton was convinced that "[t]he general power, whatever be its form, if it preserves itself, must swallow up the State powers. Otherwise it will be swallowed up by them."[5] Hamilton complained, "The States have constantly shown a disposition rather to regain the powers delegated by them than to part with more, or to give effect to what they had parted with. The ambition of their demagogues is known to hate the control of the General Government."[6] This combative language signaled the deep hostility that some proponents of the Virginia Plan harbored toward the state governments.

The Political Strategy of the Virginia Plan's Opponents

The delegates from the vulnerable states immediately began to construct an alternative to Virginia's agenda by questioning the need for such far-reaching changes. John Dickinson tried to shift the agenda on the day Randolph introduced the Virginia Plan. He focused on narrowing the agenda for effective national power, advocating incremental steps to fix the Confederation government instead of the sweeping changes proposed by Virginia: "The enquiry should be," first, "What are the legislative powers which we should vest in [the existing Confederation] Congress"? Second, "What judiciary powers"? Third, "What executive powers"? Dickinson thought the Convention should begin by resolving "That the confederation is defective; and then proceed to the definition of such powers as may be thought adequate to the objects for which it was instituted."[7] Roger Sherman agreed on the need for major changes, but was not "disposed to Make too great inroads on the existing system." The states very well could defeat the entire plan if the Convention inserted objectionable provisions.[8]

Even within Madison's coalition, Pierce Butler of South Carolina was concerned "that the taking so many powers out of the hands of the States as was proposed, tended to destroy all that balance and security of interests among the States which it was necessary to preserve."[9] Elbridge Gerry worried about a provision to create new electoral districts because "it would alarm & give a handle to the State partisans, as tending to supersede altogether the State authorities. He thought the Community not yet ripe for stripping the States of their powers," even those not required for local management. "He was for waiting till people should feel more the necessity of it."[10]

Several of the delegates from the vulnerable states began to construct a vision of narrow nationalism to counter the broad nationalists. They touted the states as a necessity and a virtue. They argued that the states were entrenched in American culture, and that they were strong, vital, and widely accepted. Though "We are a nation," said Dickinson, the nation consisted "of parts or States—we are also confederated," and he hoped "we shall always remain confederated."[11] The existence of distinct states was a "principal source of stability" in the nation, so "[t]his division ought therefore to be maintained, and considerable powers to be left with the States. . . . Without this, and in case of a consolidation of the States into one great Republic, we might read its fate in the history of smaller ones," said Dickinson. One of the "remedies" for the diseases that plagued republics was "the accidental lucky division of this country into distinct States; a division which some seemed desirous to abolish altogether."[12]

Oliver Ellsworth insisted that the survival of republican government depended on maintaining the vital role of the states. He invoked the argument that republican governments worked best in small geographical areas (later, the Anti-Federalists would take up the "small republic" argument in their battle against ratification).[13] Citizens were "warmly attached to their several Constitutions," said Ellsworth. Large states like Virginia and Massachusetts evidently could not exercise effective control over areas far away from their capitals, he said. He doubted that republican government could exist on a national scale.[14] Ellsworth also doubted whether the national government could deal adequately with the local tasks on which domestic happiness depended. From the states "alone he could derive the greatest happiness he expects in this life. His happiness depends on their existence, as much as a newborn infant on its mother for nourishment."[15]

These philosophical defenses of the states dovetailed with many states' specific interests. The narrow nationalists fought to preserve many state prerogatives, recognizing that each state had a stake in one prerogative or another. South Carolina's delegates, for example, rebelled against the idea that there would be national courts located in states. John Rutledge, a South Carolina judge, claimed that these "inferior" national courts were "an unnecessary encroachment" on the states that created "unnecessary obstacles" to state ratification of a new national government. Sherman added that these new courts would make the national government more expensive to operate.[16] Madison defended these satellite national courts, asking what would happen if the state courts made "improper verdicts . . . under the biased directions of a dependent Judge, or the local prejudices of an undirected jury?" The new government needed a judiciary as strong as its legislature, because "a Government without a proper Executive & Judiciary would be the mere trunk of a body without arms or legs to act or move."[17]

On June 6, while debating Virginia's proposal for the direct election of the U.S. House of Representatives, James Wilson counterattacked. The principle opposition to the Virginia Plan, Wilson argued, would come from state officials who stood to lose their power and position: "The opposition was to be expected . . . from the *Governments*, not from the Citizens of the States." The people themselves "would be rather more attached to the national Government than to the

State Governments as being more important in itself, and more flattering to their pride."[18] Sherman tried to shift the debate by arguing for robust state governments and for limiting the scope of national power in the new system. Like Ellsworth, he suggested that the largest states were too big to govern well—implying that a national government of even broader scope would prove even harder to govern.[19]

New Jersey's William Paterson disputed the broad nationalists. "A confederacy supposes sovereignty in the members composing it & sovereignty supposes equality," said Paterson. "If we are to be considered as a nation, all State distinctions must be abolished, the whole must be thrown into hotchpot, and when an equal division is made, then there may be fairly an equality of representation."[20] General Pinckney of South Carolina began to argue for a practical approach to the existing states, wishing "to have a good national Government & at the same time to leave a considerable share of power in the States." General Pinckney thought that the state legislatures "would be more jealous, & more ready to thwart the National Government if excluded from a participation in it. The Idea of abolishing these Legislatures would never go down."[21] The narrow nationalists began to invent a new theory of federalism in which the national and state governments shared sovereignty (see chapter 12).

When Wilson again complained about too much state power ("In all confederated systems ancient & modern," the power of the general government was "destroyed gradually by the usurpations of the parts composing it"), his opponents turned this argument around on Wilson.[22] To protect the republican values all the delegates shared, the reconstituted government had to retain substantial state government power. Dickinson moved that state legislatures choose the members of the U.S. Senate. Sherman supported the motion, observing "that the particular States would thus become interested in supporting the National Government and that a due harmony between the two Governments would be maintained. He admitted that the two ought to have separate and distinct jurisdictions, but that they ought to have a mutual interest in supporting each other."[23] Dickinson appealed to the delegates' consensus about the separation of powers, asserting that state agency was indispensable, and would provide "that collision between the different authorities which should be wished for in order to check each other." Abolishing the states "would degrade the Councils of our Country, would be impracticable, would be ruinous." He compared the proposed "National System to the Solar System, in which the States were the planets, and ought to be left to move freely in their proper orbits." He complained that Wilson "wished . . . to extinguish these planets."[24] Paterson, who was "attached strongly to the plan of the existing confederacy," believed that "[n]o other amendments were wanting than to mark the orbits of the States with due precision, and provide for the use of coercion, which was the great point."[25] Wilson answered that he simply wanted to keep the states "from devouring the national

Government." He did not want to extinguish "these planets," but he also did not "believe that they would warm or enlighten the Sun. Within their proper orbits they must still be suffered to act for subordinate purposes for which their existence is made essential by the great extent of our Country."[26]

Sherman and Dickinson had forced a crack in Madison's coalition. Now Virginia's George Mason conceded that the states needed protection and that a "certain portion" of authority "must necessarily be left in the States." Mason argued, "The State Legislatures also ought to have some means of defending themselves against encroachments of the National Government. In every other department we have studiously endeavored to provide for its self-defense. Shall we leave the States alone unprovided with the means for this purpose?" He pointed out that there was danger on both sides, but "we have only seen the evils arising on the side of the State Governments. Those on the other side remain to be displayed." He admitted that it would be impossible for a central government to bring "equal justice" to distant parts of the nation.[27] The following week, Sherman used Mason's words against the Virginia Plan, insisting that "each State ought to be able to protect itself."[28]

An Alternative Agenda: New Jersey's Plan

In mid-June, delegates from Connecticut, New York, New Jersey and Delaware (and perhaps Maryland) drew up an alternative to the Virginia Plan.[29] It became known as the New Jersey Plan because New Jersey's William Paterson formally presented it. This plan continued the Confederation Congress. It proposed a very limited increase in national powers, adding only specific authority to ensure adequate national revenue through tariffs, to regulate foreign and interstate commerce, and to allow a national court to hear some appeals from state courts. The system of national requisitions could continue, though national officials could arrange for direct collection of taxes in states that did not comply. The national government would have a new national executive (potentially more than one person, and limited to a single term) and a single national court, appointed by the executive for an unlimited term. All acts of Congress would be "the supreme law of the respective States so far forth as those Acts or Treaties shall relate to the said States or their Citizens, and that the Judiciary of the several States shall be bound thereby in their decisions." If a state resisted, the national executive could use force against it. The plan provided for new states and a national rule of naturalization. A person committing a crime in a state would be guilty even if he were from another state.[30]

Delegates from the states left out of Madison's coalition rallied around this alternative plan. John Lansing of New York declared that New Jersey's propositions sustain "the sovereignty of the respective States," while the Virginia Plan would wreck the states by absorbing "all power except what may be exercised in the little local matters of the States which are not objects worthy of the supreme cognizance." Paterson claimed that the strong national government envisioned by the Virginia Plan obliged the delegates to eradicate completely the states and their boundaries. He dared the delegates from the larger states to try it: "we shall see whether the Citizens of Massachusetts, Pennsylvania & Virginia accede to it."[31]

The broad nationalists vigorously counterattacked New Jersey's proposals. Wilson emphasized that the Virginia Plan proposed to protect republican values while establishing a government capable of dealing with the nation's problems much more effectively. Unlike the New Jersey Plan, which depended on strengthening the existing Congress, the new national government would implement republican checks through restraints on the state legislatures and would guarantee that a majority of Congress would represent a majority of the American people. "The people themselves" would ratify Virginia's Plan for a Constitution, but the New Jersey Plan would require ratification by the state legislatures. The Virginia Plan provided for more extensive national powers, "a single Executive Magistrate," and a supreme court as well as lower ("inferior") national courts.[32] Randolph objected that the Confederation government already had proved the "insufficiency" of the New Jersey approach. A "rooted distrust of Congress pretty generally prevailed," Randolph believed, and said that "A National Government alone, properly constituted, will answer the purpose; and he begged it to be considered that the present is the last moment for establishing one. After this select experiment, the people will yield to despair."[33]

On June 18, Hamilton launched into a day-long speech attacking the New Jersey proposals. The people had to have "an active & constant interest in supporting" a government, but under the New Jersey Plan, states would continue to enjoy popular support because of their parochialism. Merely enhancing the Confederation Congress would not create a national government strong enough to inspire "All the passions . . . of avarice, ambition, interest, which govern most individuals, and all public bodies." These passions would remain with the states, and without them the national government would never be able to take over the political support currently enjoyed by the state governments. Without this popular political support, the new national government could not be effective. Citizens would remain attached to their state governments because the states currently administer the judicial system, take all the actions "which familiarize & endear Government to a people," and provide the honors and awards "which produce an attachment to the Government." An effective government needed powers that would animate potential leaders' political ambition and love of power; without consequential national offices, this ambition would remain concentrated in the states, where demagogues would fight to protect their parochial powers.

"How then are all these evils to be avoided?" asked Hamilton. "Only by such a complete sovereignty in the general Government as will turn all the strong principles & passions above mentioned on its side."[34] Hamilton insisted, "[W]e ought to go as far in order to attain stability and permanency, as republican principles will admit." He offered a plan that put more distance between the people and their government than the Virginia Plan, which, he thought, did not go far enough to create a strong national government. Members of the House would be elected for a three-year term, and members of the Senate selected by electors chosen by the people for a term to last for life (during "good behavior"). A national "Governor" also would be selected by electors chosen by the people and would serve for a lifetime term. This governor could veto any law and appoint heads of key departments without Congressional interference. The Senate could declare war, approve treaties, and reject the appointment of lesser officers. The top national judges would serve lifetime terms.[35]

In his final comments before the crucial vote on the New Jersey Plan the next day, Madison argued that the New Jersey Plan simply could not accomplish the necessary task: "to preserve the Union" and "to provide a Government that will remedy the evils felt by the States both in their united and individual capacities." Madison gave eight reasons for why the New Jersey Plan could not satisfy these two fundamental Convention goals. First, it could not prevent states from violating treaties and the law of nations, "which if not prevented must involve us in the calamities of foreign wars." Second, the plan would not stop the states from encroaching on national authority, a rampant problem; Massachusetts, without Congress's consent, had raised troops to put down Shays's Rebellion, and public lands (the "Western Reserve" in the northeast corner of present-day Ohio) were "dealt out to Connecticut to bribe her acquiescence in the decree constitutionally awarded against her claim on the territory of Pennsylvania."[36] Third, the New Jersey Plan would not stop the states from encroaching on each other through debt relief, credit, and other policies. Fourth, it would not "secure the internal tranquility of the States," a danger underscored by Shays's Rebellion. Fifth, it would not "secure a good internal legislation & administration" for the individual states. States were enacting too many unjust and ineffective laws and changing their laws too frequently. Sixth, the plan would not prevent the states from falling under "the influence of foreign powers." Seventh, the plan would leave the smaller states with the burden of paying for their representation in Congress, which would result in debilitating absences in Congress. Eighth, if two or more confederacies should emerge after a failure of the Convention, the large states would insist on proportional representation in them anyway.[37]

The Convention tabled New Jersey's Plan indefinitely. Madison's coalition—the three largest states and three Southern states—voted against the plan. Connecticut, Delaware (two states that helped write the plan), and Maryland also voted against it. The delegates agreed to a motion that Virginia's Plan was "preferable" to New Jersey's.[38]

These actions killed the New Jersey Plan. But its advocates had severely damaged Madison's strategy by showing that there was strong support for an alternative approach to building a republican national government. The broad nationalists would have to argue on the much more tangible battlefield of political interests, a battlefield on which the three largest states were outnumbered.

The New Jersey Plan's Consequences

Narrow nationalists now fought to include individual elements of the plan in the Convention's final product. This conflict spilled over into specific battles over representation, national power, and national institutions for the rest of the Convention. On June 20, Ellsworth immediately proposed to drop the word "national" from the phrase, establishing "a supreme legislative, Executive and Judiciary" in the first Virginia resolution.[39] When the Convention adopted this change, Lansing assaulted the entire concept of the Virginia Plan, asking "whether the Convention would adhere to or depart from the foundation of the present Confederacy." Instead of creating a new national bicameral legislature, Lansing moved to expand the powers of the existing Confederation Congress, as the New Jersey Plan proposed. He asserted, "It could not be expected that those possessing Sovereignty could ever voluntarily part with it. It was not to be expected from any one State, much less from thirteen." With the broad nationalists' arguments gnawing at him, Lansing argued that the states would not agree to surrender their offices to the federal government so that ambitious men could focus on the national government. Lansing "doubted whether any General Government equally beneficial to all can be attained" and said the Virginia Plan was "utterly unattainable." He condemned the system laid out by Virginia as "too novel and complex. No man could foresee what its operation will be either with respect to the General Government or the State Governments."[40]

George Mason (who "did not expect this point would have been reagitated") reaffirmed that "he never would agree to abolish the State Governments or render them absolutely insignificant. They were as necessary as the General Government and he would be equally careful to preserve them."[41] Luther Martin, Maryland's Attorney General and one of the strongest advocates of state sovereignty at the Convention, exploited the political opening Mason gave him. Martin argued that Americans had proved they "preferred the Establishment of themselves into thirteen separate sovereignties instead of incorporating themselves into one." They trusted these thirteen governments to protect their lives, liberty, and property. The national government was created to protect this arrangement, and to guard smaller states from larger ones. The people could only change this arrangement by dissolving their own governments.[42] According to Lansing, Martin attacked the ambitions of broad nationalists like Hamilton, saying, "Happiness is preferable to the Splendors of a national Government."[43]

Shrewdly, Roger Sherman steered the anger of the small state delegates and the wavering support of some Madison allies to the advantage of the narrow nationalists. First, Sherman argued that there existed no need to overhaul the national government as thoroughly as the Virginia Plan proposed. Next, Sherman twisted the larger states' top priority—proportional representation—by framing "[t]he disparity of the States" in population as "the main difficulty." He made change seem more risky by noting that consolidation into a single government would create difficulties for the nation's foreign relations. Sherman granted an important concession to the Virginia Plan's authors, laying the groundwork for the "Connecticut" or "Great" Compromise: "If the difficulty on the subject of representation can not be otherwise got over, he would agree to have two branches, and a proportional representation in one of them, provided each State had an equal voice in the other." In making this concession on one house of Congress, Sherman insisted that the other house (the future Senate) had to represent the states equally, as in the current Confederation Congress. Seizing on Mason's willingness to protect the states, Sherman argued this arrangement of the Senate "was necessary to secure the rights of the lesser States; otherwise three or four of the large States would rule the others as they please." By attaching hard numbers to relative state power in Congress for the first time, Sherman invited the delegates to conclude that as many as ten states could be damaged by Virginia's proposed new government.[44]

Sherman anchored his argument in a most effective defense of state sovereignty: he used the delegates' shared belief in republican values to defend the role of the states. He said, "Each State like each individual had its peculiar habits usages and manners, which constituted its happiness. It would not therefore give to others a power over this happiness, any more than an individual would do, when he could avoid it."[45] Sherman thus tried to use republican values against the Virginia Plan. Sherman's fellow Connecticut delegate, William Samuel Johnson, expanded on this argument the next day, suggesting that the states needed to protect some of their sovereignty and "individuality." Johnson said that if the proponents of the Virginia Plan could show how the states might "be secured against" the national government to the satisfaction of "the patrons of the New Jersey propositions . . . many of their objections would no doubt be removed."[46] Later, Johnson tried to keep the delegates focused on this fundamental disagreement about state and national sovereignty, pointing out that the debate on representation would be endless while some viewed "the States as districts of people composing one political Society" while those on the other side viewed States "as so many political societies." Both were true. As Johnson said, "The States do exist as political Societies, and a Government is to be formed for them in their political capacity, as well as for the individuals composing them."[47]

The claim that large states would try to dominate the rest put the Virginia Plan's proponents on the defensive. Wilson denied that the large states would form a coalition against the rest of the states. If large states did coalesce, it "would produce a general alarm among the rest" and these other states would join to block the attempt. Wilson was drawn onto the ground prepared by Sherman's effort to equate states' rights and individual citizens' rights: the national government, he claimed, "will be as ready to preserve the rights of the States as the latter are to preserve the rights of individuals" because, as representatives of all the people, national officials will have an interest in leaving "the State Governments in possession of what the people wish them to retain."[48] Massachusetts delegate Nathaniel Gorham criticized the smaller states' suspicions about the intentions of the larger states. Massachusetts originally consisted of three separate colonies, and although there were similar apprehensions about merging them into a single colony, "all parties were safe & satisfied; and every distinction is now forgotten."[49] His colleague Rufus King "was for preserving the States in a subordinate degree, and as far as they could be necessary for the purposes stated by Mr. Ellsworth" and suggested that "[e]xpedients might be devised" to provide additional protections to the states.[50] Charles Pinckney of South Carolina acknowledged that the states "are the instruments upon which the Union must frequently depend for the support & execution of their powers, however immediately operating upon the people, and not upon the States."[51]

Madison understood that it was urgent to counter the charge that the large states aimed to dominate the rest. Even if the states became completely dependent on the national government, he asked, "why should it follow that the General Government would take from the States any branch of their power as far as its operation was beneficial, and its continuance desirable to the people?" After all, local governments were wholly dependent on the states, and the states respected the local autonomy because the people were attached to it. Even if the national government encroached on the states, it would be less harmful than encroachments by the states on national power. The critics of the Virginia Plan, said Madison, complained that the national government could not exert its authority effectively across the wide expanse of the nation. If it proved impractical, both the national government and the people would agree to maintain the "subordinate governments." But if it were practical to govern from the center, "the people would not be less free as members of one great Republic than as members of thirteen small ones."[52] Later, Madison said he "agreed with Johnson that mixed nature of the Government ought to be kept in view," but he "thought too much stress was laid on the rank of the States as political societies." The Articles of Confederation already limited state sovereignty, and under *any* plan, state power "will be much farther reduced." Madison contended that all the members agreed that the new national government "will have powers far beyond those exercised by the British Parliament when the States were part of the British Empire. It will in particular have the power, without the consent of the State Legislatures, to levy money directly on the people themselves."[53] Madison concluded that the small states' self-interest required them to embrace a government that would place the states in a relationship to the national government comparable to the relation of the counties to the states.[54]

Crossroads

The Convention was moving toward a critical juncture. The narrow nationalists' stiffening resistance to Virginia's propositions was wearing down some of Madison's allies. The more the delegates from the large states denied that national power threatened the smaller states, the more they seemed to plant doubts about the consequences of the Virginia Plan. Madison's opponents argued with increasing force that state governments were too deeply rooted to cut down. Luther Martin argued that "the language of the States being *Sovereign & independent*, was once familiar & understood," though the debate had made it seem "so strange & obscure."[55] Ellsworth expressed this reality more succinctly and memorably than anyone else at the Convention: "We were partly national; partly federal."[56]

For Madison, the success of the Virginia Plan depended on the acceptance of legislative representation based on population. Without that agreement, the plan's ambition to greatly increase national authority would run into increased resistance from large and Southern states. With proportional representation in both the House and the Senate, the states in Madison's coalition could more easily defend their interests. Without proportional representation in both houses, more of the delegates from these states would doubt the wisdom of investing the national government with the broad power he sought.

As the debates ground on, the narrow nationalists were putting the broad nationalists on the defensive. Clearly, representation in Congress was the most coveted prize. As Madison said after his lengthy dissection of the New Jersey Plan's shortcomings, "The great difficulty lies in the affair of Representation; and if this could be adjusted, all others would be surmountable."[57]

PART TWO

THE POLITICS OF BUILDING GOVERNMENT INSTITUTIONS

‖ 7 ‖

Selecting U.S. Representatives

The delegates considered the rules for selecting government officials to be critically important. Whoever selected these officials would greatly influence the officials' behavior. The Virginia Plan placed the House of Representatives in the center of the new government; it would select the Senate and share in choosing the president. The voters would directly elect the members of the new House of Representatives, and each state's population size would determine the number of representatives it would send to Congress.

The debate on the method for selecting members of the U.S. House of Representatives began as a detached discussion of the requirements of republicanism, but it evolved into a very pragmatic discussion of the allocation of political power. Though the advocates of the Virginia Plan generally won their points, the debates strengthened the position of the narrow nationalists. The concrete allocation of seats in the new House of Representatives, and the difficulties in allocating seats to new states that would join the union in the future began to fracture Madison's coalition, undermining support for the principle of proportional representation in the Senate and for broad national powers.

Why Was the Selection of Members of Congress So Crucial?

The delegates viewed the rules for selecting government officials as their most momentous task. These officials' careers would depend on those who put them in office, and the delegates expected them generally to serve as the faithful agents of their patrons. The process for selecting the members of Congress was especially important. The delegates believed that the House and Senate would be the voice and advocate of whatever group selected them.

The new House of Representatives would provide the most direct voice of the people. George Mason envisioned the House as "the grand depository of the democratic principle of the Government"; it would be "our House of Commons."[1]

The House "ought to know & sympathize with every part of the community; and ought therefore to be taken not only from different parts of the whole republic, but also from different districts of the larger members of it . . . different interests and views arising from difference of produce, of habits" and so on.[2] For him, the people should select their representatives because these legislators "should think as they think, & feel as they feel."[3] In the final debates on the New Jersey Plan, Mason passionately argued against the existing Confederation Congress in favor of direct election of members to the House of Representatives, asserting that the American people "never will" and "never ought" to "surrender both the sword and the purse, to the same body, and that too not chosen immediately by themselves."[4]

James Wilson wanted "vigor in the Government . . . to flow immediately" from the people, "the legitimate source of all authority." The new "Government ought to possess not only first, the *force*, but second, the *mind* or *sense* of the people at large. The Legislature ought to be the most exact transcript of the whole Society. Representation is made necessary only because it is impossible for the people to act collectively."[5] Wilson emphasized that "the representative ought to speak the Language of his Constituents, and . . . his language or vote should have the same influence as though the Constituents gave it."[6]

The Virginia Plan proposed that voters would directly select their representatives in the "people's house," and that the House of Representatives would play the pivotal, driving role in the new government. When the Convention decided the issue, it still seemed likely that the House would choose the Senate and set the national policy agenda. Each delegate had to weigh carefully the impact of any method of selecting members of House on the nation's immediate crisis, the nation's foreseeable future, and the interests of the state that sent him to Philadelphia. The rules had to be carefully drawn for the very first Congress, which would enact "the principal acts of Government."[7]

The Direct Election of U.S. Representatives

On May 31, the Convention took up Virginia's proposal for the direct election of members of the future House of Representatives. Roger Sherman immediately opposed the idea, preferring that the state legislatures elect members of the House, as they currently elected members of the Confederation Congress. Elbridge Gerry did not like the idea but agreed to accept it if it encouraged "men of honor and character" to serve in Congress.[8]

At this early moment in the Convention, the Virginia Plan's proponents countered Sherman by invoking republican values to defend direct election. Mason "argued strongly for an election of the larger branch by the people."[9] Wilson asserted that direct election was "peculiarly essential" for public confidence in republican government. Because he "was for raising the federal pyramid to a considerable altitude," Wilson "wished to give it as broad a basis as possible."[10] James Madison "considered the popular election of one branch of the national Legislature as essential to every plan of free Government." If the state legislatures chose members of the House of Representatives, "the people would be lost sight of altogether; and the necessary sympathy between them and their rulers and officers, too little felt."

Madison advocated "the policy of refining the popular appointments by successive filtrations," that is, he supported the idea that the selection of government leaders other than representatives would be made by other institutions rather than directly by the people. "Successive filtrations" would screen out volatile passions of pure democracy. But "it might be pushed too far" by removing voters' control over the House and giving that control to the state legislatures. The "expedient" of "successive filtrations" should "be resorted to only" in the selection of the Senate, the executive, and judicial branches. Like Wilson, he believed "that the great fabric to be raised would be more stable and durable if it should rest on the solid foundation of the people themselves, than if it should stand merely on the pillars of the Legislatures."[11] The Convention approved direct election of the House after this discussion, but New Jersey and South Carolina voted against it while Delaware and Connecticut were divided.

Charles Pinckney forced the delegates to reconsider the issue a week later, when he proposed that the state legislatures choose the members of the House of Representatives. Sherman, supporting Pinckney's proposal, believed the peoples' influence would be "sufficiently secured" if the state legislatures, which were themselves subject to popular control, elected the members of the House. Sherman then framed the issue as a stark choice: direct election was appropriate "[i]f it were in view to abolish the State Governments," but "If the State Governments are to be continued, it is necessary in order to preserve harmony . . . that the elections to the former should be made by the latter."[12] John Dickinson and William Pierce supported direct election of the House but argued that the state legislatures should elect the Senate.[13] General Pinckney of South Carolina objected to direct election as "totally impracticable" in his state, and as undesirable because many voters supported paper money.[14] Madison utilized republican principles to defend direct election of the House but now introduced more practical criticism of the Confederation and the states. Direct election, he said, would avoid "too great an agency of the State Governments in the General one."[15] The delegates rejected Pinckney's proposal.[16]

After the New Jersey Plan's defeat, General Pinckney moved to let the state legislatures to choose U.S. Representatives any way they liked.[17] His South Carolina colleague, John Rutledge, believed that the "sense of the whole community" would be equally well registered whether popularly elected state legislatures chose members of Congress or the people elected them directly. Rutledge noted that the state-selected delegates to the Convention and to Congress had been "fitter men" than those that the people would have chosen directly.[18]

Mason, conceding that direct election might cause problems, nevertheless "urged the necessity of retaining the election by the people. Whatever inconveniency may attend the democratic principle, it must actuate one part of the Government. It is the only security for the rights of the people."[19] Other proponents of direct election made much more forceful political arguments. Wilson viewed the difference between state legislative election and direct election as "immense." He berated the state legislatures, who had an official attitude of opposition to "the General Government and perhaps to that of the people themselves."[20] Rufus King complained that the state legislatures "would constantly choose men subservient to their own views as contrasted to the general interest."[21] Alexander Hamilton argued that the proposal "would increase that State influence which could not be too watchfully guarded against" and suggested that if the state governments "gradually dwindle into nothing," there would be no system for choosing U.S. Representatives.[22] Sherman finally acquiesced to direct election to the lower house, and the delegates rejected any role for the state legislatures in the process of electing House members.[23] This conflict over direct election of the House, however, was only a skirmish compared to the battle over proportional representation.

The Struggle for Proportional Representation in the House

Proportional representation in the House—that is, apportioning House seats among the states according to population size—clearly would redistribute national policy-making influence to Virginia, Pennsylvania, Massachusetts, and the growing Southern states, at the expense of the remaining states. This redistribution of power was essential for keeping the coalition of broad nationalists together. When Madison tried to maneuver the delegates into agreeing to proportional representation in the new national legislature on May 30, he ran into resistance immediately.[24] George Read of Delaware tried to postpone discussion of Madison's proposal because Delaware had instructed its delegates not to accept "any change of the rule of suffrage."[25] Madison's strategy for the Convention depended on this provision, and he insisted that there would be no reason for equal state votes in the new Congress.[26] Madison suggested more ambiguous wording that would not put the Delaware delegates in an awkward position, but in an ominous development for Madison's strategy, the delegates adjourned without resolving the issue.[27]

On June 9, New Jersey's David Brearley launched a direct attack on the principle of proportional representation as politically dangerous for states like his. A proportional ratio of representation seemed fair on its face, but Brearley argued "on a deeper examination was unfair and unjust." The three large states, Massachusetts, Pennsylvania, and Virginia, would dominate all the votes, so, to have any influence at all, a small state would be forced to cast its lot with a large state.[28] William Paterson of New Jersey "considered the proposition for a proportional representation as striking at the existence of the lesser States." A large state that contributes much revenue to the national government should not have more votes than a small state, he said, any more than "a rich individual citizen should have more votes than an indigent one." Wealth in both cases gave a greater need for government protection. Paterson said he would "rather submit to a monarch, to a despot" and added that he "would not only oppose the plan here but on his return home do everything in his power to defeat it there."[29] Wilson responded with a simple republican formula: "equal numbers of people ought to have an equal number of representatives, and different numbers of people different numbers of representatives." But he also matched his opponents' threats: "If the small States will not confederate on this plan, Pennsylvania & he presumed some other States, would not confederate on any other."[30]

Roger Sherman opened the next session with an offer of political compromise: seats in the House would be apportioned according to population, but as a condition, the states would have an equal number of representatives in the Senate. This plan would allow states to defend themselves, he said. Otherwise the large states would "rule the rest."[31] This compromise seemed to splinter the delegates. South Carolina's Rutledge and Pierce Butler wanted to base representation in the House of Representatives on the requisition quotas established in the Confederation. This proposal would help South Carolina because it was wealthier than less affluent Northern states with similar populations (and some of its wealth was held in the form of slaves). Butler frankly contended "that money was power; and that the States ought to have weight in the Government in proportion to their wealth."[32] Dickinson urged that, instead of basing representation on a state's wealth, each state's representation in Congress should be based on the "*actual* contributions of the States" to the national government's revenue.[33] Other delegates countered that these suggestions were impractical.[34]

To sidestep the problems of representing wealth and slaves, Wilson and Charles Pinckney proposed that representatives would be apportioned according to the population of whites and free citizens, and three-fifths of "other persons," that is, slaves. This rule was very familiar to the delegates: the Confederation Congress used it to allocate requisitions across the states. The Convention accepted this refinement (see chapter 13).[35] On proportional representation, the delegates only agreed to the abstract principle "that the right of suffrage in the first branch of the national Legislature ought not to be according to the rule established in the articles of Confederation, but according to some equitable ratio of representation." Sherman pressed for a vote on equal representation in the Senate, making it clear that the smaller states could acquiesce to proportional representation in one branch only if equal representation of the states were guaranteed in the second. This proposition lost.[36]

The delegates from the smaller, more vulnerable states had solidified into an opposition bloc committed to narrow nationalism. They had not surrendered to the superior numbers of Madison's coalition as he had hoped. Instead, they were going on the offensive. Paterson, defending equal state representation in the Confederation, pointedly asked, "If a proportional representation be right, why do we not vote so here," in the Constitutional Convention, where each state had an equal vote?[37] Sherman argued that "the large States had not yet suffered from the equality of votes enjoyed by the small ones."[38] Cracks were spreading in Madison's own coalition, as Benjamin Franklin joined George Mason in floating the idea of compromise.[39]

More and more, the broad nationalists based their counterarguments on political expediency. Charles Pinckney boldly questioned New Jersey's motives: "the whole comes to this ... [g]ive New Jersey an equal vote, and she will dismiss her scruples, and concur in the National system."[40] Hamilton tried to answer the fear that three large states would dominate the rest, holding that Massachusetts, Pennsylvania, and Virginia "were separated from each other" not only by physical distance but also by their different interests, which precluded them from conspiring together against the rest.[41] Wilson condemned equal representation as "a poison contaminating every branch of Government."[42]

Madison conceded that representation had become the Convention's central problem. He tried to paint the advocates of the New Jersey Plan into a logical corner. If New Jersey and Delaware thought that they would be advantaged by "an equalization of the States," why not allow them the freedom to merge if they wanted to do so? New states to the west would seek admission to the United States, and if "they should be entitled to vote according to their proportions of inhabitants," it would be safe to admit them into the union without fear that their vote would "give law to the whole."[43]

The delegates began their final debate on proportional representation in the House on June 28. In a mirror image of Madison's May 30 effort to force the delegates to go on record in favor of proportional representation, John Lansing of New York and Jonathan Dayton of New Jersey moved to establish equal state representation in the new House of Representatives—the same arrangement as in the current Confederation Congress. Sherman used republican values as a weapon, asserting, "The question is not what rights naturally belong to men; but how they may be most equally & effectually guarded in Society." No one could complain if "some give up more than others" to achieve this noble goal (that is, if the large states sacrificed proportional representation). "To do otherwise, to require an equal concession from all, if it would create danger to the rights of some, would be sacrificing the end to the means."[44]

Madison explained the urgent need for proportional representation in the new Congress, arguing that it did not pose a threat to the smaller states. He argued that in the states, counties were represented according to their numbers because large counties "have a greater stake." The mere size of the large states would not be sufficient to allow them to coalesce against the rest, because of their different circumstances: "they could not have been more effectually separated from each other by the most jealous citizen of the most jealous State." Among large and powerful nations like France and Britain, "rivalships were much more frequent than coalitions." History showed that it was easier for large governments to dominate smaller governments where central control was lax than where it was strong.

Madison framed the Convention's choice as a stark alternative: "a perfect separation & a perfect incorporation, of the 13 States." This way of framing the problem aimed to make the alternative unacceptable. If the Convention chose separation, "they would be independent nations subject to no law, but the law of nations" and would have "everything to fear from the larger states." But if it chose incorporation, the states "would be mere counties of one entire republic, subject to one common law" and the small states "would have nothing to fear" from the larger ones. A weak national government would convince large states to maintain their "own size and strength" and to prohibit their western settlements from forming new, independent states.[45]

Recognizing the mounting frustrations and the growing possibility of an impasse "after 4 or five weeks close attendance & continual reasonings with each other," Franklin tried to defuse the conflict by an appeal to God and a call for daily prayer. But now even prayer became controversial. Hamilton and others thought that the addition of a clergyman and a prayer at this point in the Convention would stoke dissension among the delegates and signal outsiders that the Convention was in danger of failing.[46]

The next day, Connecticut's William Samuel Johnson again suggested that delegates from the smaller, more vulnerable states would accept proportional representation in the House of Representatives if all the states had equal representation in the future Senate. Johnson pointed out that states already were well-established, and, explicitly using George Mason's argument against the Virginia Plan's supporters, it seemed "to follow, that if the States as such are to exist they must be armed with some power of self-defense." If some delegates regarded the states as political units and other delegates regarded the states "as districts of individual citizens, the two ideas embraced on different sides, instead of being opposed to each other, ought to be combined; that in *one* branch the *people*, ought to be represented; in the *other*, the *States*."[47]

Madison "entreated the gentlemen representing the small States to renounce" equal representation of states, "a principle which was confessedly unjust, which could never be admitted, & if admitted must infuse mortality into a Constitution which we wished to last forever." He emphasized that the national government would have the power to tax citizens, without the consent of the state legislatures.[48] Hamilton said, "Nothing could be more preposterous or absurd than to sacrifice the" individuals in the states to the interests of the states themselves, adding, "It has been said that if the smaller States renounce their *equality*, they renounce at the same time their *liberty*. The truth is it is a contest for power, not for liberty."[49] On the final vote on proportional representation in the House of Representatives, Madison's coalition held together. The six states on which Madison depended—the three large states and the three southern states—outvoted the other five states present to maintain proportional representation in the House. On this vote, New Hampshire's delegates had not yet arrived (and Rhode Island never sent delegates).[50]

Apportioning House Seats among the States

Politics dominated the debate about the allocation of House seats in the first Congress. Even one seat could significantly add to any state's influence in designing the fundamental laws this first Congress would produce. The committee that proposed the Connecticut Compromise recommended one seat in the House of Representatives "for every 40,000 inhabitants."[51] Gouverneur Morris quickly objected to this formula, because it would allow new western states enough votes in the House of Representatives to swamp the older states. Morris proposed to fix the number of representatives to ensure the existing states remained dominant, a provision he believed to be both fair and politically expedient.[52] John Rutledge moved that they set a specific number of seats for each state in the first Congress, to be adjusted in the future. Morris proposed a special committee to specify the exact number of seats each state would receive in the first House of Representatives.[53] The Convention created the five-member committee and filled it with members from states allied with Madison: Morris of Pennsylvania, Gorham and King of Massachusetts, Randolph of Virginia, and Rutledge of South Carolina.

This committee on House apportionment recommended an initial House of Representatives with fifty-six seats. Virginia would have nine seats, Pennsylvania eight, Massachusetts seven, North Carolina, South Carolina, and New York five seats each, Connecticut and Maryland four each, New Jersey three, New

Hampshire and Georgia two, and Rhode Island and Delaware one each. The three largest states would control 43 percent of the votes in this first House of Representatives. If any one of the next three largest—South Carolina, North Carolina, or New York—joined with these three large states, the four states together would have a majority vote in the new Congress.[54]

Sherman instantly challenged this apparently self-serving proposal from Massachusetts, Pennsylvania, Virginia, and South Carolina. "It did not appear to correspond with any rule of numbers" or precedent from the Confederation Congress, he said. He proposed another new committee to review the formula, this time including a member from each state. Randolph and Morris both agreed quickly.[55] The next day, this new committee recommended a House of Representatives with sixty-five seats instead of fifty-six: Virginia would have nine seats, Pennsylvania and Massachusetts would have eight seats, New York and Maryland would have six, Connecticut, North and South Carolina five each, Georgia three, and Delaware and Rhode Island one each. In this plan, smaller states gained seats relative to larger ones, and the Northern states gained relative to the South. The six states Madison counted as allies gained only three seats, while the rest gained six. Four states alone could no longer form a majority in the House, severely weakening the pivotal role of either South or North Carolina.

This report inflamed sectional rivalry and sparked a bald struggle for more House seats. South Carolina's General Pinckney asserted that the first report, with fifty-six seats, "was more favorable to the Southern States than as it now stands." Though pleased with the additional delegates added for Virginia and Georgia, he insisted on an equal distribution of seats between the Southern states and the rest.[56] Hugh Williamson of North Carolina concluded, "The Southern Interest must be extremely endangered by the present arrangement" because the majority in Congress could threaten slavery.[57] South Carolina's delegates moved to cut one of the representatives for New Hampshire, whose delegates had still not arrived. Williamson "was not for reducing New Hampshire from 3 to 2, but for reducing some others."[58] Rufus King rushed to defend the seat of Massachusetts' New England neighbor. Though he was prepared "to yield something in the proportion of representatives for the security of the Southern" states, no "principle would justify the giving them a majority. They were brought as near an equality as was possible."[59] Morris opposed any reduction in New Hampshire's House delegation and "regretted the turn of the debate" to a parochial jockeying for voting power. The delegates rejected Southern proposals to cut one of New Hampshire's representatives, rejected proposals to add a representative each for North Carolina, South Carolina, and Georgia, and accepted the committee recommendation for the apportionment of seats in the first House of Representatives.[60]

Recognizing the threat posed by regional enmity and endless quarrelling, Madison struggled to find some rule that would reduce conflict. He proposed to double the number of representatives, an idea that would allow the delegates to more easily compromise on House apportionment. The delegates rebuffed Madison's idea, however, because it would make the new House too big and expensive.[61] When Madison and his allies again advocated enlarging the House near the end of the Convention, Hamilton spoke "with great earnestness and anxiety in favor of the motion" because he thought the size to be "really dangerous, and to warrant a jealousy in the people for their liberties."[62] But the Convention refused to consider this proposal.

As late as September 15, New Hampshire's John Langdon tried to add a seat for North Carolina and Rhode Island, but as more delegates spoke up for other changes, the Convention again refused to consider these incremental adjustments in the allocation of House seats.[63] On the Convention's final day, George Washington stepped away from his role as Convention president explicitly to support a proposal to allow Congress to draw House districts for as few as 30,000 people (instead of 40,000). In effect, this provision allowed Congress to enlarge its membership. The Convention made the change.[64] It was the final substantive change to the text of the Constitution.

Determining House Seats in the Future

But what rule would be used to apportion House seats in the future? If Congress apportioned seats in the House as it pleased, when it pleased, it could redistribute votes unfairly, benefiting some states at the expense of others. As soon as the delegates established the number of seats each state would receive in the first Congress, Randolph demanded a Constitutional guarantee of an official census soon after the startup of the new government, and regularly thereafter.[65] The census was essential for establishing an objective population count on which to base the apportionment of representatives. Mason pointed out that, without a fair, periodic census as the population shifted, the North could continue to dominate the South politically even if the South had more people. He did not want the North's advantage to continue indefinitely, and he did not trust future legislators to change it.[66] Nathaniel Gorham challenged the delegates to reflect on the lessons of this debate for future Congresses: "If the Convention who are comparatively so little biased by local views are so much perplexed, how can it be expected that the Legislature hereafter under the full bias of those views, will be able to settle a standard?"[67] Though Sherman did not want to shackle Congress with a required census, "he had been convinced . . . that the *periods* & the *rule* of revising the Representation ought to be fixed by the Constitution."[68]

But the census proposal was caught up in the divisive issue of admitting new states. Williamson feared that equal representation would tempt the small, poor states added in the west to coalesce to advantage themselves, outvoting "the old States" and placing additional burdens on them.[69] South Carolina's delegates agreed that the original states should dominate in the House, and that the apportionment needed to protect slavery. Butler spoke for "some balance . . . between the old & New States" and "contended strenuously that property was the only just measure of representation. This was the great object of Government, the great cause of war, the great means of carrying it on."[70] This property criterion would advantage the old states, especially Southern states, in future apportionment. Williamson thought the Western states only deserved the same representation as the East if the value of their property were comparable.[71] Gouverneur Morris, making it clear that he wanted the old states "to keep a majority of votes in their own hands," complained that a regular census would impose too much of a constraint on Congress, and that the reapportionment should be left to Congress's discretion.[72] Morris warned that the Western states "would not be able to furnish men equally enlightened" to share in national governance. "The Busy haunts of men, not the remote wilderness, was the proper School of political Talents," said Morris. "If the Western people get the power into their hands they will ruin the Atlantic interests. The Back[country] members are always most averse to the best measures."[73] Rutledge did not believe the Atlantic states would accept the Constitution if the Western states were treated equally.[74]

Other delegates, however, insisted on equal treatment of new states in the West. King already had pointed out that the newly enacted Northwest Ordinance of 1787 (creating territories north of the Ohio River and west of Pennsylvania) promised that these potential states would be admitted on equal terms with the old states.[75] Randolph argued that the new states should join the union as equals of the old states, and that the Northwest Ordinance "pledged the public faith to New States, that they shall be admitted on equal terms. They never would nor ought to accede on any other."[76] Charles Pinckney observed that it simply was impractical to base representation on property values.[77] Mason reasserted that the Northern states would hold on to their majority even after the South and West grew more populous.[78] Madison argued that the Western states had to be admitted as equals with the other states as a matter of justice and public policy. These agricultural states eventually would provide substantial revenues to the national government. While population size was not always a measure of wealth, these two measures were "sufficiently" close in the United States to allow representation to be based on population alone. Madison sarcastically expressed surprise "to hear this implicit confidence" in Congress "urged by a member [Morris] who on all occasions, had inculcated So strongly, the political depravity of men, and the necessity of checking one vice and interest by opposing to them another vice & interest." While Morris was telling the South to trust the North, "he was still more zealous in exhorting all to a jealousy of a Western majority.

To reconcile the gentleman with himself it must be imagined that he determined the human character by the points of the compass."[79] The delegates agreed to a census every ten years, adjusting different states' representation as relative population changes warranted.[80]

This agreement on the census did not kill the hope that the Constitution would advantage the original states. Gerry proposed to place in the Constitution a provision that the number of representatives apportioned to the new states "shall never exceed" the number of seats apportioned to the states that would ratify the original Constitution.[81] Wilson had tried to head off this proposal, asserting that majority rule should prevail, and if the West acquired a majority, "they will not only have the right, but will avail themselves of it whether we will or no."[82] Sherman thought the possibility that "the number of future States would exceed that of the Existing States" was remote, and that "[b]esides, We are providing for our posterity, for our children & our grand Children, who would be as likely to be citizens of new Western States, as of the old States."[83] By a bare majority, five states to four, the framers rejected the idea that the thirteen original states would dominate the rest in perpetuity.[84]

The Path of Representation in the House

The selection of the House of Representatives was a protracted battle. It began as a theoretical disagreement over the popular election of representatives, and then evolved into a struggle over the relative power of the states in national policy-making.

Congressional elections have been held on the Constitution's regular schedule since 1789 (112 elections).[85] As anticipated at the Convention, the admission of new states soon became deeply divisive. Missouri, a slave territory, applied for statehood in 1818, jeopardizing the political balance between the slaveholding Southern states and the Northern states. A series of political compromises between 1820 and the 1850s aimed to maintain the balance of power, but by the late 1850s, the erosion of slave state representation helped fuel secession and the Civil War.[86] The Thirteenth Amendment (1865) made the "three-fifths" clause moot by abolishing slavery, and the Fourteenth Amendment (1868) provided that apportionment of House seats would simply depend on the population in each state (excluding Indians who were not taxed).

As the population and the number of states increased, the number of U.S. Representatives increased. By 1912, there were 435 representatives, a number fixed by law in 1929.[87] The number of people in the average district increased from 33,000 in 1790 to over 710,000 after the 2010 census. Because the total number of seats is now fixed, and some states make large population gains relative to others, seats are shifted toward these states and from slower growing states. After the 2010 census, eight states gained seats in the House, while ten states lost seats.[88]

States with more than one seat in the U.S. House of Representatives still draw the boundaries of all their House districts. Well into the twentieth century most states drew these districts in a way that gave rural voters more seats than urban voters. Until the 1960s, there were no requirements for redistricting to equalize the population of House districts within each state. In 1964, the Supreme Court ruled that the House districts had to be as equal in population as possible.[89]

The delegates faced an even more difficult problem. The agreement on proportional representation in the House made the selection of members of the U.S. Senate, and the distribution of Senate seats, so controversial that it threatened to wreck the Convention.

|| 8 ||

Selecting U.S. Senators

The delegates initially imagined that the U.S. Senate would be an institutional barrier, a small body of select leaders who could block the unruly democratic urges of the House of Representatives. Some hoped it would be a bastion of elite wisdom or propertied privilege. But the struggle over representation in the House made it increasingly clear that representation in the Senate would be determined by political compromise.

Representation in the Senate became the principal political battleground between the broad and narrow nationalists. The proponents of the New Jersey Plan dug in to defend equal representation in the Senate. James Madison and his closest allies fought for proportional representation with equal intensity. As antagonism over representation in the Senate grew more intense, a few delegates who supported the Virginia Plan began to waver and seek compromise. The delegates came to an impasse in July and turned the problem over to a special committee. This committee reported the Connecticut Compromise that provided for proportional representation in the House, equal state representation in the Senate, and the House control of initial tax and spending proposals. Even as this compromise won acceptance, it changed the path of the Convention by irreversibly fracturing the coalition Madison hoped to sustain.

Envisioning the Senate

At the start of the Convention, delegates envisioned the Senate as a political levee that would restrain the flood of democratic passions expected to swamp the House of Representatives. Edmund Randolph, worried about the policy impact of "the passionate proceedings" of a large body like the House, believed the Senate would check the "turbulence and follies of democracy."[1] Unless the Senate were strong, the House of Representatives, "being more numerous, and coming immediately from the people, will overwhelm it." The state legislatures' "Democratic licentiousness" proved the need for an effective check on the House, and the potential "encroachments of the Executive who will be apt to form combinations with the demagogues of the popular branch."[2]

Some delegates went further, and idealized a Senate that would represent the nation's elites. John Dickinson expressly stated that the "formation of the Senate" should "assimilate it as near as may be to the House of Lords in England."[3] Though the United States had no lords or nobles to represent, the states could send their most prominent statesmen to the Senate. Gouverneur Morris believed that the Senate "must have great personal property, it must have the aristocratic spirit; it must love to lord it through pride, pride is indeed the great principle that actuates both the poor & the rich." The senators should serve for life, Morris believed, to ensure the Senate's firmness and independence. Morris believed that political influence of the wealthy was inevitable, but this influence could be controlled if it were concentrated in a single government body. The "[r]ich will strive to establish their dominion & enslave the rest. They always did. They always will." The best protection against this inevitable threat was to allow them to establish a separate interest in a representative body. "By thus combining & setting apart, the aristocratic interest, the popular interest will be combined against it. There will be a mutual check and mutual security."[4]

This vision of a plainly aristocratic Senate did not receive much explicit support at the Convention. Charles Pinckney challenged the need for such a body precisely because the United States lacked British class distinctions.[5] But the need for a strong legislative house to brake the instability of the House of Representatives, and especially to protect liberty and property from the urges of a popular majority, was widely taken for granted.

Who Selects the Senators?

Political differences quickly surfaced when the Convention took up the proposal to make the House of Representatives responsible for choosing the senators. Richard Dobbs Spaight of North Carolina suggested that the state legislatures choose the Senate instead. Randolph objected to this departure from Virginia's plan, arguing that the Senate would not effectively check the House unless the House selected the senators.[6] Rufus King observed that if each state chose senators, proportional representation in the Senate would be impractical "unless it was to be very numerous, or *the idea of proportion* among the States was to be disregarded" (emphasis in original). King pointed out that "there must be 80 or 100 members to entitle Delaware to the choice of one of them."[7] This problem haunted advocates of proportional representation in the Senate.

To answer King's problem, James Wilson proposed direct election of the Senate, in areas large enough to encompass several House districts. Wilson "opposed both a nomination by the State Legislatures, and an election by the first branch of the national Legislature" because these mechanisms would leave the senators too dependent on one or the other.[8] Madison immediately recognized that Wilson's proposal would further antagonize the states outside his coalition because it "would destroy the influence of the smaller States associated with larger ones in the same district."[9] Roger Sherman exploited this disagreement among the Virginia Plan's proponents, suggesting a Senate consisting of "one member by each of the State Legislatures." Sherman turned Wilson's logic against Randolph, arguing that if the House appointed the Senate, it would make the Senate *too* dependent on the House.[10] Mason admitted the validity of Sherman's point.[11] But Sherman's formula would wreck Madison's plan for proportional representation in the Senate. The delegates moved on without resolving the issue.

Several days later, Dickinson argued that the Senate "should be chosen by the Legislatures of the States. This combination of the State Governments with the National Government was as politic as it was unavoidable."[12] Dickinson held that state legislatures would provide a better "sense of the States" and were more likely to choose "the most distinguished characters, distinguished for their rank in life and their weight of property, and bearing as strong a likeness to the British House of Lords as possible."[13] Dickinson defended the role of state governments in checking national power and argued that House selection of the Senate "would only unite the 13 small streams into one great current pursuing the same course without any opposition whatever."[14] William Pierce of Georgia believed that, if the state legislatures chose the Senate, the citizens of the states would "be represented both *individually* & *collectively*."[15] Madison recognized that state selection of senators opened the problem identified by Wilson: if the delegates accepted Dickinson's idea, Madison said, "we must either depart from the doctrine of proportional representation; or admit into the Senate a very large number of members. The first is inadmissible, being evidently unjust. The second is inexpedient." Because the Senate was intended to proceed with "more coolness, with more system, & with more wisdom" than the House, a large number of senators would create the very "vices which they are meant to correct," such as the divisiveness spawned by "their own indiscretions or the artifices of the opposite factions."[16] Madison contended that the "great evils" of the nation were the schemes of the state legislatures themselves. Through their agents in the Senate, the state legislatures, "instead of checking a like propensity in the National Legislature, may be expected to promote it."[17]

This dispute seemed to put other delegates on guard. Pierce Butler "was anxious to know the ratio of representation before he gave any opinion," and Hugh Williamson "wished that each State should have at least one" senator (he suggested a fixed maximum of twenty-five senators).[18] Sherman invoked the desire for a more elite Senate by saying that direct election would be unlikely "to produce such fit men as elections by the State Legislatures."[19] Other delegates from large states supported Dickinson's idea. Elbridge Gerry concluded that state legislatures would "be most likely" to provide protection for the commercial interests against the landed interests. Gerry expected that "the commercial & monied interest would be more secure in the hands of the State Legislatures, than of the people at large. The former have more sense of character, and will be restrained by that from injustice."[20] Charles Pinckney thought the selection of U.S. Senators by the state legislatures would make the Senate more stable and independent, and suggested that proportional representation could be realized by dividing the states into classes by size, and giving the group of small states one senator, the middle-sized states two, and the large states three.[21]

The Convention unanimously approved Dickinson's proposal that the state legislatures select the members of the Senate. Madison and Wilson were not ready to concede defeat, however. In late June, Wilson insisted that the national government was meant to serve individuals rather than the states, so that "*individuals . . . not the States*, ought to be represented in" both chambers of Congress (emphasis in original).[22] Connecticut's Oliver Ellsworth emphasized the need to protect "the existence & agency of the States," seeing no reason to reverse the earlier vote, anticipating that, inevitably, parochial "views & prejudices . . . will find their way into the general councils, through whatever channel they may flow."[23] Mason agreed that the states needed some power of self-defense and that "the only mode left of giving it to them" was through the appointment of senators.[24] Madison tried to delay the vote until the Convention settled the issue of proportional representation in the Senate, but too many of his allies were persuaded. The Convention again voted overwhelmingly that the state legislatures would choose the members of the Senate.[25] Madison and his allies were losing the battle over representation in the Senate—the foundation of Madison's plan for enhanced national power. His opponents' insistence on equal state representation would finally defeat that plan.

Apportioning Senate Seats

The problem of apportioning Senate seats brought the Convention to the breaking point in July. The broad nationalists insisted that seats in both the Senate and House be proportional to population, while narrow nationalists adamantly insisted that each state have the same Senate representation regardless of size. Only four days after Randolph introduced the Virginia Plan, Dickinson proposed a "mutual concession": House seats would be allocated by population size, but "each State would retain an equal voice" in the Senate.[26] When Sherman again proposed equal state representation in the Senate at the beginning of the Convention's third week, he said, "Every thing . . . depended on this. The smaller States would never agree to the plan on any other principle than an equality of suffrage in this branch."[27] Madison's coalition held together to defeat this motion, six states to five, and to approve a motion that ratio of representation in the Senate be the same as the ratio in the House.

But Madison's hope that the small states would begin to surrender plainly had failed. On the contrary, a few delegates from states essential to Madison's strategy began to waver in their support for proportional representation in the Senate. On the Monday after the rejection of the New Jersey Plan, Nathaniel Gorham of Massachusetts conceded that the small states had a point, and that he was "inclined to a compromise" because experience within his state "had shown the provision to be expedient."[28] Two days later, Luther Martin drove home the intensity of the opposition to broad nationalism. Martin accused Virginia of proposing "a system of slavery for 10 States" because "Virginia, Massachusetts & Pennsylvania have 42/90 of the votes" in Congress, so "they can do as they please without a miraculous Union of the other ten."[29] Martin's estimate more clearly specified the threat of large state domination in Congress.

Anger grew as June ended. When the delegates defeated Lansing's last-ditch motion to give each state equal representation in the House of Representatives on June 29, Ellsworth moved that the states be represented equally in the Senate. "Proportional representation in the first branch" conformed to "the national principle & would secure the large States against the small," said Ellsworth; state equality in the Senate conformed "to the federal principle and was necessary to secure the Small States against the large." He argued that "the power of self-defense was essential to the small states." Nature had given even the "smallest insect of creation" the power of self-defense. Without compromise, the states would not accept the Constitution, and the nation would divide. Ellsworth made a powerful argument against the claim that the large states could not coalesce against the rest: these states "will like individuals find out and avail themselves of the advantage to be gained by it." While he "was not in general a half-way man, yet he preferred doing half the good we could, rather than do nothing at all. The other half may be added, when the necessity shall be more fully experienced."[30] Georgia's Abraham Baldwin expressed doubt about the Senate, and wished that Congress's authority "had been defined, before the mode of constituting it had been agitated."[31]

On Saturday, June 30, James Wilson, aiming to alleviate fears that the large states would collude in Congress, took a calculated risk by drawing attention to this "imaginary combination" of the three large states. He virtually dared his opponents to specify what this supposed coalition of large states could actually agree upon. Instead, he supposed that a minority of the population would dominate a majority if the states were represented equally in the Senate. He estimated that, in the Convention, the votes against proportional representation in the Senate were cast by states with only a quarter of the American population. In a new Senate with equal state representation, states representing a third of the population could outvote states with two-thirds of the population. Unless the rule of apportionment was the same in the House and Senate, Wilson warned, the foundation of the government "can be neither solid nor lasting."[32]

Ellsworth countered Wilson forcefully. It was not true that the minority would rule the majority, because the House of Representatives would protect the interests of large states. The British House of Lords proved the value of a minority imposing a check on a majority, he said, and no confederacy had failed to provide for an "equality of voices." Ellsworth complained that the Virginia Plan proposed to run "from one extreme to another. We are razing the foundations of the building, when we need only repair the roof." He then badly damaged one of Wilson's central claims by arguing that the "danger of combinations among" the three large states "is not imaginary," and adding that "the possibility of them would be sufficient to alarm him." The three large states could combine to appoint powerful government officers, or to restrict trade solely to "Boston, Philadelphia and some port in the Chesapeake." He assured the delegates that his views were not unduly parochial because Connecticut was an average-sized state.[33]

Madison responded to Ellsworth just as forcefully. He denied that all confederacies treated units as equals, noting that other confederacies were not durable anyway. Madison harshly criticized Connecticut's past behavior. "Of all the States . . . Connecticut was perhaps least able" to complain about other states' actions because it had failed "to perform the stipulated acts from which no State was free." The Connecticut legislature had "*positively refused* to pass a law for complying with the Requisitions of Congress." Madison argued, "If the Senate represented the states equally, the majority of states could still injure a majority of the people" by obstructing needed measures, extorting measures "repugnant to the wishes & interest of the majority," and imposing measures that were just as repugnant because they were likely to have greater power than the House. Madison then gambled by injecting slavery into the discussion, asserting that slaveholding was an important and intractable interest. Madison conceded that every interest

> Madison (recording his own words) ought to be secured as far as possible. Wherever there is danger of attack, there ought be given a constitutional power of defense. But he contended that the States were divided into different interests not by their difference of size, but by other circumstances;

the most material of which resulted partly from climate, but principally from the effects of their having or not having slaves. These two causes concurred in forming the great division of interests in the United States. It did not lie between the large & small States: it lay between the Northern & Southern, and if any defensive power were necessary, it ought to be mutually given to these two interests. He was so strongly impressed with this important truth that he had been casting about in his mind for some expedient that would answer the purpose.[34]

Madison speculated that House seats might be apportioned on the basis of a state's free population alone, and Senate seats apportioned on the basis of a state's free and slave population.

Stung by Madison's blunt criticism of Connecticut, Ellsworth assured the Convention that his state entirely supported the national government, reminding them of "her great exertions" in the Revolution "in supplying both men & money."[35] Sherman attacked Madison's diagnosis that the states were the root cause of the nation's problems. Madison, he said, had veered off into complaints about "the delinquency of the States," when he had "to prove that the Constitution of Congress was faulty. Congress is not to blame for the faults of the States. Their measures have been right, and the only thing wanting has been, a further power in Congress to render them effectual."[36] William Richardson Davie of North Carolina, who did not understand how proportional representation would allow each state a senator, now preferred equal representation in the Senate at the moment. Davie, like Ellsworth, saw the union as "partly federal, partly national," and did not see a convincing argument for either equal representation or proportional representation.[37]

James Wilson recommended Senate representation based on categories of size, as first suggested by Charles Pinckney.[38] Benjamin Franklin proposed that the states vote equally on any issue that involved "the Sovereignty of individual States" or appointment to the executive branch, but proportionally on issues involving national government taxes, spending, and salaries.[39] Emotions rising, Rufus King was amazed "that when a just Government founded on a fair representation of the *people* of America was within our reach, we should renounce the blessing, from an attachment to the ideal freedom & importance of *States*." King's "fears [were] more agitated for his Country than he could express." King would accept Wilson's expedient solution, but go no further.[40] Madison also agreed to accept Wilson's solution if the Senate's independence were guaranteed. As currently framed, he complained, the Senate "is only another edition of" the Confederation Congress.[41]

New Jersey's Jonathan Dayton heatedly answered, "When assertion is given for proof, and terror substituted for argument, he presumed they would have no effect however eloquently spoken." The Virginia Plan's advocates had not shown that the nation's problems resulted from equality in Congress, and he "considered the system on the table as a novelty, an amphibious monster; and was persuaded that it never would be received by the people."[42] Gunning Bedford of Delaware inflamed the meeting by attacking Madison's coalition:

> If political Societies possess ambition, avarice, and all the other passions which render them formidable to each other, ought we not to view them in this light here? Will not the same motives operate in America as elsewhere? If any gentleman doubts it let him look at the votes. Have they not been dictated by interest, by ambition? Are not the large States evidently seeking to aggrandize themselves at the expense of the small? They think no doubt that they have right on their side, but interest had blinded their eyes. . . . We have been told with a dictatorial air that this is the last moment for a fair trial in favor of a good Government. It will be the last indeed if the propositions reported from the Committee go forth to the people. . . . The Large States dare not dissolve the confederation. If they do the small ones will find some foreign ally of more honor and good faith, who will take them by the hand and do them justice.[43]

According to another delegates' notes, Bedford told his opponents, "I do not, gentlemen, trust you."[44]

On Monday, July 2, the Convention deadlocked. Five states voted for equal representation in the Senate, and five of the states in Madison's coalition voted to defeat it. The Georgia delegation divided.[45] Charles Pinckney tried to revive his proposal to sort the states into classes, with larger states in a group receiving more senators and smaller states fewer. But even Pinckney now conceded that the large states might coalesce to pursue policies that benefited them.[46] General Pinckney was willing to consider this proposal, but he preferred Franklin's approach because "[s]ome compromise seemed to be necessary."[47]

General Pinckney proposed that a committee, with one member from each state, might bridge the political chasm.[48] Sherman instantly embraced the suggestion. "We are now at a full stop," said Sherman, and none of the delegates wanted the Convention to "break up without doing something."[49] Many delegates from the larger and Southern states supported the idea of a grand committee. Hugh Williamson warned, "If we do not concede on both sides, our business must soon be at an end."[50] Gouverneur Morris agreed that a committee was wise but advised the committee to propose a lifetime term for the Senate. "Loaves & fishes must bribe" the state "Demagogues," he said. "They must be made to expect higher offices under the general than the State Governments. A Senate for life will be a noble bait."[51]

Madison and Wilson alone tried to stop the creation of this committee by suggesting that similar committees in Congress were not very useful.[52] But the Convention overwhelmingly approved the creation of the grand committee. The membership of this committee was stacked against Madison. Of the eleven delegates chosen to serve, five represented states that had voted for equal representation in the Senate. A sixth, Abraham Baldwin of Georgia, also had voted for equal state representation. Franklin, Gerry, Mason, and Davie were chosen to represent large and Southern states. All had previously spoken out in favor of finding some kind of accommodation with the smaller states. Neither Madison nor Wilson served on this crucial committee.

The Connecticut Compromise

Three days later, on July 5, the special committee recommended the "Connecticut" (or "Great") compromise, proposing proportional representation in the House and equal state representation in the Senate. It also provided "that all bills for raising or appropriating money, and for fixing the Salaries of the Officers of the Government of the United States, shall originate in the [House of Representatives]" and could not be changed by the Senate.[53] Randolph and other Virginia Plan supporters believed that this provision would give the House of Representatives, in which large states had greater influence, effective control over spending and taxes. These supporters accepted equal state representation in the Senate on the belief that the House, not the Senate, would effectively control the national government's finances.

Clearly the Connecticut Compromise gravely threatened Madison's vision of a strong national government. Equal state representation in the Senate severely weakened the incentive for the large states to surrender substantial authority to the new national government. Madison attacked the provision for House origination of money bills as insignificant, and urged the delegates not to sacrifice "a just & judicious plan" to accommodate the smaller states.[54]

Tempers flared again. Gouverneur Morris, "as a Representative of America," vehemently objected to the compromise. He urged the delegates to look beyond their state constituencies; the delegates did not really mean "to truck and bargain for our particular States." Morris asserted that the United States would be united, if not by the force of reason, then by the force of the sword.[55] Morris's remarks gave Gunning Bedford an opportunity to soften his own impassioned prediction that the states would seek foreign allies. Bedford only had meant that foreign nations would seek to work with the smaller states to ensure that existing agreements would be upheld. But, he asked, would Morris not apologize for saying "that the sword is to unite" the country, and Gorham for suggesting that

"Delaware must be annexed to Pennsylvania and New Jersey divided between Pennsylvania and New York"? The small states had conceded on the House of Representatives and control of money bills, but, Bedford said, "If they be not gratified by correspondent concessions as to the 2nd branch is it to be supposed they will ever accede to the plan?"[56]

William Paterson pointed out that Morris's ominous prediction would not persuade the delegates, and he "complained of the manner in which Mr. Madison & Mr. Morris had treated the small States."[57] Williamson urged the delegates not to exaggerate or misconstrue the emotional language, but he felt the compromise proposals were "the most objectionable of any he had yet heard."[58] Committee members Mason and Gerry, both from large states, begged their fellow delegates to consider the compromise seriously. The committee did not mean to offer its propositions for adoption, said Mason, "but merely as a general ground of accommodation." He "would bury his bones in this city rather than expose his Country to the Consequences of dissolution of the Convention without any thing being done."[59] Gerry had "material objections" to the compromise, but a bargain was essential to prevent a breakup of the union and the intervention of a foreign army.[60]

Two days later, Sherman emphasized that equal representation in the Senate would help ensure the new government's success. Again turning the Virginia proponents' arguments against them, he argued that if the states had an equal vote in the Senate, the new government would have the "necessary vigor" to carry out essential tasks; without it, the implementation of national laws would be more difficult.[61] Gouverneur Morris objected that the committee report simply created another Confederation Congress, "a mere wisp of straw." He saw no provision "for supporting the dignity and splendor of the American Empire."[62] Wilson, while "was not deficient in a conciliating temper," believed that "firmness was sometimes a duty of higher obligation."[63] Just as firmly, Paterson emphasized, "There was no other ground of accommodation" than equal representation in the Senate.[64]

The battle over Senate apportionment came to a head on Saturday, July 14. When John Rutledge called for a separate vote on House control of money and equal representation in the Senate, Sherman played to the delegates' frustrations, suggesting that any change in any part of the compromise would prolong the debate by forcing the delegates to start from scratch.[65] Charles Pinckney again put forward his idea for dividing the states into groups. He proposed a Senate of 36 members, slightly more than half the size of the House: Virginia would be represented by five senators; Massachusetts and Pennsylvania by four; Connecticut, New York, Maryland, and North and South Carolina by three; New Hampshire and Georgia by two; and Rhode Island and Delaware by one. Madison called Pinckney's proposal a "reasonable compromise."[66] But the Virginia Plan's opponents blasted this idea.[67] Sherman "urged the equality of votes, not so much as a security for the small States, as for the State Governments which could not be preserved unless they were represented & had a negative in the General Government."[68]

Massachusetts' deeply conflicted delegation held the balance of power. Rufus King preferred to do nothing rather than allow "an equal vote to all the States"; he could not think of a reason that "the same rule of representation should not prevail" in both houses of Congress. King offered to support a national takeover of state debts to entice the smaller states.[69] Though sympathetic to Pinckney's proposal, Gerry "could see no hope of success."[70] Massachusetts delegate Caleb Strong took Gerry's side against King.[71]

Madison made a final push to hold support. He insisted that proportional representation in the Senate was necessary for expanded national authority. If "the proper foundation of Government was destroyed," with equal representation in the Senate, "no proper superstructure would be raised. If the small States really wish for a Government armed with the powers necessary to secure their liberties, and to enforce obedience on the larger members as well as on themselves he could not help thinking them extremely mistaken in their means." Madison emphasized, "The practicability of making laws, with coercive sanctions, for the States as political bodies, had been exploded on all hands." Paterson, said Madison, rightly argued that "Representation was an expedient by which the meeting of the people themselves was rendered unnecessary; and that the representatives ought therefore to bear a proportion to the votes which their constituents if convened, would respectively have." This principle should be applicable to both chambers of Congress. "In all cases where the General Government is to act on the people, let the people be represented and the votes be proportional," said Madison, who "called for a single instance in which the General Government was not to operate on the people individually." Defiantly, he said that "the people of the large States would in some way or other secure to themselves a weight proportioned to the importance accruing from their superior numbers." He then summarized the arguments against equal representation in the Senate: a minority of the people "could negative the will of the majority," extort policy, and impose policy on that a majority opposed. These problems would worsen with every new state admitted to the union, and "the perpetuity it would give to the preponderance of the Northern against the Southern Scale was a serious consideration."[72] Wilson added that equal representation of the states in the Senate created a fundamental institutional flaw that would not be corrected over time.[73]

Madison and Wilson's final arguments failed. When the Convention rejected Pinckney's proposal, Rufus King wrote that the proposition lost, "to my mortification by the Vote of Massachusetts."[74] On July 16, with Massachusetts divided, the delegates approved equal representation in the Senate for the final time.[75] Dismayed by the success of equal state representation in the Senate, some of Madison's allies seriously considered withdrawing from the Convention. Randolph said the final vote "had embarrassed the business extremely" and pointed out that all the powers given to the national government in the Virginia Plan assumed that "a Proportional representation was to prevail in both branches of the Legislature." Randolph suggested the Convention "adjourn, so that the large States might consider the steps proper to be taken in the present solemn crisis of the business, and that the small States might also deliberate on the means of conciliation."[76] Paterson agreed that it was high time to adjourn indefinitely, so that the delegates' constituents could discuss their work.[77]

The delegates now confronted the possible collapse of the Convention. General Pinckney "could not think of going to South Carolina, and returning again to this place. Besides it was chimerical to suppose that the States if consulted would ever accord separately, and beforehand."[78] Jacob Broom of Delaware thought "Such a measure . . . would be fatal. Something must be done by the Convention though it should be by a bare majority."[79] Randolph backtracked, assuring the delegates that he did not mean to suggest an indefinite postponement. He only sought a day's delay so that "some conciliatory experiment might if possible be devised, and that in case the smaller States should continue to hold back, the larger might then take such measures, he would not say what, as might be necessary."[80] Gerry "saw no new ground of compromise."[81] The influential John Rutledge of South Carolina thought the proponents of proportional representation should surrender.[82]

The Path of Representation in the Senate

When Madison joined several delegates from larger states in a strategy meeting the next morning, he watched his coalition fall apart. These delegates wasted time in "vague conversation . . . without any specific proposition or agreement." Some believed it preferable for the "side comprising the principal States, and a majority of the people of America," to propose a suitable government plan. But others were "inclined to yield to the smaller States." Madison's coalition of supporters could no longer win proportional representation in the Senate.[83] Madison and his allies reluctantly accepted the compromise and worked through the rest of the necessary provisions for the new government. The delegates later agreed there would be two senators for each state, and they would cast individual votes rather than a single state vote.[84]

At the end of the Convention, the delegates made the provision for equal representation of the states in the Senate the only permanent provision in the

Constitution that could not be amended. The process for selecting senators, however, gradually became more democratic. In the first decades after ratification, the state legislatures had only mixed success in their efforts to determine the way their senators would vote on important issues. By the mid-1800s, many aspiring senators campaigned among the voters for enough support to compel state legislatures to appoint them to the Senate. Famously, for example, Abraham Lincoln and Stephen A. Douglas in Illinois debated as part of their public campaign for an Illinois Senate seat in 1858. Congress began to debate direct popular election of senators in the late 1800s, and by the time it approved a Constitutional amendment that replaced the state legislature's selection of senators with the direct, popular election of senators, thirty-seven of the state legislatures themselves "had, by memorial to Congress or by institution of senatorial primaries, indicated that they no longer wanted to elect senators." This Seventeenth Amendment, ratified in 1913, in effect confirmed a change in the selection of senators that already was becoming widely accepted.[85]

Whether the equal representation of the states in the Senate is a flaw (as James Wilson suggested) or a strength of the Constitution, it remains an unshakable cornerstone of American government. While representation in the House of Representatives is roughly proportional to population, the number of senators per person is more uneven than ever. California, with over 37 million people in the 2010 census, had 53 U.S. Representatives and 2 U.S. Senators. Wyoming, with about 564,000 people, has 1 representative but, like California, 2 senators. The one-fifth of the American population who live in the 26 least populous states have more votes in the Senate than the four-fifths of the population who live in the 24 largest states.[86]

The Connecticut Compromise marked the rejection of the keystone of Madison's strategy. The acceptance of equal state representation in the Senate profoundly changed the path of the Convention thereafter. With equal state representation in the Senate, delegates from the smaller states pressed for more Senate power. Without equal state representation in both houses of Congress, the large state supporters of the compromise fought tenaciously for House control of national finances, the slave-state representatives fought to protect slavery and limit national authority, and Madison began to assert that the president should have more power to pursue the nation's interests.

Congressional Independence

Once the delegates agreed to the Connecticut Compromise, Congress's potential threats became more tangible. Supporters of proportional representation fought to strengthen the powers of the House of Representatives, while their opponents fought to strengthen the Senate's powers. This conflict surfaced during the prolonged and frustrating battle over House control of taxing and spending, and appeared in a different form when the Convention debated whether to prohibit national legislators from holding Cabinet or other posts. The delegates also disagreed about who could vote for members of Congress, who could serve in it, how long they would serve, and who would pay them. The delegates decided these separate issues in a way that increased the isolation, defensive powers, and complexity of Congress.

The Power of the Purse

No government power is more fundamental than the power to tax and spend. Taxes are necessary to fund any government action. But taxes also can hurt individuals, groups, states, or entire regions. Some delegates believed government tax and spending powers were so important that only the popularly elected House of Representatives should control them. But in mid-June, when Elbridge Gerry moved to prohibit the Senate from originating money bills because the new House of Representatives "was more immediately the representatives of the people, and . . . the people ought to hold the purse-strings," other delegates attacked the idea as ineffective and undesirable.[1] Pierce Butler "saw no reason" to limit Senate power. He expected the House to exploit this power by adding other substantive laws to money bills, thus negating the Senate's check.[2] James Madison said that the mere power of *originating* money bills would make no difference, and even if it did, it would be wrong to disable the "more capable set of men" in the Senate from any part in revenue and spending. Roger Sherman agreed, arguing, "We establish two branches in order to get more wisdom, which is particularly needed in the finance business."[3] The delegates defeated Gerry's proposal handily. Two weeks later, the delegates made the House and Senate equally powerful when they unanimously agreed that each enjoy "the right of originating acts."[4]

The Connecticut Compromise resurrected the proposal that the House would originate money bills and the Senate could not alter or amend them. Now, this idea served a political purpose: it aimed to win over the committee's large–state delegates (such as Mason and Gerry) to equal representation in the Senate. Large-state delegates on the committee believed that if the proportionally elected House controlled taxes and spending, large states effectively could control government actions.

But other supporters of proportional representation in the Senate again attacked the provision as a worthless concession. Since the Senate still had to agree to any bill before it became law, it could extort its preferences by refusing to accept any bill that lacked the tax and spending provisions it desired.[5] James Wilson thought the concession was "a trifle light as air," and he suggested that the Senate, rather than the House, should originate money bills.[6] If the provision actually enhanced the power of the House, Gouverneur Morris warned, it would "take away the responsibility of the" Senate, "the great security for good behavior."[7] General Pinckney, "astonished that this point should have been considered as a concession," recalled that when Gerry had suggested the provision in mid-June, it had been rejected "on the merits."[8]

The authors of the Connecticut Compromise from the large states stoutly defended this provision. George Mason agreed that it was politically expedient: "some points must be yielded for the sake of accommodation."[9] Gerry "would not say that the concession was a sufficient one on the part of the small States," but characterized it as a real concession.[10] The Convention fractured over the proposal. The delegates retained the provision on a vote of five smaller states for, three against, with three states (including Massachusetts) divided.[11] When John Rutledge appealed for a reconsideration of the provision on July 14, Gerry defended it as "the corner stone of the accommodation."[12]

Proponents of the provision remained unyielding after the Committee of Detail report included it in its August report. Charles Pinckney tried to eliminate it, as "giving no clear advantage to the House of Representatives, and clogging the Government."[13] But Mason feared the Senate. As "an aristocratic body," said Mason, the Senate would function "like the screw in mechanics, working its way by slow degrees, and holding fast whatever it gains" and "should ever be suspected of an encroaching tendency—the purse strings should never be put into its hands."[14] John Francis Mercer of Maryland "considered the exclusive [House] power of originating Money bills as so great an advantage, that it rendered the equality of votes in the Senate ideal & of no consequence."[15] While Oliver Ellsworth "did not think the clause of any consequence," he acknowledged that because "some members from the larger States" thought the clause mattered, "he was willing it should stand."[16] The Convention dropped the provision, and when it did, its supporters smoldered. Hugh Williamson insisted that the North Carolina delegation "had agreed to an equality in the Senate" because of the clause, and "was surprised" that smaller states like Connecticut were willing to surrender "the condition on which they had received their equality."[17] Edmund Randolph threatened to reopen the paralyzing issue of Senate representation if the section on House origination of money bills was not reinstated.[18] Wilson, Ellsworth, and Madison again asserted the clause made no difference, and Gouverneur Morris thought that Randolph and Mason simply were trying to bully the smaller states.[19] Unmoved by these arguments, the delegates approved equal representation in the Senate without the provision.

Randolph next proposed to prohibit the Senate from amending or altering revenue or appropriations bills in a way that would "increase or diminish" the amount set by the House. The "large States would require this compensation at least," he said, and it would "make the plan more acceptable to the people."[20] Mason strongly emphasized again that "the purse strings should be in the hands of the Representatives of the people."[21] John Dickinson, anticipating the later Anti-Federalist criticisms of the Constitution, suggested that the provision would serve the political purpose of deflecting criticism of the Constitution raised by "popular leaders." He pointed out that this requirement already existed in eight of the state constitutions.[22] Charles Pinckney "considered it a mere waste of time." John Rutledge could see no political advantage in the provision because a similar one in South Carolina merely encouraged political games and manipulation.[23] Madison forcefully attacked the idea of limiting Senate power over money, and he predicted that legislators would quarrel over the meaning of ambiguous terms like "revenue," "alter," "amend," and "increase or diminish" to get their way.[24] Randolph's motion lost, but even George Washington supported it, solely to mollify its supporters.[25] Hugh Williamson bitterly commented, "We have now got a House of Lords which is to originate money-bills," and claimed that the decision would haunt the Convention.[26]

Massachusetts' Caleb Strong proposed a solution originally suggested by Nathaniel Gorham: the House would originate revenue and spending bills, "but the Senate may propose or concur with amendments as in other cases."[27] Mason quickly seconded the motion, "extremely earnest to take this power from the Senate," and Hugh Williamson urged the delegates to indulge the members who thought the provision "essential to liberty."[28] When the delegates later considered very similar wording, Roger Sherman urged the delegates to accept the clause to give "immediate ease to those who looked on this clause as of great moment . . . trusting to their concurrence in other proper measures."[29] The Convention approved the language, then, solely to appease potential opponents of the Constitution.[30]

Forbidding Multiple Office-Holding

Should members of Congress be forbidden to hold offices in the executive branch? If legislators could also serve in executive positions such as secretary of a Cabinet department, the executive and legislative branches would be closely intertwined, as they were in Britain. Republican theory provided no clear guidance on this question, and the delegates had different ideas about the problem.

The delegates initially accepted the Virginia Plan's proposal to ban U.S. Representatives and Senators from serving in other national or state offices.[31] But after the defeat of the New Jersey Plan, Gorham argued that the ban was "unnecessary & injurious"; he conceded that Britain had abused multiple office-holding, but he suggested that it also might have saved the British government.[32] Wilson agreed, suggesting that the ban would make "perhaps the best Commanders ineligible" to take military leadership (subtly invoking Washington, the Convention president).[33] Rufus King warned that the ban "would discourage merit," and Alexander Hamilton thought it would discourage ambition.[34]

The very idea of importing British office-holding practices appalled other delegates. Butler contended that "this precaution against intrigue was necessary" because "[t]his was the source of the corruption that ruined" the British government.[35] Mason, firmly "for shutting the door . . . against corruption," regarded this ban "as a cornerstone in the fabric."[36] The Convention divided on Gorham's proposal, rejecting it on a tie vote of four states to four states, with three states too divided to decide.[37]

Madison struggled to find a way to permit members of Congress to serve simultaneously in the executive branch. He tried to allay fears that members would abuse this power to create new offices and pad their pay. When he proposed that U.S. Representatives be ineligible for offices created during their term and for a year thereafter, other delegates quickly conjectured the ways in which politicians would evade this rule.[38] Sherman anticipated that "[a] new Embassy might be established to a new court & an ambassador taken from another, in order to *create* a vacancy for a favorite member" (although he admitted "that inconveniencies lay on both sides").[39] Gerry expected that the proposal would "produce intrigues of ambitious men for displacing proper officers, in order to create vacancies for themselves."[40] King thought that it would be impossible to limit the hunt for offices, asking if the proposal would stop a legislator from seeking "appointments . . . for his son, his brother, or any other object of his partiality?"[41] The Convention banned multiple office-holding; it narrowly rejected a ban on legislators from holding other offices for a year after the end of their final term. But the delegates lifted the ban on U.S. Representatives holding *state* offices after Sherman complained about the unnecessary separations that were beginning to permeate the new government.[42] Similarly, the delegates banned U.S. Senators from other national offices, but they permitted them to hold state offices.[43]

After the Committee of Detail report, Charles Pinckney picked up the fight against the ban on holding more than one national office, arguing that it was degrading to the senators and discouraging to first-rate candidates. Pinckney hoped that the Senate would become "a School of Public Ministers, a nursery of Statesmen." He proposed that members of Congress be allowed to hold Cabinet and other executive positions, on the condition that they perform these duties without pay.[44] John Francis Mercer agreed that the president needed the power to appoint legislators to a Cabinet, and without it he would become "a mere phantom of authority." Mercer anticipated a war between the aristocracy (the Senate) and the people (the House), and he preferred the inevitable war to be waged between "the Aristocracy & the Executive" because "[n]othing else can protect the people against those speculating Legislatures which are now plundering them throughout the United States."[45] Wilson complained that the state governments had so much influence in the Senate now that "nothing seemed to be wanting to prostrate the National Legislature" to the states "but to render its members ineligible to National offices, & by that means take away its power of attracting those talents which were necessary to give weight to the Government and to render it useful to the people."[46]

Opponents of multiple office-holding refused to budge. Mason, defeated on the House control of money bills the previous day, sarcastically proposed to drop all limitations on appointments to encourage "that exotic corruption which might not otherwise thrive so well in the American Soil" and, given "the present state of American morals & manners," the Constitution would not lose much support if it encouraged such "mercenary & depraved ambition."[47] Gerry "was not so fond of" ministers and ambassadors "as to wish to establish nurseries for them."[48] Hugh Williamson "had scarcely seen a single corrupt measure in the Legislature of North Carolina, which could not be traced up to office hunting."[49] Sherman concluded that the nation would produce an ample supply of able leaders, so no provision for multiple offices was necessary.[50] Ellsworth also thought there would be no shortage of "Ambitious minds," and warned that the rule might discourage meritorious individuals outside of Congress.[51]

By the narrowest of votes, a five-to-five deadlock, the Convention upheld the ban on multiple office-holding—barely avoiding the possibility of a more British-style Cabinet system. Proponents of multiple office-holding mounted a final effort to win their point in September, but they lost again.[52] The final language prohibited members of Congress from serving in the executive or judicial branches. It also prohibited national legislators from receiving an appointment to an office they had created or whose salary they had increased. The provision did not prohibit future members of Congress from serving in the executive or judicial branches if they abandoned their position in Congress first. The Constitution did not ban simultaneous service in Congress and state office. These provisions raised the barriers between the legislative and executive branches, further isolating each from the other.

Controlling Elections

The rules for Congressional election were critical for balancing democracy and stability. Nearly all the delegates had served in state legislatures, where most members of the larger chamber served for no more than a year. The delegates believed that the shorter the term, the more closely the U.S. Representatives would mirror the preferences of their constituents. Those delegates who thought the state legislatures were *too* closely tied to the voters sought longer Congressional terms, especially for the Senate. Early in the Convention, Sherman and Ellsworth proposed a one-year term for U.S. Representatives. Elbridge Gerry "considered annual Elections as the only defense of the people against tyranny," and thought New England would insist on them.[53] Rutledge proposed a two-year term. Maryland's Daniel of St. Thomas Jenifer proposed a three-year term, arguing that elections held too frequently made "the people indifferent to them, and made the best men unwilling to engage in so precarious a service."[54] Madison supported the three-year term as a remedy for the instability that plagued republics and as a necessity in the enlarged government, in which representatives had to gain "knowledge of the various interests of" other states.[55] The delegates temporarily approved a three-year term.[56] The Virginia Plan had proposed that voters could recall members of the House of Representatives, but the Convention dropped that provision.[57]

After they rejected the New Jersey Plan, Randolph suggested shortening the Representatives' term to two years, recognizing that shorter terms were popular and that other checks on "popular intemperance" would allow it.[58] This proposal reopened the dispute over legislators' responsiveness. Ellsworth, noting, "The people were fond of frequent elections," again proposed a one-year term.[59] Wilson also liked the one-year term because it was "most familiar & pleasing to the people" and would provide "effectual representation."[60] But Madison, Dickinson, and Hamilton fought to retain the three-year term. Hamilton expected that the shortened term would dull interest in elections and "facilitate the success of little cabals."[61] Madison argued that, while U.S. Representatives worked at the capital, their political rivals would be free to cultivate support among the representatives' constituents back home. Representatives would try to prevent rivals from gaining this advantage by returning home too frequently.[62] Sherman "preferred annual elections," although he "would be content with biennial;"

he liked the idea that a representative would "return home and mix with the people," rather than stay in the capital, acquiring habits "which might differ from those of their Constituents." The delegates finally settled on a two-year House term, the midpoint between the Sherman and Madison positions.[63]

Because the delegates wanted a strong, elite Senate that would resist the momentary passions that had riled up the state legislatures, all supported longer terms for senators than for representatives. North Carolina's Richard Dobbs Spaight proposed a seven-year term for U.S. Senators. Madison agreed, arguing that this term would help stabilize republican government, and prevent the House from overwhelming the Senate. In states where state senators had shorter terms, he said, the senators did not serve as an effective check on the lower house.[64] Sherman preferred five years.[65] William Pierce of Georgia, concerned that a seven-year term "would raise an alarm" about the Constitution, proposed three years.[66] The Convention temporarily accepted the seven-year term. Two weeks later, George Read and Gouverneur Morris proposed that senators "hold their offices 'during good' behavior," that is, serve for an unlimited term, potentially decades long.[67] Hamilton hoped that senators, like judges, would hold their jobs for life to check "the amazing violence & turbulence of the democratic spirit" brought to life in the new House of Representatives.[68]

Gorham proposed a four-year term and, to better ensure stability, suggested that the Senators' selection "rotate," so that one-quarter would be chosen each year and so that most would stay in office after any election.[69] Rotation in office, Wilson added, would ensure that Senators elected in different years would act "under the influence of different views, and different impulses."[70] The delegates quickly embraced the idea of rotation, but rotation made a seven-year term awkward.[71] Williamson, Sherman, and Gorham proposed the six-year term for Senators, with one-third of the members rotating out of office every other year.[72] Read proposed a nine-year term, "the longest term that could be obtained," and Madison agreed.[73] After initially agreeing to a nine-year term, the Convention settled on six years.[74] Governors would fill Senate vacancies temporarily if the state legislatures could not do so.[75]

Who would be eligible to vote for the U.S. Representatives? The Committee of Detail provided that the same voters who elected the lower house of the state legislatures also would be able to vote for members of the U.S. House of Representatives. Gouverneur Morris proposed to limit the right to vote in House elections to "freeholders," that is, people who owned land.[76] Dickinson agreed that freeholders were "the best guardians of liberty."[77] Other delegates objected strongly. Ellsworth warned that "the people" would not support the Constitution "if it should subject them to be disfranchised." Moreover, the rule would disenfranchise merchants and manufacturers who did not own land.[78] John Rutledge warned that the idea "would create division among the people & make enemies of all those who should be excluded."[79] Wilson pointed out how difficult it would be to agree on a uniform rule for all the states, and he objected that any property qualification would be an "unnecessary" innovation.[80] For Benjamin Franklin, the "lower class of freemen" without property simply deserved the vote because of their "hardy Virtues and great Integrity."[81] A majority of states already had "extended the right of suffrage beyond the freeholders," said Mason, and he distrusted Congress with the "dangerous power" to determine who could or could not vote for its members.[82] Morris suggested that those without property would sell their votes to the wealthy, and that merchants and manufacturers could purchase property if they desired to vote. Mason answered that "The true idea . . . was that every man having evidence of attachment to & permanent common interest with the Society ought to share in all its rights & privileges . . .," and he asked whether merchants, manufacturers, and others would be "viewed as suspicious characters, and unworthy to be trusted with the common rights of their fellow Citizens?"[83] Madison was concerned about the provision's effect on ratification. He also worried about a future in which most Americans would have no property, and either combine to threaten those with property or, more likely, "become the tools of opulence & ambition."[84] Without dissent, the Convention accepted the original proposal, basing suffrage in House elections on the states' existing rules for legislative elections.

Which level of government would set times of the elections and other rules for electing members of the House of Representatives? If the states could control these rules, they could manipulate elections by providing times and places for casting votes in elections that either encouraged or discouraged voter turnout. Madison, eager to disconnect the states from the national government at every opportunity, cautioned that the states would write the laws "to favor the candidates they wished to succeed."[85] Gouverneur Morris thought the states would rig their reported results.[86] King suggested that without the ability to set rules for elections, the House might not be able to control the qualifications of new members.[87] Sherman, who "had himself sufficient confidence in the State Legislatures," thought that it "might be best" to enable the U.S. House to regulate the election of its members.[88] The delegates authorized Congress to make or alter national electoral regulations as they saw fit.[89]

Controlling Members' Qualifications and Pay

Several delegates believed that Congress would face fewer temptations to make bad policy if young persons, debtors, the propertyless, and most immigrants were prohibited from serving in the House or Senate. Without debate, the delegates set 25 as the minimum age for representatives (despite Wilson's objection to any minimum) and 30 as the minimum age for senators.[90] Mason recommended that only debt-free property owners be permitted to serve in the Senate to "secure the rights of property."[91] Gerry demanded even stricter limitations, while Charles Pinckney and General Pinckney wanted to apply the requirement to the executive and judicial branches.[92] But Madison urged that different interests needed their own representatives: "It was politic as well as just that the interests & rights of every class should be duly represented & understood in the public Councils." The commercial and manufacturing interests "should not be left entirely to the care, or the impartiality" of the landed interests.[93] Dickinson thought it was impractical and improper to disqualify "any man of merit" in a republican nation.[94] Gouverneur Morris charged that Mason's proposal "was but a scheme of the landed against the monied interest."[95] The delegates instructed the Committee of Detail to require property qualifications for Congress.

The Committee of Detail, however, could not come to any agreement on property qualifications for national legislators.[96] Charles Pinckney proposed that the president be required to own property worth a $100,000, judges $50,000, and "like proportion" for members of Congress.[97] Madison objected to giving Congress discretion to set these rules. Williamson warned that with this discretion, if "a majority of the Legislature be composed of any particular description of men, of lawyers for example, which is no improbable supposition, the future elections might be secured to their own body."[98] Ellsworth wanted to give Congress the authority to set these rules. Wilson expected that the legislators would never agree on property qualifications anyway. With some reluctance, the Convention evaded the problem of property qualifications by leaving it to Congress.[99]

How long should a person be a citizen of the nation and a resident of his state before he could serve in Congress? An immigrant from abroad might be more loyal to another country than the United States, and could use his power in Congress to enact policies more beneficial to a foreign nation than the United States. The Committee of Detail proposed that every member of Congress be a state resident, a representative be a U.S. citizen for at least three years, and a senator a citizen for four years. Mason proposed seven years to prevent "foreigners and adventurers" from making "laws for us & govern[ing] us," and the Convention agreed. Rutledge proposed that U.S. Representatives be required to be state residents for seven years. Though Mason thought seven years was too long, he insisted that state residency for a period be required to prevent rich men from one state from engineering election to office in a neighboring state. Read complained "that we were now forming a *National* Government and such a regulation would correspond little with the idea that we were one people."[100] Williamson was willing to specify that a person simply be a state resident, without any time limit, because new residents would be "most zealous" to "conform to the will of their constituents" to ally their suspicions.[101] Gouverneur Morris "moved to insert 14 instead of 4 years citizenship as a qualification for Senators; urging the danger of admitting strangers into our public Councils."[102] Madison worried that the restriction would give the Constitution a "tincture of illiberality "and send a bad signal to "great numbers of respectable Europeans" ready to emigrate to the U.S."; he was not apprehensive about the possibility that the state legislatures would appoint a "dangerous number" of immigrants to the Senate.[103] Wilson, an immigrant from Scotland himself, poignantly discussed the mortifying possibility "of his being incapacitated from holding a place under the very Constitution which he had shared in the trust of making."[104] The delegates finally settled on a nine-year U.S. citizenship requirement for Senators, seven years for members of the House, and a simple requirement of state residence for both offices.[105] To further protect against foreign influence, Charles Pinckney convinced the delegates to add a provision that "No person holding any office of profit or trust under the U. S. shall without the consent of the Legislature, accept of any present, emolument, office or title of any kind whatever, from any King, Prince or foreign State."[106]

The delegates considered the source of legislators' pay a powerful determinant of their loyalty. Broad nationalists asserted that the *national* government had to compensate legislators because, if the states paid them, they would be more dedicated to their own state's narrow interests than those of the nation as a whole. Madison observed that state government salary would create an "improper" and potentially "dangerous" dependence on the states. Madison wanted the Constitution to set a fixed salary for members of Congress.[107] Wilson also argued against state provision of legislators' salaries (though he opposed fixing the level of compensation because "circumstances would change and call for a change of the amount").[108] Hamilton insisted that the "State legislatures ought not . . . to be the pay masters" of the national government.[109] Ellsworth, who strongly urged that the states pay U.S. Senators, countered that "If we are jealous of the State Governments they will be so of us. If on going home I tell them we gave the General Government such powers because we could not trust you, will they adopt it?"[110] Madison argued that the proposal would undermine the intent of creating a firm, independent Senate, and make it instead "the mere Agents & Advocates of State interests & views, instead of being the impartial umpires & Guardians of justice and general Good."[111] Some delegates thought that senators should receive no compensation from any source because *any* salary would encourage individuals from the less privileged classes of society to seek Senate seats.[112] The delegates initially refused to provide a salary for senators.[113]

The Committee of Detail provided that the *states*, rather than the national government, would pay the U.S. Representatives and Senators. By this point in the Convention, even Ellsworth thought the provision might encourage "too much dependence on the States."[114] Mason thought that state-paid salaries would make the House and Senate "the instruments of the politics of the States whatever they may be."[115] Gouverneur Morris proposed that Congress simply set its own salaries, paid from national funds ("There could be no reason to fear that they would overpay themselves," he said), but Madison still favored a salary set by the Constitution rather than delegated to Congress.[116] Other delegates also opposed state funding because of the cost.[117] A few delegates who favored national compensation struggled to find an acceptable way to set a limit on Congress. Ellsworth suggested a clause pegging the compensation to "the present value" of some amount of money. Sherman proposed five dollars a day (a sum that states could supplement). Dickinson proposed a requirement that Congressional salaries be set every dozen years.[118] The delegates agreed finally that members of Congress would draw their salary from the national government and Congress would set that salary by law.[119]

Legislative Rules

The delegates gradually added rules that strengthened the autonomy of the House and Senate from each other and from other branches of government. They designated the leading office in the House of Representatives as "Speaker" (a title already used in the British House of Commons and American state legislatures) and required the members of the House itself—not the president or voters—to select this Speaker.[120] The House and the Senate separately would determine their own rules, punish their members for "disorderly behavior," administer their own internal elections, and judge the qualifications of their members. "Freedom of speech and debate in the Legislature" would not be "impeached or questioned in any Court or place out of the Legislature." Members of the House and Senate would "be privileged from arrest" when going to, attending, and returning from a session of Congress (except in cases of treason, felony, and disturbing the peace) to prevent the executive from intimidating Congress by arresting its members.[121] The House and Senate would be permitted to expel members, but to prevent a majority from throwing out its opponents, the Convention accepted Madison's proposal that a large, two-thirds majority be required for any vote expelling a member.[122]

To deal with other difficult questions, the Convention simply delegated discretion to the new Congress. For example, it was crucially important for the Congress to meet regularly to maintain its influence and counterbalance the executive branch—a sensible rule, given the power-grabbing history of European monarchs. The Committee of Detail draft *required* Congress to meet on a specific date, the first Monday in December each year. Both Sherman and Wilson supported a Constitutional provision to fix the day. But Madison and Mason thought it was impractical to set a specific date.[123] Randolph suggested that the Constitution could set a date but allow Congress to change it. The delegates accepted this idea—and then quibbled about the provisional date to set.[124] The debate over *where* Congress would be required to meet opened a flood of jealousy over the final location of the nation's capital city. Madison wrote that the delegates simply avoided a decision "after some further expressions from others denoting an apprehension" that the capital might be fixed in a place like Philadelphia or New York.[125]

Setting a rule for the size of a quorum, that is, the minimum number of members required to do business, required a careful balance. A quorum that was too small would allow an unrepresentative group of legislators to make law, but one that was too big could be immobilized by legislators' absences. The Committee on Detail proposed simply that a majority of members in the House and Senate had to participate to establish a quorum. The problem mushroomed into a complicated dispute, however. The delegates evaded the problem by delegating it to Congress and allowing each house to compel members' attendance.[126] The delegates explicitly required the houses of Congress to publish journals, but by a narrow margin gave them discretion to "except such parts thereof as may in their Judgment require secrecy."[127] Mason sought to require the annual publication of public spending, but the difficulty of doing so pushed the delegates to substitute the more flexible requirement that the information be published "from time to time."[128]

The Path of Congressional Development

The delegates built the new Congress incrementally, and as they did, they fortified the House and Senate. Their negotiations ensured the independent, coequal power of the houses and isolated Congressional office-holders from the executive branch. They allowed each house to make its own rules, and members of Congress to serve for as long as they could be reelected.

The Constitutional rules that ensure the independence of the House and Senate have been reinforced over time. Powerful, permanent committees in the House and Senate became the backbone of the law-making process in each house. Political parties soon organized Congress into majorities and minorities, and the leaders of the Senate and the House became party leaders. Both the committees and the party leaders have a strong interest in maintaining the independent power of the House and Senate.[129]

As a larger body, the House developed more extensive, formal rules and hierarchy.[130] The House of Representatives still guards its power to originate revenue, and custom has established that the House takes the lead on both revenue and spending bills. But the House does not control money bills. The Senate's coequal power allows it to change revenue and appropriations bills sent from the House; differences are resolved by conference committees consisting of both representatives and senators.[131]

The Senate developed as a deliberative body. Compared to the House, the Senate is more informal, allows for more debate, and treats members as equals. The filibuster, a delaying tactic unique to the Senate, allows one or more Senators to hold the floor indefinitely, speaking on topics both relevant and irrelevant to the issue. These speeches aim to delay and prevent action on a measure.[132] Because the filibuster can only be stopped by an extraordinary majority of three-fifths of the Senate, it has become practically impossible to act on controversial measures without the support of sixty of the Senate's one hundred members.

The right to vote already was relatively widespread in the United States in 1787. States removed most of the restrictions on white adult males by the 1840s.[133] Voting rights for African Americans, nominally protected by the Fifteenth Amendment (1870), were only ensured in the 1960s (see chapter 14). The Nineteenth Amendment (1920) guaranteed women the right to vote.[134] The Twenty-Sixth Amendment (1971) established 18 as the legal voting age.

The House and Senate have refused to seat some elected members of Congress, but the Supreme Court trimmed back this power in 1969. In *Powell v. McCormack*, the House of Representatives excluded Representative Adam Clayton Powell Jr. from membership in Congress after Powell, among the nation's most prominent African American office-holders, had been involved in scandals but reelected to office. Powell sued the Speaker of the House, John McCormack, and others to regain the office. The Court ruled that Congress can only *expel* members consistent with procedure specified in the Constitution, and that its effort to merely *exclude* Powell violated the Constitution.[135]

Constitutional amendments have had a marginal impact on Congressional rules and procedures. The Twentieth Amendment (1933) set January 3 as the meeting date for Congress, a date more closely aligned with the inauguration of the president. The Twenty-Seventh Amendment (proposed in 1789 but not ratified until 1992), provided that a change in Congressional pay may not take effect until a new Congress has been sworn in, thus preventing members of a current Congress from raising their own salaries.

As the delegates constructed this independent Congressional power, they also were working through a more difficult problem: the design of the executive for a republican national government.

10

Selecting the President

An effective national government clearly needed a national executive. But executive power created serious challenges for republican ideals. If the executive were too weak, scheming political opportunists in the Congress could overwhelm him and corrupt republican government for selfish ends. If the executive were given too much power, an ambitious demagogue in the office could usurp republican government and impose personal despotism. At first, most delegates were content to allow Congress to choose and control the executive. Some favored a multiple executive (that is, three individuals serving in the office) to control executive power and protect regional interests. As the design of Congress developed, the delegates raised more concrete concerns about the power of the executive relative to Congress. This chapter focuses only on the development of the process of using electors to select the president.[1] In the debates, the president's term and his eligibility for reelection were closely intertwined with the process of presidential election, because all three affected the president's independence of Congress. The president's term and eligibility are discussed in the next chapter.

After the Connecticut Compromise, James Madison and other broad nationalists demanded a process for choosing the president that would better ensure his independence of Congress. Roger Sherman and many other narrow nationalists supported Congressional selection of the president. For months, the delegates left Congress in control of choosing the executive, while they continued to discuss and refine an alternative process to bypass Congress. Finally, in September, a committee that included Madison and Sherman pulled these alternative ideas together and produced a compromise. Special electors, chosen by the states, would select the president. To solve the knotty problem of apportioning state votes in presidential selection, the delegates simply set the number of electors for each state equal to the number of U.S. Senators and U.S. Representatives that served each state in Congress.

The compromises on the presidency made the president much more independent and isolated from Congress. The separation of the president from Congress, in turn, made American government much more complex and difficult to use.

Envisioning a Republican Executive

Most delegates believed that the lack of a national executive was a critical failing of the Confederation government, and they quickly agreed to institute "a National Executive."[2] But the problem of executive power within a strong republican government deeply vexed the delegates. Gouverneur Morris put the problem as succinctly as any delegate: "It is the most difficult of all rightly to balance the Executive."

"Make him too weak: The Legislature will usurp his powers," said Morris, but "[m]ake him too strong" and "[h]e will usurp on the Legislature." Morris speculated that, if denied the opportunity to continue in office, the executive "will be in possession of the sword, a civil war will ensue, and the Commander of the victorious army on whichever side, will be the despot of America."[3] Charles Pinckney wanted "a vigorous Executive" but was afraid of adding executive powers that would "render the Executive a Monarchy, of the worst kind, that is, an elective one."[4] This ambivalence ultimately shaped the very title of the office. The Committee of Detail considered naming the American executive "Governor of the united People & States of America" but settled on the title "president," a label that connoted somewhat less active direction of government.[5]

Alexander Hamilton doubted that an effective executive could "be established on Republican principles" at all, but belived that the executive should be as steady and lasting as possible within republican principles. Hamilton urged the Convention to allow the executive to serve in office for life.[6] Some delegates suspected that Hamilton, and perhaps other delegates, hoped to establish a monarchy in the United States.[7] John Dickinson, another delegate who emphasized the limitations of republicanism, advised that "Secrecy, vigor & Dispatch," associated with monarchs, "are not the properties of Republics—we cannot have them in that Form—but Responsibility is the great point."[8]

The Virginia Plan simply made the executive the agent of the legislature. Congress would name the executive and grant him the "general authority to execute the National laws" and other powers it chose to delegate. In Sherman's view, Congress embodied the "supreme will of the Society," and the executive was "nothing more than an institution for carrying the will of the Legislature into effect." Sherman believed that Congress should even have the power to choose one or more executives if it liked, "as experience might dictate."[9] But James Madison was concerned that an executive chosen by Congress would be too weak, and would not have the ability to defend the prerogatives of the office. In a different political system, a hereditary monarch would enjoy "pre-eminence in the eyes of the rest" of society, as well as the "weight of property" and a "personal interest against betraying the National interest." In a republic, however, the executive would have none of these advantages. "In a Republic personal merit alone could be the ground of political exaltation, but it would rarely happen that this merit would be so pre-eminent as to produce universal acquiescence."[10] Madison thought the executive's powers should be "confined and defined" in the Constitution itself, and that "probably the best plan will be a single Executive of long duration with a Council, with liberty to depart from their Opinion at his peril."[11]

Edmund Randolph vigorously asserted that an executive shared by three people, rather than a single executive, offered the best solution to the problem of a republican executive for the United States. Randolph anticipated that the three co-executives would represent different regions—New England, the middle states, and the South, respectively.[12] This multiple executive would strengthen the independence of the office without sacrificing "vigor, dispatch & responsibility," which were "the great requisites for the Executive department."[13] John Rutledge objected that the executive required a single person who "would feel the greatest responsibility and administer the public affairs best."[14] Randolph, with "great earnestness," countered that such a single executive would expand executive power and never win public confidence. James Wilson and Pierce Butler both claimed that a single person in the office would be more accountable. Butler suggested that "if three or more should be taken from as many districts, there would be a constant struggle for local advantages"—an especially serious problem for military affairs.[15] Elbridge Gerry described it as "a general with three heads."[16] Wilson pointed out that each of the thirteen states, despite their differences, had put a single executive at the head of their state governments. "Among three equal members, he foresaw nothing but uncontrolled, continued, & violent animosities" that would poison the government.[17] The delegates settled on a single executive, although George Mason warned that his colleagues "mean to pave the way to hereditary Monarchy."[18] The New Jersey Plan allowed for a multiple executive—a point James Wilson used to attack the entire proposal. In late June, the delegates again approved the single executive. Hugh Williamson still complained about a single executive, arguing that the office could unfairly advantage the Northern states.[19]

The Connecticut Compromise transformed theoretical concerns about a republican executive into tangible political dilemmas for Madison and his allies. The compromise wrecked the value of Congress as a vehicle for the national interests Madison initially envisioned, and it thrust states' parochial interests into the powerful Senate. As soon as the delegates made the Senate a representative of the states, the broad nationalists forcefully argued that only the executive would champion truly *national* goals (as the "general Guardian of the National interests," in Gouverneur Morris's words) and that the executive's institutional independence and power were critical for the government's success.

The day after the final victory of the Connecticut Compromise, Madison emphasized that it was "absolutely necessary to a well constituted Republic" that the executive be completely independent of Congress because "[t]he collective interest & security were much more in the power belonging to the Executive" than in the judiciary's power, and the executive necessarily would have more discretion than judges.[20] Two days later, Gouverneur Morris strongly emphasized the need for autonomous executive power:

> It has been a maxim in political Science that Republican Government is not adapted to a large extent of Country, because the energy of the Executive Magistracy can not reach the extreme parts of it. Our Country is an extensive one. We must either then renounce the blessings of the Union, or provide an Executive with sufficient vigor to pervade every part of it. . . . One great object of the Executive is to control the Legislature. . . . It is necessary then that the Executive Magistrate should be the guardian of the people, even of the lower classes, against Legislative tyranny, against the Great & the wealthy who in the course of things will necessarily compose the Legislative body.[21]

For Morris, "The Executive therefore ought to be so constituted as to be the great protector of the Mass of the people."[22] The presence of George Washington, who many expected to serve as the first national executive, enabled the delegates to envision such a noble leader.[23] But, cautioned Benjamin Franklin, "No body knows what sort" of person would follow the first "good man" to serve in the office. Franklin expected that "the Executive will be always increasing here, as elsewhere, till it ends in a monarchy."[24]

Dual Tracks for Choosing the President

The uncertain and contentious problem of selecting the president had "greatly divided" the Convention and would divide the public, said James Wilson in September. "It is in truth the most difficult of all on which we have had to decide."[25] Because the delegates viewed the officials as the agents of those who selected them, they believed that the process for choosing the president would more powerfully shape his behavior than any other decision they could make.

During the Convention, the delegates concurrently developed two alternative processes for choosing the president. The first process, proposed in the Virginia Plan, simply delegated the selection to Congress, and prohibited him from being selected a second time. The second process, an alternative to Congressional selection, took shape incrementally. This second alternative originated in James Wilson's bold suggestion on June 1 that the voters, rather than Congress, might choose the president. This idea, used in New York and Massachusetts, aimed to give the executive more independence and to "produce more confidence among the people." Wilson proposed to divide the states into districts, and the voters in each district would choose an "elector." These electors in turn would meet and choose the executive.[26] Wilson's idea immediately drew criticism. Sherman, favoring Congressional selection, complained that executive independence was "the very essence of tyranny."[27] Williamson "could see no advantage" in electors chosen by the same voters as the state legislatures.[28] Unhappy with both Wilson's proposal and Congressional selection, Gerry suggested that the state legislatures could nominate, and the electors appoint, an executive.[29] Rutledge suggested that the Senate alone might choose the executive, because it represented more elite and propertied interests.[30] By a lopsided vote, the Convention on June 2 set aside Wilson's suggestion and voted to give Congress the responsibility to choose the executive.

But many delegates remained deeply uneasy about trusting Congress to select the executive. Gerry claimed it would "give birth to intrigue and corruption between the Executive & Legislature previous to the elections and to partiality in the Executive afterwards to the friends who promoted him." Gerry proposed that the states' governors should have the power to choose the executive.[31] Randolph thought Gerry's idea was terrible. The state executives could not be expected to support the power of the national executive, he believed, because "[t]hey will not cherish the great Oak which is to reduce them to paltry shrubs."[32]

After the Connecticut Compromise, Madison and his allies battled fiercely for a selection process that would insulate the executive from Congress. The day after the final vote on the Connecticut Compromise, Gouverneur Morris contended that if the executive could be "appointed & impeachable by" Congress, the executive "will be the mere creature of the Legislature," and presidential appointment "will be the work of intrigue, of cabal, and of faction." Reviving James Wilson's idea, Morris proposed that the U.S. citizens, instead of Congress, directly choose the executive.[33] Wilson enthusiastically favored this proposal, and now he emphasized the danger of putting executive selection at the mercy of the political schemers in Congress: if Congress chose the executive, he would be "too dependent to stand the mediator between the intrigues & sinister views of the Representatives and the general liberties & interests of the people."[34]

Too many delegates objected to any popular election of the executive. Charles Pinckney worried that the people would "be led by a few active & designing men. The most populous States by combining in favor of the same individual will be able to carry their points."[35] Mason pointed out the inconsistency that "[a]t one moment we are told that the Legislature is entitled to thorough confidence, and to indefinite power. At another, that it will be governed by intrigue & corruption, and cannot be trusted at all."[36] Sherman suggested that Congress would better express the "sense of the Nation" than the people, because the people "will never be sufficiently informed of characters, and besides will never give a majority of votes to any one man." Instead, they would vote for a fellow resident of their state, giving an unfair advantage to the largest state.[37] Wilson suggested that, if that happened, Congress could make the selection—a solution that "would restrain the choice to a good nomination at least, and prevent in a great degree intrigue & cabal."[38] Luther Martin tried to turn the notion of electors to the advantage of the states by proposing "that the Executive be chosen by Electors appointed by the several Legislatures of the individual States."[39] Though the Convention rejected both a popular vote for the executive and Martin's proposal, the system of electors as an alternative to Congressional selection was taking shape.

The executive's eligibility for a second term further complicated the delegates' calculations. Gouverneur Morris warned that denying the executive additional terms "will destroy the great incitement to merit public esteem by taking away the hope of being rewarded with a reappointment." Because "[t]he love of fame is the great spring to noble & illustrious actions," blocking the "road to Glory" in this way may force a future executive to "seek it by the sword." It may "tempt him to make the most of the Short space of time allotted him, to accumulate wealth and provide for his friends."[40] But an executive appointed by Congress and eligible for its reappointment, would likely become a subservient lackey. Randolph believed that if the executive could be reappointed, "he will be no check on" Congress at all.[41] To many delegates, it was obvious that an executive chosen by Congress could not be eligible for a second term.

On July 19, as the delegates debated whether or not to limit the president to a single term, Rufus King said he would "prefer any other reasonable plan that could be substituted" for allowing Congress to choose the president. He thought that "an appointment by electors chosen by the people for the purpose, would be liable to fewest objections."[42] William Paterson, a chief defender of the New Jersey Plan, conspicuously agreed with King, proposing for "[e]lectors to be chosen by the States in a ratio that would allow one elector to the smallest and three to the largest States."[43] Madison emphasized that the executive had to have "free agency" apart from Congress because a coalition of the legislature and the executive "would be more immediately & certainly dangerous to public liberty." Though Madison preferred popular election, he conceded that the idea of electors made it possible to overcome the problem of differences in the suffrage between the North and South.[44] Gerry still hoped the state governors would choose the electors to nurture "a strong attachment in the States to the National System."[45]

Oliver Ellsworth tried to move forward by fleshing out Paterson's proposal.[46] The system for using electors to choose the president was now almost fully developed and was gaining acceptance. Only Rutledge expressed adamant opposition "to all the modes except the appointment by the National Legislature."[47] All the states north of the Carolinas voted for a system of electors, and all the states but Virginia and South Carolina endorsed the plan to allow the state legislators to choose the electors.[48] When doubts were raised about "undue influence" on these electors, Ellsworth underscored their independence of Congress, anticipating that "any persons might be appointed Electors, excepting solely, members of the National Legislature."[49]

Electors seemed to solve the problem of executive selection—until the delegates faced the problem of choosing the *electors* and weighting the states' relative influence in the selection process.[50] When Gerry tried to specify the number of electoral votes each state would receive in the first national election, the delegates began to haggle over the number of votes allocated to New Hampshire and Georgia, much as they had done over the allocation of votes in the first House of Representatives. The delegates temporarily agreed that the electoral votes be proportioned to votes in the House.[51]

These difficulties sapped support for the idea of electors. Richard Dobbs Spaight of North Carolina and William Houstoun of Georgia sought to reconsider selection by Congress.[52] Caleb Strong complained the government plan was becoming too complicated.[53] Gerry warned that the change would unravel other difficult compromises about the executive, such as his eligibility for reelection.[54] Gerry proposed that the state legislatures choose the national executive, with states' votes weighing in the same proportion as their votes in the House of Representatives. He also proposed that, if no candidate received a majority, the U.S. House of Representatives would choose two candidates from the four candidates who received the most votes, and then the House would choose between these two.[55]

The delegates temporarily restored Congress's power to choose the executive. Desperate for some alternative to Congressional selection, Wilson thought out loud about the possibility of literally drawing names of members of Congress out of a hat, and allowing this group to choose the executive or the electors.[56] Gouverneur Morris was willing to consider Wilson's or any other scheme that would take the selection of the executive out of Congress's hands, because "[o]f all possible modes of appointment that by the Legislature is the worst." Wilson's idea "deserved consideration. It would be better that chance should decide than intrigue."[57] For Gerry, Wilson's idea was "committing too much to chance. If the lot should fall on a set of unworthy men, an unworthy Executive must be saddled on the Country."[58] King, worried that "[t]he lot might fall on a majority from the same State which would ensure the election of a man from that state," observed, "We ought to be governed by reason, not by chance."[59] Frustrated, Gerry admitted, "We seem to be entirely at a loss on this head" and suggested that they simply turn over the problem to the Committee of Detail: "Perhaps they will be able to hit on something that may unite the various opinions which have been thrown out."[60]

The next day, Ellsworth proposed that Congress select the executive initially, but after the completion of his term, state-appointed electors would decide whether to reelect him.[61] Madison inventoried the options available for choosing the executive, including the courts, the Congress, state institutions, and the people. He concluded that the most acceptable options remaining "lay between an appointment by Electors chosen by the people, and an immediate appointment by the people." The delegates had resoundingly defeated the idea of electors, he reasoned, so "the remaining mode was an election by the people or rather by the qualified part of them at large. With all its imperfections he liked this best."[62] These imperfections, he admitted, included a bias toward candidates from large states (a problem Ellsworth called "unanswerable").[63] Williamson suggested "as a cure for this difficulty, that each man should vote for 3 candidates. One of these he observed would be probably of his own State, the other 2 of some other States; and as probably of a small as a large one."[64] Gouverneur Morris "liked the idea, suggesting as an amendment that each man should vote for two persons one of whom at least should not be of his own State."[65] But Gerry cautioned that direct election might put the choice of the president in the hands of a semi-secret, hereditary elite group like the Society of the Cincinnati.[66] Butler complained that the plan was becoming "so complex & unwieldy as to disgust the States."[67] Mason concluded that selection by Congress was, after all, the best option, as long as the executive was ineligible for reelection. Once again, the Convention laid aside the alternative plan and accepted Congressional selection.[68]

The Compromise on the Presidency

The Committee of Detail's plan dutifully provided that Congress would choose the president, but added yet another problem by specifying that the House of Representatives and Senate "shall, in all cases, have a negative on the other."[69] This formula put two deeply divisive issues on the table. First, should the Senate, with equal representation of the states and already formidable powers, have a veto over the presidential preference of the "people's" house? Second, what influence should the relative size of a state's population have in the selection of the president?

Quarrelling broke out immediately. Mason questioned "the propriety of giving each branch a negative on the other 'in all cases,'" including appointments.[70] Sherman "*hoped*" for this veto, because it would allow the Senate (where the states enjoyed equal representation) to negate the presidential choice of the House of Representatives (where larger states could combine to elect their candidate).[71] Nathaniel Gorham warned that separate ballots could result in "great delay, contention & confusion."[72] Madison successfully moved to eliminate the provision.[73] After the delegates had hacked their way through a thicket of provisions on Congressional powers and procedures, Rutledge proposed that the Constitution specify that the House and Senate would cast a joint ballot. Sherman "objected to it as depriving the *States* represented in the *Senate* of the negative intended them in that house."[74] Angered, Gorham replied that "it was wrong to be considering, at every turn whom the Senate would represent. The public good was the true object to be kept in view."[75] Jonathan Dayton rushed to Sherman's defense, charging that "a *joint* ballot would in fact give the appointment to one House."[76]

Sherman's frank comment about maintaining state influence forced the relative influence of the states to the center of the discussion. David Brearley of New Jersey opposed a joint House and Senate ballot because the "argument that the small States should not put their hands into the pockets of the large ones did not apply in this case."[77] John Langdon supported a joint ballot by the House and Senate because "[t]his general officer ought to be elected by the joint & general voice." Langdon also noted that the "Negative of the Senate would hurt the feelings of the man elected by the votes of the other branch."[78] Wilson urged that it was only reasonable to give "the larger States a larger share of the appointment" and added that the Senate "had peculiar powers balancing the advantage given by a joint ballot."[79] Madison pointed out that a joint ballot "will give to the largest State, compared with the smallest, an influence as 4 to 1 only, although the population is as 10 to 1. This surely cannot be unreasonable as the President is to act for the *people* not for the *States*."[80] The delegates approved the joint ballot, and narrowly turned back a proposal to require that each state cast only a single vote in a joint ballot.

The delegates stumbled onto more problems and reached an impasse. What if the votes were so split that a minority of Congress elected the president? The delegates approved Charles Pinckney's motion that a Congressional majority was required to win the presidency. What if the vote resulted in a tie? George Read proposed that the president of the Senate cast the deciding vote in the case of a tie, but the Convention rejected this idea.[81] Gouverneur Morris again attacked any Congressional involvement in presidential selection.[82] The Convention narrowly rejected an effort to move to electors, six states to five. On a tie vote, the Convention refused to turn the problem of presidential selection over to a special committee, again rejected electors (now on a tie vote), and moved on.[83] On the last day of August, the delegates finally turned the problem over to a special Committee on Postponed Matters. This committee, consisting of eleven members from each state then represented at the Convention, included Sherman, Madison, King, Dickinson, Williamson, Brearley, and Gouverneur Morris.

This Committee on Postponed Matters stitched together the many ideas about an alternative to Congressional selection of the president and blended them with agreements already reached about Congressional selection. The committee proposed a process based on electors, who would be chosen in any way a state decided. Each state would have the same number of electors as it had senators and representatives in Congress—a formula that provided exactly the same relative influence in presidential balloting that each state would have exercised in a joint ballot of Congress. The electors would meet in their home states, to reduce the opportunity for them to conspire together in a single national "cabal" to select the president. Electors would vote for two presidential candidates; the candidate that received the largest number of votes, *if* it were a majority, would be president. The runner-up would become vice-president, a new office that would automatically provide a replacement for a president who died or was removed from office (the Committee report stated that if the president could not exercise his duties, the "vice-president shall exercise those powers and duties until another President be chosen, or until the inability of the President be removed"). If no candidate received an outright majority, or if there were a tie vote, the Senate would choose the president from among the five candidates receiving the most electoral votes.[84]

The Convention generally accepted this proposal as an adequate way to free the president from Congress. Butler "thought the mode not free from objections, but much more so than an election by the Legislature, where as in elective monarchies, cabal faction & violence would be sure to prevail."[85] Hamilton liked the changes better than the "Monster" created by Congressional selection.[86] Charles Pinckney did not think that the electors would be familiar with several candidates, but Wilson expected that the number of nationally known candidates would multiply.[87] Other delegates hesitated. Gerry served notice that his support depended on presidential powers.[88] Mason "confessed that the plan of the Committee had removed some capital objections, particularly the danger of cabal and corruption"; his remaining "great objection" to the plan would evaporate if it deprived "the Senate of the eventual election."[89] Rutledge, who "was much opposed to the plan reported by the Committee" because "[i]t would throw the whole power into the Senate," moved to restore Congressional selection. But the delegates refused to go back this time.[90] To head off potential corruption of the electors, the Convention unanimously agreed that no one could serve as an elector if they served in Congress or held "any office of profit or trust under the U.S."[91]

Many delegates, however, demanded an alternative to the Senate as the fallback if the electoral vote failed to produce a presidential winner. Mason believed that the electors often would fail to produce a majority for one presidential candidate, so that the Senate ultimately would choose most future presidents.[92] Mason also believed that the president and Senate would conspire with each other to manipulate the election. Charles Pinckney was convinced that the president "will become fixed for life under the auspices of the Senate."[93] Madison expected that large states would try to control the pool of candidates, and he worried that electors would generate so many candidates that the election invariably would be turned over to the Senate to choose among the five finalists with the highest vote totals. He "considered it as a primary object to render an eventual resort to any part of the Legislature improbable."[94] (Sherman "reminded the opponents . . . that if the Small States had the advantage in the Senate's deciding among the five highest candidates, the Large States would have in fact the nomination of these candidates").[95]

The delegates flailed about for an acceptable alternative to the Senate if the electors did not provide a majority for any candidate. Williamson thought at least the Senate's choice "ought to be restrained to the *two* highest on the list," and Mason proposed three.[96] Sherman preferred seven or thirteen, and Spaight and Rutledge proposed to expand the Senate's choices to the thirteen top vote-getters. Both proposals were defeated.[97] Mason and others unsuccessfully moved that the candidate with a plurality of the electors' votes—that is, more votes than anyone else—would win.[98] When the Convention rejected Wilson's proposal to turn the choice over to the whole of Congress instead of the Senate, Gerry "suggested that the eventual election should be made by six Senators and seven Representatives chosen by joint ballot of both Houses," and then proposed that Congress, not electors, decide whether to *re*elect an incumbent president.[99]

Frustration overflowed. Mason viewed the current provision as "utterly inadmissible. He would prefer the Government of Prussia to one which will put all power into the hands of seven or eight men, and fix an Aristocracy worse than absolute monarchy."[100] Wilson blasted the Senate, objecting that "the President will not be the man of the people as he ought to be, but the Minion of the Senate. He cannot even appoint a tide-waiter without the Senate." Conniving Senators, "sitting in Conclave, can by holding up to their respective States various and improbable candidates, contrive so to scatter their votes, as to bring the appointment of the President ultimately before themselves."[101]

Roger Sherman suggested a way to cut through the problem by allowing each state's Representatives and Senators to gather to cast a single, state vote for president if the presidential electors produced no winner.[102] This solution would trim Senate power while ensuring equal state influence in presidential selection. To prevent a coalition of smaller states from choosing the president, Madison successfully suggested that at least two-thirds of the Senators had to be present when voting to select the president.[103] When Williamson proposed Sherman's idea that the entire Congress vote on the president if necessary, Sherman himself proposed that the decision be lodged in the House of Representatives alone, with "the members from each State having one vote." Mason liked this plan best because it reduced "the aristocratic influence of the Senate."[104] Sherman's idea received overwhelming support and became the backup plan to the system of electors. The Convention delegates agreed to require that representatives of two-thirds of the states be present if the House chose the president, so that a few states would not dominate, and they required an absolute majority of the states to choose the president in the House.

The Path of Presidential Selection

From the start, the delegates struggled to establish an executive who would be safe for a national republic, one with enough power to advance the national interests, but not so much power that he undermined republicanism itself. The selection of this chief executive was critical for balancing his role, they believed. But they found it difficult to commit to either of two models: first allowing Congress to make the choice, and second, finding a way to route the choice around Congress. Driven by the evolving design of Congress, they embraced a more independent president, and a complicated path to selecting the president through a system of electors, described as the "Electoral College" by the early 1800s. This system aimed to filter popular will through state legislatures and special electors chosen only to vote for president. The growth of political party competition soon encouraged the states to provide for the direct voter selection of presidential electors. By 1804, most states provided for voters directly to influence electoral votes. By 1828, only South Carolina did not make such a provision.[105]

The United States has had remarkable success conducting regular elections for president.[106] From 1792 through 2008, American presidential elections had been held on the Constitution's regular four-year schedule fifty-six times without interruption, even during the Civil War and World War II. Some of the presidential elections have marked critical turning points in the development of American government.[107] It is even more remarkable that there has been a peaceful and orderly transfer of power from one political party to another after twenty of these elections.

The Electoral College system, however, has sparked many intense controversies.[108] In the 1800 election, the Electoral College broke down. Because electors could vote for two candidates for president and were pledged to party candidates for president and vice president, two candidates received an identical number of Electoral College votes. In 1800, political parties were emerging and organizing the contest for the presidency. Thomas Jefferson, the candidate of the Democratic-Republicans, challenged incumbent President John Adams (the candidate of the rival Federalist Party) in a very bitterly fought campaign. Jefferson won the election, but his vice-presidential running mate, Aaron Burr, received exactly the same number of electoral votes as

Jefferson. Because Jefferson and Burr tied, under the existing Constitution, the choice between the two Democratic-Republicans had to be decided by the House of Representatives. The ambitious Burr refused to defer to Jefferson. After much wrangling, the House of Representatives chose Jefferson. The Twelfth Amendment remedied this problem by requiring electors to specify their vote for president and vice president.[109]

The House next resolved an election in 1824, when a fractious Democratic-Republican Party split the electoral votes. In 1876, 1888, and 2000, one presidential candidate received more popular votes in the national ballot, while his opponent won a majority of the electoral vote and thus the presidency. A special Electoral Commission resolved disputes over the validity of states' electoral votes in 1876. The U.S. Supreme Court settled challenges over the ballot count in Florida in 2000.

After the 2000 election, experts engaged in lively discussions of the weaknesses and strengths of the Electoral College.[110] Members of Congress have introduced hundreds of proposed Constitutional amendments to reform the Electoral College—more proposed Constitutional amendments than on any other subject.[111] In 1961, the ratification of the Twenty-Third Amendment allowed the District of Columbia to cast electoral votes.

While they struggled with the process for selecting the president, the delegates were also trying to balance effectiveness and republicanism in designing the president's powers, the length of the president's term in office, his eligibility for reelection, and the process of presidential succession. Their compromises gradually increased both the president's independence and his isolation.

Presidential Independence and Isolation

The delegates' aspirations for a stronger national government and a republican government collided on the problem of defining the executive's power. Republican theory offered no clear guidance about whether the president should be completely subservient to the popular will as embodied in Congress, or enjoy the independence and muscle to check Congress. Republican ideas required the separation of the executive from other institutions, but they did not stipulate how separate institutions would restrain one another. The delegates worked out these issues piece by piece, trying to balance executive powers with constraints.

By incremental steps, the delegates gradually increased the president's independent authority, and at the same time they isolated him within the government and established checks on his powers. The president must share powers with institutions that are independent of his authority. But the precise extent of this authority, and the limits on his powers, remained unclear and ambiguous.

After the Connecticut Compromise, the struggle for executive independence spilled over into decisions about the president's term, removal, successor, appointment power, and veto. The delegates agonized over the length of the president's term because it would help determine the autonomy of the office. Presidential impeachment, succession, appointments, and veto authority each required the compromises to fine-tune the balance between presidential and Congressional power.

The Executive's Term and Qualifications

How long should the president serve in office? If a president served for a fixed term but could be reelected for an additional term, he would focus on securing reelection and scheme to win it. If a president served a longer term, he could be more independent—but he also could become settled in office, a potential tyrant who would refuse to leave office and use his powers to subvert the republic.

In 1787, the idea that a national leader would peacefully surrender power to his successor seemed visionary. Alexander Hamilton expected that "[a]t the period which terminates the duration of the Executive there will be always an awful crisis in the National situation."[1] To ensure the president would not depend on Congress if Congress chose him, then, he could not be allowed to run for reelection, but if he was permitted to run for reelection, he could not be chosen by Congress and still enjoy sufficient independence.

On June 1, James Wilson proposed a three-year executive term, assuming that the individual could be reelected.[2] Roger Sherman, who wanted the executive closely tethered to Congress, supported this three-year term and rejected any limit on the number of times a president could be reelected "as throwing out of office the men best qualified to execute its duties."[3] Charles Pinckney and George Mason countered with a seven-year term, and Mason wanted to limit the executive to one term to prevent Congress from accepting "unfit characters" and the executive from engaging in "intrigue with the Legislature for a re-appointment."[4] Gunning Bedford of Delaware "strongly opposed" the long term, for fear that the nation would be saddled with a bad or incapacitated leader.[5] The delegates approved a seven-year term.

In July, William Houstoun of Georgia proposed that the executive be eligible to serve a second seven-year term. Sherman and Gouverneur Morris endorsed the idea. Morris cautioned that ineligibility for an additional term would invite the executive to abuse power in the short run, to "make hay while the sun shines."[6]

The delegates approved presidential reelection, but once they did, some became uncomfortable with the length of the executive term. Jacob Broom felt that, if the executive had been prohibited from reelection, he would have "preferred a longer term," but now Broom "was for a shorter term."[7]

Virginia's James McClurg proposed an unlimited presidential term, allowing the president to serve "during good behavior," like judges.[8] Before the Connecticut Compromise, only Alexander Hamilton had argued for an unlimited executive term.[9] Now, with "great pleasure," Gouverneur Morris embraced a lifetime appointment for the executive. "This was the way to get a good Government," said Morris.[10] Madison personally doubted that more than three or four delegates supported a term of "good behavior" for the executive, but the idea had a political purpose: it served "to alarm" supporters of Congressional selection and to "facilitate" agreement on more executive autonomy.[11] Madison himself used the discussion to emphasize that the "Executive could not be independent of the Legislature, if dependent on the pleasure of that branch for a re-appointment." If the executive were so dependent on Congress, it "would render it the Executor as well as the maker of laws," and the result would be "tyrannical laws may be made that they may be executed in a tyrannical manner."[12] Sherman considered such lifetime tenure neither "safe" nor "admissible." The incentive to seek periodic reelection would ensure the necessary "good behavior."[13] George Mason emphasized that a lifetime term would "be an easy step to hereditary Monarchy." It would be "impossible to define" executive misbehavior to bring him to justice, and "impossible to compel" such a chief executive "to submit to a trial."[14] McClurg's proposal lost, but four states supported it.

Edmund Randolph next urged the Convention to limit the executive to a single term, so that he "not be left under a temptation to court a re-appointment." Responding to Morris's concern that the executive would refuse to leave office at the end of his term, Randolph argued that he could get away with it only if "the people be corrupt to such a degree as to render all precautions hopeless."[15] The Convention rejected a limit of one term, and then rejected a seven-year term. Rufus King did not want too short a term, and Pierce Butler "was against a frequency of the elections" because "Georgia & South Carolina were too distant to send electors often."[16] Gouverneur Morris now "was for a short term, in order to avoid impeachments, which would be otherwise necessary."[17] Oliver Ellsworth proposed a six-year term, so that the president could weather duties that made him momentarily unpopular.[18]

Once the Convention accepted this six-year presidential term, supporters of a one-term executive fought to prevent reelection. Hugh Williamson said he would accept a ten- or twelve-year presidential term if the executive could serve only one term. Elbridge Gerry thought it would be better for the executive "to continue 10, 15, or even 20 years and be ineligible afterwards."[19] Luther Martin proposed that the president serve an eleven-year term, a proposal that set off a frenzied effort to find a suitable term for a president who could not be re-elected. William Davie proposed an eight-year term. Gerry "suggested fifteen." Sarcastically, Rufus King suggested twenty years because "[t]his is the medium life of princes."[20]

James Wilson pulled the Convention back to the underlying problem: Congressional selection created too many problems. Wilson "would agree to almost any length of time in order to get rid of the dependence which must result from it." If he could not be reelected, an experienced executive could be "cast aside like a useless hulk."[21] Gouverneur Morris said that banning reelection "was as much as to say we should give" the executive "the benefit of experience, and then deprive ourselves of the use of it."[22] Morris made a final appeal for presidential appointment for an unlimited presidential term, warning, "A change of men is ever followed by a change of measures," and arguing that a term of good behavior would ensure needed stability and continuity in the office.[23] Charles Pinckney suggested "that no person be eligible for more than 6 years in any twelve years."[24] Mason and Elbridge Gerry liked the idea, but it got no further support.[25] With appeals from elder statesmen Mason and Benjamin Franklin, the delegates reinstated a single seven-year term without re-eligibility for a second term.[26]

In September, the Committee on Postponed Matters proposed a four-year term and eligibility for reelection. This solution received considerable support, in part because the delegates were weary of fighting over it.[27] Charles Pinckney and Hugh Williamson specifically objected to the potential reelection of the president. The Convention rejected efforts by John Rutledge, Richard Dobbs Spaight, and Williamson to delay the report and extend the president's term. It overwhelmingly approved the four-year presidential term without any term limits.[28]

With virtually no disagreement, the delegates gradually applied the basic template of other Congressional qualifications to the presidency. They set the minimum age at 35, 10 years older than a U.S. Representative and 5 years older than a U.S. Senator. The president would be "a natural born citizen or a Citizen of the United States at the time of the adoption of this Constitution" and a fourteen-year resident.[29] Like members of Congress, the president would receive a fixed compensation, paid out of the national treasury, and could receive no other pay from the national government or the states during his term.[30]

Removing and Replacing the Executive

Early on, Mason insisted, "Some mode of displacing an unfit magistrate is rendered indispensable by the fallibility of those who choose, as well as by the corruptibility of the man chosen," and Madison asserted that all executive officials should be held accountable.[31] But this provision for peaceful and orderly removal of the nation's chief executive was perhaps the most exceptional and hopeful republican feature of Constitution. Getting rid of national leaders had a bloody history around the world.

As the delegates became more sensitive to the political impact of the evolving Constitution, the problem of removing the president required them to fine-tune the president's independence of Congress. Would Congress use impeachment as a political hammer to manipulate the president? The power to impeach the executive was, for Gouverneur Morris, "the dangerous part of the plan" because this threat would make him too afraid to check the Congress or serve his role as "a firm guardian of the people and of the public interest."[32] Which risk was worse: making it too easy, or too difficult, to remove a controversial president?

Sherman, who sought an executive to serve as the agent of Congress, wanted the legislature to be able to remove him at will. Mason objected to this idea, viewing Congressional removal at will "as a violation of the fundamental principle of good Government."[33] John Dickinson proposed that the president be removable on the application of a majority of state legislatures. The delegates provisionally approved Dickinson's proposition, although Madison and Wilson opposed it because it gave the state governments too much power (it "enabled a minority of the people" to block the removal of a criminal president), invited intrigue, and encouraged the executive to curry favor with particular state leaders.[34]

Determined to fortify the president's independence of a Congress they now believed to be deeply flawed, some broad nationalists proposed to strike out executive impeachment altogether, so that the executive could not be removed at all. Gouverneur Morris thought the president's vulnerability to impeachment was "dangerous" and believed that president's reelection would be "sufficient proof of his innocence."[35] For Charles Pinckney, a given Congress would hold its impeachment power "as a rod over the Executive and by that means effectually destroy his independence," and ruin the value of the executive veto over legislation.[36] For Rufus King, republican principles argued against any provision for impeachment, because "the vigor of the Executive" was necessary "as a great security for the public liberties."[37]

The many proponents of presidential impeachment swiftly answered these critics. "Shall any man be above Justice?" asked Mason, and most especially the executive, "who can commit the most extensive injustice?" If an executive manipulated his first election, should he be allowed to escape punishment and be allowed to repeat it?[38] Gerry thought "A good magistrate will not fear" impeachments, while "[a] bad one ought to be kept in fear of them."[39] Without the threat of removal, an executive "will spare no efforts or means whatever to get himself re-elected," warned William Davie.[40] Randolph pointed out, "The Executive will have great opportunities of abusing his power; particularly in time of war when the military force, and in some respects the public money will be in his hands."[41] Madison "thought it indispensable that some provision should be made for defending the Community against the incapacity, negligence or perfidy of the chief Magistrate"; an executive could abuse his powers for personal gain, oppression, or to sell out the nation to a foreign power.[42]

These strong arguments clearly changed minds. Gouverneur Morris now admitted that impeachment was necessary. "This Magistrate is not the King but the prime-Minister," said Morris. "The people are the King."[43] Morris warned:

> In all public bodies there are two parties. The Executive will necessarily be more connected with one than with the other. There will be a personal interest therefore in one of the parties to oppose as well as in the other to support him. Much had been said of the intrigues that will be practiced by the Executive to get into office. Nothing had been said on the other side of the intrigues to get him out of office. Some leader of [a political faction] will always covet his seat, will perplex his administration, will cabal with the Legislature, till he succeeds in supplanting him.[44]

The Convention voted by a large margin to make "the Executive be removable on impeachments."[45] The Committee of Detail provided that the House of Representatives would impeach (that is, indict) the president and other officers of the government, and that the Supreme Court would conduct the trial on the charges of impeachment.[46]

The Committee on Postponed Matters proposed that the House of Representatives could impeach the president, but it provided that the Senate, rather than the Supreme Court, would hold the trial of a president impeached by the House. Its proposal allowed the president to be impeached for treason or bribery, but dropped "corruption," a charge included by the Committee of Detail.[47] Madison, trying to limit the Senate's power, objected that this arrangement still made the president too dependent on Congress; he still preferred impeachment be tried in the Supreme Court.[48] Gouverneur Morris responded that "no other tribunal than the Senate could be trusted" because there were too few Supreme Court justices, so that it would be too easy for them to be "warped or corrupted."[49] Sherman "regarded the Supreme Court as improper to try the President, because the Judges would be appointed by him."[50]

George Mason objected that the definition of impeachable offences was too limited, and he proposed to add "maladministration" to the list.[51] When Madison objected that "[s]o vague a term will be equivalent to a tenure during pleasure of the Senate," Mason changed his proposal to "other high crimes & misdemeanors" (but the Convention did not further define this phrase, derived from medieval British law).[52] The delegates approved this wording, as well as a Senate trial. They later required the Chief Justice of the Supreme Court to preside over an impeachment trial and allowed the president to serve in office while the trial took place.[53]

Presidential removal required the delegates to designate someone as the president's successor. A leaderless nation invited political turmoil that could wreck the government. A succession crisis would invite factions to battle to place their favored candidate in the vacant office. When the Committee of Detail designated the president of the Senate as the president's successor, many delegates found this provision very troubling. Madison objected because "the Senate might retard the appointment of a President" so that they could override vetoes more easily. Madison suggested that "the Council to the President" exercise executive powers during a vacancy, Gouverneur Morris suggested the Chief Justice of the Supreme Court succeed the president, and Hugh Williamson wanted Congress to fill the open position.[54] John Dickinson commented that a provision for a temporary president "until the disability . . . be removed" "was too vague." Dickinson asked, "who would judge whether the president were disabled?"[55]

The vice presidency was invented to make the *president* more independent of Congress. The Committee on Postponed Matters recommended the runner-up in the presidential election serve as vice-president, and this newly invented officer would fill the presidency "in case of [the president's] removal, . . . death, absence, resignation or inability to discharge the powers or duties of his office." Instead of designating the president of the Senate as the president's successor, this plan made the president's successor the president of the Senate, providing a check on that chamber. The vice president would preside over Senate proceedings (except impeachment trials), and even cast a vote if the Senators' vote deadlocked in a tie.[56]

From the moment it was proposed, the delegates disparaged the office of vice president. Nathaniel Gorham thought the office could be filled by "a very obscure man with very few votes" (Sherman disagreed).[57] Williamson "observed that such an officer as vice-President was not wanted. He was introduced only for the sake of a valuable mode of election which required two to be chosen at the same time."[58] Equally worrisome was the vice president's role in the legislature, which for some delegates violated orthodox principles of the separation of powers. "We might as well put the President himself at the head of the Legislature," complained Gerry, and Mason thought "that it mixed too much the Legislative & Executive."[59] Morris answered that if Gerry were right about the political devotion of the vice president to the president, "The vice president then will be the first heir apparent that ever loved his father."[60] Sherman simply "saw no danger in the case. If the vice-President were not to be President of the Senate, he would be without employment, and some member by being made President must be deprived of his vote, unless when an equal division of votes might happen in the Senate, which would be but seldom."[61] The delegates approved the office, and authorized Congress to establish a hierarchy of legal successors to the presidency if neither the incumbent nor the vice president could fill the job.[62]

The Executive's Council and Appointments

Presidential control of appointments would give the president significant power independent of Congress. At the same time, it could allow the president to favor his cronies with valuable jobs. Benjamin Franklin viewed executive appointment cynically, as an opportunity for building the executive's power; "all profitable offices will be at his disposal."[63] Initially, the Convention entrusted the Senate with the appointment of top executive officials and judges, and largely ignored Wilson's argument that the executive, "a single, responsible person," should make these appointments.[64]

The delegates began to deal seriously with executive appointments only after the Connecticut Compromise. Gorham defended executive appointments, noting that the president "would certainly be more answerable for a good appointment" than the Senate, while the penalty for a bad appointment would only be "public censure, which with honorable minds was a sufficient one."[65] Wilson complained about the "notorious" corruption that attended legislative appointments.[66] For the time being, the Convention left key appointments to the Senate, but allowed the executive to appoint officers not specified by law.[67] Sherman disliked even this concession to presidential appointment: "If the Executive can model the army, he may set up an absolute Government; taking advantage of the close of a war and an army commanded by his creatures."[68]

The Committee on Postponed Matters proposed that the president appoint "ambassadors, and other public Ministers," along with judges, but that the Senate would have to provide its "advice and Consent" to these appointments.[69] Gouverneur Morris explained that "as the President was to nominate, there would be responsibility, and as the Senate was to concur, there would be security."[70] Wilson objected to any Senate consent at all, arguing that this shared power destroyed responsibility.[71] Gerry dismissed the "idea of responsibility in the nomination to offices" as "chimerical" because the president could always claim that he lacked full knowledge of his nominees.[72] Despite these objections, the Convention accepted presidential appointment with Senate approval, adding that the president could make temporary appointments when the Senate was not in session. Some delegates, concerned about political manipulation, tried to restrict the appointment power as the Convention neared its end, but they had no success.[73] The delegates accepted, reluctantly, Morris's proposal that Congress could vest "the appointment of such inferior Officers as they think proper, in the President alone, in the Courts of law, or in the heads of Departments."[74] Though the Committee of Detail had proposed an entirely separate office of Treasurer appointed by Congress, the Convention ultimately allowed a Treasurer to be appointed like any other executive officer.[75]

For many of the delegates, an executive council—one imposed on the president as a Constitutional requirement—was essential for republican government. This "privy" council (a body of government officials who would provide advice to the president) could improve executive decision-making, monitor the president and limit his actions, as such councils did in the states. At the start of the Convention, Gerry believed a council of wise advisors would "give weight & inspire confidence" in the executive.[76] Sherman felt this council was essential to ensure popular confidence of the people, and he reminded the delegates that state executives could not act without the assent of their councils.[77] Madison agreed that a single executive should have the help of such a council, but he did not believe that such a council should have any control over executive authority.[78] Wilson emphatically did not want a Council because it more often "serves to cover, than prevent malpractices."[79]

In August, Ellsworth proposed a Council "composed of the President of the Senate, the Chief-Justice, and the Ministers as they might be established for the departments of foreign & domestic affairs, war finance, and marine" to advise the president but not determine his actions.[80] Gerry did not like the idea of judges participating in lawmaking, and Charles Pinckney wanted the president to have discretion to "call for advice or not as he might choose. Give him an able Council and it will thwart him; a weak one and he will shelter himself under their sanction."[81] A committee suggested a "Privy Council" that included the speaker of the House of Representatives, the chief justice, and heads of executive departments, without any power to determine the president's decisions. But the Committee on Postponed Matters simply gave the president the power to "require the opinion in writing of the principal Officer in each of the Executive Departments, upon any subject relating to the duties of their respective offices."[82] It made no mention of legislators or judges. Although this wording was accepted, Mason complained that, "in rejecting a Council to the President, we were about to try an experiment on which the most despotic Governments had never ventured."[83]

The Executive Veto and Policy Influence

The debate over the presidential veto was a microcosm of the Convention's uncertain groping for a balance between a presidential and legislative power. The veto aimed to check the policy-making passions of the legislature, especially for "a variety of pernicious measures," as Madison put it.[84] But a power to veto legislation would give the president the power to override the citizen's representatives. The issue thus forced the delegates to define the meaning of "separation of powers" in practice. The executive veto power was not a central tenet of republicanism or the separation of powers. Instead, in Wilson's words, "The revisionary duty was an extraneous one, calculated for collateral purposes."[85]

The Virginia Plan proposed that the executive and "a convenient number of the National Judiciary" share the power to veto laws. Gerry proposed to replace this "revisionary" council with a simple executive veto, one which Congress could override.[86] Wilson wanted the executive and the judiciary jointly to exercise a Congress could not override veto, because "tempestuous moments" could require the executive "to defend itself." Wilson believed that "this power would seldom be used" because Congress would not test it, so that "[i]ts silent operation would therefore preserve harmony and prevent mischief."[87] Wilson's proposal shocked Pierce Butler, who observed that "Executive power" was constantly expanding "in all countries," and that the United States was not immune to an authoritarian military leader.[88] Benjamin Franklin feared that the executive would use this power to extort a salary increase, cash, or a grant of power from the legislature.[89] Mason believed it would be sufficient to give the executive merely the power "to suspend offensive laws, till they shall be coolly revised," and then the executive's objections overridden by an extraordinarily large majority in Congress.[90] Sherman, championing legislative power, opposed any presidential veto at all, because he "was against enabling any one man to stop the will of the whole. No one man could be found far above all the rest in wisdom."[91] Gunning Bedford agreed because he "was opposed to every check" on Congress, the voice of the people: "The two branches would produce a sufficient control within the Legislature itself."[92] The Convention adopted a simple executive veto on June 4 and allowed Congress to override it with a two-thirds vote. After the Connecticut Compromise, they reaffirmed this decision without further debate.[93]

From the start, Madison fought to require that Supreme Court judges join the president in vetoing Congressional laws. This joint veto would have forced the institutional cooperation of the executive and judiciary. In Madison's view, "the utility of annexing the wisdom and weight of the Judiciary to the Executive seemed incontestable." In a republican government, "The Executive Magistrate would be envied & assailed by disappointed competitors: His firmness therefore would need support . . . An association of the Judges in his revisionary function would both double the advantage and diminish the danger."[94] Mason agreed that it was essential to give "all possible weight to the revisionary institution . . . The purse & the sword ought never to get into the same hands, whether Legislative or Executive."[95] Charles Pinckney, however, did not want to bring "Judges into the business"; the executive could simply consult his ministers on potential vetoes.[96] King thought that it was inconsistent to prefer a single executive "for the sake of responsibility" and at the same time to support a veto power shared with other officials.[97] Dickinson, building on this argument, suggested that the principle of executive responsibility required that he "singly . . . discharge" the functions of his office. Dickinson said that the participation of judges "involved an improper mixture of powers."[98] Gerry "thought the Executive, whilst standing alone would be more impartial than when he could be covered by the sanction & seduced by the sophistry of the Judges."[99] The delegates rejected the joint veto in early June.

After the Connecticut Compromise, Wilson and Madison redoubled their efforts to include the Supreme Court in the veto. Wilson cautioned that "Laws may be unjust, may be unwise, may be dangerous, may be destructive; and yet not be so unconstitutional as to justify the Judges in refusing to give them effect" after reviewing them in court.[100] The separation of powers required only that different branches "should act separately," even if "on the same objects." After all, the two branches of Congress were "separate and distinct, yet they are both to act precisely on the same object."[101] Madison argued that the joint veto would be useful to all three branches and "to the Community at large as an additional check against a pursuit of those unwise & unjust measures which constituted so great a portion of our calamities." It was necessary, he claimed, to give "every defensive authority to the other departments that was consistent with republican principles."[102] On this issue, Ellsworth agreed "heartily" with Madison.[103] Gouverneur Morris doubted that the joint veto would help to strengthen the executive against Congress, but he supported it.[104]

Opposition to the joint veto remained too strong, however. Luther Martin viewed the proposal as "a dangerous innovation" and he raised a practical problem: "in what mode & proportion are they to vote in the Council of Revision?"[105] Gerry argued, "It was establishing an improper coalition between the Executive & Judiciary department."[106] Gorham thought that Madison and his allies had failed to explain how the judges could remain neutral if they had helped to write the laws, and that, since the "Judges will outnumber the Executive, the revisionary check would be thrown entirely out of the Executive hands, and instead of enabling him to defend himself, would enable the Judges to sacrifice him."[107] A prominent judge himself, Rutledge "thought the Judges of all men the most unfit to be concerned in the revisionary Council. The Judges ought never to give their opinion on a law till it comes before them."[108] A deeply fractured Convention defeated it, three states for, four states against, and two divided. The indefatigable Madison pressed for a modified joint veto again in mid-August, but Sherman dismissed it, disapproving of "Judges meddling in politics and parties. We have gone far enough in forming the negative as it now stands."[109] The Convention rejected it again on a more decisive vote. The president would exercise the veto alone.

When the Convention defeated Madison's final effort to engineer a joint veto, Gouverneur Morris tried again to strengthen the president by giving him an absolute veto that Congress could not override. Legislatures could not be trusted, said Morris: "The most virtuous citizens will often as members of a legislative body concur in measures which afterwards in their private capacity they will be ashamed of." Inevitably, Congress would "contrive to soften down the President."[110] Sherman stood against any change, asking whether one man could "be trusted better than all the others if they all agree?"[111] Hugh Williamson moved to require three-fourths, rather than just two-thirds, of senators and representatives to override the president. Wilson strongly approved, cautioning that the distrust of presidential power was misplaced; he "insisted that we had not guarded against the danger" of legislative tyranny "by a sufficient self-defensive power either to the Executive or Judiciary department."[112] Apparently convinced that the president needed a more formidable veto power, but unwilling to allow judges to participate in it, the Convention required a three-fourths vote for the House and Senate to override a presidential veto.[113] They also required that the president state his objections to a vetoed bill.

After the Convention approved the Electoral College, Williamson himself suggested that the margin required for Congress to override a presidential veto be reduced back to two-thirds. Williamson "had since been convinced" that the three-quarters override was too high a hurdle, "puts too much in the power of the President," and made it too difficult to repeal bad laws.[114] This proposal prompted the delegates to quarrel again about the precise balance between executive and legislative power. Sherman quickly agreed "that the States would not like to see so small a minority and the President, prevailing over the general voice."[115] Gerry reminded the delegates that "[t]he primary object . . . is not to protect the general interest, but to defend his own department. If ¾ be required, a few Senators having hopes from the nomination of the President to offices, will combine with him and impede proper laws. Making the vice-President Speaker increases the danger."[116] Charles Pinckney "warmly" opposed "¾ as putting a dangerous power in the hands of a few Senators headed by the President."[117] Madison gave a measured endorsement to the three-quarters override, arguing that process of selecting the president made it more imperative to allow him to defend his prerogatives.[118] Alexander Hamilton observed that the two-thirds margin had been ineffective in New York. Gouverneur Morris suggested that the change would not matter because the difference between two-thirds and three-fourths amounted to only two members in the Senate and five in the House.[119] The Convention, though, voted to restore the margin required for an override to two-thirds.

The delegates authorized presidential influence in national policy-making in other ways. They accepted Committee of Detail language that thrust the president into the initial stages of policy-making by making it the duty of the president to provide Congress information on "the state of the Union" and recommend "such measures as he shall judge necessary, and expedient."[120]

The Committee of Detail also wrote the language in the final Constitution that the president "shall take care that the laws of the United States be . . . faithfully executed," a clause that authorized latitude for the president to determine how to implement laws once Congress enacted them.

Pardons

The power to pardon opened another door for the abuse of executive power. Presidents could pardon cronies, or accept a bribe in return for a pardon. The delegates prohibited the president from pardoning an official who had been impeached and convicted, but they rejected Sherman's effort to require that the Senate consent to all presidential pardons.[121] Martin made a motion to prevent the president from granting a pardon to a person before a court convicted him, but withdrew it when James Wilson "objected that pardon before conviction might be necessary in order to obtain the testimony of accomplices."[122]

Could the president pardon traitors? This provision could give the president an opportunity to undermine the government itself. Randolph believed, "The prerogative of pardon in these cases was too great a trust. The President may himself be guilty. The Traitors may be his own instruments." Randolph moved to prohibit presidential pardons in cases of treason.[123] But would the *Congress* then be allowed to pardon in these cases? For James Madison, "the pardon of treasons was so peculiarly improper for the President that he" would be willing to give the power to Congress.[124] Gouverneur Morris "had rather there should be no pardon for treason, than let the power devolve on the Legislature."[125] Wilson held that "Pardon is necessary for cases of treason, and is best placed in the hands of the Executive. If he be himself a party to the guilt he can be impeached and prosecuted."[126] Randolph "could not admit the Senate into a share of the Power. The great danger to liberty lay in a combination between the President & that body."[127] The delegates finally agreed to vest the power to pardon even treasonable offenses in the president alone.[128]

The Path of Presidential Power

In confronting the design of the presidency, more than in any other area, the collision of a stronger government and republican ideals forced the delegates to balance their highest aspirations. Understandably, the delegates proceeded cautiously, incrementally, and with an awareness of their tangled ideals, hopes, and interests. The delegates reinforced the president's independence by assigning him a term of office different from the terms of the Representatives and Senators, allowing him to seek reelection, and giving him powers to appoint, to veto legislation, and to influence the national agenda. But these arrangements also isolated the president within the government. The delegates explicitly rejected efforts to connect the executive to other branches by defeating a joint veto, a privy council, and the possibility that members of Congress also could serve in the executive branch. On the other hand, the delegates violated orthodox principles of separate powers by allowing a presidential veto, requiring Congressional approval of executive appointments, and installing the vice president as the presiding officer of the Senate.

As political scientists Joseph Pika and John Anthony Maltese explain, the delegates' "ambivalence over executive power . . . became a permanent feature of American political culture."[129] Americans have unrealistic expectations for a president's leadership, holding him accountable for the nation's security, prosperity, and moral tone. At the same time, the powers of the office are constrained by institutions he cannot control. Presidents have taken advantage of the Constitution's ambiguities to expand the reach of the office. But presidents in the modern era remain isolated, as political scientist Sidney Milkis explains, because presidents have a weak relationship with political parties and the popular support they once provided.[130]

The president has become the dominant player in American public policy, but the growth of presidential power has occurred with very few formal changes in the Constitution.[131] A few nineteenth-century presidents like Thomas Jefferson, Andrew Jackson and Abraham Lincoln interpreted the Constitution in a way that favored broader presidential power. In the following century, Theodore Roosevelt, Woodrow Wilson, and Franklin Roosevelt greatly expanded the president's claim to authority. Congress largely acquiesced by allowing the president to take leadership on the federal government budget, the domestic agenda, economic management, and national security.

Presidents have used the veto, executive power, and even the authority to assess the state of the union as tools for expanding the scope of their power. Although President Washington only vetoed two bills (and Presidents Adams and Jefferson vetoed none), presidents gradually made the veto power a formidable tool. Presidents had used the veto power over 2,500 times by 2012. Congress had overridden only 110 of these vetoes.[132] Presidents also have used "executive orders," an instrument not suggested in the Constitution, as tools for actively shaping policy without Congressional interference. Presidents have issued over 13,000 such orders, including directives that set policies on civil rights, the environment, abortion, and other controversial topics.[133] The provision for a "state of the union" message subtly allowed the president to focus Congress on his policy agenda, providing a considerable initial advantage by framing the initial debate on his terms. While President Washington's first "state of the union" message included a number of legislative priorities, and some of his nineteenth-century successors also made suggestions, only in the twentieth century did presidents begin to set a more active agenda for Congress. An annual, formal "State of the Union" presidential speech has become common since Woodrow Wilson first presented his message in person to a joint session of Congress in 1913.[134]

Congress has delegated to the executive branch vast responsibility for implementing programs and regulations that affect every aspect of American life—but Congress retains much power to check the president. The Senate has confirmed most presidential nominees for the Federal courts and executive offices, but confirmation can be painstaking and is not inevitable. Presidents have nominated 159 individuals to serve on the U.S. Supreme Court since 1789; the Senate confirmed 123 of these nominees but never confirmed 36.[135] Senators from the home states of judges usually have expected that a president of their party will defer to them on a judicial appointment in their state (however, this practice of "Senatorial courtesy" actually involves a much wider group of senators interested in the nomination).[136] A new president typically can make about

3,000 political appointments when taking office. The executive branch, however, now employs over two and a half million civilians, and most are protected by civil service from arbitrary removal by the president and his appointees.[137] Presidents sometimes enlist federal judges for executive duties. For example, President Truman appointed Supreme Court Justice Robert Jackson as the chief prosecutor at the Nuremberg war-crimes trials after World War II, and Chief Justice Warren chaired the commission that investigated the assassination of President Kennedy.[138]

Two Constitutional amendments have affected the president's term. The urgency of the nation's Great Depression focused attention on the needlessly protracted period between the November election and the Constitutionally-set beginning of a newly elected president's term in March of the following year. The Twentieth Amendment (1933) shortened the period between the election and the start of a new president's term. After Franklin Roosevelt became the first president elected to a third and fourth term, the Twenty-Second Amendment (1951) limited the president to two terms.

The House of Representatives has deployed the impeachment process against two presidents: Andrew Johnson in 1867 and Bill Clinton in 1997. The Senate did not convict either one. The impeachment process also was underway in 1974, during the Watergate scandal, but ended when Richard Nixon became the first president to resign the office.

The rules for presidential succession have raised many Constitutional questions in American history. The Committee of Style revised the section on succession to read, "In case of the removal of the president from office, or of his death, resignation, or inability to discharge the powers and duties of the said office, the same shall devolve on the vice president."[139] This language left it unclear whether the vice president would actually become the president on the death of a predecessor, or whether he would just "act" as president. When President William Henry Harrison became the first president to die in office in 1841, Vice President John Tyler set a lasting precedent when he declared that he was president and took the oath of office. Again, the transition of power to the vice president has been remarkably orderly. Since 1841, Vice Presidents Millard Fillmore, Andrew Johnson, Chester Arthur, Theodore Roosevelt, Calvin Coolidge, Harry Truman, and Lyndon Johnson have assumed the office of the presidency on the death of the incumbent president. In 1947, Congress passed a Presidential Succession Act that established that, if neither the president nor vice president could exercise power, the speaker of the house would act as president, followed by the president pro tempore of the Senate, and then the cabinet secretaries (beginning with the oldest cabinet position, secretary of state). The Twenty-Fifth Amendment (ratified in 1967) finally established that the vice president became president when the presidency was vacant, set a procedure for filling a vacancy in the office of vice president (used in 1973 to select Vice President Gerald Ford), and provided a procedure for declaring that an incumbent president is unable to discharge the duties of the office. The latter provisions are untested and leave open important questions about establishing a president's disability. For most of American history, vice presidents played a minimal role in American government. In recent decades, however, several vice presidents have played important roles in presidential administration, and Vice President Dick Cheney had an unprecedented influence in the administration of George W. Bush. John Dickinson's question at the Convention, "who would judge whether the president were disabled?" has never been satisfactorily answered.

The delegates approved a requirement that the president take an oath "to the best of my judgment and power [to] preserve protect and defend the Constitution of the U.S." They saw the oath as another constraint on the president, whose power and autonomy they gradually had enhanced during the Convention.[140] At the same time, they were constructing a strong and independent judiciary.

12

The Courts and a Bill of Rights

The delegates agreed that the national government required a judiciary.[1] The New Jersey Plan, like the Virginia Plan, proposed a new, national Supreme Court. But how strong and independent would the delegates make the national judiciary? As the Convention proceeded, the delegates were willing to invest the national courts with more independence so that the judiciary could serve as an additional check on the political system. How many courts would there be? Broad nationalists wanted a strong system of national courts that could establish a presence across the nation. But narrow nationalists resisted this idea, because if the national court system included courts located in the states, these courts could draw power from the existing state judicial systems. The delegates evaded this problem by allowing Congress to decide the issue. Who would choose the judges? As with other offices, selection implied dependence, and the judicial branch required as much independence as possible. Ultimately, the delegates compromised and required the president and the Senate to share this power, as they shared the power of executive appointments. The Convention added explicit protections for the rights of accused criminals and for contracts, but refused to provide a more explicit and comprehensive Bill of Rights that could alarm citizens about the new government's potential powers.

The National Courts' Authority

What kinds of legal disputes would the national courts have the authority, or the jurisdiction, to judge? The narrower the courts' jurisdiction, the narrower the courts' influence and policy role. In mid-June, the Convention agreed to extend national judicial authority to impeachments, the collection of national revenue, and "questions which involve the national peace and harmony."[2] The New Jersey Plan protected the states' court systems by authorizing a single national supreme court, with only the authority to judge appeals from state courts on national issues, such as piracy, treaties, trade, or national taxes. The New Jersey Plan limited the national court's *original* jurisdiction (that is, its power to accept new disputes rather than appeals) to impeachments. James Madison criticized that limit on the national judiciary.[3] After the Connecticut Compromise, the delegates gave the courts a warrant to strike down state laws that interfered with the nation's interest in "peace & harmony," as the judges defined that interest.[4] The Committee on Detail specified the Supreme Court's jurisdiction to "all Cases arising under" Congressional laws, "to Controversies between States" (except for conflicts over jurisdiction and territory), and to impeachment trials. It also gave Congress explicit power to shape the appellate jurisdiction of the national courts.[5]

Thereafter, the Convention further enhanced federal judicial jurisdiction. The Convention gave the national judiciary the authority to settle the highly contentious issue of territorial and land disputes. The Committee of Detail had incorporated a procedure from the Articles of Confederation that provided a distinct, complicated process for settling these cases. John Rutledge argued the new national judiciary made the process unnecessary. Despite doubts about whether the national judges would be fair in deciding these controversial disputes between states, the Convention transferred jurisdiction over these conflicts to the national courts.[6] Next, the delegates accepted William Samuel Johnson's proposal to extend judicial authority to equity, which allowed the courts more flexibility to deal with disputes involving damages to individuals and organizations.[7] Dickinson proposed to specify that the courts' appellate jurisdiction extended to questions "both as to law & fact," broadening the scope of judicial proceedings; Wilson said that the Committee of Detail intended that the national courts would determine questions of fact as well as of law, and the Convention approved the proposal to insert this explicit provision in the Constitution.[8] To clarify that even inferior courts would have the jurisdiction specified, the Convention agreed to Madison and Morris's motion to replace the phrase "The jurisdiction of the supreme Court" with the more inclusive phrase, "the Judicial power."[9]

The delegates clearly understood that the new national courts would have the authority to strike down *state* laws that violated the U.S. Constitution. The provision that the Constitution and national laws were the "supreme Law of the Land" established national judicial power to review and invalidate state legislation.[10]

But the national courts' power to review the constitutionality of *national* laws—to strike down laws approved by the U.S. Congress and the president—had much more far-reaching implications for the balance of power in a republican national government. The federal judges would be appointed for an indefinite term, not elected for a set period of years. Any form of judicial review of legislation would give them some power to invalidate national laws promulgated by the people's representatives.

When Elbridge Gerry spoke out against the proposal to require the courts to join the president in vetoing legislation, he said that the national judiciary "will have a sufficient check against encroachments on their own department by their exposition of the laws, which involved a power of deciding on their Constitutionality."[11] Rufus King agreed that the judges "will no doubt stop the operation of such as shall appear repugnant to the constitution."[12] Even Luther Martin, who opposed most proposals to broaden national authority, later admitted that national judges had the right to hear questions of the constitutionality of national laws, and "in this character they have a negative on the laws."[13] George Mason, too, acknowledged that the national courts "could declare an unconstitutional law void," though they would have to accept "every law however unjust oppressive or pernicious" that was constitutional (unless judges joined the executive in the veto over Congressional laws).[14]

The Convention deliberately refused to prohibit the national courts from reviewing the constitutionality of national laws. Madison and other delegates had serious reservations about this power of judicial review of national laws, but they could provide no acceptable alternative. John Francis Mercer liked the joint presidential-judicial veto precisely because he disapproved of the notion that judges could interpret the law by declaring it void.[15] John Dickinson expressed the dilemma the delegates faced by admitting that he "was strongly impressed with the remark of Mr. Mercer as to the power of the Judges to set aside the law. He thought no such power ought to exist. He was at the same time at a loss what expedient to substitute."[16] In late August, the delegates added language that seemed to address this dilemma. William Samuel Johnson moved to rephrase the Supreme Court's jurisdiction to include "all cases arising under this Constitution and the laws."[17] Madison criticized the proposal, questioning "whether it was not going too far" to expand Supreme Court jurisdiction to constitutionality: "The right of expounding the Constitution" in cases not of a "judicial" nature "ought not to be given to that Department."[18] The delegates seemed to casually dismiss this possibility, "it being generally supposed that the jurisdiction given was constructively limited to cases of a Judiciary nature."[19] The delegates approved the change without dissent. These choices laid the groundwork for national courts to assert the power to review the constitutionality of national laws.[20]

Judicial Independence: Selection, Term, and Pay

While the delegates were allowing the national courts broader jurisdiction, they also were reinforcing the national judges' independence in exercising that authority. As soon as the Convention first took up the Virginia Plan's proposal that Congress select national judges, some delegates began to cast around for a way to guarantee more judicial autonomy. Madison trusted neither Congress nor the executive with the appointment of judges. He was "rather inclined" to vest the appointment of judges in the Senate, but he suggested that the delegates put off the decision for "maturer reflection," and the delegates agreed to drop any provision for selecting the judges.[21] When Roger Sherman and Charles Pinckney moved to restore Congress's power to appoint the justices, Madison emphatically condemned Congress as "incompetent Judges of the requisite qualifications" who were "too much influenced by their partialities" (for example, toward a candidate who was a fellow legislator). Nevertheless, the Convention gave this appointment power to the Senate.[22]

The Connecticut Compromise turned judicial appointment into yet another battleground between presidential and Senate power. James Wilson tried to distance judicial appointments from Senate control by proposing that the executive appoint judges without Senate consent at all.[23] Nathaniel Gorham "suggested that the Judges be appointed by the Executive with the advice & consent" of the Senate, as provided in Massachusetts.[24] Martin strenuously argued for Senate appointment of judges without any presidential involvement.[25] Sherman defended Senate appointment, arguing that the Senate would have "more wisdom" and "more diffusive knowledge" of candidates than the executive. He added that Senate selection would help the courts represent the nation's geographical diversity.[26] Edmund Randolph joined in support of Senate judicial appointments because it would soften opposition to the Constitution.[27] For Mason, the decision depended on other important choices, such as the rules for the trial of an impeached president.[28]

Casting about for a politically acceptable formula for executive appointment of the judiciary, Madison suggested several possible solutions. First, he proposed that the executive appoint the judges with the approval of one-third of the Senate.[29] "The principle of compromise which had prevailed in other instances," said Madison, "required in this that there should be a concurrence of two authorities, in one of which the people, in the other states, should be represented." If the Senate alone had this power, "the Judges might be appointed by a minority of the people, though by a majority, of the States, which could not be justified on any principle." Moreover, Northern states would dominate appointments, creating "a perpetual ground of jealousy & discontent" in the South.[30] Randolph now agreed, worried that legislative appointments "have generally resulted from cabal, from personal regard, or some other consideration than a title derived from the proper qualifications."[31] Gouverneur Morris suggested, "If the Executive can be safely trusted with the command of the army, there can not surely be any reasonable ground of Jealousy" in allowing him to appoint judges.[32]

For many delegates, though, Madison's proposal gave the executive too much influence over the courts. Charles Pinckney doubted that the executive would

have enough knowledge or public confidence.[33] Oliver Ellsworth, too, preferred
Senate appointment of judges, or even Senate appointment with a presidential
veto that could be overridden by two-thirds of the Senate. He cautioned, "The
Executive will be regarded by the people with a jealous eye. Every power for
augmenting unnecessarily his influence will be disliked." The Senate would not
reject the executive's nominees, thought Ellsworth, so "[a] nomination under
such circumstances will be equivalent to an appointment."[34] Mason agreed that
an executive nomination was tantamount to appointment and "considered the
appointment by the Executive as a dangerous prerogative." Mason also rejected
Madison's claim that "the difference of interest between the Northern and
Southern States could be properly brought into this argument."[35] The Convention rejected Madison's proposals, vested judicial appointments exclusively in
the Senate, and moved on.[36]

By August, when other decisions had made the Senate's powers more controversial, Gouverneur Morris and James Wilson reopened the question of Senate
judicial appointments.[37] The Committee on Postponed Matters returned to
Madison's July proposal, including national judges in the list of offices the president could fill with the "advice and consent" of the Senate. In September, the
Convention finally included judicial appointments with executive appointments,
providing for presidential nomination and Senate consent.

Both the Virginia and the New Jersey Plans proposed that judges hold their
office for an indefinite term of "good behavior" that could stretch on for life.
After it accepted the Connecticut Compromise, the Convention approved this
provision without debate.[38] In late August, a committee recommended that national judges be subject to the same rules of impeachment that applied to the
president, and that they should be tried in the Senate. Once the delegates approved the impeachment process for judges, some expressed reservations about
the indefinite length of the judges' term. Dickinson, with Sherman's support,
proposed that judges could be removed "on the application by the Senate and
House of Representatives."[39] Randolph objected that the proposal weakened
"too much the independence of the Judges."[40] Wilson observed, "The Judges
would be in a bad situation if made to depend on every gust of faction which
might prevail in the two branches of our Government."[41] Gouverneur Morris
"thought it a contradiction in terms to say that the Judges should hold their offices during good behavior, and yet be removable without a trial."[42] The Convention rejected the proposal decisively and simply allowed for the same rules for
the impeachment of judges as for other national officers.

The delegates thought the source of pay would influence judges' behavior, as
it would influence legislators. Congress could reward judges with a pay increase
after a favorable decision, and punish judges for an objectionable decision by
lowering judges' salaries. To prevent this kind of manipulation, both the Virginia

and New Jersey Plans proposed fixed salaries for national judges. After the Connecticut Compromise, Gouverneur Morris argued that Congress should be permitted to increase, but not to decrease, the judges' pay, because "[h]e thought
the Legislature ought to be at liberty to increase salaries as circumstances might
require, and that this would not create any improper dependence in the Judges."[43]
Madison resisted this change, explaining, "Whenever an increase is wished by
the Judges, or may be in agitation in the legislature," the judges may feel an inap-
propriate willingness to go along with Congress. Madison thought that the
changes in the value of money could be accommodated if the rule for pay were
pegged to a standard of "permanent value" (such as wheat), and the "increase of
business" could be addressed with more judges.[44] Morris pointed out that some
of the workload of the Supreme Court justices could not be handled by adding
more judges; it could only be addressed if the justices on the Court worked
longer, so that "additional compensation therefore ought not to be prohibited."[45]
The delegates allowed increases, but not cuts, in judicial pay. When Madison
tried to reinstate the prohibition on increasing judges' salaries while in office,
General Pinckney countered that "large salaries" would be needed to attract
"men of the first talents" to the judiciary, salaries that would be "larger than the
U.S. can allow" at the start.[46] The Convention rejected Madison's proposal.[47]

How Many National Courts?

Though the Virginia Plan proposed "one or more supreme tribunals" and an indefinite number of "inferior," or lower, national courts, Rutledge spoke strongly
against these lower courts. Rutledge, a South Carolina judge, insisted that state
courts "be left in all cases" to make the initial decisions, and that national courts
be limited to hearing appeals.[48] Sherman, a judge in Connecticut, agreed,
dwelling "chiefly on the supposed expensiveness of having a new set of Courts,
when the existing State Courts would answer the same purpose."[49] "The people
will not bear such innovations," warned Pierce Butler. "The States will revolt at
such encroachments."[50] Madison countered that appeals would overwhelm the
Supreme Court "unless inferior tribunals" with "*final* jurisdiction in *many* cases"
were dispersed throughout the nation.[51] Wilson pointed out that maritime and
similar cases should not be decided by state courts.[52] Dickinson "contended
strongly that if there was to be a National Legislature, there ought to be a national Judiciary, and that the former ought to have authority to institute the
latter."[53] The delegates temporarily compromised on this issue by leaving inferior
courts out of the Constitution but authorizing Congress to create such courts if
it chose to do so.[54] The defenders of state autonomy continued to fight against
lower national courts and excluded them from the New Jersey Plan. Martin,

Maryland's attorney general, still complained "that a national Judiciary extended into the States would be ineffectual," and if it were effective, "would be viewed with a jealousy inconsistent with its usefulness."[55]

When the delegates revisited the provision that Congress could create these lower courts, Pierce Butler again argued that he "could see no necessity for such tribunals" because the state courts could "do the business."[56] Martin added that national courts would interfere with state courts' jurisdiction and "create jealousies & oppositions."[57] But too much support had built for creating these lower-level courts. Nathaniel Gorham viewed such courts as essential "to render the authority of the National Legislature effective," and Mason suggested that unforeseen future circumstances "might render such a power absolutely necessary."[58] Randolph was much more blunt: "the Courts of the States cannot be trusted with the administration of the National laws."[59] The Convention unanimously confirmed the decision to authorize Congress to create a national court system with lower courts.[60]

Citizen Rights

As the Constitution evolved, some delegates grew more concerned about limiting the national government's power, most especially the power to criminalize political opponents. History proved that government leaders periodically rounded up, jailed, and sometimes executed their political enemies without a trial. Independent courts did not seem sufficient to protect against the government's abuse of this power. Gerry and James McHenry proposed explicitly to prohibit Congress from passing either a "bill of attainder" or an "*ex post facto* law."[61] Both types of legislation were familiar tools of government oppression. A bill of attainder is a legislative act that punishes an individual without a trial in court.[62] An *ex post facto* law is a law passed after an act occurs that makes the act illegal (or changes its legal status in some other way), so that people could be punished retrospectively for acting in a way that was legal at the time. Gerry "urged the necessity of this prohibition, which he said was greater in the National than the State Legislature, because the number of members in the former being fewer, they were on that account the more to be feared."[63]

The ban on bills of attainder passed unanimously, but several of the delegates argued against including any language banning *ex post facto* laws because they thought the words needlessly would raise suspicions about the new government.[64] Ellsworth "contended that there was no lawyer, no civilian who would not say that ex post facto laws were void of themselves. It cannot then be necessary to prohibit them."[65] When Daniel Carroll pointed out that the states had included such prohibitions in their own constitutions, Wilson answered,

"If these prohibitions . . . have no effect, it will be useless to insert them in this Constitution. Besides, both sides will agree to the principle & will differ as to its application."[66] Rutledge favored the clause, and Hugh Williamson observed, "Such a prohibitory clause is in the Constitution of North Carolina, and though it has been violated, it has done good there & may do good here, because the Judges can take hold of it."[67] The Convention explicitly prohibited *ex post facto* laws.[68]

Charles Pinckney emphasized the need to protect *habeas corpus*, an individual's right not to be held in custody unlawfully. Governments could—and had—abused this power by jailing their political opponents. But delegates recognized that an emergency might make it necessary to suspend *habeas corpus*. As soon at the delegates approved an explicit ban on bills of attainder and *ex post facto laws*, Pinckney proposed that the right of *habeas corpus* "should not be suspended but on the most urgent occasions, & then only for a limited time not exceeding twelve months."[69] Gouverneur Morris proposed, "The privilege of the writ of Habeas Corpus shall not be suspended, unless where in cases of Rebellion or invasion the public safety may require it."[70] Rutledge "was for declaring the Habeas Corpus inviolable. He did not conceive that a suspension could ever be necessary at the same time through all the States."[71] Wilson also "doubted whether in any case a suspension could be necessary, as the discretion now exists with Judges, in most important cases to keep in jail or admit to Bail."[72] For the time being, the delegates prohibited any suspension of *habeas corpus* without any exception for national emergencies.

The Committee of Style, however, inserted wording that habeas corpus would not be suspended "unless when in cases of rebellion or invasion the public safety may require it." The delegates did not debate this exception when they approved the final document, and they also required the testimony of two witnesses for conviction of the crime of treason.[73]

The Committee of Detail had included a provision protecting the right to a jury trial in criminal cases, and the delegates later changed the language to protect the right of a jury trial even when a crime occurred outside of any of the states.[74] Some believed that the right to a jury also should be guaranteed in civil cases, that is, cases in which two parties asked a judge to decide the fairness of a lawsuit over property, a contract, or other matters.[75] Nathaniel Gorham objected, "It is not possible to discriminate equity cases from those in which juries are proper," and he urged the delegates to trust Congress to deal with this issue.[76] Gerry still "urged the necessity of Juries to guard against corrupt Judges" and tried to add a specific protection for ensuring juries in civil cases. General Pinckney warned that "such a clause in the Constitution would be pregnant with embarrassments," and the Convention dropped the matter.[77]

While the Constitution prohibited bills of attainder, *ex post facto* laws, the suspension of *habeas corpus*, and the elimination of jury trials, the delegates could not agree to go further by including a broader Bill of Rights. Charles Pinckney proposed a list of such rights, including freedom of the press, a ban on religious qualifications for office, and a ban on quartering soldiers in a home in peacetime without the owner's consent. The Convention banned religious tests, though Sherman "thought it unnecessary, the prevailing liberality being a sufficient security against such tests."[78] In the final week, Mason wished that "the plan had been prefaced with a Bill of Rights" and moved to include one because "It would give great quiet to the people" and, based on existing state constitutions, could be "prepared in a few hours."[79] Sherman strongly disagreed. In Sherman's view, "The State Declarations of Rights are not repealed by this Constitution; and being in force are sufficient—The Legislature may be safely trusted."[80] Mason did not accept Sherman's reasoning, because, he said, "[t]he Laws of the United States are to be paramount to State Bills of Rights."[81] The Convention decisively rejected the motion for a committee to prepare a Bill of Rights, without a single state delegation voting in favor. Two days later, Charles Pinckney and Gerry "moved to insert a declaration 'that the liberty of the Press should be inviolably observed.'"[82] Again, it was Sherman who objected because, he said, "It is unnecessary. The power of Congress does not extend to the Press." The Convention sided with Sherman and defeated the effort.[83]

The Path of Courts and Rights

The Convention's choices about Congress and the executive made the delegates more willing to strengthen the national courts as an additional block against reckless legislation and political corruption. National courts would have extensive jurisdiction, including the power to strike down state laws—and potentially national laws—that were inconsistent with the Constitution. Though the president would choose the judges, these judges potentially could serve long after the president had left office. John Marshall, for example, was appointed Chief Justice of the Supreme Court in 1801, and served in that role for over thirty-four years.

The national judiciary became a strong, independent force in American life, and it played a major role in establishing the supremacy of the national government.[84] Although the potential jurisdiction of the courts has been controversial from the start, it gradually has expanded. Anti-Federalists like "Brutus" (a pseudonym, probably for former New York delegate Robert Yates) attacked the Constitution for allowing Congress to establish broad jurisdiction for the federal judiciary, and thus posing a threat to the final authority of state courts.[85] But as early as 1803, in *Marbury v. Madison*, the Supreme Court asserted its power of judicial review of national laws.[86] The Court did not use this power again until

1857, but since the late nineteenth century, the federal courts have used judicial review more regularly.[87]

Over time, the United States has tended toward "judicializing" public policy, allowing courts to make decisions about controversial political and policy issues. Congress *could* settle many of these disputes, but because courts are more insulated from political backlash than elected officials are, the latter have an incentive to defer controversies to judges and the courts.[88] As the United States industrialized, the Supreme Court used the power of judicial review to protect the growth of the market economy.[89] The appointed court overturned many of the important laws established by elected officials, including the Missouri Compromise, an income tax in the 1890s, child labor regulations in the 1910s, New Deal legislation in the 1930s, and abortion and capital punishment laws in the 1970s. The Supreme Court has ruled that over 160 federal statutes and nearly 1,000 state laws have violated the U.S. Constitution.[90] Political scientist Keith Whittington showed that the political system has tacitly accepted judicial review, despite the spectacular interbranch battles over the federal courts' assertion of that power.[91] Scholars have pointed out that Congress has great power to reign in the courts by limiting their appellate authority. Legal historian Henry M. Hart Jr. concluded that "the language of the Constitution must be taken as vesting plenary control"—that is, unlimited and unqualified control over jurisdiction—in Congress.[92]

The lack of a Bill of Rights became a major problem for the Constitution's authors during the fierce battle over ratification. When New York, Virginia, Massachusetts, South Carolina, and New Hampshire ratified the Constitution, they proposed seventy-five distinct constitutional amendments, most of which aimed to protect rights.[93] In his campaign for a seat in the first House of Representatives, Madison promised to propose a bill of rights. Once elected, Madison followed through. But for Madison, a bill of rights could strengthen the new national government by building its legitimacy while it set more limits on the states. Madison's proposed bill of rights dropped recommendations to limit national taxing powers, for example. But he failed to extend protections for the freedom of conscience and the press from interference by the states. The states ratified the first ten amendments to the Constitution—the Bill of Rights—in 1791.[94]

The Bill of Rights protected personal freedoms of speech, religion, the press, assembly, and petition from the federal government. These amendments also defined and protected citizens against abuses of national government power, including the surrender of weapons, the forced quartering of soldiers, and unreasonable and arbitrary searches and seizures of property, and they provided for fair and speedy trials, and fair procedures for arrest and punishment. The Ninth and Tenth Amendments established that the people and the states retained rights not specified in the Constitution. The Fourteenth Amendment (1868) established a national guarantee of "due process" for all Americans, a provision that has allowed national courts gradually to protect civil rights and liberties against interference by state governments.[95] In the 1920s, the Supreme Court began to rule that the Fourteenth Amendment protected some First Amendment freedoms from not only federal but also state government interference. Over time, court rulings have advanced this process of "incorporating" the Bill of Rights—that is, extending most of its protections as against state governments. These interpretations, in turn, have sparked many continuing political controversies.[96]

As they were building an independent judiciary into the increasingly complicated structure of political institutions, the delegates also were deciding what authority the national government would exercise over the American people.

PART THREE

THE POLITICS OF GOVERNMENT POWER

13

Federalism

While they were constructing new national governing institutions, the delegates were enlarging the national government's authority. All aspired to strengthen national government, but a strong national government also could be a menace. Too much national power could threaten republican ideals, slavery in the South, commerce in the North, expansion in the West, and well-being in any state.

At first, the delegates seemed willing to accept the wide-ranging national authority the broad nationalists sought. But as the independence and complexity of the new governing institutions took shape, it became more difficult to predict *how* the government would use its power. Uncertainty bred caution. Roger Sherman and other narrow nationalists gained ground with their arguments that the national government should be granted only a limited range of additional policy tools, leaving most of the nation's policy authority in the states. First, the delegates defeated Madison's proposed national veto of state laws, a tool he viewed as necessary for an effective national government. Second, they gradually accepted the previously inconceivable notion that the national and state governments could share sovereignty. Third, they enumerated the powers of the national government. By explicitly listing authorized national powers, the Constitution empowered opponents of national action, who could put national officials on the defensive by challenging the constitutionality of proposals that were not on the list. (Because states' powers were *not* listed, states retained authority not prohibited by other parts of the Constitution). Finally, in defining the crime of treason, the delegates firmly institutionalized the concept of *shared* national and state sovereignty.

In the end, the delegates constructed an unfinished framework for American federalism, built by a chain of compromises and incorporating elements of both broad and narrow nationalism. Broad nationalists established many new national powers, along with elastic authority that could meet future national necessities. Narrow nationalists included limitations on national power and protections for state powers. Their compromises left the dividing line between national and state power ambiguous—and this ambiguity made federalism a primary battleground in American politics ever since.

A Supreme National Government

A day after he introduced the Virginia Plan, Edmund Randolph asked the delegates to commit to the principle that neither "a Union of the States merely federal," nor any additional treaties among the states, would "accomplish the objects proposed by the articles of Confederation, namely common defense, security of liberty, & general welfare." Instead, a distinctly "*national* Government ought to be established consisting of a *supreme* Legislative, Executive & Judiciary."[1]

The words *national* and *supreme* immediately made some delegates anxious.[2] When Charles Pinckney asked if Randolph "meant to abolish the State Governments altogether," Randolph downplayed the threat to the states, explaining that he "only meant to give the national government a power to defend and protect itself" and "[t]o take therefore from the respective legislatures or States, no more sovereignty than is competent to this end."[3] George Mason felt that such a national government was necessary to "directly operate on individuals, and . . . punish those only whose guilt required it."[4] Gouverneur Morris stood for "[a] federal government . . . which has a right to compel every part to do its duty."[5] Pierce Butler had not decided how much more power the national government should have but was willing to go to "great lengths" if its powers were separated.[6] Only Roger Sherman expressed wariness of broader national power, warning against changing the Confederation too much.[7] The Convention overwhelmingly approved the creation of a supreme national government.

But the next day, Virginia's proposal to vest "Legislative power in all cases to which the State Legislatures were individually incompetent" aggravated South Carolina's conditional nationalists. Charles Pinckney and John Rutledge "objected to the vagueness of the term '*incompetent*,' and said they could not well decide how to vote until they should see an exact enumeration of the powers comprehended by this definition."[8] Butler worried that the delegates were "running into an extreme in taking away" state powers, and he called for an explanation.[9] Randolph denied "any intention to give indefinite powers to the national Legislature" and declared "that he was entirely opposed to such an inroad on the State jurisdictions."[10] Randolph and James Wilson explained that it would be hard to enumerate the powers of the new government just yet.[11]

Madison, trying to nudge the Convention toward broad national authority, said that he came to the Convention with "a strong bias in favor of an enumeration and definition" of the reconstituted national legislature's powers, but "had also brought doubts concerning its practicability" and his "doubts had become stronger. What his opinion might ultimately be he could not yet tell."[12] Sherman criticized Virginia's vague proposition as "too indefinitely expressed," though he conceded that "it would be hard to define all the powers by detail."[13] For the moment, the delegates ignored Sherman and agreed to the Virginia Plan's broad language on national authority. Nine states voted for Virginia's language, none voted against, and Connecticut was divided.[14] They reinforced this decision when they approved another Virginia proposal, requiring *state* officers to swear an oath to observe the U.S. Constitution and national law. Sherman objected that the oath was unnecessary; Elbridge Gerry objected to it, and Luther Martin moved to delete it. These objections to state loyalty oaths began to solidify the opposition. The vote for these oaths passed by a narrow margin, with Madison's coalition of six states opposed by the other five.[15] The national veto forced the delegates to confront the tangible possibilities of broad national authority more squarely.

A National Veto of State Laws

For Madison, the national government could exercise its authority effectively only if it had the power to veto state laws at will. This national veto would ensure that the national government would exercise legislative power, directly or by default, over all the significant laws that governed American citizens. For Madison's opponents, nothing jeopardized states' authority more than this proposed national veto, which threatened any meaningful state exercise of legislative discretion.

On May 31, the Convention approved the national power "to negative all State laws contravening in the opinion of the National Legislature the articles of Union." Sherman alone said the power seemed "improper."[16] Madison believed the vote validated "other clauses giving powers necessary to preserve harmony among the States." But the delegates balked when they took up the proposal to allow the national government to use the national military as the force of the whole "against a delinquent State."[17] Even Madison doubted its "practicality" and "justice," and he successfully moved to table it.[18]

Apprehensions about the national veto increased when Charles Pinckney proposed to expand the language to cover "all laws" that the new Congress "should judge to be improper." This "universal negative," Pinckney believed, was "the corner stone of an efficient national Government," one that was "indispensably necessary to render it effectual." The states, he stressed, "must be kept in due subordination to the nation."[19] Madison instantly seconded Pinkney's motion, holding that "an indefinite power" to veto state laws was "absolutely necessary to a perfect system," as the Confederation experience proved. This veto power "was the mildest expedient that could be devised for preventing these mischiefs" and its mere existence "would prevent attempts to commit them." This strong national veto of state laws would make military intervention unnecessary. For the national veto to be effective, explained Madison, "it must extend to all cases. . . . This prerogative of the General Government is the great pervading principle that must control the centrifugal tendency of the States; which, without it, will continually fly out of their proper orbits and destroy the order & harmony of the political system."[20]

James Wilson argued that the Convention had to correct the "vices" of the Confederation, adding that "[o]ne of its vices is the want of an effectual control in the whole over its parts." Wilson reasoned that

> Federal liberty is to States, what civil liberty, is to private individuals. And States are not more unwilling to purchase it, by the necessary concession of their political sovereignty, than the savage is to purchase Civil liberty by the surrender of the personal sovereignty, which he enjoys in a State of nature. A definition of the cases in which the Negative should be exercised, is impracticable. A discretion must be left on one side or the other. Will it not be most safely lodged on the side of the National Government? ... What danger is there that the whole will unnecessarily sacrifice a part? But reverse the case, and leave the whole at the mercy of each part, and will not the general interest be continually sacrificed to local interests?[21]

John Dickinson posed a stark choice: "We must either subject the States to the danger of being injured by the power of the National Government or the latter to the danger of being injured by that of the States." The danger was greater from the states. "To leave the power doubtful, would be opening another spring of discord, and he was for shutting as many of them as possible."[22] In this view, the states had to bear the burden of proof for retaining authority.

Others saw only danger in this expanded national veto. Ominously for Madison, some Southern and large state delegates argued strongly against it. North Carolina's Hugh Williamson opposed such "a power that might restrain the States from regulating their internal police."[23] Butler "was vehement against the Negative in the proposed extent, as cutting off all hope of equal justice to the distant States."[24] Gerry thought it could allow Congress to "enslave the States": because national legislators would be "ignorant of each other's interests," he said, the national veto "will be abused." According to Rufus King, Gerry warned that the veto could "enable the General Government to depress a part for the benefit of another part," nurturing "particular manufactures," or training their militias.[25]

Delaware's Gunning Bedford passionately accused the Pennsylvania and Virginia delegates of planning a government that would give their states "an enormous & monstrous influence." He emphasized that Delaware, under the proportional representation rule, might have only one-ninetieth of the seats in Congress while Pennsylvania and Virginia would control one-third of the seats. Bedford asked, "Is there no difference of interests, no rivalship of commerce, of manufactures? Will not these large States crush the small ones whenever they stand in the way of their ambitions or interested views?" He insisted that it would be impractical to suspend urgent laws while Congress ("a body who may be incapable of Judging of them") deliberated these laws, or to expect Congress to "sit continually . . . to revise the laws of the States."[26] Deftly, Sherman tried to limit the broad veto—and national authority—by suggesting that the Convention enumerate "cases in which the negative ought to be exercised. . . . He wished the point might not be decided till a trial at least should be made for that purpose."[27]

Madison tried to deflect all these objections to a stronger national veto.[28] He asked, "If the large States possessed the Avarice & ambition with which they were charged, would the small ones in their neighborhood, be more secure when all control of a General Government was withdrawn?" He suggested that the smaller (and still formless) Senate could exercise the veto. He emphasized that Britain ensured coherent policy across the empire by vetoing colonial laws (in an audience of Revolutionary War leaders, this argument may have evoked disagreeable memories of English rule).[29] The Convention, however, refused to strengthen the national veto. Only the three largest states voted for the measure—a vote that undoubtedly made the other states even more apprehensive about large states' cooperation.[30] A week later, narrow nationalists attacked the national veto. "The States will never feel a sufficient confidence in a general Government to give it a negative on their laws," said John Lansing of New York. "The Scheme is itself totally novel." Lansing also doubted whether the members of Congress would have the time or the competence to judge which state laws to veto.[31]

Opposition to the national veto intensified after the Connecticut Compromise. Sherman dismissed the provision as "unnecessary," trusting the state courts to invalidate any law "contravening the Authority of the Union."[32] Luther Martin groused that the national veto was "improper & inadmissible."[33] Even Gouverneur Morris thought the national veto was "likely to be terrible to the States, and unnecessary if sufficient Legislative authority should be given to the General Government."[34] Madison remained steadfast, asserting that only the national veto would control "the propensity of the States to pursue their particular interests in opposition to the general interest." The state courts could not be trusted to protect the national interest. Again, Madison evoked the British example: "Nothing could maintain the harmony & subordination of the various parts of the empire, but the prerogative by which the Crown, stifles in the birth every Act of every part tending to discord or encroachment." Madison conceded that the British veto "is sometimes misapplied through ignorance or a partiality," but the reasons for these misapplications did not exist in the United States.[35] Only Charles Pinckney, however, stood with Madison for "the necessity of the Negative."[36] Gouverneur Morris "was more & more opposed."[37] Sherman charged that Madison wrongly assumed that the national courts would not invalidate such laws.[38]

The Convention dropped the national veto on July 17. It substituted the more palatable "supremacy" clause, the New Jersey Plan provision that national treaties and laws were "the supreme law of the respective States."[39] This alternative to the national veto placed the responsibility for policing the states in the hands of the state and national courts, rather than Congress.[40]

A month later, Charles Pinckney and Madison made a last effort to restore the national veto. They proposed that Congress, by a two-thirds vote, could invalidate state laws that interfered "with the General interests and harmony of the Union." Pinckney pointed out that the equal vote of the states in the Senate had solved the problem that large states could dominate the use of this veto.[41] Wilson "considered this as the key-stone wanted to complete the wide arch of Government we are raising. . . . The firmness of Judges is not of itself sufficient. Something further is requisite." Noting that a court review of legislation would be slower than the national veto, Wilson said, "It will be better to prevent the passage of an improper law, than to declare it void when passed."[42] Madison, anticipating defeat, wanted to put off the vote by sending the proposal to a committee.[43] But too many others piled on objections.

Sherman argued that the national veto was unnecessary because national laws would be as "Supreme & paramount to the State laws" as the Constitution.[44] For Hugh Williamson, "the question was a waste of time."[45] Rutledge flatly declared, "If nothing else, this alone would damn and ought to damn the Constitution. Will any State ever agree to be bound hand & foot in this manner? It is worse than making mere corporations of them whose by-laws would not be subject to this shackle."[46] Mason questioned whether any road or bridge would be built without Congress's approval, and whether it would be in perpetual session to deal with state laws.[47] This last attempt to establish a national veto died. Its omission deeply disappointed Madison.[48]

Shared Sovereignty

According to prevailing wisdom in 1787, government sovereignty—public authority with a territory—was supreme and indivisible. Either the national government had full sovereignty or the states had full sovereignty; there was no middle ground.[49] At the start of the Convention, the delegates assumed that the new national government would be sovereign in the United States, and that national government sovereignty would erase state sovereignty. As John Dickinson put it, "There can be no line of separation dividing the powers of legislation between the State & General Governments. The consequence is inevitable that there must be a supreme & august national Legislature."[50] Gouverneur Morris lectured the smaller states on "the distinction between a *federal* and *national*, *supreme,* Government; the former being a mere compact resting on the good faith of the parties; the latter having a complete and *compulsive* operation. He contended that in all communities there must be one supreme power, and one only." Morris "could not conceive of a government in which there can exist two *supremes.*"[51] George Read of Delaware took this reasoning to its logical conclusion by suggesting that a "national Government must soon of necessity swallow all of" the states.[52]

Narrow nationalists contested this prevailing wisdom as they defended the states. By doing so, they began to develop a new theory of shared sovereignty, in which the national government and the states *could* exercise sovereign authority over the same citizens at the same time. The road to this new idea began with the insistence that the national government's powers be limited. Sherman believed that

> [t]he objects of the Union, he thought were few. 1. defense against foreign danger; 2. against internal disputes & a resort to force; 3. Treaties with foreign nations; 4. regulating foreign commerce, & drawing revenue from it. These & perhaps a few lesser objects alone rendered a Confederation of the States necessary. All other matters civil & criminal would be much better in the hands of the States. The people are more happy in small than large States. States may indeed be too small as Rhode Island, & thereby be too subject to faction. Some others were perhaps too large, the powers of Government not being able to pervade them. [Sherman] was for giving the General Government power to legislate and execute within a defined province.[53]

Madison agreed that these "were certainly important and necessary objects," but that the national government needed broader powers to provide "more effectually for the security of private rights, and the steady dispensation of Justice. Interferences with these were evils which had more perhaps than any thing else, produced this convention."[54]

William Paterson chopped away at Madison's argument when he defended the New Jersey Plan. The success of the new government, he said, would "depend on the quantum of power collected, not on its being drawn from the States, or from the individuals," so that it did not matter which level of government exercised power.[55] George Mason challenged Paterson, asking if he intended to maintain a national army to enforce national laws in recalcitrant states, or to march the militia "from one State to another, in order to collect the arrears of taxes from the delinquent members of the Republic?"[56] According to Rufus King, however, Mason gave ground to Paterson. Mason would never "consent to the Abolition of the State Governments. There never can be a General Government that will perform their Offices."[57]

After the rejection of the New Jersey Plan, the broad nationalists attacked the idea of shared sovereignty. Alexander Hamilton explained that Congress had to "have indefinite authority. If it were limited at all, the rivalship of the States would gradually subvert it."[58] According to Madison, Hamilton believed,

> Two sovereignties cannot co-exist within the same limits. Giving powers to [the existing Confederation Congress] must eventuate in a bad Government or in no Government. The plan of New Jersey therefore will not do. What then is to be done? Here [Hamilton] was embarrassed. The extent of the Country to be governed, discouraged him. The expense of a general Government was also formidable; unless there were such a diminution of expense on the side of the State Governments as the case would admit. If they were extinguished, he was persuaded that great economy might be obtained by substituting a general Government. He did not mean however to shock the public opinion by proposing such a measure. On the other hand he saw no *other* necessity for declining it. They [the state governments] are not necessary for any of the great purposes of commerce, revenue, or agriculture. Subordinate authorities he was aware would be necessary. There must be district tribunals: corporations for local purposes.[59]

Hamilton asked, rhetorically, who benefits from "the vast & expensive apparatus now appertaining to the States," implying that state officials resisted national power to protect their prerogatives.[60]

Rufus King denied that the states ever had any sovereignty to defend:

> The States were not "sovereigns" in the sense contended for by some. They did not possess the peculiar features of sovereignty. They could not make war, nor peace, nor alliances, nor treaties. Considering them as political Beings, they were dumb, for they could not speak to any foreign Sovereign whatever. They were deaf, for they could not hear any propositions from such Sovereign. They had not even the organs or faculties of defense or offense, for they could not of themselves raise troops, or equip vessels, for war.[61]

King "doubted much the practicability of annihilating the States; but thought that much of their power ought to be taken from them."[62] Elbridge Gerry later impatiently "urged that we never were independent States, were not such now, & never could be even on the principles of the Confederation. The States & the advocates for them were intoxicated with the idea of their *sovereignty*."[63]

King's remarks incensed Luther Martin, who argued that independence "from Great Britain placed the 13 States in a state of nature towards each other." The states met to amend the confederation on an equal and independent footing.[64] Wilson and Hamilton both objected to Martin's claim. Wilson admitted that he was "tenacious" in the idea of preserving the states because "they were absolutely necessary for certain purposes which the former could not reach" and said that "[a]ll large Governments must be subdivided into lesser jurisdictions," providing examples from Persia, Rome, and England.[65] The next day, Wilson argued that if the Virginia proposals were not implemented, the state legislatures and the national Congress would be rivals. "An individual citizen," said Wilson, "is indifferent whether power be exercised by the General or State Legislatures, provided it be exercised most for his happiness."[66]

Connecticut's William Samuel Johnson made an inconceivable concept explicit when he suggested that sovereignty be divided between the national and state governments.[67] By late June, Oliver Ellsworth had coined a slogan for this idea: "We were partly national; partly federal" (see chapter 6).[68] As they tried to hold off equal state representation in the Senate, Madison's allies came to agree that that there existed some ambiguous dividing line between national and state government authority. James Wilson reasserted that the national government would manage national defense, commerce, treaties, and other issues, while "Certain inferior and local Qualities" would remain in the states' hands. Wilson insisted that "there is a line of separation," adding that wherever "the prerogatives" are "on the side of the General Government, we are citizens of the nation or of the United States (although I think we should use a term in the singular Number), and so on the other side."[69] Once broad nationalists had conceded that the states would retain some authority, the struggle over federalism turned on defining this vague "line of separation."

The Ambiguity of National Authority

Which level of government bore the burden of proof for establishing its authority in an undefined area? Would the Constitution assume that the national government exercised powers except for those retained by the states, or would it assume that the states held authority except for those powers explicitly enumerated and granted to the national government? Luther Martin had tried to lay the burden of proof on the national government to show why it needed any particular governing power: "Whatever is internal and existing between the separate states & individuals shall belong to the particular States . . . if the object of [national] Legislation is of an external nature, the Government is federal."[70]

An enumeration of powers would hem in national authority. For Gerry, the announcement of the Connecticut Compromise increased the urgency of this enumeration of national powers.[71] Madison tried to hold off any effort to specify national authority, arguing "that it would be impossible to say what powers could be safely & properly vested in the Government" before Senate representation was settled. After the final approval of the Connecticut Compromise, Gouverneur Morris feared that equal representation in the Senate "would mix itself with the merits of every question concerning the powers."[72] He was correct.

After accepting the Connecticut Compromise, more delegates tried to narrow and restrict the national government's authority because it became harder to predict what the government would do with its power. They revisited the language they had approved quickly on May 31, authorizing Congress to "legislate in all cases to which the separate States are incompetent; or in which the harmony of the U. S. may be interrupted by the exercise of individual legislation." This wording made states bear the burden of proving that they were competent to make specific public policies without harming the nation's interest. South Carolina's Pierce Butler called "for some explanation of the extent of this power; particularly of the word *incompetent*," and his colleague John Rutledge called for an enumeration of national powers.[73] After debating potential government abuses of power for seven weeks, the clause now appeared more threatening to the conditional broad nationalists, notably the South Carolina delegates who worried that national power would jeopardize slavery and Southern exports.

Sherman seized on these fears, proposing explicit language to limit national power. He proposed that Congress have authority "to make laws binding on the people of the United States in all cases which may concern the common interests of the Union; but not to interfere with the Government of the individual States in any matters of internal police which respect the Government of such States only, and wherein the General welfare of the United States is not concerned."[74] Wilson at first agreed that Sherman's formulation better expressed "the general principle." But Gouverneur Morris perceived the broad-ranging state authority that could be protected—and abused—under the rubric "police powers."[75] Sherman answered with a list of enumerated national powers, hoping to limit national powers to this list and no more. He included "the power of levying taxes on trade, but not the power of *direct taxation*."[76] Sherman's resolution was defeated, but the ambition to limit national authority by enumerating national powers gained momentum. When Gunning Bedford proposed revised language for a broad grant of national power, Edmund Randolph broke with Madison and strongly opposed it for giving the national government "the power of violating all the laws and constitutions of the States, and of intermeddling with their police."[77] Though the Convention approved Bedford's change for the moment, the delegates were considering enumerated national powers only two weeks later.

The Committee of Detail (with Rutledge, Ellsworth, and Randolph in a majority) shifted the burden of proof for exercising power from the states to the national government. It dropped the Virginia Plan's broad language on national authority, specified a list of appropriate national powers and another list of prohibited state powers, stipulated that national laws were the supreme law of the land, and authorized the national government to make all laws "necessary and proper for carrying into (full and complete) Execution" these enumerated powers.[78] Rufus King believed that the Committee of Detail report ended all hope that the Convention was ready "to strengthen the General Government and to mark a full confidence in it."[79]

But the delegates hedged by adding language that allowed Congress room to stretch national authority. The Committee of Detail's "necessary and proper" clause generated little debate. It seemed essential to give the government some latitude to exercise its enumerated powers. It was clear, however, that some delegates believed that this "necessary and proper" language allowed much greater national authority than simply the ability to carry out its assigned tasks. When Madison proposed that the national government be given explicit power to establish "all offices" essential to implement its powers, members of the Committee of Detail "urged that the amendment could not be necessary" because "necessary and proper" already authorized the government to establish such offices.[80] Mason and Gerry refused to sign the Constitution in part because they believed the clause gave the government too much power (see chapter 17).

The delegates also gave the national government an elastic grant of power when they approved the "general welfare" clause. After some proposals to add more enumerated powers to national authority, a committee headed by John Rutledge recommended national authority "to provide, as may become necessary . . . for the well managing and securing the common property and general interests and welfare of the United States," though in a way that would not "interfere with the Governments of individual States in matters which respect only their internal Police, or for which their individual authorities may be competent."[81] The Committee on Style (a committee that included Madison) finally wrote language that seemed to expand this authority, adopting words from the Articles of Confederation allowing Congress the power to "provide for the common defense and general welfare of the United States." The Committee of Style also produced a preamble to the Constitution that envisioned broad national government responsibility "to form a more perfect union, to establish justice, insure domestic tranquillity, provide for the common defence, promote the general welfare, and secure the blessings of liberty to ourselves and our posterity."[82]

Treason and Shared Sovereignty

The delegates officially stipulated that the state and national governments would share sovereignty when they defined the crime of treason, the attempt to overthrow a sovereign government. If sovereignty were indivisible, treason could only be a crime against national government, not against a state; but if both the states and the national government had sovereignty, it was possible to commit treason against a state *or* the national government.

In August, the Committee of Detail defined treason as "levying war against the United States, *or any of them*; and in adhering to the enemies of the United States, *or any of them*" (italics added).[83] Randolph suggested redefining the crime as giving "aid and comfort" to the enemy, as in Britain. Dickinson thought Randolph's phrasing too broad.[84] Gouverneur Morris insisted that there could not be treason against any one state; the national government had to have the exclusive right to define treasonable offenses.[85] Connecticut's William Samuel Johnson supported this view, contending "that Treason could not be both against the United States and individual States" because treason was "an offence against the Sovereignty which can be but one in the same community."[86] The Convention dropped the phrase "or any of them" after "United States" to "remove the embarrassment."[87] This change left Madison unsatisfied because the states still had the authority to declare "an act to be treason against the state."[88] Clearly, Madison was challenging the concept of state sovereignty. When Johnson reasserted that "there could be no Treason against a particular State,"[89] Mason answered that the national government would "have a qualified sovereignty only. The individual States will retain a part of the Sovereignty. An Act may be treason against a particular State which is not so against the United States."[90] To defuse the question, the delegates simply struck out the phrase "against the United States," enabling both the national and state governments to outlaw and prosecute treason.[91]

With the memory of Shays's Rebellion still fresh, Rufus King pressed to give the national government the "sole" power to punish treason to exclude any idea of "treason against particular States." He claimed that "no line can be drawn between levying war and adhering to enemy against the United States and against an individual State. Treason against the latter must be so against the former."[92] Sherman firmly asserted that "resistance against the laws of the United States as distinguished from resistance against the laws of a particular State, forms the line."[93]

Ellsworth defined this new concept of federalism more forcefully, observing that "the U.S. are sovereign on one side of the line dividing the jurisdictions, the States on the other. Each ought to have power to defend their respective Sovereignties."[94] The delegates restored the phrase "against the United States" without the phrase "or any of them" (and accepted the phrase, "giving aid and comfort to the enemy").[95] By accepting the possibility that a state government could outlaw treason, the delegates wrote the doctrine of shared national and state sovereignty into the Constitution—marking a major innovation in the conception of government.

The Path of American Federalism

Their piecemeal choices constructed the concept of shared sovereignty and created, as Madison later described it in *The Federalist*, a "compound" or "federal" republic.[96] A week before the debate on treason, Sherman and Madison quarreled about whether states' laws on citizenship rules for immigrants should affect qualifications for the House of Representatives. Madison treated the issue as a touchstone of the state sovereignty problem.[97] But Madison could not persuade the delegates to reject the idea. Sherman, in turn, could not persuade the delegates to guarantee the states' authority.

On the last day of Convention debate, Sherman moved to add the wording "that no State shall without its consent be affected in its internal police, or deprived of its equal suffrage in the Senate," to prevent this provision from being changed by the constitutional amendment process. The delegates accepted the proposal, putting equal Senate representation beyond amendment, but they did not provide a similar constitutional protection for state police powers.[98] Potentially broad national power would be embodied in the Constitution's silence on state police powers, as well as the authority embodied in the "necessary and proper" and "general welfare" clauses.

Ambiguity made federalism a constant political battleground throughout American history. In effect, the ambiguities of federalism and the high stakes involved with the control of public authority have constituted "a standing invitation to contest the federal government's power," according to historian Ronald P. Formisano.[99] Madison himself anticipated political battles between the state and national governments, and he argued in *The Federalist* that these governments would protect the republic by controlling each other.[100] Opponents of national power to deal with a specific issue often invoke the Constitution as a shield against federal interference with state authority. Those who seek change often invoke Constitution and the elastic authority of the federal government to nationalize authority to deal with an issue. Racial and economic issues throughout American history demonstrate the constant use of federalism as a battleground in American politics.

The ambiguities of federalism sparked bitter conflict as soon as the Constitution was made public. Anti-Federalists attacked the proposed Constitution for creating a national government with so much power and so much potential for tyranny.[101] Madison assured readers of *The Federalist* essays that the states would be "regarded as distinct and independent sovereigns,"[102] and that "the powers delegated by the proposed Constitution to the federal government, are few and defined" while the states retained "numerous and indefinite" powers.[103] In his proposed Bill of Rights introduced in the first Congress, Madison included what would become the Tenth Amendment: "The powers not delegated to the United States by the Constitution, nor prohibited by it to the States, are reserved to the States respectively, or to the people." This Tenth Amendment aimed to reinforce the limits that enumerated powers placed on national action, but it did almost nothing to clarify the ambiguous division of state and federal power. Madison himself did not believe that the Tenth Amendment was necessary.[104] When the Supreme Court allowed citizens of South Carolina to sue the state of Georgia in a dispute over lands, Congress responded with the Eleventh Amendment (ratified in 1795), which eliminated the Supreme Court's power to allow such suits. Subsequent Supreme Court rulings denied Congress the authority to abrogate state sovereignty.[105]

Political leaders clashed over federalism when the new government came into existence. Once they held national offices, Alexander Hamilton, John Marshall, and other leaders argued that the Constitution gave the national government very broad authority. Hamilton proposed sweeping initiatives for the federal assumption of state debts, for the promotion of manufactures, and for a central bank. But these initiatives seemed to benefit Northern cities, merchants, and financiers at the expense of regions that grew and exported crops—like Virginia. Madison objected to Hamilton's plan for assuming state debts as "particularly unfriendly to the interest of Virginia."[106] To defeat the proposal for a national bank, Madison argued that it "was not possible to discover in [the Constitution] the power to incorporate a Bank." Hamilton's expansive interpretation of federal authority violated the "necessary and proper clause," which Madison now thought clearly limited federal power. Furthermore, Hamilton's national bank would interfere with state banks and "the rights of the States, to *prohibit* as well as to establish Banks, and the circulation of Bank Notes."[107] In the 1790s, Madison and Thomas Jefferson helped construct the Democratic-Republican Party, a political coalition dedicated to states' rights and a narrow interpretation of national authority. The Democratic-Republican Party and its successor, the Democratic Party, resisted the expansion of national government power through most of the nineteenth century.

Two noteworthy instances of treason against a state occurred before the Civil War. Thomas Dorr was convicted of treason against Rhode Island and imprisoned for leading the Dorr Rebellion in that state in 1841–1842. Abolitionist John Brown was convicted of treason against Virginia and hanged after his raid on Harper's Ferry, Virginia, in 1859.[108]

After the Civil War, constitutional amendments trimmed state powers and reinforced national supremacy. The Thirteenth Amendment (1865) prohibited states from legalizing slavery. The Fourteenth Amendment (1868) declared, "No State shall make or enforce any law which shall abridge the privileges or immunities of citizens of the United States; nor shall any State deprive any person of life, liberty, or property, without due process of law; nor deny to any person within its jurisdiction the equal protection of the laws."

The roles of both the national and state governments expanded in the twentieth century. During the twentieth century, new constitutional amendments expanded democracy, requiring states to use direct elections to select U.S. Senators (the Seventeenth Amendment), and denying states the authority to prevent women and 18-year-olds from voting (the Nineteenth Amendment and Twenty-Sixth Amendment), to require poll taxes for voting (the Twenty-Fourth Amendment), or to allow liquor sales (the Eighteenth Amendment, repealed by the Twenty-first Amendment in 1933). The New Deal of the 1930s broadened both national and state activism in social welfare and economic regulation. Since then, national authority expanded to address such problems as discrimination, poverty, pollution, and inequality of opportunity.

Today, American federalism is so much a part of American life that few appreciate its wide-ranging impact. State and local governments each employ far more civilians than the national government. In 2008, U.S. national government spending was nearly the same as state and local government spending.[109] States regulate nearly 20 percent of the American economy, including business incorporations, insurance, occupations, and health services.[110]

In the Convention, the debate on national authority spilled over into a series of conflicts over specific government powers: slavery, taxes, trade, money and credit, land, and national defense. Of these, slavery nearly brought the Convention to a premature end.

14

Slavery

Slavery drove the framers to compromise their ideals with hard-headed politics. The slavery issue divided Madison's Northern and Southern allies, and it threatened to unravel the possibility of a stronger national government. Many Northern delegates considered slavery morally indefensible. Many Southerners ardently defended it as essential for their region.[1] Slavery linked the apportionment of seats in Congress to the scope of national government authority. If slaves counted in estimating the relative population size of the states, the slave states—Virginia, North and South Carolina, and Georgia—would gain an important advantage in Congress, and would have a strong incentive to support broad national powers. But if the delegates refused to count the slave population, these slave states would be at a severe political disadvantage, and might not ratify the Constitution at all.

The delegates could only get past their differences over slavery with a series of political compromises that underwrote slave states' power. The compromise over representation allowed Southern states to count slaves as three-fifths of a person for the purposes of determining a state's seats in the House of Representatives and its electoral votes for president. This compromise guaranteed that the South's slave-owning whites would have a disproportionate influence in national policy-making. Other compromises ensured that slave states could continue to import slaves for a generation and would have the authority to recover their escaped slaves.

These compromises had tragic consequences for the nation. Almost four score years later, Abraham Lincoln said he considered slavery to be "a moral, social and political evil"—but in the next breath acknowledged "its actual existence amongst us and the difficulties of getting rid of it in any satisfactory way, and to all the Constitutional obligations which have been thrown about it."[2]

Slavery and Representation

James Madison recognized that slavery posed a grave threat to his plans for broad national authority. His strategy for the Constitution depended on a coalition of Southern slave states and two large Northern states, Pennsylvania and Massachusetts, whose delegates had little sympathy for slavery. Proportional representation in Congress united both elements of his coalition by increasing their national policy-making influence. On May 31, he unsuccessfully proposed to drop the words "the number of free inhabitants" from the Virginia Plan because this rule "might occasion debates which would divert the Committee from the general question" of proportional representation.[3]

How would slaves be counted in the state population tallies used to determine the allocation of seats in Congress? The debate on how to count slaves surfaced as soon as the delegates confronted the issue of whether wealth or population should constitute the basis of representation. Southerners preferred wealth to population. If wealth were used to allocate Congressional seats, the slave states would gain relatively more seats because slaves would be counted as wealth. South Carolina's Pierce Butler stated that his support for broad nationalism was conditional. If the principle of representation were "favorable to wealth as well as numbers of Free Inhabitants," Butler said he would support "abolishing the State Legislatures, and becoming one Nation instead of a confederation of Republics."[4] When Alexander Hamilton challenged the South by proposing to base representation on "the number of free inhabitants" excluding slaves, the Convention evaded the conflict by postponing the proposal.[5]

As soon as the delegates rejected the equal representation of the states in Congress on June 11, Butler and John Rutledge pushed to make wealth instead of population the basis of proportional representation. James Wilson and Charles Pinckney tried to deflect this proposal, suggesting that representation be based on the free population along with a partial count of slaves. Four years earlier, the Confederation Congress had established a rule that each state's financial obligation to the Confederation would be based on its population of free inhabitants plus three-fifths of its slaves.[6] Wilson and Pinckney proposed to insert this "three-fifths" rule into the Constitution as a way to establish an "equitable ratio of representation."[7] Elbridge Gerry of Massachusetts asked, "Why should the blacks, who were property in the South, be in the rule of representation more than the cattle & horses of the North?"[8] The delegates set aside Gerry's qualms and approved this "three-fifths" compromise by a vote of nine states to two.[9]

Southern delegates reacted to the proposed Connecticut Compromise by insisting that the Convention lock in adequate slave state representation in the

House. The day the agreement was first announced, Butler "urged warmly the justice & necessity of regarding wealth in the apportionment of Representation."[10] New Jersey's William Paterson answered that blacks were not represented in apportioning seats in the Southern state legislatures, so "why should they be represented in the General Government?" For Paterson, slaves were nothing but property put to use at the "will of the Master" with no free agency. The slave trade would be encouraged if wealth were made the basis of representation in the House. He reminded the delegates that the Confederation Congress had been too "ashamed to use the term 'Slaves'" and substituted evasive language for that word.[11] Charles Pinckney, arguing that "[t]he value of land had been found on full investigation to be an impracticable rule," tried to encourage a compromise by saying that he would accept the three-fifths ratio for representing slaves, even though he believed that blacks and whites should be counted equally when determining seats in Congress.[12] Rufus King, also trying to find grounds for compromise, had expected that the relatively wealthy Southern states would not unite with the poorer Northern states "unless some respect were paid to their superior wealth." He suggested that, in principle, the burden of taxation should be tied to the benefit of representation.[13]

These issues resurfaced on July 10, when a committee recommended the apportionment of sixty-five seats in the first House of Representatives. North Carolina's Hugh Williamson thought the plan provided too few seats to adequately protect the "Southern Interest," and General Pinckney "urged the reduction" of Northern seats, claiming that the wealthier South should have "its due weight in the Government."[14] "Property ought to have its weight," conceded Gouverneur Morris, "but not all the weight." The report gave Southern states "more than their share" of House seats. Morris observed, "If the Southern States are to supply money, the Northern States are to spill their blood. Besides, the probable Revenue to be expected from the Southern States has been greatly overrated."[15]

After the Convention accepted the plan for apportioning sixty-five House seats, Southern delegates sought more representation for their slaves than the three-fifths to which they had agreed. General Pinckney and Butler "insisted that blacks be included in the rule of Representation, *equally* with the Whites: and for that purpose moved that the words 'three fifths' be struck out."[16] Butler demanded full representation of all Southerners, because the value of work of slaves and Northern freemen were equal.[17] Charles Pinckney later commented that "blacks are the laborers, the peasants of the Southern States" and their economic contributions would strengthen the nation as much as finance and commerce in the North.[18] Gerry shot back that three-fifths was, "to say the least, the full proportion that could be admitted."[19] Nathaniel Gorham explained that the three-fifths rule had been set as a fair "rule of taxation." When the Confederation Congress adopted the three-fifths rule, the slave states sought to reduce the fraction to reduce their payments to the Confederation. But now, "when the ratio of representation is to be established, we are assured that they are equal to freemen."[20] Williamson supported the three-fifths ratio, but "reminded Mr. Gorham" that, when the formula for payments to the Confederation was established, New England had argued for fully counting the slaves.[21] George Mason conceded that slaves would increase the nation's land values, trade, and government revenues, but he could not "regard them as equal to freemen and could not vote for them as such." He also noted that slaves were a "peculiar species of property, over & above the other species of property common to all the States."[22]

The delegates rejected South Carolina's motion to count slaves equally with free whites, but a proposal to take a census of the nation's population kept the sore point open. Gouverneur Morris objected that a proposal for an annual census "fettered the Legislature too much." He argued, "If slaves were to be considered as inhabitants, not as wealth," the proposal should be rejected, but if the slaves are considered wealth, "then why is no other wealth but slaves included?" Citizens of Pennsylvania "would revolt at the idea of being put on a footing with slaves."[23] King admitted the "great force" of these objections, but "would however accede to the proposition for the sake of doing something."[24]

Would the census include wealth as well as population? Mason thought the idea of counting wealth was "too indefinite & impracticable" and gave Congress "a pretext for doing nothing."[25] Wilson was willing to leave discretion to Congress but he also "considered wealth as an impracticable rule."[26] Roger Sherman "thought the number of people alone the best rule for measuring wealth as well as representation," and although he initially supported the idea of leaving the issue to Congress, he had been persuaded that the Constitution should set a regular schedule for conducting the census.[27] Wilson also questioned the idea of representing three-fifths of the slaves, but believed these problems "must be overruled by the necessity of compromise."[28] The Convention finally accepted the proposal to include three-fifths of the slaves in the population count for seats in the House of Representatives. Morris, though, remained adamantly opposed; he "could never agree to give such encouragement to the slave trade as would be given by allowing them a representation for their negroes, and he did not believe those States would ever confederate on terms that would deprive them of that trade."[29]

Next, Gouverneur Morris proposed "that taxation shall be in proportion to Representation," so that the more seats a state had in Congress, the larger its financial obligation to the national government.[30] Madison noted that the "object was to lessen the eagerness on one side, & the opposition on the other, to the share of Representation claimed by the Southern States on account of the Negroes."[31] Though General Pinckney liked Morris's idea, he was "alarmed at what was said yesterday, concerning the Negroes" and he reasserted "that property in slaves should not be exposed to danger under a Government instituted for the protection of property."[32] Pierce Butler admitted that the principle was fair, but that representation should therefore be based on a full count of all whites and slaves.[33] For William Davie of North Carolina, "it was high time now to speak out. He saw that it was meant by some gentlemen to deprive the Southern States of any share of Representation for their blacks," and was certain that North Carolina would not join the union unless at least three-fifths of their slaves contributed to their population count for establishing representation.[34] Morris responded that it was futile for the South to insist on conditions the North would never accept.[35] Randolph "lamented that such a species of property [as slaves] existed, but as it did exist the holders of it would require this security."[36]

James Wilson suggested a subterfuge to evade the problem of writing the three-fifths compromise into the Constitution. He proposed that, in one section of the document, the Constitution would base representation on direct taxation; in a separate section, it would base direct taxation on the Confederation formula for requisitions—that is, that slaves would be counted as three-fifths of a person. According to Wilson, "less umbrage would perhaps be taken against an admission of the slaves into the Rule of representation, if it should be so expressed as to make them indirectly only an ingredient in the rule." It would achieve the same result.[37] The Convention accepted Wilson's expedient solution. Gerry proposed to proportion taxes directly to the apportionment of seats in the first Congress.[38] Madison liked Gerry's motion "because it tended to moderate the views both of the opponents & advocates for rating very high, the negroes."[39] The motion passed. Ellsworth thought the proposal added too much detail to the Constitution, and both he and Mason believed that it would be unjust until a census established the actual number of state inhabitants.[40]

Randolph proposed that a census be conducted periodically, so that representation could be rebalanced and kept fair as population shifted among the states. King worried that a Constitutional requirement to count slaves eventually would harm the North, because the South would gain population and strength, and Southerners would be able to say, "do us justice or we will separate."[41] Randolph's proposal inflamed Gouverneur Morris, who answered that "the Southern Gentleman will not be satisfied" until they establish "a majority in the public Councils." This "transfer of power from the maritime to the interior & landed interest will" result in a severe enough "oppression of commerce" that he would support an equal state vote in the Senate "to provide some defense for the Northern States against it." Morris said that, if the distinction between the North and South were as serious as Madison suggested,

> instead of attempting to blend incompatible things, let us at once take a friendly leave of each other. There can be no end of demands for security if every particular interest is to be entitled to it. The Eastern States

may claim it for their fishery, and for other objects, as the Southern States claim it for their peculiar objects. . . . If the Southern States get the power into their hands, and be joined as they will be with the interior Country they will inevitably bring on a war with Spain for the Mississippi. . . . He wished to know what security the Northern & middle States will have against this danger. It has been said that North Carolina, South Carolina, and Georgia only will in a little time have a majority of the people of America. They must in that case include the great interior Country, and every thing was to be apprehended from their getting the power into their hands.[42]

Pierce Butler bluntly replied:

The security the Southern States want is that their negroes may not be taken from them, which some gentlemen within or without doors, have a very good mind to do. It was not supposed that North Carolina, South Carolina, and Georgia would have more people than all the other States, but many more relatively to the other States than they now have. The people & strength of America are evidently bearing Southwardly & Southwestwardly.[43]

The delegates rejected a motion by Charles Pinckney to count slaves as equal to free whites and then quibbled over the frequency of the mandatory censuses. They agreed that a census would be taken within six years of the first meeting of Congress, and every ten years thereafter.[44]

Anger about slavery boiled over again after the Committee of Detail report. King complained that, despite the three-fifths compromise, the report further restricted the national government's power to limit slavery.[45] Gouverneur Morris fiercely attacked slavery and the three-fifths compromise, proposing to limit the census to free inhabitants of any state.

He never would concur in upholding domestic slavery. It was a nefarious institution. It was the curse of heaven on the States where it prevailed. Compare the free regions of the Middle States, where a rich & noble cultivation marks the prosperity & happiness of the people, with the misery & poverty which overspread the barren wastes of Virginia, Maryland & the other States having slaves. Travel through the whole Continent & you behold the prospect continually varying with the appearance & disappearance of slavery. The moment you leave the Eastern States & enter New York, the effects of the institution become visible; passing through the Jerseys and entering every criterion of superior improvement witnesses the change. Proceed Southwardly, & every step you take through the great regions of slaves, presents a desert increasing with the increasing proportion of these wretched beings. . . .

The admission of slaves into the Representation when fairly explained comes to this: that the inhabitant of Georgia and South Carolina who goes to the Coast of Africa, and in defiance of the most sacred laws of humanity tears away his fellow creatures from their dearest connections & damns them to the most cruel bondages, shall have more votes in a Government instituted for protection of the rights of mankind, than the Citizen of Pennsylvania or New Jersey who views with a laudable horror, so nefarious a practice. . . .

And what is the proposed compensation to the Northern States for a sacrifice of every principle of right, of every impulse of humanity? They are to bind themselves to march their militia for the defense of the Southern States; for their defense against those very slaves of whom they complain. They must supply vessels & seamen, in case of foreign Attack. The Legislature will have indefinite power to tax them by excises, and duties on imports, both of which will fall heavier on them than on the Southern inhabitants. . . . On the other side the Southern States are not to be restrained from importing fresh supplies of wretched Africans, at once to increase the danger of attack, and the difficulty of defense; nay they are to be encouraged to it by an assurance of having their votes in the National Government increased in proportion and are at the same time to have their exports & their slaves exempt from all contributions for the public service. . . . He would sooner submit himself to a tax for paying for all the Negroes in the United States than saddle posterity with such a Constitution.[46]

South Carolina's Charles Pinckney countered that "the fisheries & the Western frontier" were "more burdensome to the U.S. than the slaves."[47] Sherman disagreed that the three-fifths compromise caused "such insuperable objections." Only the Southern freemen were "to be represented according to the taxes paid by them, and the Negroes are only included in the Estimate of the taxes."[48] James Wilson conceded that even if the delegates forbid the representation of three-fifths of the slaves, slavery and the slave trade would endure in the South.[49]

The Convention rejected this last-ditch effort to eliminate the three-fifths rule and voted unanimously for the three-fifths rule for direct taxation.[50] In the final days of the Convention, the delegates replaced the word "servitude" with "service" in the section on counting population for House apportionment. They viewed *service* as a more evasive word that downplayed slavery by expressing "the obligations of free persons." When John Dickinson and Wilson tried to remove the term "direct taxes" from this section, Morris reminded them that "direct taxes" were included here "to exclude the appearance of counting the Negroes in the Representation."[51] The Southern states, then, successfully had ensured that their slaves gave them added influence in Congress. They battled just as tenaciously to protect their state prerogatives to govern slavery.

The Slave Trade

As Southerners grew more concerned about their influence in Congress, the delegates from South Carolina and Georgia demanded that government be prohibited from restricting imports of new slaves. To protect slavery, they linked the slave trade to the national power to make commercial treaties. These treaties were essential for Northern merchants, but delegates from all the Southern states were deeply suspicious of national authority over commerce. The new Congress could make treaties, or impose taxes, that would strangle the South's agricultural exports and the system of slavery on which it depended.

The Committee of Detail report protected Southern interests in slavery. It provided that Congress could not prohibit "the migration or importation of such persons as the several States shall think proper to admit." Congress could not tax exports, a tax that could undermine the slave economy by pricing plantation commodities out of foreign markets. The Committee also required an extraordinary two-thirds majority for approval of any commercial treaty with another country.[52] Requiring a two-thirds majority to pass such treaties would make it much more difficult to enact the commercial agreements that Northern states so desperately wanted, and it would protect Southern exports from any Northern scheme that would harm the Southern commodity trade.

When the delegates approved a provision for calculating the allocation of House seats based on the three-fifths rule, Rufus King lashed out against the slave trade as "a most grating circumstance to his mind, & he believed would be so to a great part of the people of America." Congress could neither ban slave imports nor tax the South's slave-grown exports. In King's view, "There was so much inequality & unreasonableness in all this" that Northerners would never ratify the Constitution; "either slaves should not be represented, or exports should be taxable."[53] The pragmatic Roger Sherman agreed that he "regarded the slave-trade as iniquitous," but he observed that "representation having been Settled after much difficulty & deliberation," he would not object and thought the problem could be addressed elsewhere in the Constitution.[54] For the moment, the issue was laid aside.

Two weeks later, when the delegates took up the issue of national export taxes, Luther Martin proposed a tax on slave imports. Calling on the delegates' ideals, Martin said it "was inconsistent with the principles of the revolution and dishonorable to the American character" to protect the slave trade in the Constitution. The slave trade gave the South a greater opportunity to add Congressional votes and placed a greater burden on the North to protect the South against slave revolts.[55] Other delegates outraged by the slave trade spoke out. George Mason, who himself owned dozens of slaves, blamed "[t]his infernal traffic" on "the avarice of British Merchants." Britain would not allow Virginia to end it. Stopping the slave trade was a national issue. The slave trade would thrive if South Carolina and Georgia were allowed to continue to import slaves, because Westerners would "fill that Country with slaves if they can be got through South Carolina & Georgia." According to Madison, Mason said that,

> Slavery discourages arts & manufactures. The poor despise labor when performed by slaves. They prevent the immigration of Whites, who really enrich & strengthen a Country. They produce the most pernicious effect on manners. Every master of slaves is born a petty tyrant. They bring the judgment of heaven on a Country.... By an inevitable chain of causes & effects providence punishes national sins, by national calamities.... [Mason] held it essential in every point of view, that the General Government should have power to prevent the increase of slavery.[56]

Dickinson believed it "inadmissible on every principle of honor & safety that the importation of slaves should be authorized to the States by the Constitution." The question of whether slave imports would serve "the national happiness" had to be left to the national government. Dickinson said he "could not believe that the Southern States would refuse to confederate on the account apprehended; especially as the power was not likely to be immediately exercised by the General Government."[57]

Sherman acknowledged that if Congress had the power to stop slave imports, it would use it, and said that "[h]e thought it would be its duty to exercise the power."[58] New Hampshire's John Langdon "was strenuous" for national power to stop the slave trade, explaining that he could not allow the states to exercise this power despite assurances from some Southern delegates that they were likely to stop it.[59] Wilson did not believe that the Southern states would end the slave trade on their own, or that Northerners would accept the Constitution with the provision. If all imports were to be taxed except for slaves, then the national government would in effect be subsidizing slavery.[60] King agreed with Wilson, and "thought the subject should be considered in a political light only." If Georgia and South Carolina would "not agree to the Constitution" without the provision, "he could affirm with equal belief on the other, that great & equal opposition would be experienced from the other States" if it were included.[61]

Martin's proposed tax on slave imports incited the Southerners. Rutledge insisted, "Religion & humanity had nothing to do with this question. Interest alone is the governing principle with Nations." The question was "whether the Southern States shall or shall not be parties to the Union. If the Northern States consult their interest, they will not oppose the increase of Slaves which will increase the commodities" that Northern merchant ships would carry.[62] North Carolina, South Carolina, and Georgia, he said, "will never be such fools as to give up so important an interest" as the slave trade.[63] Madison recorded Charles Pinckney's answer: "If slavery be wrong, it is justified by the example of all the world.... If the Southern States were let alone they will probably of themselves stop importations.... An attempt to take away the right as proposed will produce serious objections to the Constitution which he wished to see adopted."[64] Williamson added "that it was wrong to force anything down, not absolutely necessary, and which any State must disagree to."[65]

Abraham Baldwin of Georgia defended slavery as "one of" Georgia's "favorite prerogatives," an issue "of a local nature" that should be out of the reach of Congress. Georgia eventually "may probably put a stop to the evil" if left alone.[66] General Pinckney pointed out that Virginia "will gain by stopping the importations" because "Her slaves will rise in value, & she has more than she wants." It would be unfair "to require South Carolina & Georgia to confederate on such Unequal terms." He contended that "the importation of slaves would be for the interest of the whole Union. The more slaves, the more produce to employ the carrying trade; The more consumption also, and the more of this, the more of revenue for the common treasury."[67]

Connecticut's pragmatic delegates defended state control of the slave trade as politically expedient. Sherman

> disapproved of the slave trade: yet as the States were now possessed of the right to import slaves, as the public good did not require it to be taken from them, & as it was expedient to have as few objections as possible to the proposed scheme of Government, he thought it best to leave the matter as we find it.[68]

Ellsworth urged the Convention to "Let every State import what it pleases. The morality or wisdom of slavery are considerations belonging to the States themselves. What enriches a part enriches the whole, and the States are the best judges of their particular interest." It was not necessary for the national government to meddle in this issue.[69] In a caustic response to Mason, a slave owner, Ellsworth said,

> As he had never owned a slave could not judge of the effects of slavery on character. He said however that if it was to be considered in a moral

light we ought to go farther and free those already in the Country. As slaves also multiply so fast in Virginia & Maryland that it is cheaper to raise than import them, whilst in the sickly rice swamps foreign supplies are necessary, if we go no farther than is urged, we shall be unjust towards South Carolina & Georgia.[70]

Slavery would eventually die, Ellsworth believed, because the American population would increase over time, meaning "poor laborers will be so plenty as to render slaves useless. Slavery in time will not be a speck in our Country." The prospect of slave revolts instigated by foreigners "will become a motive to kind treatment of the slaves."[71]

Delegates scrambled for some accommodation. Gouverneur Morris suggested a political deal involving the slave trade and the extraordinary political majority required for commercial treaties. "These things," said Morris, "may form a bargain among the Northern & Southern States."[72] Randolph agreed that the problem should be sent to a committee to find "some middle ground." If the clause remained, "it would revolt the Quakers, the Methodists, and many others in the States having no slaves. On the other hand, two States might be lost to the Union."[73] Sherman, who had championed a committee to break the impasse on Congressional representation, tried to fend off this proposed committee but failed.[74] During the day's debate, Madison silently watched his coalition partners slash away at one another.

This special committee proposed a political bargain between the South and the Northern commercial states. Congress could not ban the importation of slaves until 1800, and slaves brought into the country could be taxed at an average for other items. No extraordinary majority would be required for international commercial agreements; Congress could pass such an agreement with a simple majority (see chapter 14).[75] South Carolina's General Pinckney argued in favor of an additional eight years of slave imports, urging the Convention to extend the ban on Congressional action to 1808. Now Madison weighed in, arguing, "Twenty years will produce all the mischief that can be apprehended from the liberty to import slaves." He added, "So long a term will be more dishonorable to the National character than to say nothing about it in the Constitution."[76] The delegates ignored his concerns and extended the protection for importing slaves (or in their words, "such persons as the several States now existing shall think proper to admit") to 1808.

Gouverneur Morris suggested limiting slave imports to North Carolina, South Carolina, and Georgia.[77] But his proposal would require the Constitution to use the word "slave," and too many delegates were uncomfortable inserting the indelicate word "slave" into the text to take this step. Sherman recounted that the Confederation Congress had declined to use the term *slaves*, and the term was "not pleasing to some people."[78] Mason said he "was not against using the term 'slaves' but against naming North Carolina, South Carolina & Georgia, lest it should give offence to the people of those States."[79] Williamson said he was "against slavery; but thought it more in favor of humanity, from a view of all circumstances, to let in South Carolina & Georgia on those terms, than to exclude them from the Union."[80] Morris withdrew his proposal.

Next, the delegates considered the provision allowing imported slaves to be taxed like other imports. Sherman opposed the provision because it acknowledged "men to be property, by taxing them as such under the character of slaves."[81] Madison also expressed dissatisfaction with the arrangement, because he, too, "thought it wrong to admit in the Constitution the idea that there could be property in men."[82] But most other delegates spoke in defense of the bargain. King and Langdon told Sherman that this was "the price of the first part," that is, New England agreed to protect slave imports on the condition that the imported slaves be taxed. General Pinckney "admitted that it was so," that is, that there was an explicit political bargain on importing slaves.[83] For Mason, "Not to tax, will be equivalent to a bounty on the importation of slaves."[84] The Convention ignored Madison and Sherman's sensibilities. After adjusting the language to limit the tax on imported slaves to a maximum of ten dollars per person, the Convention accepted the importation and taxation of slaves. Although the third element of this political deal—the requirement that only a simple majority, rather than a two-thirds majority, be required for commercial laws—also generated controversy the following week, key Southern delegates stuck with the bargain and provided the key votes to pass the proposition. In its final days, the Convention provided that the protection of the slave trade until 1808 could not be changed by Constitutional amendment.[85]

Fugitive Slaves

The delegates also protected slavery when they provided that slaves who ran away from their owners had to be returned to them, even when they escaped to the Northern states. When the delegates discussed the extradition of criminals fleeing from justice to be returned to the state where the offense was committed, South Carolina's Pierce Butler and Charles Pinckney moved "to require fugitive slaves and servants to be delivered up like criminals."[86] Wilson objected that the proposal "would oblige the Executive of the State to do it, at the public expense."[87] Sherman "saw no more propriety in the public seizing and surrendering a slave or servant, than a horse."[88] Butler withdrew his proposal for the moment, but the next day, the delegates accepted Butler's substitute, requiring that a slave who escaped into another state would not be considered free, "but shall be delivered up to the person justly claiming their service or labor."[89] The Committee on Style reworded this agreement in the nearly final version of the Constitution. To avoid using the troublesome word "slave," the Constitution instead refers to "person legally held to service or labor in one state, escaping into another."[90] Some delegates found the word "legally" repellent, viewing the word as an endorsement of "the idea that slavery was legal in a moral view." Before the Constitution went to the printer, therefore, the term "legally" was replaced with the more indirect phrase, "under the laws thereof."[91]

The Path of Slavery and Race in the United States

Madison believed that "where slavery exists, the Republican Theory" of majority rule "becomes still more fallacious."[92] But the delegates compromised such republican ideals during the bare-knuckles battle over slavery. Years later, Abraham Lincoln observed "that our fathers *did not* make this nation half slave and half free, or part slave and part free. I insist that they found the institution of slavery existing here. They did not make it so, but they left it so because they knew of no way to get rid of it at that time."[93]

Political pragmatism cemented the states' control of slaves, and state control of slavery made dual national and state sovereignty an indispensable feature of the new political system. The U.S. Constitution protected slavery, and it guaranteed that the South's slave-owning whites would have a disproportionate influence in national policy-making. It also clarified the operation of "the compound republic": states would have access to imported slaves for a generation, and their residents would have the authority to recover their escaped slaves anywhere in the nation. The Constitutional Convention's compromises ensured that conflict over race would be an "American dilemma" for generations.[94]

Slavery flourished in the early nineteenth century. The diverging interests of the South and North came to the breaking point in the Civil War in the 1860s. After the war, the Thirteenth Amendment (1865) banned slavery, the Fourteenth Amendment (1868) attempted to protect the citizenship rights of newly freed slaves, and the Fifteenth Amendment (1870) aimed to protect African American voting rights.[95] But for another century, the Constitution was held compatible with racial exclusion in the South.[96] Southern states mandated the segregation of whites and blacks in schools, trains, streetcars, waiting rooms, hotels, restaurants, saloons, restrooms, and courtrooms.[97] Southern states used literacy tests, poll taxes, and other rules to exclude blacks from voting.[98]

By the 1940s, rising demands for civil rights began to wash away the Constitutional supports for racial segregation.[99] The Supreme Court's decision in

Brown v. Board of Education (1954) invalidated legal segregation in elementary and secondary education, stating, "Separate educational facilities are inherently unequal."[100] The 1964 Civil Rights Act outlawed legal segregation in schools, public accommodations, and employment. The 1965 Voting Rights Act banned literacy tests and allowed the federal government to supervise voter registration and elections in several states, and the Twenty-Fourth Amendment (1964) banned poll taxes as an obstacle to voting.[101] Intense controversies still continue over current issues of racial discrimination and remedial actions for past discrimination.

In the process of making their bargains over slavery, the Convention delegates bolstered the authority of the states over their internal economies. They did the same with many of the tools of economic development.

15

Economic Authority

The delegates began to negotiate the scope of national power just as delegates were growing more wary of the policies the national government would pursue. Both broad and narrow nationalists agreed that the reconstituted national government required the power to tax and to manage money, credit, debt, commerce, land, and economic development. But these powers were double-edged. National officials could use this authority to favor one region or alliance of states and to harm others.

The delegates, then, tried to strengthen national powers selectively. Individual delegates sought stronger national powers they believed would be beneficial, and opposed granting the national powers that could harm vital interests. The Convention approved extensive taxing powers for the government, for example, but tried to make it difficult to use this power to benefit or harm any state or region. Most of the framers were determined to end the profligate currency and credit policies of the states and to boost the credit standing of the national government. The Convention strengthened national authority to pursue more conservative currency and credit policies and to restrict significantly the states' authority in these areas. It delegated such controversial issues as the state debts, bankruptcy laws, and the distribution of public land to the new Congress and courts. Finally, the delegates refused explicitly to grant new powers to the national government to dig canals, build roads, charter corporations, or establish a national university.

Taxes and Their Limits

Taxes were the lifeblood of the new national government. As James Wilson pointed out, the government's most basic tasks, including national defense and trade regulation, all depended on revenue.[1] Pierce Butler viewed taxation as one of the "distinguished marks of Sovereignty."[2] The delegates agreed that the new government needed a much more reliable source of revenue than the requisitions used in the Confederation. But the power to tax was dangerous. Leaders could abuse the taxing power, undertaking wasteful projects and costly wars, enriching themselves, destroying their political opponents, or developing one region at the expense of another. Benjamin Franklin warned that history showed "a constant kind of warfare between the Governing & Governed: the one striving to obtain more for its support, and the other to pay less."[3]

All agreed that the new government would levy tariffs on imported goods, a power long sought for the Confederation government. But, as Wilson pointed out, taxes on imports "alone will not be sufficient."[4] Additional taxes on at least some Americans would be required. To protect state government authority while providing for these additional revenues, several delegates believed that the new government should set a requisition for each state and allow each to choose how to levy internal taxes needed to fill the requisition. This solution would allow the states to choose what additional internal taxes to levy, as they did in the Confederation. The New Jersey Plan authorized national tariffs as well as postage fees, but provided for this system of requisitions when additional revenues were needed.

Broad nationalists vigorously attacked the idea of leaving so much taxing authority to the states. Alexander Hamilton denounced the unreliable requisition system discredited in the Confederation government: the "delinquency of one" state "will invite and countenance it in others."[5] Gouverneur Morris viewed requisitions as "subversive of the idea of Government."[6] By mid-July, even Roger Sherman was convinced that the Confederation's requisition system would be inadequate.[7] When Luther Martin proposed state requisitions in August, the Convention defeated the idea overwhelmingly.[8]

Instead, the Constitution authorized a formidable national power to tax. When the Committee of Detail enumerated Congress's powers, a broad national "power to lay and collect taxes, duties, imposts and excises" topped the list, and the Convention approved.[9] James Madison commented that the states were entrusting the national government "with a power over the public treasure." Sherman did not deny that the national government had extensive taxing power, but he did deny Madison's suggestion that the states had surrendered control over taxes to the national government. "In giving up that of taxation, they retain a concurrent power of raising money for their own use," a view that reinforced the shared sovereignty of the national and state governments.[10] When George Mason sought to add to national power the authority to enact sumptuary laws (that is, laws that prohibited individuals from displaying extravagance in their clothing and other choices), the delegates refused.[11] For Oliver Ellsworth, any reasonable effort to regulate eating and drinking "is provided for in the power of taxation."[12]

When given the opportunity to limit the national taxing power, the delegates also refused. First, they declined to put a time limit on these taxes. Mason was concerned that, once the government imposed taxes, it would never rescind them, and he argued for "the necessity of preventing the danger of perpetual revenue which must of necessity subvert the liberty of any Country."[13] Though a committee recommended a clause providing a time limit on most taxes, this limit was not seriously discussed or included in the Constitution.[14] Second, when Sherman tried to limit national taxing power to revenues required "for the payment of said debts and for the defraying [of] the expenses that shall be incurred for the common defense and general welfare," the Convention over-whelmingly rejected this effort to constrict national taxing authority.[15] Third, the delegates refused to eliminate the national government's power to levy direct taxes on property, sales, or income. As the Convention drew to a close, the dele-gates explicitly defeated a proposal to remove the phrase "direct taxes" after Gouverneur Morris reminded them that the phrase was intended to avoid the word "slave" in allocating House seats.[16] Fourth, the delegates rejected Elbridge Gerry's proposal that, in the first House of Representatives, direct taxes would be levied in proportion to representation.[17]

By the end of the Convention, even the most attentive delegates found it hard to identify the limits of the national taxing power. For example, Maryland's del-egates sought explicit language protecting states' authority to tax ships to main-tain harbors and lighthouses. Morris and Sherman believed that the Constitution already allowed the states to levy these taxes; James Madison believed that it did not.[18] No delegate ever took the opportunity to narrow the national taxing power by answering Rufus King's challenging question, "what was the precise meaning of direct taxation?"[19]

Although the delegates rejected limits on the national taxing power, they made it difficult to actually levy these taxes and especially to redistribute re-sources from one area to another. Most important, they agreed to shackle the national government so that it could not vary tax rates across states and regions. Delegates began to bridle at the dependence of direct taxes on representation before the Committee of Detail began its work.[20] Gouverneur Morris himself thought the same provision was "liable to strong objections" and he "hoped" the Committee would drop it because it was only meant to work through the issue of apportioning legislative seats.[21] But the delegates finally required both House seats and direct taxes be allocated on a per capita basis, and that direct taxes be based on a population census.[22] These requirements made it much more difficult to design a national direct tax, particularly a tax on property.

The intense, protracted battle over export taxes raised fears about the govern-ment's taxing power, and the Convention finally solved the problem simply by amputating *both* national and state power to tax exports. Southern delegates viewed the power to tax exports as a direct and massive danger. If Congress could tax exports, and the North enjoyed a majority in Congress, the national government could impose stiff taxes on the South's massive shipments of commodities like rice and tobacco. Butler "was strenuously opposed to a power over exports, as unjust and alarming" to states that exported crops in bulk.[23] Mason pointed out that the Northern members of Congress could outvote Southern members on this issue.[24] Ellsworth also defended the ban on export taxes because it would be hard to make these taxes impartial. Moreover, export taxes would "discourage industry" and "engender incurable jealousies."[25] Madison and his allies unsuccessfully argued that the national interest required national power to tax exports. Madison implored the delegates to consider "national and permanent views." By taxing exports of products for which there was no ready substitute abroad, such as tobacco, the government could produce more revenue, advance "domestic manufactures," and exert leverage over other nations.[26] Gouverneur Morris viewed export taxes as a valuable way to extract revenue without imposing direct taxes.[27] Despite these arguments, the delegates voted to ban the national power to tax exports.[28] A week later, King proposed to prohibit the *states* from imposing export taxes.[29] Morris "thought the regulation necessary to prevent the Atlantic States from endeavoring to tax the Western States & promote their interest by opposing the navigation of the Mississippi, which would drive the Western people into the arms of Great Britain."[30] The delegates narrowly approved King's motion.

The Convention, then, gave the national government enormous, open-ended taxing power, and with the exception of export taxes and state tariffs, refused to ban specific national or state taxes. But outside of national tariffs, they made most of this extensive revenue power difficult to use. First, their requirement that direct taxes be levied on a per capita basis made it more difficult to design tax plans that would be consistent with the Constitution. Second, any tax plan would have to negotiate its way through the complicated policy-making process designed to prevent regions and states from easily legislating advantages for themselves over others.

Commerce

National power to govern commerce was another long-sought need, and Edmund Randolph argued for robust national power over commerce when he introduced the Virginia Plan. The Committee of Detail specified Congress's power "[t]o regulate commerce with foreign nations, and among the several States" as the second enumerated power for Congress. The Convention endorsed this wording unanimously.[31]

But commercial policy divided the delegates almost as deeply as slavery. Southerners wanted low tariffs and as much free trade as possible, no matter what nation's ships carried their goods. Northerners, especially those from New England, wanted more restrictive commercial treaties that gave legal preferences to American ships, even if such treaties increased freight costs for the South. Delegates from smaller states worried that their larger neighbors would use Congress to benefit the large commercial states and harm them. Once the Convention settled on a distribution of seats in the first House of Representatives, the Northern advantage became clearer. In a meeting of the Maryland delegation, Daniel Carroll pointed out the plain fact "that the dearest interest of trade were under the control of four States or of 17 members in one branch and 8 in the other branch."[32]

The Southern and small states, then, worked to make it difficult for the national government to harm their vital interests. Many delegates from these states wanted to require that any commercial treaty had to receive a two-thirds majority for Congressional approval. Randolph announced his intent to require this extraordinary majority after the announcement of the Connecticut Compromise, and the Committee of Detail proposed it.[33] Northern delegates were deeply worried that this rule would block the trade agreements vital to *their* interests. Nathaniel Gorham argued that the New England states "had no motive to Union but a commercial one. . . . They were not afraid of external danger, and did not need the aid of the Southern States."[34]

This problem was resolved with a straightforward political deal, or as Madison called it, "an understanding on the two subjects of *navigation* and *slavery*" between the New England and the Southern states (on slave imports, see chapter 13).[35] A special committee recommended that the entire section on "navigation acts" be jettisoned, so that any commercial law would require the same simple majority required for other laws (in turn, the Northern delegates agreed to protect the slave trade).[36] Several days after the Convention had accepted the compromise on the slave trade, Charles Pinckney tried to disrupt the slave-trade bargain by proposing to restore the requirement for an extraordinarily large majority for commercial laws. Because "States pursue their interests with less scruple than individuals," argued Pinckney, the "distinct commercial interests" of the different regions "would be a source of oppressive regulations if no check to a bare majority should be provided." Answering Gorham, Pinckney insisted, "The power of regulating commerce was a pure concession on the part of the Southern States. They did not need the protection of the Northern States at present."[37] Hugh Williamson agreed, arguing that the rule would not harm any "useful measure" and that the "sickliness of" the Southern climate would deter invaders, reducing the need for an American navy.[38] Mason held, "The Southern States are the *minority* in both Houses. Is it to be expected that they will deliver themselves bound hand & foot to" New England?[39] Edmund Randolph, who like Mason was growing more impatient with the evolving Constitution, believed, "A rejection of the motion would complete the deformity of the system."[40]

Northerners immediately struck back to defend the slave-trade compromise against Pinckney's proposal. George Clymer of Pennsylvania pointed out that the nation's diverse commercial interests created enough headaches for trade policy. "Unnecessary restrictions" like the two-thirds rule would make them worse.[41] Gouverneur Morris argued that "Shipping . . . was the worst & most precarious kind of property and stood in need of public patronage." Any law benefiting American ships would spawn the growth of American shipping, resulting in more competition and lower costs for shipping Southern produce. "A navy was essential to security, particularly of the Southern States, and can only be had by a navigation act encouraging American bottoms [that is, ships] & seamen. In those points of view then alone, it is the interest of the Southern States that navigation acts should be facilitated."[42]

Political expediency decided the issue. James Madison anticipated that trade agreements eventually would bring about the development of a shipping industry in the South, and a simple majority would make it easier for Congress to retaliate against another country in a trade war. The abuse of this commercial power was "improbable," said Madison, because of the separation of legislative powers, the Senate's independence, the executive veto, and the representation of agricultural interests in the North and West.[43] Sherman believed that "the diversity" of regional commercial interests "was of itself a security" and pointed out that the rules for extraordinary majorities in such bodies as the Confederation Congress "was always embarrassing."[44] Like Madison, John Rutledge believed that any impact on the South would be temporary, and added, "As we are laying the foundation for a great empire, we ought to take a permanent view of the subject." Rutledge argued for "the necessity of securing the West [Indies] trade to this country. That was the great object, and a navigation Act was necessary for obtaining it."[45] General Pinckney appreciated the "liberal conduct" of New England "towards the views of South Carolina" on the slavery issue and opposed his colleague's motion. Butler frankly conceded that his support for the Committee compromise was grudging and motivated by political expediency.[46]

The Convention refused to reconsider a two-thirds majority for commercial treaties.[47] Later, Mason tried one last time to erect a stronger legislative barrier to commercial treaties by requiring a two-thirds majority until 1808.[48] Again, the delegates soundly rejected the proposal. It would be just as easy for Congress to enact a tariff or a commercial treaty as it would to pass any other law.

But by the time the delegates rejected the two-thirds rule for commercial treaties, they already had acted in other ways to restrict national policies that would favor the commercial interests of one region over others. First, they required all commercial rules to be uniform across the country. Maryland's delegates were particularly concerned that Congress would make laws to benefit Virginia's port of Norfolk, at the mouth of the Chesapeake Bay, at the expense of Maryland's port of Baltimore, further up the Chesapeake.[49] A committee recommended new language specifying that no "regulation of commerce or revenue" give "preference to the ports of one State over those of another, or oblige vessels bound to or from any State to enter clear or pay duties in another," and that "all tonnage, duties, imposts & excises laid by the Legislature shall be uniform throughout the U.S."[50] Madison "thought the restriction would be inconvenient," and Gorham and John Langdon "contended that the Government would be so fettered by this clause, as to defeat the good purpose of the plan."[51] But Carroll assured fellow delegates "that this was a tender point in Maryland," and the Convention unanimously approved the restriction.[52]

More importantly, the delegates permitted the states to continue to regulate commerce *within* their borders, while they restricted national government authority to foreign and interstate commerce. The Committee of Detail carefully framed the national government's commercial authority to include "foreign nations" and trade "among the several States," excluding national control of commerce *within* the states. The Committee report also prohibited the states from taxing imports or exports unless Congress approved.[53] These provisions seemed to allow the states to keep substantial authority over American trade within the United States. They were never debated explicitly. Sherman stated a position that seemed widely shared when he asserted, "The States will never give up all power over trade."[54]

James Madison, who wanted the national government to set broad rules for all the nation's commerce, believed this language left the states with too much commercial authority. On the last day of Convention debate, Madison "was more & more convinced that the regulation of Commerce was in its nature indivisible and ought to be wholly under one authority."[55] Madison unsuccessfully pressed for wording changes to further limit the states' commercial authority.[56]

The delegates greatly increased the national government's commercial authority. But to protect the states, the delegates made it difficult for the national government to tailor commercial policies if they would hurt any of the states, and they also left internal state commerce, an enormous area of economic activity, under the control of state government.

Money, Credit, and Debt

Most delegates were determined to restore the financial credibility of the national government, to enable it to ensure the repayment of debts at fair value, and to stop the states' careless currency and credit policies. Authority to regulate currency and credit would enable the national government to steer the new nation's economic prosperity in the future. The Committee of Detail specified that the Congress would have the power "To coin money," "To regulate the value of foreign coin," and "To borrow money, and emit bills on the credit of the United States."[57] The Convention approved the power to coin money without dispute, because coins usually were made out of a metal like gold that had some inherent value.[58] But the provision to emit "bills of credit" touched a raw nerve, because some of the states, and especially Rhode Island, had printed so much paper currency that few accepted these bills at face value. Gouverneur Morris tried to prohibit the national government from issuing such "bills of credit," arguing that these notes would be unnecessary if the U.S. government could borrow money, and that creditors would oppose a Constitution "if paper emissions be not prohibited."[59] Ellsworth of Connecticut—Rhode Island's neighbor—agreed, stating that this was "a favorable moment to shut and bar the door against paper money."[60] George Read warned that "the words, if not struck out, would be as alarming as the mark of the Beast in Revelations."[61] Wilson, Butler, and Langdon all endorsed the ban on national bills of credit.

Other delegates did not want to limit national credit authority, however. Despite his "mortal hatred to paper money," Mason acknowledged that the Revolution could not have been fought without it. Madison thought the power could be valuable in a future emergency. Maryland's John Francis Mercer, who explicitly favored paper money, predicted that the propertied interests "would be sure" to support the Constitution with or without such a provision, but a ban would raise the suspicions of the debtors, and "it was impolitic" to buy off the creditors at the expense of the debtors.[62] Gorham thought that the government's broad borrowing power gave it the authority to issue such notes anyway (Madison privately agreed).[63] The Convention rejected an explicit ban on national bills of credit.

Two weeks later, the delegates tried to erase any remaining *state* power to print paper money. Sherman, believing "this a favorable crisis for crushing paper money," wanted to remove Congress's authority to allow states to issue bills of credit because "the friends of paper money would make every exertion to get into the Legislature" to authorize it.[64] Although Gorham objected that "an absolute prohibition of paper money would rouse the most desperate opposition from its partisans," the Convention approved the change and proscribed state-issued paper money.[65]

As soon as the delegates prohibited the states from issuing bills of credit and paper money, King proposed that the Constitution include "a prohibition on the States to interfere in private contracts."[66] Pennsylvania's Gouverneur Morris warned, "This would be going too far. There are a thousand laws relating to bringing actions and limitations of actions . . . which affect contracts." The national courts could protect some contracts, he said, but "within the State itself a majority must rule, whatever may be the mischief done among themselves."[67] Madison tended to support the idea. Sherman, though, challenged Morris, asking, "Why then prohibit bills of credit?"[68] The Committee of Style, which wrote the nearly final draft of the Constitution in September, included a phrase that explicitly prohibited any laws "altering or impairing the obligation of contracts."[69] When the Convention approved the section, no delegate objected to the clause the Committee of Style inserted. Instead, Gerry tried, without success, to prohibit the *national* government from interfering in contracts.[70]

No one questioned that the new government would honor the debts of the Confederation government. In late August, Sherman proposed that Congress have explicit authority to pay any past debts incurred for "the common defense and general welfare."[71] The Committee on Postponed Matters added this language.[72] The new government's obligation to those who held *state*-issued securities was much more controversial. The states had borrowed money to pay for their operations during the Revolutionary War and its aftermath, and these debts burdened many states. Some states, however, had paid off many of their debts. If the national government assumed responsibility for paying off the states' debts, those with the most debt stood to gain at the expense of states with little remaining debt. This provision seemed to penalize states that had economized to pay off their debts, and reward those that had not. Moreover, if the national government took control of these debts, it would exert much more influence over all credit in the United States.

Political pragmatism drove the delegates to allow Congress the authority to take over these state debts. South Carolina's Rutledge, representing a state with substantial debts, argued that this national "assumption" of the state debt burden was fair because the states had used the money to defend the nation. "It was necessary" because the new government would take over the tariff power. "It was politic" because it would make citizens more amenable to ratification.[73] King also believed that an explicit authorization would be politically expedient, because "State Creditors, an active and formidable party, would otherwise be opposed to a plan which transferred to the Union the best resources of the States without transferring the State debts at the same time."[74] Sherman was willing to authorize Congress to assume these debts; Ellsworth believed that the Constitution already gave Congress such power.[75] The final Constitution simply mandated that Congress "*shall* fulfill the engagements and discharge the debts of the United States."[76]

The Convention also evaded the question of whether or not the original recipients of national and state notes—particularly Revolutionary War veterans—would be compensated fully even if hardship had driven them to sell the notes to speculators for less than their value. These speculators (or "stock-jobbers") would stand to gain substantial profits if the government paid them the face value of the notes. When the Convention agreed that the new government would guarantee the debts of the old one, Butler objected that this provision would "compel payment as well to the Blood-suckers who had speculated on the distresses of others, as to those who had fought & bled for their country."[77] Mason condemned the "pestilent practice" of stock-jobbing. Gerry, however, defended these speculators for creating a market for the securities.[78] The Constitution avoided the issue by simply guaranteeing that the obligations of the Confederation would be valid under the new government.[79]

Because bankruptcy law balanced the claims of creditors against debtors, national bankruptcy law could affect prosperity as well as national politics. Government laws on bankruptcy could favor creditors by making it difficult for debtors to file for bankruptcy and by applying harsh penalties for nonpayment of debts. During the economic crisis of the 1780s, states had relaxed their penalties and made it easier for debtors to delay payments or escape their debts. Charles Pinckney moved to add explicit language that would authorize the national government to "establish uniform laws upon the subject of bankruptcies, and respecting the damages arising on the protest of foreign bills of exchange." A committee recommended similar language.[80] Sherman feared that such laws could be brutally oppressive, as in England, and Morris admitted that the subject was "extensive and delicate."[81] The Convention added the clause, and authorized Congress to prevent a person from moving from state to state to avoid a bankruptcy judgment.[82]

Land

Land disputes had plagued the nation after independence from Britain. Pennsylvania, Massachusetts, Virginia, North and South Carolina, and Georgia took possession of millions of acres of land once owned by the British king (the "Crown lands") and loyalist landholders. Landlocked states like Connecticut, New Jersey, Delaware, and Maryland could not acquire similar lands. If the Constitution required the large states to surrender control of these lands to the national government, all states would benefit. Land sales could pay off the national debt. As the discussions over state representation heated up, Delaware's George Read suggested that, if the western lands were sold and "the fund be applied fairly & equally to the discharge of the general debt, [then] the smaller States who had been injured would listen then perhaps to those ideas of just representation which had been held out."[83] The delegates only began to debate the public lands issue in earnest in mid-August, when they considered the national payment of the state war debts.

Incongruously, many of the broad nationalists insisted on protecting state authority over public lands, while the narrow nationalists demanded strong national authority over these lands. Many narrow nationalists who supported the New Jersey Plan now began to attack state prerogatives over public lands, because the large states controlled these lands. Luther Martin strongly objected to the idea that the large states would have to give their consent to any surrender of their public lands. Martin said that nothing "would so alarm the limited States as to make the consent of the large States claiming the Western lands, necessary to the establishment of new States within their limits."[84] Langdon thought a requirement for state consent would ignite "dangerous opposition" to the Constitution.[85] Delaware's John Dickinson thought such consent amounted to a requirement that smaller states "secure the large ones in their extensive claims of territory."[86] King suggested that, if the national government assumed responsibility for the states' debts, "all unallocated lands of particular States ought to be given up."[87]

Delegates from the larger, land-rich states responded vigorously—and defended states' rights. Wilson "knew of nothing that would give greater or juster alarm than the doctrine, that a political society is to be torn asunder without its own consent." He suggested that those who wanted to do so aimed to cut up the large states against their will.[88] Butler of South Carolina warned that "If new States were to be erected without the consent of the dismembered States, nothing but confusion would ensue. Whenever taxes should press on the people, demagogues would set up their schemes of new States."[89] Accusing these large state delegates of hypocrisy, Martin "wished Mr. Wilson had thought a little sooner of the value" of states. At the start of the Convention, "when the rights of the small States were in question, they were phantoms, ideal beings. Now when the Great States were to be affected, political Societies were of a sacred nature."[90]

The delegates solved this issue by delegating land controversies to Congress and the courts.[91] When Carroll made a final effort to ensure national government control of public lands, Madison asserted that the national courts would view the problem from a national perspective and would favor U.S. government claims against a state. Like Wilson and Rutledge, Madison "thought it best on the whole to be silent on the subject."[92] Morris suggested a statement that Congress could "dispose of and make all needful rules and regulations respecting the territory or other property belonging to" the United States, and that nothing in the Constitution "shall be so construed as to prejudice any claims either of the United States, or of any particular State." The Convention accepted this wording.[93] This statement authorized the national government potentially to possess huge expanses of land. The delegates also provided that Congress could develop sites for a national capital and national military installations, despite fears that the capital would be located in a large city (such as Philadelphia or New York) to the detriment of other regions.[94]

Economic Development

When the delegates considered the enumerated powers they would specify for the new government, they had little difficultly agreeing to basic powers recommended by the Committee of Detail for expediting commerce and communication, such as post offices and national standards for weights and measures. When Gerry proposed adding the potentially expensive power to build "post-roads" to connect the post offices—roads that could be used for much more than carrying letters—the delegates narrowly agreed to add this power.[95]

Madison, though, envisioned much more active national direction of the American economy. He proposed additional national power to "grant charters of incorporation in cases where the Public good may require them, and the authority of a single State may be incompetent," along with powers to enact a copyright law, establish a national university, and provide subsidies for "the advancement of useful knowledge and discoveries."[96]

The Convention authorized the national government to grant copyrights and patents, but it balked at expanding national economic authority much further.[97] In the final week, Benjamin Franklin proposed an additional national authority, "a power to provide for cutting canals where deemed necessary."[98] Sherman objected that the "expense in such cases will fall on the United States, and the benefit accrue to the places where the canals may be cut."[99] Madison moved to add a general national power to incorporate enterprises.[100] Wilson concurred with Madison, pressing the case and saying, "It is necessary to prevent a *State* from obstructing the *general* welfare."[101] Yet even Madison ally Rufus King "thought the power unnecessary," and he worried that the provision would suggest a power to establish monopolies and banks, thus multiplying opposition to the Constitution.[102] Wilson denied any political problem, asserting that western development made it important to facilitate canals and that "the power to regulate trade" already included the power to promote commercial monopolies.[103] Mason "was for limiting the power to the single case of Canals. He was afraid of monopolies of every sort, which he did not think were by any means already implied by the Constitution as supposed by Mr. Wilson."[104] Madison also proposed an explicit national power to create a university, but now Morris objected, "It is not necessary. The exclusive power at the Seat of Government, will reach the object."[105] The Convention rejected these additional powers. Its silence left authority to govern internal economic development principally to the states.[106]

The Path of Economic Authority

Soon after the Committee of Detail report, Rufus King drew a deceptively simple line between state and national authority to govern domestic affairs. King observed, "The most numerous objects of legislation belong to the States. Those of the National Legislature were but few. The chief of them were commerce & revenue. When these should be once settled, alterations would be rarely necessary & easily made."[107] But the specific boundaries of national economic power were far more elusive than King suggested. The Convention gave Congress potentially strong economic powers, including wide-ranging taxing, commercial, and financial powers, but it restricted these powers to guarantee that they would not be used to advantage some states rather than others. The Constitution also protected the states' control over their own internal commerce, allowing the states to occupy many fields of government activity. It is striking that when newly appointed Treasury Secretary Alexander Hamilton asked his advice on raising revenues in the fall of 1789, Madison urged Hamilton to consider direct taxes on liquor and a national tax on land. Madison explicitly hoped to preempt the states from establishing authority over land taxes.[108]

Later Constitutional amendments expanded national economic authority. The Sixteenth Amendment (1913) permitted the national government to tax incomes, and exempted these taxes from any per capita limitation. As revenues from tariffs became less important, the income tax gradually became an indispensable major source of revenue for federal domestic and foreign policy. By banning slavery, the Thirteenth Amendment wiped out $3 billion, or over 40 percent of the entire wealth of the Southern states before secession.[109] The Eighteenth Amendment prohibited "the manufacture, sale, or transportation of intoxicating liquors" in the United States; although it was repealed by the Twenty-First Amendment in 1933, Prohibition did away with hundreds of legal brewers, distillers, and vintners, and it laid the foundation for a more vigorous exercise of national government police power.[110]

But most of the expansion of national economic authority has resulted from changing interpretations of the Constitution's words, rather than amendments to those words. Conflicts over the indefinite and elastic boundaries of federal authority have shaped and reshaped American politics since the early days of the government. Disagreements between Thomas Jefferson and Alexander Hamilton over national economic authority sparked the beginnings of political parties. Andrew Jackson's war on the Bank of the United States helped cement the role of mass-based political parties in the United States. Though national authority seemed barely visible in the nineteenth century, the national government affected the nation's economic development with land policies, support for railroads, and benefits for veterans, among others.[111] Court interpretations of national authority in the nineteenth century corralled state restrictions on the expanding national market, and spurred the growth of the Populist movement.

In the twentieth century, national authority expanded more visibly, first in the Progressive Era, and then in the New Deal of the 1930s. In its initial "Hundred Days" in office, Franklin Roosevelt's administration signed fifteen major laws dealing with banking, farming, industry, relief and public works, home foreclosures, and the development of the Tennessee River Valley. National government spending tripled by 1939, and has exceeded state and local spending ever since. Although the Supreme Court struck down a number of New Deal laws as violations of the national government's Constitutional authority, the Court in 1937 retreated from its narrow interpretation of economic power and began to uphold wide-ranging federal regulatory power.[112] These decisions revolutionized federal power, allowing federal officials to manage much of the economic activity in the nation. Since World War II, national economic authority has expanded further. Spending on highways, public services, social insurance, and antipoverty programs grew. Environmental, safety, and consumer regulations multiplied, affecting every aspect of American life.[113] In 2012, the U.S. Supreme Court narrowly upheld the constitutionality of the Affordable Care Act of 2010. In this case, a Court majority held that there are limits to the federal government's power over commerce—a ruling that foreshadows much more political conflict over federalism.[114] Meanwhile, federal military powers also have been expanding.

National Security and Foreign Policy

The delegates were determined to strengthen the government's power to defend the nation from foreign enemies and to quell domestic uprisings such as Shays's Rebellion. Almost half of the specific Congressional powers enumerated in the Constitution authorized national security measures.

But national power to put down a rebellion also could enable national troops to impose martial law indefinitely, or quash any dissent. The relative roles of the states and the national government in national security got caught up in conflicts among republicanism, national ambitions, and state prerogatives. Broad nationalists generally sought to broaden national and presidential powers in foreign and military affairs. Narrow nationalists pressed the Convention to leave substantial military power in the hands of the existing militias under state control. The delegates' compromises on military and diplomatic power deliberately left some boundaries between state and national authority obscure while creating additional complexity in American policy-making.

The Military

The delegates sought a stronger defense against foreign invasion and internal sedition, "the great objects" of the national government.[1] In Alexander Hamilton's view, "No Government could give us tranquility & happiness at home, which did not possess sufficient stability and strength to make us respectable abroad."[2] But a strong, permanent (or "standing") national army posed a grave threat to the republic. The executive power to wage war and command the military was an invitation to tyranny. The power to make peace could result in the surrender of huge territories, or even entire states, to a foreign adversary.

The delegates agreed to vest potentially strong national military powers in the new national government. When the Convention approved the power to create and support an army and navy, Elbridge Gerry objected that "there was no check here against standing armies in time of peace," and he could not consent to allowing the size of the military to be unlimited. He proposed a fixed number of two or three thousand national troops in peacetime.[3] Delegates with actual military experience found Gerry's proposal unreasonable. General Pinckney "asked whether no troops were ever to be raised until an attack should be made on us?" George Washington allegedly "suggested a countermotion that 'no foreign enemy should invade the United States at any time, with more than three thousand troops.'"[4] Jonathan Dayton indicated that since preparations for war usually were made in peacetime, he had no objections to "restrictions consistent with these ideas."[5] Hugh Williamson thought that limiting the funds for the military would serve "as the best guard in this case."[6] The delegates unanimously rejected the motion to limit the size of the army in peacetime.

The Convention made four other decisions that strengthened national military power. First, the delegates approved Gerry's suggestion that the national government be authorized to issue "letters of marque," that is, government commissions to private ships to seize the merchant vessels of enemy nations (a normal part of naval warfare in the eighteenth century). They denied states the authority to issue these letters of marque.[7] Second, they accepted a minimal constraint on military expenditures, limiting appropriations to two years or less.[8] Gerry objected to the proposal because it "implied there was to be a standing army" which was dangerous and unnecessary.[9] Roger Sherman agreed with Gerry that there should be a reasonable restriction on the number and continuance of an army in time of peace but argued that the two-year duration of Congress made the two-year rule more practical.[10] Third, they passed up the opportunity to add language condemning a standing army. George Mason sought to strengthen the state militias by adding a statement that such support would better secure "the liberties of the people . . . against the danger of standing armies in time of peace."[11] James Madison, who used the potential danger of a standing army to emphasize the seriousness of the national crisis on June 29, supported the proposal to disapprove of a national army in peacetime.[12] Gouverneur Morris "opposed the motion as setting a dishonorable mark of distinction on the military class of Citizens."[13] The motion was defeated handily. Fourth, the delegates agreed that the national government could make laws concerning piracy, crimes at sea, the rules of military capture, and counterfeiting.[14] The delegates, then, allowed the national government substantial authority to protect national security. They were much less willing to allow that authority to intrude on the states' military prerogatives.

Domestic Rebellion and the State Militias

Inevitably, this new national military authority clashed with the determination to protect existing state militias. Some delegates wanted an effective national army prepared to quell future domestic upheavals like Shays's Rebellion. But each state already had a long-established militia, an army of citizens who could be called into military service. States cherished their militias, which helped to keep order within their and defended frontier settlements against hostile Indians. Massachusetts militiamen had fired the first shots of the American Revolution at Lexington and Concord in 1775. In South Carolina the militia served as a slave patrol. These state militias also were seen as an alternative to a permanent national army. If the military were fully nationalized, states would lose their power over the militia, as well as the appointment of militia officers, a kind of patronage appointment. Those who favored more national control of the military believed that the states had poorly prepared their militias for larger responsibilities. Edmund Randolph observed "that the Militia were every where neglected by the State Legislatures, the members of which courted popularity too much to enforce a proper discipline."[15]

The Virginia Plan's guarantee of each state's territory and its republican government authorized the national government to suppress "domestic commotions" such as Shays's Rebellion.[16] Mason argued, "If the General Government should have no right to suppress rebellions against particular States, it will be in a bad situation indeed," because domestic rebellions originated "in & against individual States." Without this authority, the national government "must remain a passive Spectator of its own subversion."[17] Luther Martin, the most jealous guardian of state power, was simply "for leaving the States to suppress Rebellions themselves."[18] Nathaniel Gorham of Massachusetts was appalled at this suggestion that the national government could not suppress domestic violence. Without this provision, "an enterprising Citizen might erect the standard of Monarchy in a particular State, might gather together partisans from all quarters, might extend his views from State to State, and threaten to establish a tyranny over the whole."[19] John Rutledge thought it unnecessary to insert any guarantee because the nature of government gave the Congress the power to subdue a rebellion, but Daniel Carroll insisted that "Some such provision is essential" to remove all doubts. The delegates modified the language, guaranteeing each state a republican government and protection against foreign and domestic violence.[20]

Would the national government need a state's permission to intervene in domestic violence inside the state? The Committee of Detail specified that the Congress had the power "[t]o subdue a rebellion in any State, on the application of its legislature." Charles Pinckney and Gouverneur Morris moved to drop the requirement that the state request assistance.[21] For Martin, this proposal to bypass the state governments gave "a dangerous & unnecessary power" to the national government.[22] Elbridge Gerry agreed with Martin: referring to Greek legend, he said he "was against letting loose the myrmidons [that is, robotic soldiers] of the United States on a State without its own consent." Gerry claimed that national government intervention in Shays's Rebellion would have made that situation worse.[23] When Oliver Ellsworth tried to find a compromise that would allow either the governor or the state legislature to request national intervention, Morris objected that a state governor himself might lead the rebellion. He emphasized, "The General Government should enforce obedience in all cases where it may be necessary."[24] Ellsworth said, "In many cases The General Government ought not to be able to interpose unless called upon," and he altered the proposal to allow the governor to request national help when the state legislature could not meet.[25] Edmund Randolph countered that this change would give Congress the power "to judge whether the State legislature can or cannot meet."[26]

The delegates finally approved Ellsworth's motion after agreeing that the clause only applied to rebellion against a state government (rather than the national government). It authorized the national government "to provide for calling forth" the state militias if needed.[27] Late in the Convention, John Dickinson tried to strike out the requirement that states invite the national government in to suppress rebellions. Jonathan Dayton said the "Conduct of Rhode Island" showed the need to permit "the power of the United States on this subject." The delegates, though, refused to make the change.[28]

The most heated dispute over national security turned on the autonomy of the state militias. The Committee of Detail proposed that Congress have the power "[t]o call forth the aid of the militia, in order to execute the laws of the Union, enforce treaties, suppress insurrections, and repel invasions" and designated the president as commander-in-chief of not only the national military but also "of the Militia of the Several States."[29] Two weeks later, Mason proposed that the national government regulate the state militias. He argued that to avoid the creation of a standing national army, the state militias needed better preparation, discipline, and supply. "Thirteen States will never concur in any one system, if the disciplining of the Militia be left in their hands," observed Mason.[30] Madison proposed national rules to regulate and discipline the militia, leaving the states the power to appoint officers; Randolph, concurring with Madison, said that "leaving the appointment of officers to the States protects the people against every apprehension that could produce murmur."[31]

This proposal for broad national control over the state militia generated strong resistance. Ellsworth complained, "The whole authority over the Militia ought by no means to be taken away from the States." The national government could not "sufficiently pervade" the country or "accommodate itself to the local genius of the people." The militia "would pine away to nothing after such a sacrifice of power." He warned that the states would never give up control of their militias, and would "never submit to the same militia laws." He remarked, "Three or four shillings as a penalty will enforce obedience better in New England, than forty lashes in some other places." Ellsworth believed that the militia should have the "same arms & exercise and be under rules established by the General Government when in actual service of the United States," but that the U.S. government should step in only when states neglect their militias.[32] Sherman argued that state militias were important for enforcing state police powers: "the States might want their Militia for defense against invasions and insurrections, and for enforcing obedience to their laws. They will not give up this point."[33] Dickinson agreed "that the States never would nor ought to give up all authority over the Militia" and proposed that the national government discipline a fraction of the state militia at a time.[34] Gerry, angered by the powers already allocated to Congress, groused, "If it be agreed to by the Convention, the plan will have as black a mark as was set on Cain."[35]

Supporters of a strong national military were frustrated with this resistance to national military supervision. General Pinckney felt that "for a part to be under the general and a part under the State Governments, would be an incurable evil. He saw no room for such distrust of the General Government."[36] For Madison, militia regulation was a natural part of "the public defense. It did not seem in its nature to be divisible between two distinct authorities." Arguing again for broad national powers, Madison observed that national officials "who had a full view of the public situation would from a sense of the danger, guard against it," while "the States would not be separately impressed with the general situation, nor have the due confidence in the concurrent exertions of each other."[37] Charles Pinckney said he had "a scanty faith in Militia," and added, "There must be also a real military force. This alone can effectually answer the purpose."[38]

Stymied again, the delegates turned the whole matter over to yet another committee, which tried to finesse the problem by providing that Congress could "make laws for organizing, arming & disciplining the Militia" and governing any part of the militia employed in national service.[39] Rufus King, a committee member, explained that the committee had walked a fine political line on this issue: "by *organizing* the Committee meant, proportioning the officers & men; by *arming*, specifying the kind, size and caliber of arms; & by *disciplining*, prescribing the manual exercise, evolutions," and so on, including the methods of furnishing weapons.[40] Now the delegates clashed over these details of state military authority. Sherman proposed to strike out Congressional authority to "prescribe" the "discipline" for training the state militia because it was unnecessary.[41] Gerry grumbled that this national authority, "as explained, is making the States drill-sergeants. He had [as willingly] let the Citizens of Massachusetts be dis-armed, as to take the command from the States, and subject them to the General Legislature. It would be regarded as a system of Despotism."[42]

Ellsworth and Sherman tried to rephrase the proposal so that the national government would lay out militia rules while leaving the implementation to the states.[43] Dayton opposed national militia rules because, he said, "In some States there ought to be a greater proportion of cavalry than in others. In some places rifles would be most proper, in others muskets," and so on.[44] Gerry again objected. A frustrated John Langdon "could not understand the jealousy expressed by some Gentlemen. The General & State Government were not enemies to each other, but different institutions for the good of the people of America.... In transferring power from" one level of government to the other, "I only take out of my left hand what it cannot so well use, and put it into my right hand where it can be better used."[45] Madison anticipated that the states would do as poor a job disciplining their militia as they had paying their requisitions: "The States neglect their Militia now.... The Discipline of the Militia is evidently a *National* concern, and ought to be provided for in the *National* Constitution."[46]

Madison tried to bypass the problem by suggesting that the national gov-ernment control the appointment of top officers. Sherman shot back that this proposal was "absolutely inadmissible."[47] The Convention defeated Madison's proposal, accepted the states' power to appoint officers, and finally accepted the language on the militia recommended by the committee.[48] Later, Sherman successfully shaved away a bit more national power by limiting the president's command over the militia to periods "when called into the actual service of the United States."[49]

War, Peace, and Treaties

The authority to make treaties involved another crucial power for the United States government: the ability to surrender territory to another country. Mason, for example, worried that the Senate already could surrender "the whole Country" with its treaty-making power; "if Spain should possess herself of Georgia, therefore, the Senate might by treaty dismember the Union."[50] James Wilson suggested that if the Senate alone could make a treaty, it could require "all the Rice of South Carolina to be sent to some one particular port."[51] The treaty power also raised practical problems for a republican government, as Nathaniel Gorham pointed out. If treaties had to go through the regular republican law-making process, the United States would experience foreign policy delays and complications, and put American officials at a great disad-vantage in international negotiations. Representatives of foreign governments would receive instructions from the leader who could approve the agreement quickly, while American negotiators would receive instructions from a president without authority to ratify the agreement.[52]

The struggle over war-making, peace-making and treaty power were complicated by the delegates' differences about the relative power of governing institutions. Compromise resulted in an ambiguous line between the war powers of the branches. The Committee of Detail gave Congress the power to enforce treaties and the "power to make war," and gave the Senate power to "make treaties, and to appoint Ambassadors."[53] Charles Pinckney objected that Congress would be too slow to make war, and that war-making power should reside in the Senate alone.[54] Pierce Butler "was for vesting the power in the President, who will have all the requisite qualities, and will not make war but when the Nation will support it."[55] Madison and Gerry proposed to reduce Congress's authority from making war to simply declaring it, thus "leaving to the Executive the power to repel sudden attacks."[56] Sherman supported the original wording because the change would narrow Congress's power too much.[57] All options troubled Mason; the president could not "be trusted with" war-making, he said, and the Senate was "not so constructed as to be entitled to it." He said he "was for clogging rather than facilitating war; but for facilitating peace."[58] The delegates agreed overwhelmingly to change "make" to "declare," a change that seemed to limit Congressional military power. Congress would make a formal declaration of war, but the president would conduct warfare.

Peace-making and treaties posed another divisive problem. "There is a material difference between the cases of making *war*, and making *peace*," Ellsworth said. "It should be more easy to get out of war, than into it. War also is a simple and overt declaration. Peace [is] attended with intricate & secret negotiations."[59] Butler proposed that Congress, and not the Senate alone, should control the peace-making process. Gerry supported the idea, fearing that a small number of Senators could agree to surrender part of the nation to a foreign power (a common occurrence in Europe).[60] The delegates rejected this motion, only to confront the problem again when they debated the treaty-making process.

Madison "observed that the Senate represented the States alone, and that for this as well as other obvious reasons it was proper that the President should be an agent in Treaties."[61] Gouverneur Morris proposed that the House and Senate together, not just the Senate, should ratify treaties that imposed binding, legal obligations on the United States.[62] Madison objected that this change would make it more difficult to require "a legal *ratification* of treaties of alliance for the purposes of war" and similar decisions.[63] Morris admitted that he wanted treaties to be hard to make, because "[t]he more difficulty in making treaties, the more value will be set on them."[64] Gorham worried about foreign diplomats in the United States, warning that treaty negotiations "will be generally influenced by two or three men, who will be corrupted by the Ambassadors here. In such a Government as ours, it is necessary to guard against the Government itself being seduced."[65] William Samuel Johnson thought it simply was absurd to provide "that the acts of a Minister with plenipotentiary powers from one Body, should depend for ratification on another Body."[66] The delegates, however, left treaty ratification in the hands of the Senate.

After Madison suggested that different kinds of treaties might be handled in different ways, the Committee on Postponed Matters recommended another compromise that required shared presidential and Senate power: "The President by & with the advice and consent of the Senate shall have power to make Treaties," and treaty approval would require an extraordinary two-thirds majority of the Senate.[67] This proposal reenergized the debate on the treaty power. Wilson moved to require House of Representatives' approval for any treaty because treaties "ought to have the sanction of laws also," a fact that outweighed the need for secrecy in treaty negotiations.[68] Sherman disagreed, believing that "the power could be safely trusted to the Senate," and noting "that the necessity of secrecy in the case of treaties forbade" the involvement of the House.[69] The delegates overwhelmingly defeated the idea of requiring House consent for treaties and agreed to the compromise on presidential treaty-making with the approval of the Senate alone.

Next, the Convention struggled to find a politically acceptable balance between making treaty approval too difficult and making it too easy. Wilson objected to the requirement for a large, two-thirds majority for approving treaties in the Senate because it "puts it in the power of a minority to control the will of a majority."[70] Agreeing with Wilson, King noted that the role of the president in checking the Senate made an extraordinary majority unnecessary.[71] Madison proposed making an exception for peace treaties, so that a simple majority vote could expedite treaties that would end hostilities. When the delegates approved this exception to the two-thirds barrier, Madison next moved to exclude the president entirely from peace treaties because "[t]he President . . . would necessarily derive so much power and importance from a state of war that he might be tempted, if authorized, to impede a treaty of peace."[72] Pierce Butler "was strenuous for" Madison's proposal "as a necessary security against ambitious & corrupt Presidents."[73] Gorham thought that Madison's precaution was not needed because "the means of carrying on the war would not be in the hands of the President, but of the Legislature."[74] Morris, who thought "the power of the President in this case harmless," also believed "that no peace ought to be made without the concurrence of the President," who represented the general interest of the nation.[75] Gerry wanted to keep a high barrier to peace treaties, which involved "the dearest interests" such as "the fisheries, territories & so on. In treaties of peace also there is more danger to the extremities of the Continent, of being sacrificed, than on any other occasions."[76] The Convention finally refused to exclude the president from peace treaties, and affirmed that a simple majority in the Senate could ratify these kinds of treaties.

The debate rekindled the next day, when King moved to reconsider the lower threshold for peace treaties. Wilson insisted on dropping the large majority for peace treaties. He cautioned, "If two thirds are necessary to make peace, the minority may perpetuate war, against the sense of the majority."[77] Gouverneur Morris agreed with Wilson, adding that the large majority for peace treaties would cause Congress to "be unwilling to make war for that reason, on account of the Fisheries or the Mississippi, the two great objects of the Union. Besides, if a Majority of the Senate be for peace, and are not allowed to make it, they will be apt to effect their purpose in the more disagreeable mode, of negativing the supplies for the war."[78] Sherman proposed to limit the Senate's power to alter the terms of the treaty that ended the Revolutionary war with Britain.[79] The Convention, however, soundly defeated the effort to strike out the two-thirds majority for any treaty.[80] Instead, the delegates reversed themselves and restored the requirement that ratification of a *peace* treaty require a two-thirds vote (while rejecting efforts to stiffen further the two-thirds requirement).[81]

The relationship with Native Americans was an afterthought at the Convention. Madison suggested national authority "[t]o regulate affairs with the Indians as well within as without the limits of the United States," and a similar provision was added with no debate.[82] Though delegates such as Sherman tenaciously protected the states' internal police powers, they did not challenge the surrender of specific powers to deal with Native Americans.

The Path of National Security and Foreign Policy

The problem of creating a national government strong enough to suppress rebellion and defend the nation, but not strong enough to suppress Americans' liberty, created a huge problem for the delegates. While they agreed on the need to empower the federal government in military and foreign affairs, they could not agree on the best way to prevent the abuse of that power. The delegates resolved the issue by substantially extending national military authority, while imposing institutional restraints on the use of that power. Their negotiations deliberately left obscure boundaries between state and national military power, and between the Congressional and presidential roles in foreign policy. Anti-Federalists raised the specter of a standing Army in the ratification debates. In *The Federalist*, Hamilton and Madison defended the indefinite national power to raise armies in the proposed Constitution.[83] Madison later would differ from

Hamilton on whether President Washington could unilaterally issue his 1793 Proclamation of Neutrality.[84]

The United States has grappled with the ambiguity of national diplomatic and military power since 1789, but the nation has not changed the Constitutional provisions for these powers. Instead, the national government has greatly strengthened the military and expanded the president's role in foreign policy without adding to its formal authority in the original Constitution.[85] After the outbreak of Civil War in 1861, but before Congress could meet to authorize his actions, President Abraham Lincoln declared Southern states in rebellion, established a naval quarantine of those states, called out the state militias, and suspended habeas corpus in Maryland. Congress later authorized most of these actions, and the courts generally upheld the exercise of emergency powers during the Civil War. Both the North and South conducted military drafts during the war (and the draft sparked a massive riot in New York City in July 1863).[86]

A series of laws enacted after the Spanish-American War transformed the state militias into the National Guard system under greater federal government control. During World War I, Woodrow Wilson expanded the national direction of military and domestic war efforts. Franklin Roosevelt further expanded national power during World War II, and since then, the United States has maintained a large, formidable, and technologically advanced military. In World Wars I and II, the Korean War, and the Vietnam War, the U.S. military used conscription to help fill its ranks. The military draft became bitterly controversial during the Vietnam War, and the U.S. military has become an all-volunteer force (though registration for the draft continues).

Both Congress and the Supreme Court have given the president wide—but not unlimited—latitude to exercise war powers. The United States has committed troops abroad hundreds of times since the 1790s, but Congress has issued a formal declaration of war in only five of these conflicts, and none since 1941.[87] Congress has authorized other military actions without a formal declaration of war, and the president has ordered even more. The Vietnam-era War Powers Resolution attempted to limit presidential power to commit troops, but its impact has largely been symbolic, in part because of the difficulty in enforcing it and also because it may not be constitutional. After the attack on the World Trade Center in 2001, President George W. Bush asserted wide-ranging presidential powers to combat terrorism with surveillance, detention, and interrogation. As a candidate, President Obama promised to scale back these powers, but in office, the Obama administration continues to claim wide-ranging powers. In early 2012, Attorney General Eric Holder declared that the U.S. government could lawfully kill American citizens without judicial sanction if administration officials determined that the citizens were planning Al Qaeda attacks on the United States and could not be captured alive.[88]

Presidents have asserted strong diplomatic powers as well, concluding many executive agreements with other nations. These agreements are easier to achieve than a formal treaty because they do not require Senate approval. There are now many more executive agreements than formal treaties. Many executive agreements address narrow issues, but others, such as the Vietnam peace accords (1973) and the Sinai agreements (1975) had a large impact on American foreign relations.[89]

‖ 17 ‖

The End Game

The delegates wanted to make it likely that the nation would ratify their Constitution and put it into effect, while making it difficult to change their Constitution after it did go into effect. For James Madison and his allies, asking the state legislatures to ratify the Constitution was a prescription for failure. If the state legislatures had the power to ratify the Constitution, it was likely that some of them would reject it. The delegates agreed to Virginia's proposal to require special state ratifying conventions. The delegates ultimately provided for four different ways to amend the Constitution. All required extraordinary majorities to succeed, and all required state approval. In contrast, the delegates made it relatively easy to add new states to the Union.

George Mason, Elbridge Gerry, and Edmund Randolph were so unhappy with the final Constitution that they refused to sign it. Many of the delegates who did sign the Constitution also expressed disappointment with it, and none expressed the view that the Constitution was the best solution to the problems they had set out to solve. Yet most of the delegates signed the Constitution because they believed all the realistic alternatives to it were far worse.

The Ratification Process

The delegates were keenly aware that it would take much effort to convince a majority of Americans to accept their Constitution.[1] George Mason, Elbridge Gerry, and Edmund Randolph previewed many of the principled objections that would be raised after the Constitution's provisions became public. They knew that the diverse, parochial problems of thirteen states would guarantee that some provisions of the Constitution would be controversial in each state. Moreover, state governments everywhere were likely to fight against losing power to a stronger national government. Ratification would bog down in one or both houses of several of the state legislatures.

The Virginia Plan addressed the last of these obstacles by proposing special state ratifying conventions that would bypass the state legislatures entirely. Popularly elected delegates to these ratifying conventions, rather than the state legislatures, would commit the state to the Constitution on behalf of the people. This special ratification process plainly was designed for political expediency, but it also aimed to place the Constitution on a foundation of public consent and to make a clean break with the Articles of Confederation. James Madison was adamant that this special, streamlined ratification process was "essential" and "indispensable" because "the new Constitution should be ratified in the most unexceptionable form, and by the supreme authority of the people themselves."[2] Pierce Butler agreed and cautioned that the state legislatures had "sworn to support the Government under which they act."[3] James Wilson warned that this ratification process was necessary to ensure that needed reforms were not "defeated by the inconsiderate or selfish opposition of a few States." Wilson hoped that the Constitution would take effect even if fewer than all thirteen states ratified it (Madison noted that the last comment was "probably meant" to frighten "the smaller States of New Jersey & Delaware. Nothing was said in reply").[4]

The plan for special ratifying conventions met immediate resistance, particularly from the narrow nationalists who sought to protect the state governments' prerogatives. Roger Sherman claimed this provision was "unnecessary" because the Articles of Confederation already had a process for approving fundamental changes—"with the assent of Congress and ratification of State Legislatures."[5] Gerry thought the special conventions were an unwise innovation for New England, where "The people . . . have, at this time, the wildest ideas of Government in the world."[6] Several delegates cited the word "perpetual" in the Articles of Confederation and insisted "upon the main principles of the confederacy"— that is, "that the several States should meet in the general Council on a footing of complete equality each claiming the right of sovereignty."[7] The decision to establish special ratifying conventions was put off.

The New Jersey Plan proposed that the Convention's work should be ratified by a unanimous vote of the state legislatures, like any other amendment to the Articles of Confederation. New Jersey's William Paterson defended this approach and rejected the idea that the Constitution could take effect without ratification by all the states. The Articles required unanimous consent, like "all treaties. What is unanimously done, must be unanimously undone."[8] Madison answered that, if the Confederation were actually a treaty, then "a breach of any one article, by any one party," dissolves the agreement—and violations of the Articles "had been numerous & notorious," with "New Jersey herself" a leading violator that "*expressly refused* to comply with a constitutional requisition of Congress."[9] Oliver Ellsworth denied that "a breach of any of the federal articles could dissolve the whole." Ellsworth disliked these ratifying conventions because "[t]hey were better fitted to pull down than to build up Constitutions."[10] Luther Martin complained that "the people have no right to do this without the consent of those to whom they have delegated their power for State purposes; through their tongue only they can speak, through their ears, only, can hear."[11]

The delegates settled the ratification issue just before they sent their work to the Committee of Detail in late July. Ellsworth moved that the state legislatures ratify the Constitution, as in the New Jersey Plan.[12] Gerry calculated that it was more dangerous to rely on state ratifying conventions than the state legislatures because the special conventions would create too much confusion. The people "would never agree on anything. He could not see any ground to suppose that the people will do what their rulers will not."[13]

But Ellsworth's opponents recited a litany of problems with ratification by state legislatures. Mason argued that the state "Legislatures have no power to ratify it. They are the mere creatures of the State Constitutions, and cannot be greater than their creators." Ratification had to depend on "the people with whom all power remains that has not been given up in the Constitutions derived from them." This doctrine was "cherished as the basis of free Government."[14] Randolph said that political pragmatism made it imperative to bypass the state legislatures:

> One idea has pervaded all our proceedings, to wit, that opposition as well from the States as from individuals, will be made to the System to be proposed. Will it not then be highly imprudent, to furnish any unnecessary pretext by the mode of ratifying it? . . . Whose opposition will be most likely to be excited against the System? That of the local demagogues who will be degraded by it from the importance they now hold. These will spare no efforts to impede that progress in the popular mind which will be necessary to the adoption of the plan, and which every member will find to have taken place in his own, if he will compare his present opinions with those brought with him into the Convention. It is of great importance therefore that the consideration of this subject should be transferred from the Legislatures where this class of men, have their full influence to a field in which their efforts can be less mischievous.[15]

Nathaniel Gorham observed, "Men chosen by the people for the particular purpose, will discuss the subject more candidly than members of the Legislature who are to lose the power which is to be given up to the General Government." State legislatures might delay ratification indefinitely. And, asked Gorham, "will any one say that all the States are to suffer themselves to be ruined, if Rhode

Island should persist in her opposition to general measures?"[16] Gouverneur Morris believed that Ellsworth "erroneously supposes" that the Convention was amending the Confederation, but claimed that "This Convention is unknown to the Confederation."[17] Rufus King praised state ratifying conventions as "the most certain means of obviating all disputes & doubts concerning the legitimacy of the new Constitution; as well as the most likely means of drawing forth the best men in the States to decide on it."[18] Madison "thought it clear that the Legislatures were incompetent to the proposed changes. . . . He considered the difference between a system founded on the Legislatures only, and one founded on the people, to be the true difference between a *league* or *treaty*, and a *Constitution*."[19]

The Convention defeated Ellsworth's motion to refer the matter to the state legislatures, and also rejected Morris's proposal for a national ratifying convention.[20] At the end of August, a few delegates tried to derail the requirement for special state ratifying conventions.[21] King, however, complained "that striking out ratifying conventions . . . was equivalent to giving up the business altogether" and encouraged the delegates to put aside their scruples about necessary changes.[22] The people, added Madison, as the source of all power, "could alter" their existing "constitutions as they pleased."[23] The delegates rejected this final effort to derail the ratifying conventions.

But how many states would be enough to ratify the Constitution and put it into effect? The Committee of Detail did not suggest a specific number, and the delegates found it very difficult to negotiate one. Wilson proposed that only seven states—a simple majority of the existing thirteen—be required "for the commencement of the plan."[24] Randolph proposed nine states be required as "a respectable majority of the whole" and a number used to pass important issues in the Confederation Congress.[25] Roger Sherman suggested ten states be required.[26] Daniel Carroll proposed that all thirteen states ratify before the Constitution take effect.[27] Madison worried that the small states might ratify and leave larger states behind. Gouverneur Morris, who was concerned about the possibility that key states like New York would refuse to ratify, wanted a larger number in case the states that did ratify were small and dispersed.[28] Wilson answered, "The House on fire must be extinguished, without a scrupulous regard to ordinary rights."[29]

Determined to prevent states with a minority of the population from ratifying the Constitution, Madison proposed that ratification would be completed with the agreement of seven states that together would have at least a majority of the seats in the new House of Representatives. This formula would assure the "concurrence of a majority of both the States and people."[30] Sherman did not think it was proper to allow "less than all the States to execute the Constitution" and speculated that "Perhaps all the States may concur, and on that supposition it is needless to hold out a breach of faith."[31] After more discussion, Sherman and

Jonathan Dayton proposed ten states, and Wilson and George Clymer coun-tered with "requiring a majority both of the people and of States."[32] The Conven-tion finally adopted the threshold of nine states for ratification, and all the states but Maryland accepted this number.[33]

During these discussions, John Dickinson raised another question: did the Confederation Congress also have to approve the Constitution?[34] The existing Congress might recommend changes or even kill it before it reached the states, ruining the Convention's arduous work. The Committee of Detail recommended that the Constitution include specific language that "This Constitution shall be laid before the United States in Congress assembled for their approbation" before being submitted to the states.[35] As soon as the delegates began to discuss this provision, Gouverneur Morris and Charles Pinckney "moved to strike out the words 'for their approbation,'" so that Congress could not block the Consti-tution's adoption by refusing to approve it. The Convention approved this change without debate.[36]

A week before the end of the Convention, Gerry moved to reconsider the issue. Bypassing Congress was "improper" and would offend Congress, said Gerry, who "urged the indecency and pernicious tendency of dissolving in so slight a manner, the solemn obligations of the Articles of Confederation."[37] Alex-ander Hamilton agreed with Gerry that Congressional approval was "a necessary ingredient in the transaction."[38] But an exasperated Wilson vehemently dis-agreed, declaring, "After spending four or five months in the laborious & arduous task of forming a Government for our Country, we are ourselves at the close throwing insuperable obstacles in the way of its success."[39] King doubted that if Congress refused to approve the Constitution, the state legislatures would sub-mit the plan to ratifying conventions, "and all our labor be lost."[40] King suggested a solution, that "it would be more respectful to Congress to submit the plan gen-erally to them" rather than in a form that required them to accept or reject it, and Sherman agreed.[41] The delegates rejected the effort to restore a veto role for the existing Congress. They published a separate set of resolutions laying out the transition from the Confederation to the new government (see appendix 2).[42]

Amendments

The prospect that the Constitution could be amended in the future made it easier for delegates to accept an imperfect plan. During the heated debate on the New Jersey Plan, George Mason appealed to its proponents, saying that "we cannot form a perfect System. There will be faults. We can trust our successors with farther amendments."[43] Some of the delegates initially doubted that they should make any provision for changing their Constitution after it took effect.

Charles Pinckney did not think it was proper or necessary.[44] For Gerry, though, "The novelty & difficulty of the experiment requires periodical revision." Gerry also pointed out that state constitutions provided for amendments.[45] The delegates postponed the discussion for the time being. The following week, several members again failed to "see the necessity" for amendments, or the Virginia proposal that amendments bypass the new Congress.[46] Again, George Mason urged the need for some way to correct the inevitable problems in the Constitution, saying it would be better to establish a process for amendment "in an easy, regular and Constitutional way than to trust to chance and violence."[47] The delegates approved the idea of Constitutional amendments in principle.[48]

In late August, the Convention took up the Committee of Detail's proposal for amending the Constitution. If two-thirds of the states formally requested amending the Constitution, Congress would call a special national "Convention for that purpose."[49] The delegates agreed to this state-driven process without debate, although Gouverneur Morris suggested that Congress have the power to call for such a Convention "whenever they please."[50] A week before the end of the Convention, Elbridge Gerry moved to reconsider this process, worried that a simple majority of the states at any future constitutional convention could "bind the Union to innovations that may subvert the State Constitutions altogether."[51] Hamilton also sought to reconsider the process; he sought an "easy mode" for "supplying defects which will probably appear in the new System" and worried that in the process approved, the state legislatures would only apply for changes "to increase their own powers."[52] Madison simply thought the process was too unclear.[53] Sherman proposed a second option, allowing Congress to propose amendments, but requiring the consent of "the several States" before the amendments took effect.[54]

This proposal opened questions similar to those raised by ratification: how many states would be required to ratify amendments? The Convention narrowly rejected a rule allowing two-thirds of the states to ratify amendments and unanimously approved a higher, more difficult threshold of three-quarters of the states.[55] Madison now proposed four options for amending the Constitution. Amendments could be proposed by either two-thirds of the House and Senate or by two-thirds of the state legislatures; these proposed amendments, in turn, could then be ratified either by three-fourths of the state legislatures, or by special state ratifying conventions.[56] Mason thought this plan was "exceptionable and dangerous" because it gave Congress too important a role.[57] To accommodate Mason's concern and ensure that Congress would not stand in the way of amendments desired by the people, the Convention changed the rule so that a Constitutional Convention would be required if two-thirds of the states applied for one.[58] Sherman tried to change the rule for state ratification so that future authors of amendments could, like the present Convention, set the margin for state approval at a level thought appropriate, rather than at three-fourths. Gerry sought to eliminate the provisions allowing state ratifying conventions, thus requiring the state legislatures to participate in any Constitutional amendments.[59] Both motions failed.

Even this demanding amendment process was not enough security for some delegates. South Carolina's John Rutledge, concerned about the carefully constructed compromise protecting the slave trade until 1808, refused to agree to any process that would amend the slave-trade bargain. Sherman proposed that no amendment could change the Constitutional ban on a law against the slave trade before 1808.[60] When the delegates approved this provision, Sherman next proposed that no Constitutional amendment could interfere with state police powers or remove the equal representation of the states in the U.S. Senate. The delegates rejected the protection of police powers, but added the provision that the equal apportionment of Senate seats could not be amended in the future.[61]

New States

Acts of Congress, not Constitutional amendments, would formally add new states to the Union. But these new states would add new members to Congress and cast additional electoral votes for president. New states would bring new interests into Congress and the selection of the president. New states, in short, could drastically change the balance of political power in the new government. The steady growth of western population would soon increase the pressure for statehood in the Southwest Territory and the Ohio Valley. Would these new states be admitted as equals of the original thirteen states? There was considerable opposition to allowing new Western states to join the union as equals, partly because their voting power in Congress would grow (see chapter 12), and partly because they could burden the national government with new state debts and other problems.

The Committee of Detail recommended that the admission of new states require a two-thirds vote of Congress. New states would be admitted on the same terms as existing states, but Congress could set conditions on the way the prior public debts of these states would be handled at admission.[62] When the Convention debated this provision, Gouverneur Morris still resisted admitting Western states on an equal basis.[63] But Madison insisted "that the Western States neither would nor ought to submit to a Union which degraded them from an equal rank with the other States."[64] Mason advised that "the best policy is to treat them with that equality which will make them friends not enemies."[65] The Convention eliminated the two-thirds vote for admission, but also refused to adopt the guarantee that "the new States shall be admitted on the same terms with the original

States."[66] The national government could prepare the way for these new states by developing the framework of laws in the territories.[67]

Imperfections and Signing

Of the delegates who attended the final session of the Constitutional Convention, three—George Mason, Elbridge Gerry, and Edmund Randolph—refused to sign the final Constitution. On August 31, Mason declared "that he would sooner chop off his right hand than put it to the Constitution as it now stands" and indicated that he would urge a second Constitutional Convention if some unsettled issues were decided "improperly."[68] Randolph expressed the hope that the state ratifying conventions could propose amendments to a second Constitutional Convention.[69] He later complained that the republican propositions he had introduced at the start of the Convention had "much to his regret been widely, and in his opinion, irreconcilably, departed from."[70] On the last full day of debate, Randolph again proposed a second Constitutional Convention and threatened to withhold his signature if it were not approved.[71] Mason seconded Randolph's motion and also threatened not to sign the Constitution, criticizing "the dangerous power and structure of the Government, concluding that it would end either in monarchy, or a tyrannical aristocracy."[72] The delegates rejected the idea despite this ultimatum.[73]

Mason, Gerry, and Randolph each explained their reasons for refusing to sign the Constitution. All three of these large – state delegates complained about aspects of the Senate. Mason protested the absence of a bill of rights, and complained about battles he had lost at the Convention: the lack of a presidential council, the Senate's influence in money bills, the provision that treaties would be the supreme law of the land, and the prohibition on Congress's power to ban the slave trade for 20 years. For Mason, the "necessary and proper" clause allowed members of Congress to "extend their powers as far as they shall think proper; so that the State legislatures have no security for the powers now presumed to remain to them, or the people for their rights."[74] Mason and Randolph agreed that the House of Representatives was too small, that commercial treaties were too easy to pass, that the boundary between national and state authority was too vague, that states could not tax their own exports, and that the President could pardon those convicted of treason. Like Mason, Gerry feared national authority, and thought Congress could "make what laws they may please to call necessary and proper." He complained specifically that the national government could establish monopolies. Gerry objected to the vice presidency and the lack of a guarantee of jury trials. He disliked the national power to "raise armies and money without limit," the three-fifths compromise on slave representation, Massachusetts's underrepresentation in the House, and Congress's power over its own elections and compensation. Like Mason, Randolph complained that state legislative and judicial prerogatives were insufficiently safe. Randolph also believed it was too easy to override a presidential veto and did not like the provision allowing Congress to quell an uprising when the state executive asked it to do so.[75]

Though many other delegates also were disappointed with the final Constitution, thirty-nine *did* sign it on September 17. Not a single delegate left written evidence that, in private, he was perfectly satisfied with the Constitution he signed. These signers believed, however, that the Constitution came close enough to their aspirations, and that they had no practical alternative but to bring the document forward and fight for its ratification.

The delegates who signed the Constitution expressed many doubts about it. In mid-August, an impatient George Washington wrote that "it is the best that can be obtained at the present moment under such diversity of ideas as prevail."[76] Alexander Hamilton thought it "better than nothing."[77] Charles Pinckney was troubled by the criticisms of "members so respectable" as Gerry, Randolph, and Mason, but believed that a second Constitutional Convention would result in "[n]othing but confusion & contrariety." He objected to the weakness of the presidency, and the ease of passing commercial laws, but, "apprehending the danger of a general confusion, and an ultimate decision by the Sword, he should give the plan his support."[78] Hugh Williamson "did not think a better plan was to be expected and had no scruples against putting his name to it."[79]

When Mason suggested a second Constitutional Convention, Gouverneur Morris shot back that he, too, "had long wished for another Convention, that will have the firmness to provide a vigorous Government, which we are afraid to do."[80] But Morris, "considering the present plan as the best that was to be attained," would "take it with all its faults." Once the Constitution became public, doubts would be laid aside and "the great question will be, shall there be a national Government or not? And this must take place or a general anarchy will be the alternative."[81] While "there are several parts of this constitution which I do not at present approve," Benjamin Franklin admitted, "I am not sure I shall never approve them." He observed that "when you assemble a number of men to have the advantage of their joint wisdom, you inevitably assemble with those men, all their prejudices, their passions, their errors of opinion, their local interests, and their selfish views. . . . Thus I consent, Sir, to this Constitution because I expect no better, and because I am not sure, that it is not the best."[82] Other delegates agonized over its shortcomings in letters and notes.[83]

Even signing the Constitution required political maneuvering. Besides Mason, Gerry, and Randolph, other delegates seemed reluctant to write their names on the document. Franklin proposed a clever political trick to overcome their qualms. He moved that the signatures follow a statement that the Constitution was unanimously approved by "*the States* present ... In Witness whereof we have hereunto subscribed our names.'"[84] The delegates would sign the Constitution, therefore, to vouch that the *states* with representatives in the chamber consented to it, not to endorse it personally. Gouverneur Morris had written this motion "in order to gain the dissenting members" (Gerry said that he viewed the proposal as "leveled at himself and the other gentlemen who meant not to sign").[85] Ten states of the eleven state delegations present voted for Franklin's political ploy.[86] This subterfuge failed to sway Randolph, Mason, and Gerry, but it persuaded North Carolina's William Blount to sign.[87] This phrasing allowed Alexander Hamilton to sign on behalf of the state of New York, even though the rules for New York's delegates denied him the authority to act alone on behalf of the state. One delegate whose name appears on the document, John Dickinson, was not even in the room when the delegates signed it (he had asked his Delaware colleague, George Read, to sign the Constitution for him).[88]

Madison wrote, "The members then proceeded to sign the instrument."[89] The framers summarized their thinking at the close of the Convention, in their collective letter to accompany the Constitution as they sent it to the Confederation Congress (see appendix 2).[90] This letter embodied the idealism, the anguish, the ambiguity, the political concerns, and the hopes that permeated the Convention from start to finish.

The Uncertainties That Remained

Three uncertainties about the Constitution troubled the delegates as they concluded their work. First, the delegates did not know whether the states would ratify the Constitution. Several delegates had warned that one particular provision or another would make the Constitution unacceptable in their states. Gerry constantly warned that a provision under discussion would torpedo ratification in New England. Luther Martin told his fellow Maryland delegate, Daniel of St. Thomas Jenifer, "I'll be hanged if ever the people of Maryland agree to it" (Jenifer responded, "I advise you ... to stay in Philadelphia lest you should be hanged").[91] By the time the delegates were ready to sign the Constitution, Mason, Gerry, and Randolph had provided a preview of the criticisms that would be used to hammer the Constitution.[92]

Second, the delegates could not be sure that the new government would actually work. As early as June, Rufus King advised that "we were refining too much in this business."[93] In the late July discussion of presidential electors, both Caleb Strong of Massachusetts and Pierce Butler of South Carolina warned that the delegates were making the government too complex.[94] As the delegates patched together institutions, Madison, a master of institutional complexity, cautioned,

"The Senate was formed on the model of that of Maryland, [and] the Revisionary check, on that of New York. What the effect of a union of these provisions might be, could not be foreseen."[95] Madison privately wrote Thomas Jefferson in September: "I hazard an opinion nevertheless that the plan, should it be adopted, will neither effectually answer its national object, nor prevent the local mischiefs which everywhere excite disgusts against the State Governments."[96]

Third, even if the Constitution were ratified and worked reasonably well, the delegates could not be sure how long it would endure. After the Connecticut Compromise, William Blount wrote, "I must confess not withstanding all I heard in favor of this System, . . . I still think we shall ultimately end [in] not many years [and] just be separate and distinct Governments."[97] In early August, Madison objected to a ratio of one U.S. Representative to every 40,000 inhabitants (later reduced to 30,000) because it would result in too many U.S. Representatives as the population increased.[98] Nathaniel Gorham scoffed, "It is not to be supposed that the Government will last so long as to produce this effect. Can it be supposed that this vast Country including the Western territory will 150 years hence remain one nation?"[99]

The Path of Constitutional Acceptance and Development

The Confederation Congress debated the Constitution less than two weeks after receiving it. Congress debated it for two days, and Madison, King, and William Samuel Johnson—all members of Congress as well as delegates—fended off efforts to add amendments to the Constitution. Instead, Congress sent it to the states for submission to state ratifying conventions.

Mason's objections were widely circulated and used by opponents of ratification, who supporters of the Constitution described as "Anti-Federalists" (supporters were described as "federalists").[100] The Anti-Federalists had a wide range of viewpoints about the Constitution, as well as a wide range of interests. Anti-Federalist opponents in the Pennsylvania ratifying convention, or Patrick Henry in the Virginia convention, or pseudonymous authors like "Brutus," "Cato," or "The Federal Farmer," presented a wide range of principled and practical objections.[101]

Ratifying conventions in Delaware, Pennsylvania, and New Jersey approved the Constitution by the end of 1787. Georgia, Connecticut, Massachusetts, Maryland, and South Carolina ratified early in 1788, and New Hampshire became the ninth state to ratify in June. The key ratification fights now focused on Virginia and New York; realistically, without these states, the success of the Constitution was doubtful. Madison helped lead the ratification fight in Virginia, which narrowly approved the Constitution on June 25, 1788. A month later in New York, where *The Federalist* essays were only part of intense debates, ratification succeeded only by a close margin. In addition to the states that submitted a list of amendments along with ratification, New York called for a second Constitutional Convention. North Carolina did not ratify until 1789, and Rhode Island in 1790. By that time, the nation had selected George Washington as its first president, and Congress had begun its work. Most Anti-Federalists acquiesced to the Constitution when it was legally ratified. Almost all agreed to work within its boundaries once it was implemented.[102]

Over 11,000 proposals to amend the Constitution have been introduced in Congress since then. Most of these proposals never received enough support for Congressional approval. Twenty-seven amendments have been sent to the states and ratified. Six amendments were sent to the states but failed to win ratification. The Equal Rights Amendment, protecting the rights of men and women equally, fell three states short of ratification when it expired in 1982. Only sixteen of the required thirty-eight states ratified the District of Columbia Voting Rights Amendment by its 1985 expiration, the measure that would have given the District voting members in the U.S. House and Senate.[103]

Thirty-seven states joined the Union between 1791 and 1959. None successfully have seceded. The framers had made no provision for secession from the union. When Southern states did try to secede in 1860–1861, Abraham Lincoln asserted that, "in contemplation of universal law and of the Constitution the Union of these States is perpetual . . . no State upon its own mere motion can lawfully get out of the Union."[104] This secession of eleven states marked the most serious constitutional crisis in American history.[105] A Constitution that had been implemented without bloodshed survived intact because Lincoln's interpretation of the Constitution prevailed in war.

‖ 18 ‖

A Republic, If You Can Keep It

As James Madison concluded his Convention notes, he reported:

> Whilst the last members were signing it, Doctor Franklin, looking towards the President's Chair, at the back of which a rising sun happened to be painted, observed to a few members near him, that Painters had found it difficult to distinguish in their art a rising from a setting sun. I have, said he, often and often in the course of the Session, and the vicissitudes of my hopes and fears as to its issue, looked at that behind the President without being able to tell whether it was rising or setting: But now at length I have the happiness to know that it is a rising and not a setting Sun.[1]

In a letter to his sister, Benjamin Franklin wrote, "We have however done our best and it must take its chance."[2] It was said that, outside Independence Hall, "A lady asked Dr. Franklin, 'Well Doctor what have we got, a republic or a monarchy?' 'A republic,' replied the Doctor, 'if you can keep it.'"[3]

The framers' Constitution could have turned out differently. The Convention likely would have failed, or produced a Constitution that could not be ratified, if the broad nationalists had abandoned the Convention after the final vote on the Connecticut Compromise, or if the narrow nationalists had followed the New York delegates who left, or if the conditional nationalists representing South Carolina and Georgia had walked out because of the slave issue. The Convention could have produced a Constitution with some significantly different provisions. Madison's coalition might have held together long enough to win the critical July 14 vote on a form of proportional representation in the Senate. On that vote, Nathaniel Gorham of Massachusetts was absent, and in his absence Elbridge Gerry and Caleb Strong decided Massachusetts's vote against modified proportional representation in the Senate.[4] If the delegates had accepted proportional representation in both the Senate and the House, the broad nationalists would have been more likely to win votes on other Constitutional provisions. Other close votes made a difference. The Convention closely divided on proposals to allow members of Congress to serve in executive branch offices; had legislators been able to do so, the U.S. government would have had some of the characteristics of a parliamentary system. But these things did not happen.

What Drove the Constitution's Design?

This book shows how the delegates' intertwined aspirations and interests shaped the U.S. Constitution. Ideals, negotiations, the clash of broad and narrow nationalism, and the sequence of the Convention's choices shaped its provisions.

Ideas and Interests

It is impossible to separate the framers' ideals and interests. The delegates championed principles that usually matched their political goals. Madison showed a resolute dedication to a republican national government throughout the Convention, and the Virginia Plan reflected this dedication; but the Virginia Plan also corresponded to Virginia's interests and Madison's ambitions. Roger Sherman and other narrow nationalists insisted that fairness required equal state representation in the Senate; but they also had an interest in protecting their states' existing influence and authority. Ideas and interests together drove the intense politics of the Convention.

Politics

The Constitution is built on compromises engineered by accomplished political leaders who had thrived in the republican politics that American independence set free. Their negotiations produced a document that thirty-nine of them endorsed. No such agreement would have occurred without major and minor political agreements and concessions throughout.

The delegates fully understood that future politicians would use the government they were building. These future politicians would use their skills to assemble majority coalitions by shrewdly framing problems and structuring choices. They would deftly use persuasion, rhetoric, pressure, threats, ambiguous wording, and deals to keep these coalitions together—just as the framers had done. The Convention sought a government ruled by majorities, knowing that some of the future politicians would build majorities for unscrupulous purposes. Farrand's *Records* show that the delegates constantly reminded each other about the way politicians would exploit this or that provision to pursue selfish goals, to "intrigue" and "cabal."[5]

Put another way, the delegates aspired to build an effective republican national government and aimed to make it safe. They endeavored to filter the energy of direct democracy through institutions only indirectly influenced by
popular demands. They aimed to protect the interests of their individual states
and regions, and to produce a Constitution that the states would ratify and that
harmonized with their ideals about the way government *should* work.

Broad and Narrow Nationalism

Two different policy strategies organized many of the conflicts of ideas and interests in the Convention. James Madison, James Wilson, Gouverneur Morris,
Alexander Hamilton, Rufus King, and their allies advocated a broad nationalism
that aimed to give the reconstituted national government expansive authority
and reduce the states to a minor role in American governance. The Virginia Plan,
authored largely by Madison, proposed a broad nationalist agenda: proportional
representation in both houses of a bicameral legislature, broad national economic and military authority, and a veto over state laws. Other delegates, including Roger Sherman, Oliver Ellsworth, William Paterson, Luther Martin, and
Gunning Bedford, were just as determined to maintain as many existing state
government powers as possible and to grant only limited authority to the
national government. These narrow nationalists immediately questioned the
Virginia Plan, and by mid-June introduced their own alternative agenda, the New
Jersey Plan, which aimed to protect equal state representation in the national
legislature and to authorize only a restricted range of new national powers.

These two strategies collided again and again, over proportional representation
in Congress, the national veto of state laws, the relative power of the Senate and the
president, the ratification process, and specific areas of authority such as commerce,
the military, and economic development. Neither strategy decisively defeated the
other. Indeed, a number of swing delegates voted with the broad nationalists on
some issues and the narrow nationalists on others. Key Southern delegates initially
were conditional "broad nationalists"—that is, they supported Madison's plan for
broad national authority on the condition that seats in the new Congress were apportioned on the basis of population, a formula that seemed to protect Southern
interests. Once the Connecticut Compromise created a Senate that distilled Southern votes in Congress, delegates from South Carolina demanded adequate representation in the House and protections for slavery and state policy authority.

The Sequence of Constitutional Choice

Constitutional design was incremental, the product of an evolving web of
agreements about who each branch would represent, what influence each institution would wield in policy-making, and what new authority the national

government would have. The delegates quickly embraced a national government with separate legislative, executive, and judicial branches, and they agreed to a bicameral legislature. Early on, the delegates settled on the basic method for electing the House and agreed that the state legislatures would choose the Senate. But they could not agree on the proportional representation in the House of Representatives until late June, or the apportionment of the Senate until mid-July. They did not begin serious work on national authority until August, and only settled on the method for selecting the president and appointing judges in September.

These incremental steps ensured that the framing of the Constitution was a cumulative process. Early decisions influenced later ones. Once they won a Senate based on equal representation of the states, the advocates of narrow nationalism fought for Senate power. Once the broad nationalists lost the battle for a proportionally based Senate, many fought for a strong and independent presidency, while some (like Randolph) fought for House control of national spending and revenues. The United States Constitution, then, is not the product of a careful plan, but rather the cumulative by-product of a sequence of political negotiations and compromises. The result was not foreordained. No delegate viewed the result as a perfect answer to their original aspirations.

The Results of the Constitutional Convention

The framers created a national government with the authority to lead the nation into its future, while they armed the states and ambitious officials with the means to defend existing governing arrangements. Both broad and narrow nationalists wanted and got a national government with more power than the Confederation, including the power to tax, to defend the nation, and to govern commerce between the United States and other countries. The broad nationalists won a House of Representatives based on proportional representation, as well as an independent executive and ambiguous language that would allow the national government to push for more power on a case-by-case basis. The narrow nationalists limited the initial reach of this national power and ensured that the states would retain substantial authority to govern themselves. They also added some defensive weapons, such as equal representation in the Senate, that states could use to hold off the accretion of power by the national government.

As the Convention wore on, the delegates grew less certain about the consequences of their accumulating agreements. Especially after the Connecticut Compromise, they strengthened the institutions that were most likely to defend their interests. While they did not agree on the precise limits of national government authority, they did agree that by building separate defenses for their favored institutions, they could reduce the risk that the national government would harm their constituents. The narrow nationalists fought for a powerful Senate, because small and large states would have an equal vote in the Senate. Several of the broad nationalists fought for an independent and influential executive, because they viewed this institution as the most likely vehicle for the active pursuit of national interest. The slave states sought favorable rules of representation in the House and limits on national authority to harm slavery. Those broad nationalists who had helped write the Connecticut Compromise fought to ensure House predominance in taxes and spending.

This logic produced a government of separate institutions, each with the will and ability to defend its independence. The Senate received unique powers that the House did not share: the power to ratify treaties, to consent to presidential appointees, and to hold impeachment trials. The House gained nominal authority to initiate revenue measures. The president received substantial influence over the policy agenda, major appointments, and foreign affairs. Courts gained more power to construe state and potentially national laws. The Convention rejected efforts to ensure more formal collaboration among these institutions in the national policy-making process. The delegates refused to create a privy council that included legislators, refused to allow U.S. Representatives and Senators to serve in executive offices, and refused to allow judges to join the president in exercising the veto.

In this way, the Constitution created an ingenious national government of separated institutions *sharing* powers, as political scientist Richard Neustadt put it. The president's veto and agenda-setting powers make the executive a part of the legislative process; Congress's budget and oversight powers make it part of the executive process.[6] They invented a new concept of shared state and national sovereignty, creating a compound republic in which the state and national governments shared the most fundamental powers of government, even "the sword and the purse."

They produced a government in which majorities ruled, but which made it very hard actually to construct majorities and govern actively. The national government had potentially strong powers, but the framers ensured that these powers would be very difficult to use in the absence of an extraordinarily large majority of public support. As the delegates armed institutions with more autonomy, they gradually built a complex government with a cumbersome policy-making process. Making national policy usually would be difficult and time-consuming, because it had to survive a gauntlet of different institutions, each intentionally anchored to different constituencies, electoral calendars, and powers. Different majorities, representing somewhat different constituencies, would have to be built in the House and the Senate, and yet these two houses of Congress would have to come to total agreement on legislation. The president, chosen by yet another different group of voters, could veto the law. If the law survived a veto, it could be challenged in court, and the Supreme Court, appointed by past presidents as well as the incumbent, might rule that the law was invalid. Congress would declare war, but the president would wage war.

Gouverneur Morris expressed frustration with this evolving system: "We first form a strong man to protect us, and at the same time wish to tie his hands behind him."[7] Madison turned Morris's frustration into a positive feature of the Constitution in *The Federalist* Number 51:

> In order to lay a due foundation for that separate and distinct exercise of the different powers of government, which to a certain extent is admitted on all hands to be essential to the preservation of liberty, it is evident that each department should have a will of its own; and consequently should be so constituted that the members of each should have as little agency as possible in the appointment of the members of the others.
>
> ... Were the executive magistrate, or the judges, not independent of the legislature in this particular, their independence in every other would be merely nominal. But the great security against a gradual concentration of the several powers in the same department, consists in giving to those who administer each department the necessary constitutional means and personal motives to resist encroachments of the others. The provision for defense must in this, as in all other cases, be made commensurate to the danger of attack. Ambition must be made to counteract ambition. The interest of the man must be connected with the constitutional rights of the place.[8]

These institutional features were not the product of abstract, dispassionate, and systematic reasoning process, as Madison's essay can imply. Rather, Madison was rationalizing a Constitution built on the core aspirations of a stronger republican national government, and produced incrementally through a process of negotiation and compromise.

The Enduring Republic

Constitution-making in 1787 was a profoundly human process, and it tested all the political skills that the framers brought to Philadelphia. For all their improvisations, and compromises, they produced a path-breaking republican Constitution for the nation, a government charter so forward-looking that it influenced constitutional thought around the world.[9] Government authority was derived from the American people, and government institutions that could harm the people were designed to check one another. The nation's leader could be deposed and replaced through an orderly process.

The enduring achievements of the Convention's Constitution are remarkable. Before the Constitution, republican governments had been rare and fragile, but the Constitution laid the foundation for a strong and durable republican government for a large nation. Through its history, the United States has held regular elections, even during the Civil War and World Wars. Transitions of power from one leader to the next have been peaceful. The Constitution has withstood a huge expansion and diversification of the nation's population and physical area. While federalism has evolved and national government power greatly expanded, the states retain a significant role in governing the nation. The United States government maintains a standing military so large that it would stun every delegate in the Convention Hall—and deeply trouble many of them.

The Constitution has accommodated vast changes in the rules for American government. Important amendments have made formal changes in the Constitution, adding a Bill of Rights, expanding democracy, making an effort to protect African Americans and ensure rights against the states, and authorizing the income tax. But these explicit amendments are overshadowed by the changes that have taken place without any formal, written alteration of the Constitution at all. The organization of politics by political parties, the rise of interest groups, the expansion of national economic and military power, the development of much more complex intergovernmental relations, the increasing power of the president, the role of the Supreme Court as a referee of the Constitution's meaning, and many other changes are the product of political developments that work within the framework of the Constitution's original words. Indeed, in the case of the Bill of Rights, the vote for women, alcohol prohibition, and the income tax, Constitutional amendments validated changes that already had gained a strong foothold in American culture.

The Original Compromise

The framers' Constitution was deliberately unfinished, an incomplete framework for the future play of republican politics. The framers' compromises left many major issues unsettled. What exactly was the limit of national government authority, and what did the states control that the national government could not? What were the limits of presidential power? How much direct influence could the people exercise over the government? What was the meaning of citizenship? Who could be considered a citizen? What rights and duties did citizenship entail?

The records of the Constitutional Convention show indefinite words and phrases, rather than clear bright lines, mark the frontiers of national and state power and the powers of the main branches of the national government. Words like "slavery" and "judicial review" never even appear in the Constitution, but their impact on the Constitution is clear in the Convention debates. Some delegates, like George Mason, called attention to these ambiguities and condemned the Constitution because of them. But the people's conventions ratified the Constitution with all these ambiguities in place.

The framers, like many politicians before and since, left these ambiguities to be worked out in the future, through negotiation and compromise within the political rules they drafted. They were sure that there were going to be enormous changes—though they could not be sure about the nature of these changes, and they could not agree about the best way to steer them. The Constitution was designed to structure vigorous, evolving politics—not to fix all specific boundaries for all time.

This political truth *is* the original meaning of the Constitution: the framers left it to us to determine what is necessary and proper for the general welfare, and to determine the answer politically, within the general rules laid out in the document. Political leaders have struggled to gain advantage by pushing on these boundaries ever since the Constitution took effect. Both conservatives and liberals, for example, have defended federalism or "states' rights" when it has suited their political objectives. Both liberals and conservatives have insisted on nationalizing policy when it achieves a substantive outcome they seek.[10] The framers, all republicans, certainly anticipated and implicitly sanctioned these struggles. Republican politics, not the etymology of the Constitution's words, have determined the meaning of the Constitution's provisions.

The Unfinished Republic

The Constitutional Convention records prove that the framers were both idealistic and practical politicians who sustained a resolute optimism about their nation despite, or even because of, their personal political experience, forged in bare-knuckle republican politics. Nobility surfaced in the Convention debates, a nobility that I believe is inherent (though not always triumphant) in collective political reasoning on occasions of momentous public choice.

Americans inherit an unfinished republic. To keep their republic, Americans must better understand the logic behind it and appreciate much better that its authority derives from its citizens. American citizenship requires Americans to engage in politics. The enduring Constitution—and the enduring questions the Constitutional Convention confronted—still challenge Americans. In a time filled with uncertainly and conflict, their best hope is to rediscover and to renew the framers' pragmatic political idealism.

Appendix 1

CHRONOLOGICAL SEQUENCE OF CONSTITUTIONAL CONVENTION DECISIONS

May 14 (M): Date fixed for the Convention; too few delegates have arrived to begin.

May 25 (F): Convention begins.

May 28 (M): Convention approves its rules of procedure.

May 29 (Th): Virginia Plan proposed.

May 30 (W): Convention meets as Committee of the Whole, approves a national government with three branches.

June 1 (F): Debate on national executive.

June 2 (Sa): Committee of the Whole approves an executive chosen by the legislature for seven years; debates removal of executive, and an executive consisting of more than one person.

June 4 (M): Committee of the Whole approves a one-person executive, and an executive veto of legislation, requiring a two-thirds vote in both houses to override; rejects veto cast jointly by the executive and judiciary.

June 5 (Tu): Committee of the Whole approves a national judiciary with a supreme and lesser courts; approves admission of new states; transition to a new national government and provision for constitutional amendments.

June 6 (W): Committee of the Whole approves direct election of Representatives; rejects adding the judiciary to the executive veto of Congressional acts.

June 7 (Th): Committee of the Whole approves election of Senate by state legislatures.

June 8 (F): Committee of the Whole rejects a broader national power to veto state laws.

June 9 (Sa): Committee of the Whole rejects plan for presidential selection by state executives; debates proportional representation in Congress.

June 11 (M): Committee of the Whole approves proportional representation in House and Senate, guarantee of republican government to each state, requirement that state officials take oaths to support the Constitution.

June 12 (Tu): Committee of the Whole approves ratification by the people of the states, a two-year term for representatives, seven-year term for senators, fixed compensation for legislators.

June 13 (W): Committee of the Whole approves Virginia Plan as amended.

June 14 (Th): New Jersey Plan proposed; delegates adjourn to consider it.

June 15 (F): New Jersey Plan debated.

June 16 (Sa): New Jersey Plan debated.

June 18 (M): Hamilton speech and plan.

June 19 (Tu): Convention rejects New Jersey Plan; takes up amended Virginia Plan.

June 20 (W): Convention approves a new government with "a supreme legislative, Executive and Judiciary."

June 21 (Th): Convention approves a bicameral legislature, and direct election of the members of the House of Representatives for a two-year term.

June 22 (F): Convention debates House compensation, disqualification from other offices; approves minimum age of 25 for Representatives.

June 23 (Sa): Convention debates House compensation; approves disqualification of Representatives from other national offices.

June 25 (M): Charles Pinckney speech; Convention approves election of senators by state legislatures, and a minimum age of 30 for senators.

June 26 (Tu): Convention debates compensation for senators, approves a six-year term for senators, disqualification of senators from other national offices.

June 27 (W): Luther Martin speech.

June 28 (R): Convention debates proportional apportionment of seats in the House of Representatives.

June 29 (F): Convention debates proportional apportionment of seats in the House of Representatives; rejects equal representation of states in the House, accepts proposition for a different apportionment of seats.

June 30 (Sa): Convention debates apportionment of seats in the Senate.

July 2 (M): Convention deadlocks on equal apportionment of Senate seats, appoints a committee to resolve issue.

July 5 (Th): Committee reports "Connecticut" (or "Great") Compromise: proportional representation in House, equal state representation in Senate, House origination of money bills.

July 6 (F): Convention appoints a committee of five members to apportion House seats in the first Congress; approves House origination of money bills.

July 7 (Sa): Convention debates representation of states in the Senate; provisional vote in favor of equal representation.

July 9 (M): Committee of five recommends apportionment of fifty-six seats in the first House of Representatives; Convention appoints a new committee of eleven members to apportion House seats in the first Congress.

July 10 (Tu): Committee of eleven members recommends apportionment of sixty-five House seats in the first Congress.

July 11 (W): Convention debates apportionment of House seats and a periodic census of population to adjust apportionment.

July 12 (Th): Convention debates a clause linking slavery representation and direct taxation; approves a census every ten years.

July 13 (F): Convention approves a link of direct taxation to representation, and a periodic census of population.

July 14 (Sa): Convention rejects an absolute limit on the number of House seats for western states, and a thirty-six-seat Senate with proportional representation.

July 16 (M): Convention approves Connecticut Compromise; debates adjournment.

July 17 (Tu): Convention approves broad national authority, "supremacy" clause, Congressional election of a single executive; rejects a national veto of state legislation.

July 18 (W): Convention approves the executive veto of Congressional acts, a separate judiciary with lifetime terms, Congressional authority to establish inferior courts, admission of new states, and a guarantee of republican government to the states.

July 19 (Th): Convention debates executive selection and eligibility; approves a system of electors for the executive, and a seven-year executive term.

July 20 (F): Convention debates executive selection; approves executive impeachment.

July 21 (Sa): Convention rejects joint executive-judiciary veto of Congressional legislation and executive nomination of judges; approves Senate appointment of judges.

July 23 (M): Convention approves a provision for Constitutional amendments, oaths for national and state public officers, state conventions to ratify the Constitution, and two senators for each state (each senator casting an individual vote).

July 24 (Tu): Convention debates executive election; approves Congressional selection of the executive; appoints a Committee of Detail to produce a more detailed draft of a constitution.

July 25 (W): Convention debates executive election and term.

July 26 (Th): Convention approves Congressional selection of the executive, limited to a single, seven-year term; instructs Committee of Detail to set property and citizenship qualifications for members of Congress; rejects a ban on those with public debts from serving in Congress; debates a clause on the location of the national capital. Delegates turn over their work to a Committee on Detail and adjourn temporarily.

August 6 (M): Committee of Detail reports a more detailed draft of a constitution.

August 7 (Tu): Convention takes up Committee of Detail report; approves a government of the "United States of America" with separate executive, legislative, and judiciary branches, and a Congress with a separate House of Representatives and a Senate; debates annual meeting of Congress, and the qualifications for voters for elections to the House of Representatives.

August 8 (W): Convention sets qualifications for voters for the House of Representatives as the state's qualifications for voters for the directly elected state legislative houses; sets age, citizenship, and residency requirements for U.S. Representatives; approves a first House of Representatives with sixty-five members, with future adjustments in apportionment based on population changes; refuses to count only free citizens in House apportionment; guarantees each state at least one representative; strikes out provision for House origination of money bills.

August 9 (Th): Convention approves House power to impeach, to choose its officers, provision for filling House vacancies; approves a Senate with two members per state, chosen by the state legislatures for six-year terms, with each senator having one vote; approves age, citizenship, and residency requirements for senators and representatives, House and Senate control of internal rules, Congressional authority to set election rules; debates House origination of money bills.

August 10 (F): Convention rejects property qualifications for representatives; approves quorum of a majority of members in the House and Senate, and the power to compel attendance.

August 11 (Sa): Convention approves requirement that House and Senate keep a journal of proceedings, and rules for Congressional adjournment.

August 13 (M): Convention debates citizenship requirement for representatives, and House origination of money bills.

August 14 (T): Convention debates multiple office-holding for members of Congress; approves national government payment of members of Congress, to be set by law.

August 15 (W): Convention debates House origination of money bills, executive veto power; approves a three-fourths vote of the House and Senate to override executive vetoes.

August 16 (Th): Convention approves presidential power to veto most Congressional resolutions; approves Congressional power to "lay and collect taxes, duties, imposts and excises," to set a uniform rule of naturalization, to coin money and regulate the value of foreign coin, to fix standards for weights and measures, to establish post offices and post roads, and to borrow money; strikes out authority to emit bills of credit.

August 17 (F): Convention approves Congressional power to establish inferior national courts, to make rules for capture in war, to define and punish piracy, counterfeiting, and offenses against international law, and to subdue rebellion if a state requests it; rejects appointment of a separate U.S. Treasurer.

August 18 (Sa): Several delegates propose additional enumerated powers for Congress. Convention debates raising and equipping the troops and a navy, and control of the state militias.

August 20 (M): Several delegates propose changes and additions, including a list of protected rights and liberties; Convention rejects Congressional power to enact sumptuary laws; approves Congressional power to "enact all laws that shall be necessary and proper" to execute the powers authorized by the Constitution, and a provision defining treason.

August 21 (T): Convention debates slave trade; approves direct taxation based on number of free citizens and three-fifths of all others [that is, slaves], and a ban on national taxes on exports; rejects House origination of money bills with Senate concurrence, and state discretion to administer direct taxes to fulfill national requisitions.

August 22 (W): Convention debates slave imports; creates a committee on slave imports and commercial treaties; prohibits bills of attainder and ex post facto laws; approves clause requiring Congress to discharge the debts and fulfill the obligations of the United States.

August 23 (Th): Convention approves limited national power over the state militias, a ban on foreign payments and titles to U.S. office holders, and the supremacy clause; rejects national veto of state laws; debates Senate responsibility for treaties.

August 24 (F): Convention approves judicial resolution of land disputes, a single president elected by a joint vote of House and Senate, and presidential authority to recommend measures; rejects direct election of the president and a system of electors to choose the president; debates presidential appointments.

August 25 (Sa): Convention approves a national obligation to honor Confederation debts, prohibition of any ban on slave imports until 1808, authority to tax slave imports at up to $10 a head; debates import duties and laws for ports.

August 27 (M): Convention approves a presidential oath, a national judiciary, judicial terms for "good behavior," and adds to national court authority.

August 28 (T): Convention approves jury trial for offences committed out of state, protection of habeas corpus with exceptions, restrictions on state authority (including authority to emit bills of credit and to tax exports), the "privileges and immunities" clause, and extradition for accused criminals who flee the state where they are accused.

August 29 (W): Convention rejects two-thirds requirement for commercial treaties; approves requirement that fugitive slaves must be returned; debates admission of new states.

August 30 (R): Convention approves admission of new states, a guarantee of a republican government to all states, procedure for constitutional amendment, oaths for state and national officials; debates number of states required to ratify the Constitution.

August 31 (F): Convention debates ratification process; approves process for presenting the Constitution to the Confederation Congress, which will send it to the states; sets threshold for ratification at nine state constitutional conventions; approves provision that no preference be given to any port, and that all duties, tariffs and excise taxes will be uniform across the United States; appoints a committee on Postponed Matters.

September 1 (Sa): Reports of committees on several delayed items.

September 3 (M): Convention approves "full faith and credit" clause with Congressional power to define effect of state laws and judgments in other states; approves Congressional power to make national bankruptcy law; approves members of Congress resigning to fill other national office; rejects multiple office-holding.

September 4 (Tu): Committee on Postponed Matters report on presidential selection by electors, presidential powers, and presidential removal and succession; Convention approves restated clause on Congressional powers to levy taxes, pay debts, and enact laws "necessary and proper"; authorizes dealings with Indian tribes; debates presidential selection.

September 5 (W): Committee on Postponed Matters report on Congressional authority; Convention approves authority to grant letters of marque and reprisal, to provide military appropriations for two years, to create a capital district, to erect public buildings, and to grant patents and copyrights; debates presidential selection.

September 6 (Th): Convention approves election of a president and a vice-president by electors, chosen as state legislatures direct, with each elector voting in his own states for two candidates, on a date set by national law; if no candidate receives an electoral vote majority or there is a tie, the House votes by state delegation for the president.

September 7 (F): Convention approves provision that the president be a natural-born citizen and 35 years old, that the vice president serve as president of the Senate, and that the president can make treaties and appoint officials with the advice and consent of the Senate.

September 8 (Sa): Convention approves Senate treaty approval requiring a two-thirds majority; approves House authority to impeach the president for "high crimes and misdemeanors," with the Senate holding the impeachment trial; approves House origination of money bills; rejects changes in apportionment of House seats in the first Congress.

September 10 (M): Convention approves four ways to amend the Constitution; agrees that the protection of slave imports until 1808 cannot be amended;

rejects proposal to require Congress to approve the Constitution before state ratification.

September 11 (Tu): Convention adjourns early to wait for Committee of Style draft of the Constitution.

September 13 (Th): Committee on Style reports nearly final draft of the Constitution; Convention approves state inspection fees for exports.

September 14 (F): Convention rejects changes in apportionment of House seats in the first Congress; rejects appointment of a separate U.S. Treasurer, national authority to cut canals and establish a national university, and a guarantee of freedom of the press.

September 15 (Sa): Convention rejects changes in apportionment of House seats in the first Congress; rejects proposals to protect state police powers from Constitutional amendment, and to require a two-thirds margin for commercial treaties until 1808; debates presidential pardons for treason; approves Congressional delegation of power to the president to appoint to lesser executive offices; and protects equality state representation in the Senate from Constitutional amendment.

September 17 (M): Convention approves reduction of minimum size of U.S. House of Representatives districts from 40,000 to 30,000. Thirty-nine delegates sign the Constitution; three who are present refuse to sign it.

Appendix 2

THE UNITED STATES CONSTITUTION AND ACCOMPANYING DOCUMENTS FROM THE CONSTITUTIONAL CONVENTION

We the People of the United States, in Order to form a more perfect Union, establish Justice, insure domestic Tranquility, provide for the common defence, promote the general Welfare, and secure the Blessings of Liberty to ourselves and our Posterity, do ordain and establish this Constitution for the United States of America.

Article. I.

Section. 1.

All legislative Powers herein granted shall be vested in a Congress of the United States, which shall consist of a Senate and House of Representatives.

Section. 2.

The House of Representatives shall be composed of Members chosen every second Year by the People of the several States, and the Electors in each State shall have the Qualifications requisite for Electors of the most numerous Branch of the State Legislature.

No Person shall be a Representative who shall not have attained to the Age of twenty five Years, and been seven Years a Citizen of the United States, and who shall not, when elected, be an Inhabitant of that State in which he shall be chosen.

Representatives and direct Taxes shall be apportioned among the several States which may be included within this Union, according to their respective Numbers, which shall be determined by adding to the whole Number of free Persons, including those bound to Service for a Term of Years, and excluding Indians not taxed, three fifths of all other Persons. The actual Enumeration shall be made within three Years after the first Meeting of the Congress of the United States, and within every subsequent Term of ten Years, in such Manner as they shall by Law direct. The Number of Representatives shall not exceed one for every thirty Thousand, but each State shall have at Least one Representative; and until such enumeration shall be made, the State of New Hampshire shall be entitled to chuse three, Massachusetts eight, Rhode-Island and Providence Plantations one, Connecticut five, New-York six, New Jersey four, Pennsylvania eight, Delaware one, Maryland six, Virginia ten, North Carolina five, South Carolina five, and Georgia three.

When vacancies happen in the Representation from any State, the Executive Authority thereof shall issue Writs of Election to fill such Vacancies.

The House of Representatives shall chuse their Speaker and other Officers; and shall have the sole Power of Impeachment.

Section. 3.

The Senate of the United States shall be composed of two Senators from each State, chosen by the Legislature thereof for six Years; and each Senator shall have one Vote.

Immediately after they shall be assembled in Consequence of the first Election, they shall be divided as equally as may be into three Classes. The Seats of the Senators of the first Class shall be vacated at the Expiration of the second Year, of the second Class at the Expiration of the fourth Year, and of the third Class at the Expiration of the sixth Year, so that one third may be chosen every second Year; and if Vacancies happen by Resignation, or otherwise, during the Recess of the Legislature of any State, the Executive thereof may make temporary Appointments until the next Meeting of the Legislature, which shall then fill such Vacancies.

No Person shall be a Senator who shall not have attained to the Age of thirty Years, and been nine Years a Citizen of the United States, and who shall not, when elected, be an Inhabitant of that State for which he shall be chosen.

The Vice President of the United States shall be President of the Senate, but shall have no Vote, unless they be equally divided.

The Senate shall chuse their other Officers, and also a President pro tempore, in the Absence of the Vice President, or when he shall exercise the Office of President of the United States.

The Senate shall have the sole Power to try all Impeachments. When sitting for that Purpose, they shall be on Oath or Affirmation. When the President of the United States is tried, the Chief Justice shall preside: And no Person shall be convicted without the Concurrence of two thirds of the Members present.

247

Judgment in Cases of Impeachment shall not extend further than to removal from Office, and disqualification to hold and enjoy any Office of honor, Trust or Profit under the United States: but the Party convicted shall nevertheless be liable and subject to Indictment, Trial, Judgment and Punishment, according to Law.

Section. 4.

The Times, Places and Manner of holding Elections for Senators and Representatives, shall be prescribed in each State by the Legislature thereof; but the Congress may at any time by Law make or alter such Regulations, except as to the Places of chusing Senators.

The Congress shall assemble at least once in every Year, and such Meeting shall be on the first Monday in December, unless they shall by Law appoint a different Day.

Section. 5.

Each House shall be the Judge of the Elections, Returns and Qualifications of its own Members, and a Majority of each shall constitute a Quorum to do Business; but a smaller Number may adjourn from day to day, and may be authorized to compel the Attendance of absent Members, in such Manner, and under such Penalties as each House may provide.

Each House may determine the Rules of its Proceedings, punish its Members for disorderly Behaviour, and, with the Concurrence of two thirds, expel a Member.

Each House shall keep a Journal of its Proceedings, and from time to time publish the same, excepting such Parts as may in their Judgment require Secrecy; and the Yeas and Nays of the Members of either House on any question shall, at the Desire of one fifth of those Present, be entered on the Journal.

Neither House, during the Session of Congress, shall, without the Consent of the other, adjourn for more than three days, nor to any other Place than that in which the two Houses shall be sitting.

Section. 6.

The Senators and Representatives shall receive a Compensation for their Services, to be ascertained by Law, and paid out of the Treasury of the United States. They shall in all Cases, except Treason, Felony and Breach of the Peace, be privileged from Arrest during their Attendance at the Session of their respective

Houses, and in going to and returning from the same; and for any Speech or Debate in either House, they shall not be questioned in any other Place.

No Senator or Representative shall, during the Time for which he was elected, be appointed to any civil Office under the Authority of the United States, which shall have been created, or the Emoluments whereof shall have been encreased during such time; and no Person holding any Office under the United States, shall be a Member of either House during his Continuance in Office.

Section. 7.

All Bills for raising Revenue shall originate in the House of Representatives; but the Senate may propose or concur with Amendments as on other Bills.

Every Bill which shall have passed the House of Representatives and the Senate, shall, before it become a Law, be presented to the President of the United States: If he approve he shall sign it, but if not he shall return it, with his Objections to that House in which it shall have originated, who shall enter the Objections at large on their Journal, and proceed to reconsider it. If after such Reconsideration two thirds of that House shall agree to pass the Bill, it shall be sent, together with the Objections, to the other House, by which it shall likewise be reconsidered, and if approved by two thirds of that House, it shall become a Law. But in all such Cases the Votes of both Houses shall be determined by yeas and Nays, and the Names of the Persons voting for and against the Bill shall be entered on the Journal of each House respectively. If any Bill shall not be returned by the President within ten Days (Sundays excepted) after it shall have been presented to him, the Same shall be a Law, in like Manner as if he had signed it, unless the Congress by their Adjournment prevent its Return, in which Case it shall not be a Law.

Every Order, Resolution, or Vote to which the Concurrence of the Senate and House of Representatives may be necessary (except on a question of Adjournment) shall be presented to the President of the United States; and before the Same shall take Effect, shall be approved by him, or being disapproved by him, shall be repassed by two thirds of the Senate and House of Representatives, according to the Rules and Limitations prescribed in the Case of a Bill.

Section. 8.

The Congress shall have Power To lay and collect Taxes, Duties, Imposts and Excises, to pay the Debts and provide for the common Defence and general Welfare of the United States; but all Duties, Imposts and Excises shall be uniform throughout the United States;

To borrow Money on the credit of the United States;

To regulate Commerce with foreign Nations, and among the several States, and with the Indian Tribes;

To establish an uniform Rule of Naturalization, and uniform Laws on the subject of Bankruptcies throughout the United States;

To coin Money, regulate the Value thereof, and of foreign Coin, and fix the Standard of Weights and Measures;

To provide for the Punishment of counterfeiting the Securities and current Coin of the United States;

To establish Post Offices and post Roads;

To promote the Progress of Science and useful Arts, by securing for limited Times to Authors and Inventors the exclusive Right to their respective Writings and Discoveries;

To constitute Tribunals inferior to the supreme Court;

To define and punish Piracies and Felonies committed on the high Seas, and Offences against the Law of Nations;

To declare War, grant Letters of Marque and Reprisal, and make Rules concerning Captures on Land and Water;

To raise and support Armies, but no Appropriation of Money to that Use shall be for a longer Term than two Years;

To provide and maintain a Navy;

To make Rules for the Government and Regulation of the land and naval Forces;

To provide for calling forth the Militia to execute the Laws of the Union, suppress Insurrections and repel Invasions;

To provide for organizing, arming, and disciplining, the Militia, and for governing such Part of them as may be employed in the Service of the United States, reserving to the States respectively, the Appointment of the Officers, and the Authority of training the Militia according to the discipline prescribed by Congress;

To exercise exclusive Legislation in all Cases whatsoever, over such District (not exceeding ten Miles square) as may, by Cession of particular States, and the Acceptance of Congress, become the Seat of the Government of the United States, and to exercise like Authority over all Places purchased by the Consent of the Legislature of the State in which the Same shall be, for the Erection of Forts, Magazines, Arsenals, dock-Yards, and other needful Buildings;—And

To make all Laws which shall be necessary and proper for carrying into Execution the foregoing Powers, and all other Powers vested by this Constitution in the Government of the United States, or in any Department or Officer thereof.

Section. 9.

The Migration or Importation of such Persons as any of the States now existing shall think proper to admit, shall not be prohibited by the Congress prior to the Year one thousand eight hundred and eight, but a Tax or duty may be imposed on such Importation, not exceeding ten dollars for each Person.

The Privilege of the Writ of Habeas Corpus shall not be suspended, unless when in Cases of Rebellion or Invasion the public Safety may require it.

No Bill of Attainder or ex post facto Law shall be passed.

No Capitation, or other direct, Tax shall be laid, unless in Proportion to the Census or enumeration herein before directed to be taken.

No Tax or Duty shall be laid on Articles exported from any State.

No Preference shall be given by any Regulation of Commerce or Revenue to the Ports of one State over those of another; nor shall Vessels bound to, or from, one State, be obliged to enter, clear, or pay Duties in another.

No Money shall be drawn from the Treasury, but in Consequence of Appropriations made by Law; and a regular Statement and Account of the Receipts and Expenditures of all public Money shall be published from time to time.

No Title of Nobility shall be granted by the United States: And no Person holding any Office of Profit or Trust under them, shall, without the Consent of the Congress, accept of any present, Emolument, Office, or Title, of any kind whatever, from any King, Prince, or foreign State.

Section. 10.

No State shall enter into any Treaty, Alliance, or Confederation; grant Letters of Marque and Reprisal; coin Money; emit Bills of Credit; make any Thing but gold and silver Coin a Tender in Payment of Debts; pass any Bill of Attainder, ex post facto Law, or Law impairing the Obligation of Contracts, or grant any Title of Nobility.

No State shall, without the Consent of the Congress, lay any Imposts or Duties on Imports or Exports, except what may be absolutely necessary for executing it's inspection Laws: and the net Produce of all Duties and Imposts, laid by any State on Imports or Exports, shall be for the Use of the Treasury of the United States; and all such Laws shall be subject to the Revision and Controul of the Congress.

No State shall, without the Consent of Congress, lay any Duty of Tonnage, keep Troops, or Ships of War in time of Peace, enter into any Agreement or Compact with another State, or with a foreign Power, or engage in War, unless actually invaded, or in such imminent Danger as will not admit of delay.

Article. II.

Section. 1.

The executive Power shall be vested in a President of the United States of America. He shall hold his Office during the Term of four Years, and, together with the Vice President, chosen for the same Term, be elected, as follows:

Each State shall appoint, in such Manner as the Legislature thereof may direct, a Number of Electors, equal to the whole Number of Senators and Representatives to which the State may be entitled in the Congress: but no Senator or Representative, or Person holding an Office of Trust or Profit under the United States, shall be appointed an Elector.

The Electors shall meet in their respective States, and vote by Ballot for two Persons, of whom one at least shall not be an Inhabitant of the same State with themselves. And they shall make a List of all the Persons voted for, and of the Number of Votes for each; which List they shall sign and certify, and transmit sealed to the Seat of the Government of the United States, directed to the President of the Senate. The President of the Senate shall, in the Presence of the Senate and House of Representatives, open all the Certificates, and the Votes shall then be counted. The Person having the greatest Number of Votes shall be the President, if such Number be a Majority of the whole Number of Electors appointed; and if there be more than one who have such Majority, and have an equal Number of Votes, then the House of Representatives shall immediately chuse by Ballot one of them for President; and if no Person have a Majority, then from the five highest on the List the said House shall in like Manner chuse the President. But in chusing the President, the Votes shall be taken by States, the Representation from each State having one Vote; A quorum for this purpose shall consist of a Member or Members from two thirds of the States, and a Majority of all the States shall be necessary to a Choice. In every Case, after the Choice of the President, the Person having the greatest Number of Votes of the Electors shall be the Vice President. But if there should remain two or more who have equal Votes, the Senate shall chuse from them by Ballot the Vice President.

The Congress may determine the Time of chusing the Electors, and the Day on which they shall give their Votes; which Day shall be the same throughout the United States.

No Person except a natural born Citizen, or a Citizen of the United States, at the time of the Adoption of this Constitution, shall be eligible to the Office of President; neither shall any Person be eligible to that Office who shall not have attained to the Age of thirty five Years, and been fourteen Years a Resident within the United States.

In Case of the Removal of the President from Office, or of his Death, Resignation, or Inability to discharge the Powers and Duties of the said Office, the Same shall devolve on the Vice President, and the Congress may by Law provide for the Case of Removal, Death, Resignation or Inability, both of the President and Vice President, declaring what Officer shall then act as President, and such Officer shall act accordingly, until the Disability be removed, or a President shall be elected.

The President shall, at stated Times, receive for his Services, a Compensation, which shall neither be increased nor diminished during the Period for which he shall have been elected, and he shall not receive within that Period any other Emolument from the United States, or any of them.

Before he enter on the Execution of his Office, he shall take the following Oath or Affirmation:—"I do solemnly swear (or affirm) that I will faithfully execute the Office of President of the United States, and will to the best of my Ability, preserve, protect and defend the Constitution of the United States."

Section. 2.

The President shall be Commander in Chief of the Army and Navy of the United States, and of the Militia of the several States, when called into the actual Service of the United States; he may require the Opinion, in writing, of the principal Officer in each of the executive Departments, upon any Subject relating to the Duties of their respective Offices, and he shall have Power to grant Reprieves and Pardons for Offences against the United States, except in Cases of Impeachment.

He shall have Power, by and with the Advice and Consent of the Senate, to make Treaties, provided two thirds of the Senators present concur; and he shall nominate, and by and with the Advice and Consent of the Senate, shall appoint Ambassadors, other public Ministers and Consuls, Judges of the supreme Court, and all other Officers of the United States, whose Appointments are not herein otherwise provided for, and which shall be established by Law: but the Congress may by Law vest the Appointment of such inferior Officers, as they think proper, in the President alone, in the Courts of Law, or in the Heads of Departments.

The President shall have Power to fill up all Vacancies that may happen during the Recess of the Senate, by granting Commissions which shall expire at the End of their next Session.

Section. 3.

He shall from time to time give to the Congress Information of the State of the Union, and recommend to their Consideration such Measures as he shall judge necessary and expedient; he may, on extraordinary Occasions, convene both Houses, or either of them, and in Case of Disagreement between them, with Respect to the Time of Adjournment, he may adjourn them to such Time as he shall think proper; he shall receive Ambassadors and other public Ministers; he shall take Care that the Laws be faithfully executed, and shall Commission all the Officers of the United States.

Section. 4.

The President, Vice President and all civil Officers of the United States, shall be removed from Office on Impeachment for, and Conviction of, Treason, Bribery, or other high Crimes and Misdemeanors.

Article III.

Section. 1.

The judicial Power of the United States shall be vested in one supreme Court, and in such inferior Courts as the Congress may from time to time ordain and establish. The Judges, both of the supreme and inferior Courts, shall hold their Offices during good Behaviour, and shall, at stated Times, receive for their Services a Compensation, which shall not be diminished during their Continuance in Office.

Section. 2.

The judicial Power shall extend to all Cases, in Law and Equity, arising under this Constitution, the Laws of the United States, and Treaties made, or which shall be made, under their Authority;—to all Cases affecting Ambassadors, other public Ministers and Consuls;—to all Cases of admiralty and maritime Jurisdiction;—to Controversies to which the United States shall be a Party;—to Controversies between two or more States;—between a State and Citizens of another State,—between Citizens of different States,—between Citizens of the same State claiming Lands under Grants of different States, and between a State, or the Citizens thereof, and foreign States, Citizens or Subjects.

In all Cases affecting Ambassadors, other public Ministers and Consuls, and those in which a State shall be Party, the supreme Court shall have original Jurisdiction. In all the other Cases before mentioned, the supreme Court shall have appellate Jurisdiction, both as to Law and Fact, with such Exceptions, and under such Regulations as the Congress shall make.

The Trial of all Crimes, except in Cases of Impeachment, shall be by Jury; and such Trial shall be held in the State where the said Crimes shall have been committed; but when not committed within any State, the Trial shall be at such Place or Places as the Congress may by Law have directed.

Section. 3.

Treason against the United States, shall consist only in levying War against them, or in adhering to their Enemies, giving them Aid and Comfort. No Person shall be convicted of Treason unless on the Testimony of two Witnesses to the same overt Act, or on Confession in open Court.

The Congress shall have Power to declare the Punishment of Treason, but no Attainder of Treason shall work Corruption of Blood, or Forfeiture except during the Life of the Person attainted.

Article. IV.

Section. 1.

Full Faith and Credit shall be given in each State to the public Acts, Records, and judicial Proceedings of every other State. And the Congress may by general Laws prescribe the Manner in which such Acts, Records and Proceedings shall be proved, and the Effect thereof.

Section. 2.

The Citizens of each State shall be entitled to all Privileges and Immunities of Citizens in the several States.

A Person charged in any State with Treason, Felony, or other Crime, who shall flee from Justice, and be found in another State, shall on Demand of the executive Authority of the State from which he fled, be delivered up, to be removed to the State having Jurisdiction of the Crime.

No Person held to Service or Labour in one State, under the Laws thereof, escaping into another, shall, in Consequence of any Law or Regulation therein, be discharged from such Service or Labour, but shall be delivered up on Claim of the Party to whom such Service or Labour may be due.

Section. 3.

New States may be admitted by the Congress into this Union; but no new State shall be formed or erected within the Jurisdiction of any other State; nor any State be formed by the Junction of two or more States, or Parts of States, without the Consent of the Legislatures of the States concerned as well as of the Congress.

The Congress shall have Power to dispose of and make all needful Rules and Regulations respecting the Territory or other Property belonging to the United

States; and nothing in this Constitution shall be so construed as to Prejudice any Claims of the United States, or of any particular State.

Section. 4.

The United States shall guarantee to every State in this Union a Republican Form of Government, and shall protect each of them against Invasion; and on Application of the Legislature, or of the Executive (when the Legislature cannot be convened), against domestic Violence.

Article. V.

The Congress, whenever two thirds of both Houses shall deem it necessary, shall propose Amendments to this Constitution, or, on the Application of the Legislatures of two thirds of the several States, shall call a Convention for proposing Amendments, which, in either Case, shall be valid to all Intents and Purposes, as Part of this Constitution, when ratified by the Legislatures of three fourths of the several States, or by Conventions in three fourths thereof, as the one or the other Mode of Ratification may be proposed by the Congress; Provided that no Amendment which may be made prior to the Year One thousand eight hundred and eight shall in any Manner affect the first and fourth Clauses in the Ninth Section of the first Article; and that no State, without its Consent, shall be deprived of its equal Suffrage in the Senate.

Article. VI.

All Debts contracted and Engagements entered into, before the Adoption of this Constitution, shall be as valid against the United States under this Constitution, as under the Confederation.

This Constitution, and the Laws of the United States which shall be made in Pursuance thereof; and all Treaties made, or which shall be made, under the Authority of the United States, shall be the supreme Law of the Land; and the Judges in every State shall be bound thereby, any Thing in the Constitution or Laws of any State to the Contrary notwithstanding.

The Senators and Representatives before mentioned, and the Members of the several State Legislatures, and all executive and judicial Officers, both of the United States and of the several States, shall be bound by Oath or Affirmation, to support this Constitution; but no religious Test shall ever be required as a Qualification to any Office or public Trust under the United States.

Article. VII.

The Ratification of the Conventions of nine States, shall be sufficient for the Establishment of this Constitution between the States so ratifying the Same.

The Word, "the," being interlined between the seventh and eighth Lines of the first Page, the Word "Thirty" being partly written on an Erazure in the fifteenth Line of the first Page, The Words "is tried" being interlined between the thirty second and thirty third Lines of the first Page and the Word "the" being interlined between the forty third and forty fourth Lines of the second Page.

Attest William Jackson Secretary

Done in Convention by the Unanimous Consent of the States present the Seventeenth Day of September in the Year of our Lord one thousand seven hundred and Eighty seven and of the Independence of the United States of America the Twelfth In witness whereof We have hereunto subscribed our Names,

G. Washington
Presidt and deputy from Virginia

State	Signatories
Delaware	Geo: Read
	Gunning Bedford jun
	John Dickinson
	Richard Bassett
	Jaco: Broom
Maryland	James McHenry
	Dan of St Thos. Jenifer
	Danl. Carroll
Virginia	John Blair
	James Madison Jr.
North Carolina	Wm. Blount
	Richd. Dobbs Spaight
	Hu Williamson
South Carolina	J. Rutledge
	Charles Cotesworth Pinckney
	Charles Pinckney
	Pierce Butler
Georgia	William Few
	Abr Baldwin
New Hampshire	John Langdon
	Nicholas Gilman

Massachusetts	{	Nathaniel Gorham
		Rufus King

Connecticut	{	Wm. Saml. Johnson
		Roger Sherman

New York . . . . Alexander Hamilton

New Jersey	{	Wil: Livingston
		David Brearley
		Wm. Paterson
		Jona: Dayton

Pennsylvania	{	B Franklin
		Thomas Mifflin
		Robt. Morris
		Geo. Clymer
		Thos. FitzSimons
		Jared Ingersoll
		James Wilson
		Gouv Morris

(Source of transcript: U.S. National Archives, http://www.archives.gov/ exhibits/charters/constitution_transcript.html, accessed January 9, 2010)

In Convention Monday September 17th. 1787
Present
The States of

New Hampshire, Massachusetts, Connecticut, Mr. Hamilton from New York, New Jersey, Pennsylvania, Delaware, Maryland, Virginia, North Carolina, South Carolina and Georgia.

Resolved,

That the preceding Constitution be laid before the United States in Congress assembled, and that it is the Opinion of this Convention, that it should afterwards be submitted to a Convention of Delegates, chosen in each State by the People thereof, under the Recommendation of its Legislature, for their Assent and Ratification; and that each Convention assenting to, and ratifying the Same, should give Notice thereof to the United States in Congress assembled.

Resolved, That it is the Opinion of this Convention, that as soon as the Conventions of nine States shall have ratified this Constitution, the United States in Congress assembled should fix a Day on which Electors should be appointed by the States which shall have ratified the same, and a Day on which the Electors

should assemble to vote for the President, and the Time and place for com-
mencing Proceedings under this Constitution. That after such Publication the
Electors should be appointed, and the Senators and Representatives elected:
That the Electors should meet on the Day fixed for the Election of the President,
and should transmit their votes certified signed, sealed and directed, as the Constitution requires, to the Secretary of the United States in Congress assembled,
that the Senators and Representatives should convene at the Time and Place
asigned; that the Senators should appoint a President of the Senate, for the sole
Purpose of receiving, opening and counting the Votes for President; and, that
after he shall be chosen, the Congress, together with the President, should, without Delay, proceed to execute this Constitution.

By the Unanimous Order of the Convention
Go: Washington Presidt.
W. Jackson Secretary

(Source: RFC September 17, II: 665–666)

[Letter to Congress]

In Convention, September 17, 1787.

   Sir,
   WE have now the honor to submit to the consideration of the United States
in Congress assembled, that Constitution which has appeared to us the most
adviseable.
   The friends of our country have long seen and desired, that the power of
making war, peace and treaties, that of levying money and regulating commerce,
and the correspondent executive and judicial authorities should be fully and effectually vested in the general government of the Union: but the impropriety of
delegating such extensive trust to one body of men is evident—Hence results
the necessity of a different organization.
   It is obviously impracticable in the fœderal government of these States, to
secure all rights of independent sovereignty to each, and yet provide for the interest and safety of all—Individuals entering into society, must give up a share of
liberty to preserve the rest. The magnitude of the sacrifice must depend as well
on situation and circumstance, as on the object to be obtained. It is at all times
difficult to draw with precision the line between those rights which must be surrendered, and those which may be reserved; and on the present occasion this
difficulty was increased by a difference among the several States as to their situation, extent, habits, and particular interests.

In all our deliberations on this subject we kept steadily in our view, that which appears to us the greatest interest of every true American, the consolidation of our Union, in which is involved our prosperity, felicity, safety, perhaps our national existence. This important consideration, seriously and deeply impressed on our minds, led each State in the Convention to be less rigid on points of inferior magnitude, than might have been otherwise expected; and thus the Constitution, which we now present, is the result of a spirit of amity, and of that mutual deference and concession which the peculiarity of our political situation rendered indispensable.

That it will meet the full and entire approbation of every State is not perhaps to be expected; but each will doubtless consider, that had her interest alone been consulted, the consequences might have been particularly disagreeable or injurious to others; that it is liable to as few exceptions as could reasonably have been expected, we hope and believe; that it may promote the lasting welfare of that country so dear to us all, and secure her freedom and happiness, is our most ardent wish.

> With great respect,
> We have the honor to be.
> SIR,
> Your Excellency's most
> Obedient and humble Servants,
> GEORGE WASHINGTON, PRESIDENT.

By unanimous Order of the Convention.

HIS EXCELLENCY

The President of Congress.

(Source: RFC September 17, II: 666–667)

NOTES

Chapter 1

1. Rogan Kersh, *Dreams of a More Perfect Union* (Ithaca, NY: Cornell University Press, 2001), 32–68.
2. *Journals of the Continental Congress, 1774–1789* [hereafter, *JCC*], ed. Worthington C. Ford et al., 34 vols. (Washington, DC: Government Printing Office, 1904–1937), http://memory.loc.gov/ammem/amlaw/lwjc.html, September 25, 1783, 618. The Committee consisted of James Duane, John Rutledge, Thomas Fitzsimons, Elbridge Gerry, and Stephen Higginson. Rutledge, Fitzsimons, and Gerry were delegates to the Constitutional Convention.
3. George Washington, "Circular to the States," June 8, 1783, in *The Writings of George Washington*, ed. John C. Fitzpatrick (Washington, DC: Government Printing Office, 1938), 26, 483–96.
4. David Brian Robertson, "Constituting a National Interest: Madison Against the States' Autonomy," in *James Madison: The Theory and Practice of Republican Government*, ed. Samuel Kernell (Stanford, CA: Stanford University Press, 2003), 184–216. In *The Federalist* Number 51, Madison aspires to a government that serves the national interest, a national government with "a will independent of the society itself." In an extended republic, "a coalition of a majority of the whole society could seldom take place on any other principles than those of justice and the general good." Alexander Hamilton, James Madison, and John Jay, *The Federalist*, ed. Jacob E. Cooke (Middletown, CT: Wesleyan University Press, 1961), 352–53. Originally titled *The Federalist* when first published in 1788, the collection of essays often has appeared under the title *The Federalist Papers* over the past century.
5. Madison to James Monroe, August 7, 1785, in *The Papers of James Madison*, ed. William T. Hutchinson et al., 17 vols. (Chicago: University of Chicago Press and Charlottesville: University of Virginia Press, 1962–1991) [hereafter, *PJM*], ed. William T. Hutchinson et al., 17 vols. (Chicago: University of Chicago Press and Charlottesville: University of Virginia Press, 1962–1991), 8, 333–36, and "Vices of the Political System of the United States," *PJM* 9, 348–50; Lance Banning, *The Sacred Fire of Liberty: James Madison and the Founding of the Federal Republic* (Ithaca, NY: Cornell University Press, 1995), 54–55, 72.
6. *The Records of the Federal Convention of 1787* [hereafter, *RFC*], ed. Max Farrand, 4 vols. (New Haven, CT: Yale University Press, 1937), *RFC* May 31, I, 53. Decades later, Madison remembered that public opinion was rapidly growing supportive of a national government with stronger powers; James Madison, "Preface to Debates in the Convention of 1787," in *RFC* III, 545. On growing support for a stronger national government, see David Brian Robertson, *The Constitution and America's Destiny* (Cambridge and New York: Cambridge University Press, 2005), 65–73.

7. Jefferson, minister to France at the time, was frustrated by the Barbary Pirates, who preyed on merchant ships and demanded tribute from the U.S. and other governments. Letter, Jefferson to James Monroe, August 18, 1786, cited in Library of Congress, "America and the Barbary Pirates: An International Battle Against an Unconventional Foe," http://memory.loc.gov/ammem/collections/jefferson_papers/mtjprece.html (accessed March 24, 2012).

8. "Debates and Resolutions Related to the Regulation of Commerce . . .," *PJM* 8, 406–409.

9. On republicanism, see Robert E. Shalhope, "Republicanism and Early American Historiography," *William and Mary Quarterly*, 3rd Series, 39:2 (April 1982), 334–56; J. G. A. Pocock, *The Machiavellian Moment: Florentine Political Thought and the Atlantic Republican Tradition*, rev. ed. (Princeton, NJ: Princeton University Press, 2003); Bernard Bailyn, *The Ideological Origins of the American Revolution* (Cambridge, MA: Belknap Press, 1967); Gordon S. Wood, *The Creation of the American Republic, 1776–1787* (Chapel Hill: University of North Carolina Press, 1969), 46–90, and *The Radicalism of the American Revolution* (New York: Alfred A. Knopf, 1991), 95–228. On the way in which republicanism melded with American economic interests, see Cathy Matson and Peter Onuf, "Toward a Republican Empire: Interest and Ideology in Revolutionary America," *American Quarterly* 37:4 (Autumn 1985): 496–531.

10. *RFC* June 20, I, 346.

11. *PJM* 9, 348–50, 353–54.

12. Wood, *The Creation of the American Republic, 1776–1787*, 55; Bailyn, *The Ideological Origins of the American Revolution*, 280–86.

13. Jack N. Rakove, *Original Meanings: Politics and Ideas in the Making of the Constitution* (New York: Alfred A. Knopf, 1996), 203.

14. *JCC* May 15, 1776, 4, 358.

15. James Morone, *The Democratic Wish: Popular Participation and the Limits of Democratic Government* (New York: Basic Books, 1990), 53.

16. Wood, *The Radicalism of the American Revolution*, 187.

17. Charles-Louis de Secondat, baron de Montesquieu, *The Spirit of the Laws* (New York: Hafner Press, 1948), Book 9, 150–60, was the most prominent authority on the separation of powers most often cited by the framers. Montesquieu wrote that "the legislature is the general will of the state—the executive is the execution of that general will." The delegates often invoked Montesquieu at the Convention; see *RFC* June 7, I, 71; June 18, I, 308; June 23, I, 391; June 30, I, 485, 495; July 11, I, 579–80; July 17, II, 34; September 6, II, 534. Madison and his allies usually enlisted Montesquieu to defend the Constitution in *The Federalist* Number 47, 324–27 (see also 52–56, 292, 295, 523). Opponents of the Constitution also cited Montesquieu; see Luther Martin, "Genuine Information" (delivered to the Maryland legislature November 29, 1787) in *RFC* III, 197.

18. Roger H. Brown, *Redeeming the Republic: Federalists, Taxation, and the Origins of the Constitution* (Baltimore, MD: Johns Hopkins University Press, 1993), 171–83; M. J. C. Vile, *Constitutionalism and the Separation of Powers* (Oxford: Clarendon Press, 1967), 153–54; Gerhard Casper, *Separating Power: Essays on the Founding Period* (Cambridge, MA: Harvard University Press, 1997), 7–8.

19. Vile, *Constitutionalism and the Separation of Powers*, 128; Wood, *The Creation of the American Republic, 1776–1787*, 150–61. The constitutions of Maryland, Virginia, North Carolina, and Georgia specifically separated government powers, and the rest of the states implicitly separated powers.

20. *RFC* III, 585.

21. Morone, *The Democratic Wish*, 33–34, 63.

22. *RFC* May 31, I, 48.

23. *RFC* June 23, I, 423.

24. *RFC* June 29, I, 475.

25. Robertson, *The Constitution and America's Destiny*, 37–45.

26. James Madison to Thomas Jefferson, July 18, 1787, in *RFC* III, 60; James Madison, "Preface to Debates in the Convention of 1787," *RFC* III, 550.

27. When I cite these notes in this book, I cite Madison's notes simply as *RFC*, date, volume and page. When I cite other delegates' notes and records, I also indicate the delegate's name.

28. James L. Hutson discusses the objectivity of Madison's records in "The Creation of the Constitution: The Integrity of the Documentary Record," *Texas Law Review* 65:1 (November 1986): 1–39, and in James L. Huston, ed., *Supplement to Max Farrand's The Records of the Federal Convention of 1787* [hereafter, *RFC 1987 Supplement*] (New Haven, CT: Yale University Press, 1987), xx–xxiv. Robert Yates took notes on the proceedings until July. Yates's notes were edited later to advance partisan goals. I do not believe Yates's notes, as they exist, can be accepted as a fair and reliable record of the proceedings. For that reason, I use only one quote from Yates's notes in chapter 7 below; this quote from Gunning Bedford is one of the most widely cited quotes from the Convention.

29. New York Governor George Clinton had asked that Jay, a supporter of a much stronger national government, be excluded from the Convention. While Jay wrote four of the first five essays in *The Federalist*, he fell ill and wrote only one additional *Federalist* essay. Richard B. Morris, *Witness at the Creation: Hamilton, Madison, Jay and the Constitution* (New York: Henry Holt, 1985), 22, 56–58.

30. Pauline Maier, *Ratification: The People Debate the Constitution, 1787–1788* (New York: Simon and Schuster, 2010), 84.

31. Bernard Bailyn, *To Begin the World Anew: The Genius and Ambiguities of the American Founders* (New York: Alfred A. Knopf, 2003), 100.

32. Bailyn, *To Begin the World Anew*, 103–104.

33. Rakove, *Original Meanings*, 350. The author was Hamilton, who had been nominated to serve as the first secretary of the treasury.

34. Andrew Burstein and Nancy Isenberg, *Madison and Jefferson* (New York: Random House, 2010), 586.

35. Working Group on Federalism of the Domestic Policy Council, "The Status of Federalism in America" (unpublished mimeo, c. November, 1987), 1–2, 7–9.

36. Glenn Beck, *The Original Argument: The Federalists' Case for the Constitution, Adapted for the 21st Century* (New York: Threshold Editions, 2011), xxv.

37. *Printz v. United States*, 521 U.S. 898 (1997).

38. Melvyn R. Durschlag, "The Supreme Court and the Federalist Papers: Is There Less Here Than Meets the Eye?," *William & Mary Bill of Rights Journal* 14:1 (2005): 243–349, quote 315. See also Matthew J. Festa, "Dueling Federalists: Supreme Court Decisions with Multiple Opinions Citing *The Federalist*, 1986–2007," *Seattle University Law Review* 31:1 (Fall 2007): 75–106; Pamela C. Corley, Robert M. Howard, and David C. Nixon, "The Supreme Court and Opinion Content: The Use of the Federalist Papers," *Political Research Quarterly* 58:2 (June 2005): 329–40. In their opinions on the constitutionality of Affordable Care Act of 2010 (*National Federation of Independent Business et al. v. Sibelius*, June 28, 2012), the Supreme Court justices make eight separate references to *The Federalist*.

39. Richard B. Morris, *Witnesses at the Creation: Hamilton, Madison, Jay and the Constitution* (New York: Holt, Rinehart, and Winston, 1985), 23; Richard B. Bernstein, "Charting the Bicentennial," *Columbia Law Review* 87:8 (December 1987): 1588; Bailyn, *To Begin the World Anew*, 103; Richard Beeman, *Plain, Honest Men: The Making of the American Constitution* (New York: Random House, 2009), 407.

40. James W. Ducayet, "Publius and Federalism: On the Use and Abuse of *The Federalist* in Constitutional Interpretation," *New York University Law Review* 68 (1993): 821–69; John P. Roche, "The Founding Fathers: A Reform Caucus in Action," *American Political Science Review* 55:4 (December 1961): 799–816; Garry Wills, *Explaining America: The Federalist* (Garden City, NY: Doubleday, 1981); Samuel Kernell, "'The True Principles of Republican Government': Reassessing James Madison's Political Science," in *James Madison: The Theory and Practice of Republican Government*, ed. Samuel Kernell (Stanford, CA: Stanford University Press, 2003), 92–125.

41. *The Federalist* Number 2, 10–11.

42. Clinton Rossiter, *1787: The Grand Convention* (New York: Macmillan, 1966), 165, 188, 237; *RFC* September 17, II, 648–49; *RFC* III, 588, 590.

43. Indeed, the word "slavery" is used only in reference to the political servitude of all citizens under a dictatorship, as occurred in ancient Athens (*The Federalist* Number 18, 112) and could occur in the United States (*The Federalist*, Number 29, 186). The words "slave" or

"slaves" receive relatively brief mentions. In *The Federalist* Number 38 (247) and Number 42 (279, 281–82), Madison briefly addresses the provision that permits the importation of slaves until 1808, arguing that the possibility of banning the slave trade in 1808 is a "great point gained in favor of humanity." In *The Federalist* Number 54 (366–69), Madison uses the word "slave" or "slaves" fourteen times in six paragraphs, defending the provision that slaves be counted at a ratio to whites of three-fifths to one in apportioning of seats in the House of Representatives according to population. Madison also uses "slave" as a synonym for "dupe" (*The Federalist*, Number 58, 396). Compare to chapter 14 in this volume.

44. *The Federalist* Number 58, 394.
45. RFC August 8, II, 224; August 13, II, 280. In their dissenting opinion in *National Federation of Independent Business et al. v. Sibelius*, four Supreme Court justices utilize James Madison's *Federalist* 58 essay to argue that the House of Representatives' power to originate tax measures is very important (24–25).
46. James Madison to Thomas Jefferson, October 24, 1787, in *PJM*, 10: 209–14; Charles F. Hobson, "The Negative on State Laws: James Madison, the Constitution and the Crisis of Republican Government," *William and Mary Quarterly* 36 (1979): 217; Richard K. Matthews, *If Men Were Angels: James Madison and the Heartless Empire of Reason* (Lawrence: University Press of Kansas, 1995), 15.
47. Morris, *Witness at the Creation*, 19.
48. Bailyn, *To Begin the World Anew*, 124.
49. Rossiter, *1787: The Grand Convention*; Catherine Drinker Bowen, *Miracle at Philadelphia: The Story of the Constitutional Convention, May to September, 1787* (Boston: Little, Brown, 1966); Christopher Collier and James Lincoln Collier, *Decision in Philadelphia: The Constitutional Convention of 1787* (New York: Random House, 1986); Carol Berkin, *A Brilliant Solution: Inventing the American Constitution* (New York: Harcourt, 2002); Richard Beeman, *Plain, Honest Men: The Making of the American Constitution* (New York: Random House, 2009).
50. Wood, *The Creation of the American Republic, 1776–1787*; Rakove, *Original Meanings*; Charles Beard, *An Economic Interpretation of the Constitution of the United States* (New York: Macmillan, 1913); George Bancroft, *History of the Formation of the Constitution of the United States of America* (New York: D. Appleton, 1882). See also R. B. Bernstein, *The Founding Fathers Reconsidered* (Oxford and New York: Oxford University Press, 2009), 12–38. Political scientist John R. Vile edited a very helpful research tool for the Constitutional Convention; see *The Constitutional Convention of 1787: A Comprehensive Encyclopedia of America's Founding*, 2 vols. (Santa Barbara, CA: ABC-CLIO, 2005).
51. Thornton Anderson, *Creating the Constitution: The Convention of 1787 and the First Congress* (University Park: Pennsylvania State University Press, 1993); Calvin C. Jillson, *Constitution Making: Conflict and Consensus in the Federal Convention of 1787* (New York: Algora Publishing, 2008). See also Keith L. Dougherty and Jac C. Heckelman, "A Pivotal Voter from a Pivotal State: Roger Sherman at the Constitutional Convention," *American Political Science Review* 100 (2006): 297–302.
52. Roche, "The Founding Fathers: A Reform Caucus in Action"; Forrest McDonald, *E Pluribus Unum: The Formation of the American Republic, 1776–1790*, 2nd ed. (Indianapolis, IN: Liberty Press, 1979), *Novus Ordo Seclorum: The Intellectual Origins of the Constitution* (Lawrence: University Press of Kansas, 1985), and *States' Rights and the Union: Imperium in Imperio, 1789–1876* (Lawrence: University Press of Kansas, 2000); David Hendrickson, *Peace Pact: The Lost World of the American Founding* (Lawrence: University Press of Kansas, 2003). My own work also emphasized political realism, but it, too, makes a larger point about American political development and provided only an abbreviated narrative of the delegates' political reasoning during the Convention. See *The Constitution and America's Destiny* and "Madison's Opponents and Constitutional Design," in *American Political Science Review* 99:2 (May 2005): 225–43.
53. Bernard Bailyn, *The Ideological Origins of the American Revolution* (Cambridge, MA: Belknap Press, 1967); Wood, *The Creation of the American Republic, 1776–1787*; Trevor Colbourn, ed., *Fame and the Founding Fathers: Essays by Douglass Adair* (New York: W. W. Norton for the Institute of Early American History and Culture at Williamsburg, 1974); Donald Lutz, *The Origins of American Constitutionalism* (Baton Rouge: Louisiana State University Press, 1988).
54. Beard, *An Economic Interpretation of the Constitution*, 188.

55. Forrest McDonald, *We the People: The Economic Origins of the Constitution* (Chicago: University of Chicago Press, 1958); Robert E. Brown, *Charles Beard and the Constitution: A Critical Analysis of "An Economic Interpretation of the Constitution"* (New York: W. W. Norton, 1965); E. James Ferguson, *The Power of the Purse: A History of Public Finance, 1776–1790* (Chapel Hill: University of North Carolina Press, 1961), 251–86.

56. Robert A. McGuire, *To Form a More Perfect Union: A New Economic Interpretation of the United States Constitution* (New York: Oxford University Press, 2003).

57. McDonald, *E Pluribus Unum.*

58. Jillson, *Constitution Making,* ix–xi.

59. Rakove, *Original Meanings,* 15. See also Rakove, *The Beginnings of National Politics: An Interpretive History of the Continental Congress* (New York: Alfred Knopf, 1979); "The Great Compromise: Ideas, Interests, and the Politics of the Constitution," *William and Mary Quarterly,* Third Series, 44:3 (July 1987): 424–57; *James Madison and the Creation of the American Republic* (Glenview, IL: Scott, Foresman/Little, Brown, 1990).

60. See, for example, Madison's argument about admitting Western states into the Union on equal terms with the states on the Atlantic coast; *RFC* July 11, I, 584–85.

61. Edmund S. Morgan, *Inventing the People: The Rise of Popular Sovereignty in Early America* (New York: W. W. Norton, 1988), 256; *The Federalist* Number 53, 360–62.

62. "Resolution of Congress," February 21, 1787, *RFC* III, 13–14. In 1787, the term "federal government" was used to refer to the national government established under the Articles of Confederation of 1781. The delegates to the Constitutional Convention used the term in this sense, and the first sentence of the first number of *The Federalist* refers to "inefficiency of the subsisting federal government." In the United States today, the term "federal government" commonly refers to the U.S. national government established by the Constitution. To avoid confusion, I regularly use the term "national government" to refer to the object of the Convention's work, and the "Confederation government" as the national governing authority under the Articles of Confederation.

63. I discuss policy strategy further in *Capital, Labor, and State: The Battle for American Labor Markets from the Civil War to the New Deal* (Lanham, MD: Rowman and Littlefield, 2000), xiii–xvii, 13–27, and in *The Constitution and America's Destiny,* 17–25.

64. The following two paragraphs draw on David Brian Robertson, *Federalism and the Making of America* (Abingdon, UK, and New York: Routledge, 2011), 21–25.

65. Political scientist Paul Pierson describes this process as "path dependence," a tendency for a commitment, once established, to become self-reinforcing because more people accustom themselves to the commitment and resist changing it. On path dependence and sequence, see Paul Pierson, *Politics in Time: History, Institutions, and Social Analysis* (Princeton, NJ: Princeton University Press, 2005), 17–78.

66. *RFC* August 8, II, 224.

67. In presidential selection, the delegates went back and forth between Congressional selection and election by a special set of electors. The latter plan itself evolved through a long sequence of decisions. See chapter 10 in this volume.

68. See Robertson, *The Constitution and America's Destiny,* 97, 127, 163.

69. *RFC* August 15, II, 301.

70. Robertson, *The Constitution and America's Destiny,* 131–236.

71. *RFC* June 23, I, 386.

72. Wilbourn E. Benton made an effort simply to reorganize Farrand's *Records* verbatim and arrange them by Articles and sections of the Constitution itself. This compilation of the debates is nearly as long as Farrand's *Records* (1,558 pages with appendices) and provided no analytical context. Wilbourn E. Benton, ed., *1787: Drafting the U.S. Constitution* (College Station: Texas A&M University Press, 1986).

Chapter 2

1. James Madison to William Short, June 6, 1787, *RFC* III, 37.

2. George Mason to George Mason Jr., May 20, 1787, *RFC* III, 23.

3. Clinton Rossiter, *1787: The Grand Convention* (New York: Macmillan, 1966), 79–156; James H. Charleton and Robert G. Ferris, eds., *Framers of the Constitution* (Washington,

DC: Smithsonian Institution Press, 1986); Patrick T. Conley and John P. Kaminski, eds., *The Constitution and the States: The Role of the Original Thirteen in the Framing and Adoption of the Federal Constitution* (Madison, WI: Madison House, 1988).

4. David Brian Robertson, *The Constitution and America's Destiny* (Cambridge and New York: Cambridge University Press, 2005), 73–80; David Brian Robertson, "Madison's Opponents and Constitutional Design," *American Political Science Review* 99:2 (May 2005): 225–43.

5. Jeremiah Wadsworth to Rufus King, June 3, 1787, *RFC* III, 33–34.

6. William Pierce, "Character Sketches of Delegates to the Federal Convention," *RFC* III, 89.

7. Robertson, "Madison's Opponents and Constitutional Design."

8. Richard Beeman, *Plain, Honest Men: The Making of the American Constitution* (New York: Random House, 2009), 40; Rossiter, *1787: The Grand Convention*, 248–49.

9. *RFC* August 16, II, 307.

10. *RFC* June 8, I, 167.

11. *RFC* June 30, I, 491.

12. *RFC* June 11, I, 197.

13. *RFC* June 28: I, 467.

14. George Washington to David Stuart, July 1, 1787, *RFC* III, 52.

15. George Washington to Thomas Jefferson, May 30, 1787, *RFC* III, 31.

16. *RFC* July 14, II, 8.

17. James Madison to Edmund Pendleton, May 27, 1787, *RFC* III, 27.

18. Lansing notes, *RFC 1987 Supplement*, June 16, 78.

19. *RFC* June 26, I, 426. See Calvin C. Jillson and Rick K. Wilson, *Congressional Dynamics: Structure, Coordination, and Choice in the First American Congress, 1774–1789* (Stanford: Stanford University Press, 1994), 134–63; Keith L. Dougherty, *Collective Action under the Articles of Confederation* (Cambridge and New York: Cambridge University Press, 2001).

20. *RFC* July 14, II, 10. See Merrill Jensen, *The Articles of Confederation: An Interpretation of the Social-Constitutional History of the American Revolution, 1774–1781* (Madison: University of Wisconsin Press, 1940); James Ferguson, *The Power of the Purse: A History of Public Finance, 1776–1790* (Chapel Hill: University of North Carolina Press, 1961), 46–47, 61; Jack N. Rakove, *The Beginnings of National Politics: An Interpretive History of the Continental Congress* (New York: Alfred Knopf, 1979), 141–44, 159.

21. Allan Nevins, *The American States During and After the Revolution, 1775–1789* (New York: Macmillan, 1924), 117–70; Gordon S. Wood, *The Creation of the American Republic, 1776–1787* (Chapel Hill: University of North Carolina Press, 1969), 361; Jackson Turner Main, *The Sovereign States, 1775–1783* (New York: New Viewpoints, 1973); Samuel H. Beer, *To Make a Nation: The Rediscovery of American Federalism* (Cambridge, MA: Belknap Press, 1993), 200–206.

22. Cathy Matson, "The Revolution, the Constitution, and the New Nation," in *The Cambridge Economic History of the United States*, vol. I, *The Colonial Era*, ed. Stanley L. Engerman and Robert E. Gallman (Cambridge and New York: Cambridge University Press, 1996), 378–79; Nevins, *The American States During and After the Revolution*, 558–61; Curtis P. Nettels, *The Emergence of a National Economy, 1775–1815* (New York: Holt, Rinehart, and Winston, 1962), 69, 72–73.

23. George Washington to David Stuart, July 1, 1787, *RFC* III, 51.

24. *RFC* June 8, I, 166. See Joseph L. Davis, *Sectionalism in American Politics, 1774–1787* (Madison: University of Wisconsin Press, 1977).

25. Irwin H. Polishook, *Rhode Island and the Union, 1774–1795* (Evanston, IL: Northwestern University Press, 1969).

26. William Pierce to John Sullivan, May 24, 1787, *RFC 1987 Supplement*, 18; James Madison to James Monroe, June 10, 1787, *RFC 1987 Supplement*, 67; Paterson notes, *RFC* June 29, I, 479; George Washington to David Stuart, July 1, 1787, *RFC* III, 51; Abraham Baldwin to Joel Barlow, July 26, 1787, *RFC 1987 Supplement*, 193.

27. David P. Szatmary, *Shays's Rebellion: The Making of an American Insurrection* (Amherst: University of Massachusetts Press, 1980); Leonard L. Richards, *Shays's Rebellion: The American Revolution's Final Battle* (Philadelphia: University of Pennsylvania Press, 2002). Ronald P. Formisano argues that "Shays's Rebellion" is a misnomer and the event

is misunderstood; see *For the People: American Populist Movements from the Revolution to The 1850* (Chapel Hill: University of North Carolina Press, 2008), 27–32.

28. Main, *The Sovereign States*, 76; Gary M. Walton and Hugh Rockoff, *History of the American Economy*, 8th ed. (Fort Worth, TX: Dryden Press, 1998), 94–113, 147–50.

29. Davis, *Sectionalism in American Politics*, 13, 16–21, 76, 85–86, 92, 108–20, 125; Drew McCoy, "James Madison and Visions of American Nationality in the Confederation Period: A Regional Perspective," in *Beyond Confederation: Origins of the Constitution and American National Identity*, ed. Richard Beeman, Stephen Botein, and Edward Carter III (Chapel Hill: University of North Carolina Press, 1987), 226–60; Jensen, *The Articles of Confederation*, 218–24; Nevins, *The American States During and After the Revolution*, 566–68.

30. *RFC* June 29, I, 466.

31. *RFC* June 30, I, 486.

32. *RFC* August 29, II, 451.

33. *RFC* August 29, II, 449.

34. McCoy, "James Madison and Visions of American Nationality," 230–32.

35. Textbook discussions of the Constitutional Convention often simplify the disagreement over representation in Congress as a clash of "large" states against "small" states. In fact, the states and their votes cannot be reduced to a straightforward clash of "large" and "small" states. Virginia, Pennsylvania, and Massachusetts were considered the three largest states. North Carolina was already a large state and South Carolina expected to join the large states in the foreseeable future, so their delegations voted with the large states for proportional representation in Congress. Georgia was smaller than most of the other states; its delegates tended to vote for the Virginia Plan but sometimes were divided. Delaware, New Jersey, Connecticut, Rhode Island, and New Hampshire were considered small states. New York and Maryland were larger than average, but their delegates disagreed internally about the Virginia Plan.

36. *RFC* July 23, II, 90.

37. *RFC* June 29, I, 464–65.

38. *RFC* June 29, I, 466.

39. George Washington to George Augustine Washington, May 17, 1787, *RFC 1987 Supplement*, 6.

40. Rufus King to Jeremiah Wadsworth, May 24, 1787, *RFC* III, 26.

41. George Mason to George Mason Jr. May 27, 1787, *RFC* III, 28.

42. Peter S. Onuf, *The Origins of the Federal Republic: Jurisdictional Controversies in the United States, 1775–1787* (Philadelphia: University of Pennsylvania Press, 1983), 60–61, 142, 95–96, 205–207.

43. George Mason to George Mason Jr., May 27, 1787, *RFC* III, 28.

44. Mildred Amer, "Secret Sessions of Congress: A Brief Historical Overview," *Congressional Research Service* Report RS20145 (October 21, 2004).

45. *RFC* May 28, I, 7–13; May 29, I, 15–17.

46. A "committee of the whole" is the term used for a meeting of an entire house of a legislature— or in this case, the entire Constitutional Convention—as a committee. This common legislative device allows more informal debate than under the restricted rules that apply to formal meetings of a legislative body.

47. The Committee of Detail consisted of John Rutledge of South Carolina, Edmund Randolph of Virginia, Oliver Ellsworth of Connecticut, James Wilson of Pennsylvania, and Nathaniel Gorham of Massachusetts.

48. The Committee of Style consisted of William Samuel Johnson of Connecticut, Alexander Hamilton of New York, Gouverneur Morris of Pennsylvania, James Madison of Virginia, and Rufus King of Massachusetts. Its final report is reproduced in *RFC* II, 590-603. Madison dated his copy "Sepr. 12." Farrand compiled the Constitutional provisions approved prior to the Committee of Style's work; this undated compilation appears at *RFC* II, 565–80.

49. Elbridge Gerry to Ann Gerry, May 30, 1787, *RFC 1987 Supplement*, 33.

50. Mary Norris to—, July 4, 1787, *RFC 1987 Supplement*, 145.

51. George Mason to George Mason Jr., May 20, 1787, *RFC* III, 24; Abraham Baldwin to Joel Barlow, July 26, 1787, *RFC 1987 Supplement*, 193; Luther Martin to Nicholas Low, July 1, 1787, *RFC 1987 Supplement*, 141.

52. *RFC* III, 586–90. Gordon Lloyd has integrated many sources of information about the attendance of the delegates. See Gordon Lloyd, "Constitutional Convention Attendance Record," http://teachingamericanhistory.org/convention/attendance/ (accessed September 13, 2011).
53. William R. Davie to Richard Carswell, June 19, 1787, *RFC 1987 Supplement*, 97; Rufus King to Henry Knox, July 11, 1787, *RFC 1987 Supplement*, 163; Jonathan Dayton to William Livingston, July 13, 1787, *RFC 1987 Supplement*, 167; *RFC* August 15, II, 301; *RFC* August 18, II, 328.
54. George Mason to George Mason Jr., June 1, 1787, *RFC* III, 32–33.
55. *RFC* June 25, I, 405.
56. James Madison to Thomas Jefferson, June 6, 1787, *RFC* III, 36.
57. *RFC* June 16, I, 255.

Chapter 3

1. *RFC* May 31, I, 53.
2. *RFC* May 31, I, 53; George Washington to David Stuart, July 1, 1787, *RFC* III, 51.
3. McHenry Notes, *RFC* May 30, I, 42.
4. *RFC* May 30, I, 34–35.
5. *RFC* May 29, I, 23.
6. *RFC* June 16, I, 255.
7. Lansing notes, June 16, *RFC 1987 Supplement*, 79.
8. *RFC* June 18, I, 282–83.
9. *RFC* June 29, I, 467.
10. *RFC* July 2, I, 511.
11. *RFC* July 5, I, 532.
12. *RFC* May 30, I, 34.
13. *RFC* June 9, I, 178; June 16, I, 250.
14. *RFC* June 16, I, 249; June 20, I, 336.
15. *RFC* June 4, I, 101.
16. *RFC* June 16, I, 255.
17. *RFC* June 16, I, 253.
18. *RFC* June 16, I, 255.
19. *RFC* June 18, I, 283.
20. *RFC* August 29, II, 451.
21. Lansing notes, June 29, *RFC 1987 Supplement*, 127.
22. *RFC* June 12, I, 215.
23. *RFC* August 14, II, 285–86.
24. *RFC* June 16, I, 250.
25. *RFC* June 16, I, 249–50.
26. *RFC* June 12, I, 215.
27. *RFC* July 5, I, 529.
28. *RFC* June 20, I, 338.
29. *RFC* June 16, I, 253.
30. *RFC* July 5, I, 528.
31. *RFC* August 14, II, 287–88.
32. James Madison to Thomas Jefferson, September 6, 1787, *RFC* III, 78.
33. Gordon S. Wood, *The Creation of the American Republic, 1776–1787* (Chapel Hill: University of North Carolina Press, 1969), 46–90, 150–61.
34. *RFC* June 20, I, 339.
35. George Mason to George Mason Jr., June 1, 1787, *RFC* III, 32.
36. *RFC* June 26, I, 423.
37. Mason draft of speech, *RFC* June 4, I, 112.
38. King notes, *RFC* June 1, I, 71.
39. Pierce notes, *RFC* June 1, I, 74.
40. *RFC* June 25, I, 398, 402, 404.

41. *RFC* June 4, I, 102.
42. King notes, *RFC* June 1, I, 71.
43. *RFC* June 26, I, 425.
44. *RFC* June 2, I, 87.
45. *RFC* July 17, II, 36.
46. *RFC* June 1, I, 66; June 7, I, 153.
47. *RFC* June 18, I, 288.
48. *RFC* June 25, I, 398–99, 403.
49. *RFC* August 28, II, 439–42.
50. McHenry notes, *RFC* May 29, I, 26–27.
51. *RFC* June 18, I, 284–86.
52. *RFC* June 6, I, 135.
53. *RFC* May 31, I, 49–50.
54. *RFC* August 13, II, 276.
55. Wood, *The Creation of the American Republic*, 55–57; Bernard Bailyn, *The Ideological Origins of the American Revolution* (Cambridge, MA: Belknap Press, 1967), 280–86.
56. *RFC* August 31, II, 476.
57. *RFC* July 26, II, 120.
58. *RFC* June 4, I, 101.
59. King notes, *RFC* June 6, I, 142.
60. *RFC* June 19, I, 318.
61. *RFC* July 13, I, 605; September 8, II, 548.
62. *RFC* August 29, II, 450.
63. M. J. C. Vile, *Constitutionalism and the Separation of Powers* (Oxford, UK: Clarendon Press, 1967), 128; Wood, *The Creation of the American Republic*, 150–61.
64. *RFC* May 30, I, 34.
65. Nathaniel Gorham to Theophilus Parsons, June 18, 1787, *RFC 1987 Supplement*, 94; *RFC* May 30, I, 35; August 7, II, 196.
66. *RFC* July 19, II, 56; see Dickinson comments on the separation of powers, *RFC* June 2, I, 86.
67. *RFC* July 21, II, 77.
68. *RFC* July 2, I, 512. In *The Federalist*, Madison expressed a similar idea, writing, "Ambition must be made to counteract ambition." Alexander Hamilton, James Madison, and John Jay, *The Federalist*, ed. Jacob E. Cooke (Middletown, CT: Wesleyan University Press, 1961), Number 51, 349.
69. *RFC* July 17, II, 35. Even Thomas Jefferson, the champion of democracy, was concerned about the possibility of legislative despotism. See Madison's essay in *The Federalist* Number 48, 355.
70. *RFC* July 21, II, 74.
71. *RFC* June 16, I, 254.
72. *RFC* June 2, I, 86.
73. *RFC* June 16, I, 251.
74. *RFC* June 20, I, 341.
75. *RFC* May 31, I, 48; June 21, I, 358.
76. Vile, *Constitutionalism and the Separation of Powers*, 154.
77. On the separation of powers in the Pennsylvania Constitution, see Wood, *The Creation of the American Republic*, 449–51; Robert F. Williams, "The State Constitutions of the Founding Decade: Pennsylvania's Radical 1776 Constitution and Its Influences on American Constitutionalism," *Temple Law Review* 62 (Summer 1989): 541–74.

Chapter 4

1. *RFC* August 16, II, 307.
2. Forrest McDonald, *We the People: The Economic Origins of the Constitution* (Chicago: University of Chicago Press, 1958), 21–37.
3. *RFC* August 13, II, 273.

4. *RFC* August 21, II, 362.
5. *RFC* June 6, I, 135–36.
6. *RFC* August 13, II, 276.
7. *RFC* June 18, I, 289.
8. *RFC* July 21, II, 78.
9. *RFC* May 31, I, 48.
10. *RFC* May 31, I, 48.
11. *RFC* August 7, II, 202–203.
12. *RFC* August 7, II, 202.
13. *RFC* June 2, 1, 82.
14. *RFC* July 26, II, 122.
15. *RFC* June 6, I, 132.
16. *RFC* July 18, II, 42.
17. *RFC* July 11, I, 584.
18. *RFC* July 19, II, 52.
19. *RFC* August 13, II, 274.
20. *RFC* July 5, I, 527.
21. *RFC* July 25, II, 109.
22. *RFC* June 2, I, 80.
23. *RFC* September 4, II, 500.
24. *RFC* September 7, II, 542.
25. *RFC* June 4, I, 99.
26. *RFC* September 12, II, 587.
27. *RFC* August 27, II, 430.
28. McHenry notes, *RFC* September 6, II, 530.
29. *RFC* July 2, I, 512.
30. *RFC* July 17, II, 32.
31. *RFC* June 5, I, 119.
32. *RFC* June 23, I, 387.
33. *RFC* August 9, II, 236, 239; August 13, II, 269.
34. Butler notes, *RFC 1987 Supplement,* June 8, 61.
35. *RFC* September 15, II, 626–27. Shays himself was pardoned, and the state legislature enacted some reforms addressing the debtors' concerns. See David P. Szatmary, *Shays's Rebellion: The Making of an American Insurrection* (Amherst: University of Massachusetts Press, 1980).
36. *RFC* June 2, I, 87.
37. King notes, *RFC* June 4, I, 108.
38. James Madison, "Vices of the Political System of the United States," *PJM* 9, 354–55.
39. *RFC* June 26, I, 421–23. I replaced the word "seasonably" in Farrand's *Records* with the word "reasonably."
40. *RFC* June 26, I, 423.
41. *RFC* June 26, I, 425.
42. *RFC* June 26, I, 424.
43. *RFC* June 6, I, 134–36.
44. David Brian Robertson, "Madison's Opponents and Constitutional Design," *American Political Science Review* 99:2 (May 2005): 225–43.
45. Elsewhere, I argue that Madison, before and during the Convention, was advocating not only a physically extensive republic, but also a national government with very broad authority. After the Convention, advocating the ratification of a Constitution in a closely contested state, Madison restricted his argument to the geographical extent of the American republic. David Brian Robertson, "Constituting a National Interest: Madison Against the States' Autonomy," in *James Madison: The Theory and Practice of Republican Government,* ed. Samuel Kernell (Stanford, CA: Stanford University Press, 2003), 200–201.
46. *RFC* June 26, I, 423.
47. *RFC* July 24, II, 101.

48. *RFC* July 20, II, 66.
49. *RFC* August 14, II, 288.
50. *RFC* June 23, I, 387.

Chapter 5

1. Ralph Ketcham, *James Madison: A Biography* (Charlottesville: University Press of Virginia, 1971); Richard K. Matthews, *If Men Were Angels: James Madison and the Heartless Empire of Reason* (Lawrence: University Press of Kansas, 1995).
2. Madison to Edmund Randolph, March 11, 1787, *PJM* 9, 307.
3. Ketcham, *James Madison*, 183–85; "Notes on Ancient and Modern Confederacies," *PJM* 9, 3–25; "Vices of the Political System of the United States," *PJM* 9, 345–58; Rakove, *Original Meanings*, 46–56; Madison to Thomas Jefferson, March 19, 1787, to Edmund Randolph, April 8, 1787, and to George Washington, April 16, 1787, in *PJM* 9, 317–22, 368–71, 382–87.
4. Ketcham, *James Madison*, 191–94.
5. *RFC* May 28, I, 10–11.
6. *RFC* May 29, I, 8.
7. *PJM* 9, 348–50, 354–56.
8. Madison to George Washington, April 16, 1787, in *PJM* 9, 383–84.
9. Madison to George Washington, April 16, 1787, in *PMJ*, 9, 383.
10. *RFC* May 30, I, 34.
11. *RFC* May 30, I, 34.
12. *RFC* July 6, I, 551.
13. *RFC* May 29, I, 18.
14. *RFC* May 29, I, 18–19.
15. *RFC* May 29, I, 19; McHenry notes, *RFC* May 29, I, 25.
16. *RFC* May 29, I, 19.
17. McHenry notes, *RFC* May 29, I, 25.
18. *RFC* May 29, I, 19.
19. McHenry notes, *RFC* May 29, I, 25–26.
20. *RFC* May 29, I, 19.
21. McHenry notes, *RFC* May 29, I, 26.
22. *RFC* May 29, I, 19.
23. McHenry notes, *RFC* May 29, I, 26.
24. *RFC* May 29, I, 19.
25. McHenry notes, *RFC* May 29, I, 26–27.
26. *RFC* May 29, I, 19.
27. *RFC* May 29, I, 20–22. Ketcham, *James Madison*, 194–95; Jack N. Rakove, *James Madison and the Creation of the American Republic* (Glenview, IL: Scott, Foresman/Little, Brown, 1990), 55, 59.

Chapter 6

1. George Read to John Dickinson, May 21, 1787, *RFC* III, 25–26.
2. *RFC* May 30, I, 34.
3. *RFC* July 5, I, 530.
4. *RFC* July 7, I, 552–53.
5. *RFC* June 18, I, 287.
6. *RFC* June 18, I, 284.
7. *RFC* May 30, I, 42.
8. *RFC* May 30, I, 35.
9. *RFC* May 31, I, 51.
10. *RFC* June 2, I, 80.
11. McHenry notes, *RFC*, May 30, I *RFC*, 42.
12. *RFC* June 2, I, 86–87.

13. Herbert J. Storing, *What the Anti-Federalists Were For* (Chicago: University of Chicago Press, 1981), 15–23.
14. Lansing notes, *RFC 1987 Supplement*, June 25, 112–13.
15. *RFC* June 30, I, 492.
16. *RFC* June 5, I, 124–25.
17. *RFC* June 5, I, 124.
18. *RFC* June 6, I, 133.
19. *RFC* June 6, I, 133.
20. *RFC* June 9, I, 178.
21. *RFC* June 6, I, 137.
22. *RFC* June 6, I, 137.
23. *RFC* June 7, I, 150.
24. *RFC* June 7, I, 152–53.
25. *RFC* June 9, I, 179.
26. *RFC* June 7, I, 153–54.
27. *RFC* June 7, I, 155–56.
28. *RFC* June 11, I, 196.
29. *RFC* June 15, I, 242n. According to Madison, "Connecticut and New York were against a departure from the principle of the Confederation, wishing rather to add a few new powers to Congress than to substitute, a National Government. The States of New Jersey and Delaware were opposed to a National Government because its patrons considered a proportional representation of the States as the basis of it."
30. *RFC* June 15, I, 242–45.
31. *RFC* June 16, I, 249, 251.
32. *RFC* June 16, I, 252–53.
33. *RFC* June 16, I, 255–56.
34. *RFC* June 18, I, 284–86.
35. *RFC* June 18, I, 289, 291–92. Some delegates believed that this plan was more monarchical than republican, and Hamilton himself admitted, "As to the Executive, it seemed to be admitted that no good one could be established on Republican principles" (289). In *The Federalist* Numbers 67–77, Hamilton earnestly defended a much different design of the presidency embodied in the Constitution; see *The Federalist*, 452–521.
36. *RFC* June 19, I, 316–17. On Connecticut's Western Reserve, see Christopher Collier, *Roger Sherman's Connecticut: Yankee Politics and the American Revolution* (Middletown, CT: Wesleyan University Press, 1971), 146–48.
37. *RFC* June 19, I, 315–21.
38. *RFC* June 19, I, 322.
39. *RFC* June 20, I, 335.
40. *RFC* June 20, I, 336–38.
41. *RFC* June 20, I, 338, 340.
42. *RFC* June 20, I, 340–41.
43. Lansing notes, *RFC Supplement*, June 28: 125.
44. *RFC* June 20, I, 342–43.
45. *RFC* June 20, I, 343.
46. *RFC* June 21, I, 355.
47. *RFC* June 29, I, 461.
48. *RFC* June 21, I, 356.
49. *RFC* June 29, I, 462.
50. *RFC* June 30, 492–93.
51. *RFC* June 25, I, 404.
52. *RFC* June 21, I, 358.
53. *RFC* June 29, I, 464.
54. *RFC* June 28, I, 449.
55. *RFC* June 29, I, 468.
56. *RFC* June 29, I, 468.
57. *RFC* June 19, I, 321.

Chapter 7

1. The "House of Commons" was the title of the house of the British Parliament whose members were elected by local communities.
2. *RFC* May 31, I, 48–49.
3. *RFC* June 6, I, 133–34.
4. *RFC* June 20, I, 338–39.
5. *RFC* June 6, I, 132–33.
6. King notes, *RFC* June 9, I, 185.
7. *RFC* August 21, II, 357.
8. *RFC* May 31, I, 50.
9. *RFC* May 31, I, 48.
10. *RFC* May 31, I, 49.
11. *RFC* May 31, I, 49–50.
12. *RFC* June 6, I, 133.
13. *RFC* June 6, I, 136–37.
14. *RFC* June 6, I, 137.
15. *RFC* June 6, I, 134.
16. *RFC* June 6, 137–38.
17. *RFC* June 21, I, 358.
18. *RFC* June 21, I, 359.
19. *RFC* June 21, I, 359.
20. *RFC* June 21, I, 359.
21. *RFC* June 21, I, 359.
22. *RFC* June 21, I, 358–59.
23. *RFC* June 21, I, 359–60.
24. *RFC* May 30, I, 36.
25. *RFC* May 30, I, 37.
26. *RFC* May 30, I, 37.
27. *RFC* May 30, I, 37–38.
28. *RFC* June 9, I, 177.
29. *RFC* June 9, I, 177–79.
30. *RFC* June 9, I, 179–80.
31. *RFC* June 11, I, 196.
32. *RFC* June 11, I, 196.
33. *RFC* June 11, I, 196.
34. *RFC* June 11, I, 197.
35. *RFC* June 11, I, 201.
36. *RFC* June 11, I, 201–202.
37. *RFC* June 16, I, 250.
38. *RFC* June 20, I, 342.
39. Mason, *RFC* June 20, I, 340; for Franklin, see *RFC* June 11, I, 197–200.
40. *RFC* June 16, I, 255.
41. *RFC* June 19, I, 325.
42. *RFC* June 16, I, 253.
43. *RFC* June 19, I, 321–22.
44. *RFC* June 28, I, 450.
45. *RFC* June 28, I, 446–49.
46. *RFC* June 28, I, 451–52.
47. *RFC* June 29, I, 461–62.
48. *RFC* June 29: I, 464.
49. *RFC* June 29: I, 466.
50. *RFC* June 29, I, 468.
51. *RFC* July 5, I, 526.
52. *RFC* July 5, I, 533–34; King notes, *RFC* July 5, I, 536.
53. *RFC* July 5, I, 534.

54. *RFC* July 9, I, 559.
55. *RFC* July 9, I, 559, 561.
56. *RFC* July 10, I, 566–67.
57. *RFC* July 10, I, 567.
58. *RFC* July 10, I, 567.
59. *RFC* July 10, I, 566.
60. *RFC* July 10, I, 567.
61. *RFC* July 10, I, 568–70.
62. *RFC* September 8, II, 553–54. In *Federalist* Number 55, Madison defended the smaller size of the initial House of Representatives (375–78).
63. *RFC* September 15, II, 623.
64. *RFC* September 17, II, 644.
65. *RFC* July 10, I, 570–71.
66. *RFC* July 11, I, 578.
67. *RFC* July 11, I, 583.
68. *RFC* July 11, I, 582.
69. *RFC* June 28, I, 446.
70. *RFC* I, July 6, I, 542.
71. *RFC* July 9, I, 560.
72. *RFC* July 10, I, 571.
73. *RFC* July 11, I, 583.
74. *RFC* July 11, I, 582.
75. *RFC* July 6, I, 541.
76. *RFC* July 11, I, 580.
77. *RFC* July 6, I, 542.
78. *RFC* July 11, I, 586.
79. *RFC* July 11, I, 584–85.
80. *RFC* July 12, I, 596.
81. *RFC* July 14, II, 2–3.
82. *RFC* July 13, I, 605.
83. *RFC* July 14, II, 3.
84. *RFC* July 14, II, 3.
85. On Congressional elections, see David W. Brady, *Critical Elections and Congressional Policy Making* (Stanford, CA: Stanford University Press, 1988); David Mayhew, *Congress: The Electoral Connection*, 2nd ed. (New Haven, CT: Yale University Press, 2004); Paul S. Herrnson, *Congressional Elections: Campaigning at Home and in Washington*, 5th ed. (Washington, DC: CQ Press, 2007), and *Electing Congress*, 2nd ed. (Washington, DC: CQ Press, 2008).
86. Robert Pierce Forbes, *The Missouri Compromise and Its Aftermath: Slavery and the Meaning of America* (Chapel Hill: University of North Carolina Press, 2007).
87. After the 1910 census, Congress apportioned 433 seats in the House; Arizona and New Mexico joined the union in 1912, adding one seat each for a total of 435. The Republican majority in Congress in 1921 enacted no reapportionment bill after the 1920 census (that census showed a substantial increase in the urban population, and thus reapportionment would have worked to the benefit of the Democrats). In 1929, Congress passed a Reapportionment Act that fixed the number of House seats at 435. Charles A. Kromkowski and John A. Kromkowski, "Why 435? A Question of Political Arithmetic," Polity 24:1 (Autumn 1991): 129–45.
88. U.S. Census Bureau, "Census 2010 Apportionment Results," http://usgovinfo.about.com/od/censusandstatistics/a/Census-2010-Apportionment-Results.htm (accessed March 23, 2012).
89. *Wesberry v. Sanders*, 376 U.S. 1 (1964). On apportionment, see Charles A. Kromkowski, *Recreating the American Republic: Rules of Apportionment, Constitutional Change, and American Political Development, 1700–1870* (Cambridge and New York: Cambridge University Press, 2002); Robert G. Dixon Jr., "The Courts, The People, and 'One Man, One Vote,'" in *Reapportionment in the 1970s*, ed. Nelson Polsby (Berkeley: University of California Press, 1971), 7–46.

Chapter 8

1. *RFC* May 31, I, 51.
2. *RFC* June 12, I, 218.
3. *RFC* June 6, I, 136.
4. *RFC* July 2, I, 512–13.
5. *RFC* June 25, I, 403.
6. Pierce notes, *RFC* May 31, I, 58.
7. *RFC* May 31, I, 51–52.
8. *RFC* May 31, I, 52.
9. *RFC* May 31, I, 52.
10. *RFC* May 31, I, 52; Pierce Notes, *RFC* May 31, I, 59.
11. Pierce Notes, *RFC* May 31, I, 59.
12. *RFC* June 6, I, 136.
13. *RFC* June 6, I, 136; June 7, I, 150.
14. *RFC* June 7, I, 153.
15. *RFC* June 6, I, 137.
16. *RFC* June 7, I, 151–52.
17. *RFC* June 7, I, 154. In *The Federalist* Number 63, Madison argues that the Senate will defend liberty and republicanism against the "temporary errors and delusions" of the people. The Senate was different from the British House of Lords and would "never be able to transform itself, by gradual usurpations, into an independent and aristocratic body" (425, 430–31).
18. *RFC* June 7, I, 150–51.
19. *RFC* June 7, I, 154.
20. *RFC* June 7, I, 152, 154.
21. *RFC* June 7, I, 155.
22. *RFC* June 25, I, 406.
23. *RFC* June 25, I, 406–407.
24. *RFC* June 25, I, 407.
25. *RFC* June 25, I, 408.
26. *RFC* June 2, I, 87.
27. *RFC* June 11, I, 196, 201.
28. *RFC* June 25, I, 404–405.
29. *RFC* June 27, I, 438.
30. *RFC* June 29, I, 468–69.
31. *RFC* June 29, I, 469.
32. *RFC* June 30, I, 482–84.
33. *RFC* June 30, I, 484–85.
34. *RFC* June 30, I, 485–86.
35. *RFC* June 30, I, 487.
36. *RFC* June 30, I, 487.
37. *RFC* June 30, I, 488.
38. *RFC* June 30, I, 488.
39. *RFC* June 30, I, 489.
40. *RFC* June 30, I, 489–90.
41. *RFC* June 30, I, 490.
42. *RFC* June 30, I, 490.
43. *RFC* June 30, I, 490–92. After listening to Bedford's implied threat to find allies abroad, Rufus King denied that he had "uttered a dictatorial language"; *RFC* June 30, I, 493.
44. Yates's notes, *RFC* June 30, I, 500.
45. *RFC* July 2, I, 510.
46. *RFC* July 2, I, 510–11.
47. *RFC* July 2, I, 511.
48. *RFC* July 2, I, 511.
49. *RFC* July 2, I, 511.
50. *RFC* July 2, I, 515.

51. *RFC* July 2, I, 511, 513–14.
52. *RFC* July 2, I, 515.
53. *RFC* July 5, I, 526.
54. *RFC* July 5, I, 527–29.
55. *RFC* July 5, I, 529–30.
56. *RFC* July 5, I, 531–32.
57. *RFC* July 5, I, 532.
58. *RFC* July 5, I, 532.
59. *RFC* July 5, I, 532–33.
60. *RFC* July 5, I, 532.
61. *RFC* July 7, I, 550.
62. *RFC* July 7, I, 551–52.
63. *RFC* July 7, I, 550.
64. *RFC* July 7, I, 551. Six states, including North Carolina, voted in favor of equal representation in the Senate on a test vote. However, Madison noted that "several votes were given here in the affirmative or were divided because another final question was to be taken on the whole report" (551).
65. *RFC* July 14, II, 4.
66. *RFC* July 14, II, 5.
67. *RFC* July 14, II, 5.
68. *RFC* July 14, II, 5.
69. *RFC* July 14, II, 6.
70. *RFC* July 14, II, 5.
71. *RFC* July 14, II, 7–8.
72. *RFC* July 14, II, 8–10.
73. *RFC* July 14, II, 10–11.
74. King Notes, *RFC* July 15, II, 12. Nathaniel Gorham was absent; had he been present, his vote might have split this Massachusetts vote and negated it.
75. *RFC* July 16, II, 15.
76. *RFC* July 16, II, 17–18.
77. *RFC* July 16, II, 18.
78. *RFC* July 16, II, 18.
79. *RFC* July 16, II, 19.
80. *RFC* July 16, II, 18.
81. *RFC* July 16, II, 19.
82. *RFC* July 16, II, 19.
83. *RFC* July 16, II, 19–20.
84. *RFC* July 14, II, 5; July 23, II, 94; August 9, II, 233–34.
85. Christopher Hyde Hoebeke, *The Road to Mass Democracy: Original Intent and the Seventeenth Amendment* (New Brunswick, NJ: Transaction Publishers, 1995); Daniel Wirls, "Regionalism, Rotten Boroughs, Race, and Realignment: The Seventeenth Amendment and the Politics of Representation," *Studies in American Political Development* 13:1 (Spring 1999): 1–30; William H. Riker, "The Senate and American Federalism," *American Political Science Review* 49:2 (June 1955): 452–69. Given this history, it is highly unlikely that the repeal of the Seventeenth Amendment would make senators more attentive to states' prerogatives, as some reformers hope.
86. See Frances E. Lee and Bruce I. Oppenheimer, *Sizing Up the Senate: The Unequal Consequences of Equal Representation* (Chicago: University of Chicago Press, 1999).

Chapter 9

1. *RFC* June 13, I, 233.
2. *RFC* June 13, I, 233.
3. *RFC* June 13, I, 234.
4. *RFC* June 26, I, 429.
5. *RFC* July 5, I, 527.

6. *RFC* July 6, I, 544.
7. *RFC* July 6, I, 545.
8. *RFC* July 6, I, 546.
9. *RFC* July 6, I, 544.
10. *RFC* July 6, I, 545.
11. *RFC* July 6, I, 547.
12. *RFC* July 14, II, 5.
13. *RFC* August 8, II, 224.
14. *RFC* August 8, II, 224.
15. *RFC* August 8, II, 224.
16. *RFC* August 8, II, 224.
17. *RFC* August 9, II, 233.
18. *RFC* August 9, II, 230, 232.
19. *RFC* August 9, II, 233–34.
20. *RFC* August 11, II, 263.
21. *RFC* August 13, II, 273–74.
22. *RFC* August 13, II, 278.
23. *RFC* August 11, II, *RFC* 263; August 13, II, 279–80.
24. *RFC* August 13, II, 276–77.
25. *RFC* August 13, 280.
26. *RFC* August 14, II, 287.
27. *RFC* August 8, II, 224; August 15, II, 297.
28. *RFC* August 15, II, 297.
29. *RFC* September 5, II, 508, 510.
30. *RFC* September 8, II, 552.
31. *RFC* June 12, I, 217, 219.
32. *RFC* June 22, I, 375–76.
33. *RFC* June 22, I, 376.
34. *RFC* June 22, I, 376.
35. *RFC* June 22, I, 376.
36. *RFC* June 22, I, 376.
37. *RFC* June 22, I, 377.
38. *RFC* June 23, I, 386.
39. *RFC* June 23, I, 387–88.
40. *RFC* June 23, I, 388.
41. *RFC* June 23, I, 387.
42. *RFC* June 23, I, 386, 390.
43. *RFC* June 26, I, 429.
44. *RFC* August 14, II, 283–84.
45. *RFC* August 14, II, 284–85.
46. *RFC* August 14, II, 288.
47. *RFC* August 14, II, 284.
48. *RFC* August 14, II, 285–86.
49. *RFC* August 14, II, 287.
50. *RFC* August 14, II, 287.
51. *RFCRFC* August 14, II, 288.
52. *RFCRFC* August 14, II, 289; September 3, II, 489–92.
53. *RFCRFC* June 12, I, 214–15.
54. *RFCRFC* June 12, I, 214.
55. *RFCRFC* June 12, I, 214.
56. *RFCRFC* June 12, I, 215.
57. *RFCRFC* June 12, I, 217.
58. *RFC* June 21, I, 360.
59. *RFC* June 21, I, 361.
60. *RFC* June 21, I, 361.
61. *RFC* June 21, I, 362.

62. *RFC* June 21, I, 360–61.
63. *RFC* June 21, I, 362.
64. *RFC* June 12, I, 218–19.
65. *RFC* June 12, I, 218.
66. *RFC* June 12, I, 218.
67. *RFC* June 25, I, 409.
68. *RFC* June 18, I, 289.
69. *RFC* June 24, I, 408.
70. *RFC* June 26, I, 426.
71. *RFC* June 25, I, 409.
72. *RFC* June 25, I, 409; June 21, I, 421.
73. *RFC* June 26, I, 421–23.
74. *RFC* June 26, I, 426.
75. *RFC* August 9, II, 231–32.
76. *RFC* August 7, II, 201.
77. *RFC* August 7, II, 202.
78. *RFC* August 7, II, 202.
79. *RFC* August 7, II, 205.
80. *RFC* August 7, II, 201.
81. *RFC* August 7, II, 204–5; King notes, August 7, II, 208.
82. *RFC* August 7, II, 201–2.
83. *RFC* August 7, II, 203.
84. *RFC* August 7, II, 203–4.
85. *RFC* August 9, II, 241.
86. *RFC* August 9, II, 241.
87. *RFC* August 9, II, 241.
88. *RFC* August 9, II, 241.
89. *RFC* August 9, II, 242.
90. *RFC* June 12, I, 217; June 22, I, 375; June 25, I, 408.
91. *RFC* June 26, I, 428.
92. *RFC* July 26, II, 122–23.
93. *RFC* July 26, II, 122–24.
94. *RFC* July 26, II, 123.
95. *RFC* July 26, II, 122.
96. *RFC* August 10, II, 249.
97. *RFC* August 10, II, 248–49.
98. *RFC* August 10, II, 249–50.
99. *RFC* August 10, II, 250–51.
100. *RFC* August 8, II, 217–18.
101. *RFC* August 8, II, 218.
102. *RFC* August 9, II, 235.
103. *RFC* August 9, II, 236.
104. *RFC* August 9, II, 237.
105. *RFC* August 13, II, 269–72.
106. *RFC* August 23, II, 389.
107. *RFC* June 12, I, 216.
108. *RFC* June 22, I, 373.
109. *RFC* June 22, I, 374.
110. *RFC* June 22, I, 374; June 26, I, 427.
111. *RFC* June 26, I, 427–28.
112. *RFC* June 26, I, 426–27; July 2, I, 513.
113. *RFC* June 26, I, 428.
114. *RFC* August 14, II, 290.
115. *RFC* August 14, II, 291.
116. *RFC* August 14, II, 290–91.
117. *RFC* August 14, II, 291.

118. *RFC* August 14, II, 290–92.
119. *RFC* August 14, II, 293.
120. *RFC* August 9, II, 231, 239.
121. *RFC* August 10, II, 254.
122. *RFC* August 10, II, 254.
123. *RFC* August 7, II, 197–99.
124. *RFC* August 7, II, 199–200.
125. *RFC* August 11, II, 261–62.
126. *RFC* August 10, II, 251–53.
127. *RFC* August 11, II, 260.
128. *RFC* September 14, II, 618–19.
129. On the development of Congress, see David Brady, "Incrementalism in the People's Branch: The Constitution and the Development of the Policy-making Process," and Charles Stewart III, "Responsiveness in the Upper Chamber: The Constitution and the Institutional Development of the Senate" in *The Constitution and American Political Development: An Institutional Perspective*, ed. Peter F. Nardulli (Urbana: University of Illinois Press, 1992), 35–96; Neal Devins and Keith E. Whittington, eds., *Congress and the Constitution* (Durham, NC: Duke University Press, 2005); Paul J. Quirk and Sarah A. Binder, eds., *The Legislative Branch* (Oxford and New York: Oxford University Press, 2005); Eric Schickler and Frances E. Lee, *The Oxford Handbook of the American Congress* (Oxford and New York: Oxford University Press, 2009); Eric Schickler, *Disjointed Pluralism: Institutional Innovation and the Development of the U.S. Congress* (Princeton, NJ: Princeton University Press, 2001); Joseph Cooper, *The Origins of the Standing Committees and the Development of the Modern House* (Houston, TX: Rice University Studies, 1971); Sarah A. Binder, *Minority Rights, Majority Rule: Partisanship and the Development of Congress* (Cambridge and New York: Cambridge University Press, 1997); Keith T. Poole and Howard Rosenthal, *Congress: A Political-Economic History of Roll Call Voting* (Oxford and New York: Oxford University Press, 1997); Barbara Sinclair, *The Transformation of the U.S. Senate* (Baltimore, MD: Johns Hopkins University Press, 1989).
130. Eric Schickler, "Institutional Development of Congress," in *The Legislative Branch*, ed. Paul J. Quirk and Sarah A. Binder (Oxford and New York: Oxford University Press, 2004), 35–62.
131. Allen Schick and Felix LoStracco, *The Federal Budget: Politics, Policy, Process*, rev. ed. (Washington, DC: Brooking Institution, 2000), 146.
132. On the development of the U.S. Senate, see Elaine K. Swift, *The Making of an American Senate: Reconstitutive Change in Congress, 1787–1841* (Ann Arbor: University of Michigan Press, 1996); Daniel Wirls and Stephen Wirls, *The Invention of the United States Senate* (Baltimore, MD: Johns Hopkins University Press, 2004); Sarah Binder and Steven S. Smith, *Politics or Principle? Filibustering in the United States Senate* (Washington, DC: Brookings Institution, 1996).
133. Alexander Keyssar, *The Right to Vote: The Contested History of Democracy in the United States* (New York: Basic Books, 2000), 26–76.
134. Eleanor Flexner and Ellen Fitzpatrick, *Century of Struggle: The Woman's Rights Movement in the United States*, enlarged ed. (Cambridge, MA: Belknap, 1996), 169–70, 208–17, 255–317; Suzanne M. Marilley, *Woman Suffrage and the Origins of Liberal Feminism in the United States, 1820–1920* (Cambridge, MA: Harvard University Press, 1996).
135. *Powell v. McCormack*, 395 U.S. 486 (1969).

Chapter 10

1. The term "electoral college" was not included in the Constitution. The term came into usage in the early nineteenth century. National Records and Archives Administration, Electoral College, "Frequently Asked Questions," http://www.archives.gov/federal-register/electoral-college/faq.html#history (accessed August 19, 2011).
2. *RFC* June 1, I, 66.
3. *RFC* July 24, II, 105.

4. *RFC* June 1, I, 64–65.
5. *RFC* August 6, II, 145, 185.
6. *RFC* June 18, I, 289.
7. McHenry Notes, *RFC* August 6, II, 191–92.
8. King Notes, *RFC* June 6, I, 144.
9. *RFC* June 1, I, 65.
10. *RFC* June 6, I, 138.
11. King notes, *RFC* June 1, I, 70.
12. *RFC* June 2, I, 88.
13. *RFC* June 1, I, 66.
14. *RFC* June 1, I, 65.
15. *RFC* June 1, I, 65; June 2, I, 88–89.
16. *RFC* June 4, I, 97.
17. *RFC* June 4, I, 96.
18. *RFC* June 4, I, 101–102.
19. *RFC* July 16, II, 29; July 24, II, 100–101.
20. *RFC* July 17, II, 34–35.
21. *RFC* July 19, II, 52.
22. *RFC* July 19, II, 52.
23. *RFC* June 4, I, 103; Alexander Hamilton to Jacob Duché, September 8, 1787, *RFC 1987 Supplement*, 263.
24. *RFC* June 4, I, 103.
25. *RFC* September 4, II, 501.
26. *RFC* June 1, I, 69; June 2, I, 80.
27. *RFC* June 1, I, 68.
28. *RFC* June 2, I, 81.
29. *RFC* June 2, I, 80.
30. *RFC* June 1, I, 69.
31. *RFC* June 9, I, 175–76.
32. *RFC* June 9, I, 176.
33. *RFC* July 17, II, 29.
34. *RFC* July 17, II, 29–30.
35. *RFC* July 17, II, 30.
36. *RFC* July 17, II, 31.
37. *RFC* July 17, II, 29.
38. *RFC* July 17, II, 30.
39. *RFC* July 17, II, 32.
40. *RFC* July 19, II*RFC*, 52.
41. *RFC* July 19, II, 55.
42. *RFC* July 19, II, 55–56.
43. *RFC* July 19, II, 56.
44. *RFC* July 19, II, 56–57.
45. *RFC* July 19, II, 57.
46. *RFC* July 19, II, 57.
47. *RFC* July 19, II, 57.
48. *RFC* July 19, II, 58.
49. *RFC* July 19, II, 58.
50. *RFC* July 20, II, 63.
51. *RFC* July 20, II, 63–64.
52. *RFC* July 23, II, 95.
53. *RFC* July 24, II, 100.
54. *RFC* July 24, II, 100.
55. *RFC* July 24, II, 101.
56. *RFC* July 24, II, 103, 105.
57. *RFC* July 24, II, 103–105.
58. *RFC* July 24, II, 105.

59. *RFC* July 24, II, 105–6.
60. *RFC* July 24, II, 103.
61. *RFC* July 25, II, 108–109.
62. *RFC* July 25, II, 109–11.
63. *RFC* July 25, II, 111.
64. *RFC* July 25, II, 113.
65. *RFC* July 25, II, 113.
66. *RFC* July 25, II, 114. The Society of the Cincinnati, created in 1783, was a fraternal society of former Continental Army officers. George Washington was its first president. The organization was controversial because membership was passed down through the eldest son, which smacked of hereditary nobility. See Joseph Ellis, *His Excellency: George Washington* (New York: Vintage Books, 2004), 158–60. The Society of the Cincinnati still exists; see http://societyofthecincinnati.org/ (accessed March 24, 2012).
67. *RFC* July 25, II, 112.
68. *RFC* July 26, II, 118–19.
69. *RFC* August 6, II, 177.
70. *RFC* August 7, II, 196.
71. *RFC* August 7, II, 196.
72. *RFC* August 7, II, 196.
73. *RFC* August 7, II, 196–97.
74. *RFC* August 24, II, 401.
75. *RFC* August 24, II, 402.
76. *RFC* August 24, II, 402.
77. *RFC* August 24, II, 402.
78. *RFC* August 24, II, 402.
79. *RFC* August 24, II, 402.
80. *RFC* August 24, II, 403.
81. *RFC* August 24, II, 403.
82. *RFC* August 24, II, 403–404.
83. *RFC* August 24, II, 404.
84. *RFC* September 4, II, 497–98.
85. *RFC* September 4, II, 501.
86. *RFC* September 6, II, 524.
87. *RFC* September 4, II, 501–502.
88. *RFC* September 5, II, 511.
89. *RFC* September 4, II, 500; September 5, II, 512.
90. *RFC* September 6, II, 525.
91. *RFC* September 6, II, 521.
92. *RFC* September 4, II, 500; September 5, II, 511.
93. *RFC* September 5, II, 511–12.
94. *RFC* September 4, II, 500; September 5, II, 513.
95. *RFC* September 5, II, 512–13.
96. *RFC* September 4, II, 501; September 5, II, 514.
97. *RFC* September 5, II, 514–15.
98. *RFC* September 5, II, 512; 514–15; September 6, II, 526.
99. September 5, II, 514; September 6, II, 522.
100. *RFC* September 5, II, 515.
101. *RFC* September 6, II, 522–23.
102. *RFC* September 6, II, 522.
103. *RFC* September 6, II, 526–27.
104. *RFC* September 6, II, 527.
105. Akhil Reed Amar, *America's Constitution: A Biography* (New York: Random House, 2005), 152. The Supreme Court decision in *Bush v. Gore*, 531 U.S. 98 (2000) made it clear that "[t]he individual citizen has no federal constitutional right to vote for electors for the President of the United States unless and until the state legislature chooses a statewide election as the means to implement its power to appoint members of the Electoral College."

106. For overviews of the history of presidential elections, see Arthur M. Schlesinger Jr., Gil Troy, and Fred L. Israel, *History of American Presidential Elections, 1789–2008* (New York: Facts on File, 2011); *Presidential Elections 1789–2008* (Washington, DC: CQ Press, 2009); Hanes Walton, Donald Deskins Jr., and Sherman Puckett, *Presidential Elections, 1789–2008: County, State, and National Mapping of Election Data* (Ann Arbor: University of Michigan Press, 2010). Many books analyze specific presidential elections.
107. On critical elections, see Walter Dean Burnham, *Critical Elections and the Mainsprings of American Politics* (New York: W. W. Norton, 1970); James L. Sundquist, *Dynamics of the Party System: Alignment and Realignment of Political Parties in the United States*, 2nd ed. (Washington, DC: Brookings Institution, 1983); Jerome M. Clubb, William H. Flanigan, and Nancy H. Zingale, *Partisan Realignment: Voters, Parties, and Government in American History* (Beverly Hills, CA: Sage, 1980); Byron E. Shafer, ed. *The End of Realignment? Interpreting American Electoral Eras* (Madison: University of Wisconsin, 1991).
108. On the electoral college, see Wallace S. Sayre and Judith H. Parris, *Voting for President: The Electoral College and the American Political System* (Washington, DC: Brookings Institution, 1970); Walter Berns et al., *After the People Vote: A Guide to the Electoral College* (Washington, DC: AEI Press, 2004).
109. Bernard A. Weisberger, *America Afire: Jefferson, Adams, and the Revolutionary Election of 1800* (New York: William Morrow, 2000); Tadahisa Kuroda, *The Origins of the Twelfth Amendment: The Electoral College in the Early Republic, 1787–1804* (Westport, CT: Greenwood Press, 1994).
110. George C. Edwards III, *Why the Electoral College Is Bad for America*, 2nd ed. (New Haven, CT: Yale University Press, 2011); Paul D. Schumaker and Burdett A. Loomis, eds., *Choosing a President: The Electoral College and Beyond* (Washington, DC: CQ Press, 2002).
111. L. Paige Whitaker and Thomas H. Neale, "The Electoral College: An Overview and Analysis of Reform Proposals" *Congressional Research Service*, Report RL30804 (November 5, 2004), 17.

Chapter 11

1. Hamilton notes, ascribed to June 6, *RFC* I, 145.
2. *RFC* June 1, I, 68; an indication of the importance of the issue is that it was taken up almost two weeks before the debate on Congressional terms.
3. *RFC* June 1, I, 68.
4. *RFC* June 1, I, 68.
5. *RFC* June 1, I, 68–69.
6. *RFC* July 17, II, 33.
7. *RFC* July 17, II, 33.
8. *RFC* July 17, II, 33.
9. *RFC* June 18, I, 292.
10. *RFC* July 17, II, 33.
11. *RFC* July 17, II, 36n.
12. *RFC* July 17, II, 34–35.
13. *RFC* July 17, II, 33–34.
14. *RFC* July 17, II, 35.
15. *RFC* July 19, II, 54–55.
16. *RFC* July 19, II, 59.
17. *RFC* July 19, II, 59.
18. *RFC* July 19, II, 59.
19. *RFC* July 24, II, 101–102.
20. *RFC* July 24, II, 102.
21. *RFC* July 24, II, 102–103.
22. *RFC* July 24, II, 103–104.
23. *RFC* July 25, II, 112–13.
24. *RFC* July 25, II, 111–12.
25. *RFC* July 25, II, 112.

26. *RFC* July 26, II, 119–20.
27. *RFC* September 4, II, 497, 501–502.
28. *RFC* September 6, II, 525.
29. *RFC* September 4, II, 498; September 7, II, 536.
30. *RFC* July 20, II, 69; September 15, II, 626. The courts have ruled that those born in the United States and subject to its jurisdiction are "natural born" citizens. There are still unsettled questions about those born to American citizens outside the United States (such as Senator John McCain, born in Panama). Jack Maskel, "Qualifications for President and the 'Natural Born' Citizenship Eligibility Requirement," *Congressional Research Service*, Report R42097 (November 14, 2011).
31. *RFC* June 2, I, 86; Pierce notes, *RFC* June 2, I, 92.
32. *RFC* July 19, II, 53.
33. *RFC* June 2, I, 86.
34. *RFC* June 2, I, 86.
35. *RFC* July 19, II, 53; July 20, II, 64–65.
36. *RFC* July 20, II, 66.
37. *RFC* July 20, II, 66–67.
38. *RFC* July 20, II, 65.
39. *RFC* July 20, II, 66.
40. *RFC* July 20, II, 64.
41. *RFC* July 20, II, 67.
42. *RFC* July 20, II, 65–66.
43. *RFC* July 20, II, 65, 68–69.
44. *RFC* July 24, II, 104.
45. *RFC* July 20, II, 69.
46. *RFC* August 6, II, 185–86.
47. *RFC* September 4, II, 497, 499.
48. *RFC* September 8, II, 551.
49. *RFC* September 8, II, 551.
50. *RFC* September 8, II, 551.
51. *RFC* September 8, II, 550.
52. *RFC* September 8, II, 550; Michael J. Gerhardt, *The Federal Impeachment Process: A Constitutional and Historical Analysis*, 2nd ed. (Chicago: University of Chicago Press, 2000), 103–104.
53. *RFC* September 8, II, 552; September 14, II, 612–13.
54. *RFC* August 6, II, 185–86; August 27, II, 427.
55. *RFC* August 27, II, 427.
56. *RFC* September 4, II, 498–99.
57. *RFC* September 4, II, 499.
58. *RFC* September 7, II, 537.
59. *RFC* September 7, II, 536–37.
60. *RFC* September 7, II, 537.
61. *RFC* September 7, II, 537.
62. *RFC* September 7, II, 535.
63. *RFC* June 4, I, 103.
64. *RFC* June 5, I, 119.
65. *RFC* July 18, II, 43.
66. *RFC* July 17, II, 31–32.
67. *RFC* July 17, II, 33.
68. *RFC* August 24, II, 405–6.
69. *RFC* September 4, II, 498–99.
70. *RFC* September 7, II, 539.
71. *RFC* September 7, II, 538–39.
72. *RFC* September 7, II, 539.
73. *RFC* September 8, II, 550, 553; September 14, II, 613–14.
74. *RFC* September 14, II, 627–28.

75. *RFC* August 6, II, 182; August 17, II, 314–15; September 14, II, 614.
76. *RFC* June 1, I, 66.
77. *RFC* June 4, I, 97.
78. Pierce notes, *RFC* June 1, I, 74.
79. *RFC* June 4, I, 97.
80. *RFC* August 18, II, 328–29.
81. *RFC* August 18, II, 329.
82. *RFC* August 22, II, 367; September 4, II, 499.
83. *RFC* September 7, II, 541.
84. *RFC* July 25, II, 110. The word "veto" does not appear in the Constitution. Article I, Section 7 provides that "Every Bill which shall have passed the House of Representatives and the Senate, shall, before it become a Law, be presented to the President of the United States; If he approve he shall sign it, but if not he shall return it, with his Objections to that House in which it shall have originated, who shall enter the Objections at large on their Journal, and proceed to reconsider it." The phrase "executive veto" does not appear in Madison's notes on the debates, and the concept of a presidential "veto" rarely appears in Farrand's *Records* (*RFC* July 21, II, 79–80; July 24, II, 100). The term "negative" was used in the Virginia Plan and the debates.
85. *RFC* June 6, I, 140.
86. *RFC* June 4, I, 97–98.
87. *RFC* June 4, I, 98, 100.
88. *RFC* June 4, I, 100.
89. *RFC* June 4, I, 99.
90. *RFC* June 4, I, 101–102.
91. *RFC* June 4, I, 99.
92. *RFC* June 4, I, 100–101.
93. *RFC* June 4, I, 104; July 18, II, 41.
94. *RFC* June 6, I, 138–39.
95. *RFC* June 6, I, 139–40.
96. *RFC* June 6, I, 139.
97. *RFC* June 6, I, 139.
98. *RFC* June 6, I, 140.
99. *RFC* June 6, I, 139.
100. *RFC* July 21, II, 73.
101. *RFC* July 21, II, 78.
102. *RFC* July 21, II, 74.
103. *RFC* July 21, II, 73–74.
104. *RFC* July 21, II, 75–76, 78–79.
105. *RFC* July 21, II, 76–77.
106. *RFC* July 21, II, 74–75.
107. *RFC* July 21, II, 79.
108. *RFC* July 21, II, 80.
109. *RFC* August 15, II, 300.
110. *RFC* August 15, II, 299–300.
111. *RFC* August 15, II, 300.
112. *RFC* August 15, II, 300–301.
113. *RFC* August 15, II, 301–302. The delegates also allowed the president to veto Congressional resolutions as well as laws, and gave him ten days instead of seven to use the veto (before a bill became law without his signature).
114. *RFC* September 12, II, 585–86.
115. *RFC* September 12, II, 585.
116. *RFC* September 12, II, 586.
117. *RFC* September 12, II, 586.
118. *RFC* September 12, II, 586–87.
119. *RFC* September 12, II, 585.
120. *RFC* August 6, II, 185; *RFC* August 24, II, 405. The delegates added to this power by enabling the president to convene the House or Senate; *RFC* September 8, I, 553.

121. *RFC* August 25, II, 419.
122. *RFC* August 27, II, 426.
123. *RFC* September 15, II, 626.
124. *RFC* September 15, II, 627.
125. *RFC* September 15, II, 626.
126. *RFC* September 15, II, 626.
127. *RFC* September 15, II, 627.
128. On the use of the presidential pardon, see Jeffrey P. Crouch, *The Presidential Pardon Power* (Lawrence: University Press of Kansas, 2009).
129. Joseph A. Pika and John Anthony Maltese, *The Politics of the Presidency*, rev. 7th ed. (Washington, DC: CQ Press, 2010), 12.
130. Sidney M. Milkis, *The President and the Parties: The Transformation of the American Party System since the New Deal* (Oxford and New York: Oxford University Press, 1993).
131. On the development of the presidency, see Bert A. Rockman, "Entrepreneur in the Constitutional Marketplace: The Development of the Presidency," in *The Constitution and American Political Development: An Institutional Perspective*, ed. Peter F. Nardulli (Urbana: University of Illinois Press, 1992), 97–120; Sidney M. Milkis, *The American Presidency: Origins and Development, 1776–2011*, 6th ed. (Washington, DC: CQ Press, 2011); Stephen Skowronek, *The Politics Presidents Make: Leadership from John Adams to Bill Clinton* (Cambridge, MA: Belknap Press, 1997) and *Presidential Leadership in Political Time: Reprise and Reappraisal* (Lawrence: University Press of Kansas, 2008); Joel D. Aberbach and Mark A. Peterson, eds., *The Executive Branch* (Oxford and New York: Oxford University Press, 2005); George C. Edwards III and William G. Howell, *The Oxford Handbook of the American Presidency* (Oxford and New York: Oxford University Press, 2000).
132. On vetoes, see "Presidential Vetoes," *The American Presidency Project*, ed. John T. Woolley and Gerhard Peters, http://www.presidency.ucsb.edu/data/vetoes.php (accessed July 20, 2011).
133. "Executive Orders," *The American Presidency Project*, http://www.presidency.ucsb.edu/data/orders.php (accessed July 20, 2011). See Kenneth R. Mayer, *With the Stroke of a Pen: Executive Orders and Presidential Power* (Princeton, NJ: Princeton University Press, 2001).
134. George Washington, "First Annual Message to Congress on the State of the Union January 8, 1790," *The American Presidency Project*, ed. John T. Woolley and Gerhard Peters, http://www.presidency.ucsb.edu/ws/?pid=29431 (accessed March 24, 2012).
135. "Of the 36 not confirmed, 11 were rejected by the Senate (all in roll-call votes), 11 were withdrawn by the President, and 14 lapsed at the end of a session of Congress without a Senate vote cast on whether to confirm." Denis Steven Rutkus, "Supreme Court Appointment Process: Roles of the President, Judiciary Committee, and Senate," *Congressional Research Service*, Report RL31989 (February 19, 2010), 48.
136. Sarah A. Binder and Forrest Maltzman, "The Limits of Senatorial Courtesy," *Legislative Studies Quarterly* 29:1 (February 2004): 5–22.
137. Ed O'Keefe, "How Many Federal Workers Are There?" *Washington Post*, September 30, 2010, http://voices.washingtonpost.com/federal-eye/2010/09/how_many_federal_workers_are_t.html (accessed November 23, 2010); David E. Lewis, *The Politics of Presidential Appointments* (Princeton, NJ: Princeton University Press, 2008), 3. On American bureaucracy, see Michael Nelson, "A Short, Ironic History of American National Bureaucracy," *Journal of Politics* 44:3 (1982): 747–78; David H. Rosenbloom, "Democratic Constitutionalism and the Evolution of Bureaucratic Government: Freedom and Accountability in the Administrative State," in *The Constitution and American Political Development: An Institutional Perspective*, ed. Peter F. Nardulli (Urbana: University of Illinois Press, 1992), 121–49; Robert Durant, ed., *The Oxford Handbook of American Bureaucracy* (Oxford and New York: Oxford University Press, 2010).
138. Judicial participation on commissions has been controversial; see Wendy Ackerman, "Separation of Powers and Judicial Service on Presidential Commissions," *University of Chicago Law Review* 53:3 (Summer 1986): 993–1025.
139. Report of the Committee on Style, *RFC* September 12, II, 599.

140. *RFC* August 27, II, 427. The Committee of Style revised the president's oath as follows: "I—, do solemnly swear (or affirm) that I will faithfully execute the office of president of the United States, and will to the best of my judgment and power, preserve, protect and defend the constitution of the United States." Report of the Committee on Style, *RFC* September 12, II, 599.

Chapter 12

1. *RFC* June 4, I, 104; July 11, II, 41.
2. *RFC* June 13, I, 232.
3. *RFC* June 15, I, 244; June 19, I, 317.
4. *RFC* July 18, II, 46.
5. *RFC* August 6, II, 186–87.
6. *RFC* August 24, II, 400–401.
7. *RFC* August 27, II, 428.
8. *RFC* August 27, II, 431.
9. *RFC* August 27, II, 431.
10. When the plan was presented, Gunning Bedford's notes indicated that the national veto could be appealed to the federal judiciary, allowing the federal courts to umpire potential disputes between state and national legislation; *RFC 1987 Supplement*, 27; see the discussion of the national veto, *RFC* July 17, II, 28.
11. *RFC* June 4, I, 97.
12. *RFC* June 4, I, 97–98; Pierce notes, *RFC* June 4, I, 109.
13. *RFC* July 21, II, 76.
14. *RFC* July 21, II, 78.
15. *RFC* August 15, II, 298.
16. *RFC* August 15, II, 299.
17. *RFC* August 27, II, 430.
18. *RFC* August 27, II, 430.
19. *RFC* August 27, II, 430.
20. M. J. C. Vile, *Constitutionalism and the Separation of Powers* (Oxford, UK: Clarendon Press, 1967), 158.
21. *RFC* June 5, I, 120.
22. *RFC* June 13, I, 232–33.
23. *RFC* July 18, II, 41.
24. *RFC* July 18, II, 41.
25. *RFC* July 18, II, 41.
26. *RFC* July 18, II, 41, 43.
27. *RFC* July 18, II, 43.
28. *RFC* July 18, II, 41–42.
29. *RFC* July 18, II, 42–44.
30. *RFC* July 21, II, 80–81.
31. *RFC* July 21, II, 81.
32. *RFC* July 21, II, 82.
33. *RFC* July 21, II, 81.
34. *RFC* July 21, II, 81.
35. *RFC* July 21, II, 83.
36. *RFC* July 21, II, 83.
37. *RFC* August 23, II, 389.
38. *RFC* July 18, II, 44.
39. *RFC* August 27, II, 428.
40. *RFC* August 27, II, 429.
41. *RFC* August 27, II, 429.
42. *RFC* August 27, II, 428.
43. *RFC* July 18, II, 44.
44. *RFC* July 18, II, 45.

45. *RFC* July 18, II, 45.
46. *RFC* August 27, II, 429–30.
47. *RFC* August 27, II, 430.
48. *RFC* June 5, I, 119, 124.
49. *RFC* June 5, I, 124.
50. *RFC* June 5, I, 125.
51. *RFC* June 5, I, 124.
52. *RFC* June 5, I, 125.
53. *RFC* June 5, I, 125.
54. *RFC* June 5, I, 125.
55. *RFC* June 20, I, 341.
56. *RFC* July 11, II, 45.
57. *RFC* July 11, II, 45–46.
58. *RFC* July 11, II, 46.
59. *RFC* July 11, II, 46.
60. *RFC* July 11, II, 46; August 17, II, 315.
61. *RFC* August 22, II, 375.
62. The British Parliament, for example, passed a bill of attainder in 1542 that declared King Henry VIII's wife, Catherine Howard, guilty of treason and subject to execution without a trial.
63. *RFC* August 22, II, 375.
64. *RFC* August 22, II, 376.
65. *RFC* August 22, II, 376.
66. *RFC* August 22, II, 376.
67. *RFC* August 22, II, 376.
68. *RFC* August 29, II, 448–49; September 14, II, 617.
69. *RFC* August 28, II, 438. On the development of habeas corpus in Britain, see Paul D. Halliday, *Habeas Corpus: From England to Empire* (Cambridge, MA: Harvard University Press, 2010).
70. *RFC* August 28, II, 438.
71. *RFC* August 28, II, 438.
72. *RFC* August 28, II, 438.
73. *RFC* September 14, II, 617–18; *RFC* August 20, II, 348.
74. *RFC* August 28, II, 438.
75. *RFC* September 12, II, 587.
76. *RFC* September 12, II, 587.
77. *RFC* September 15, II, 628.
78. *RFC* August 30, II, 468.
79. *RFC* September 12, II, 587–88.
80. *RFC* September 12, II, 588.
81. *RFC* September 12, II, 588.
82. *RFC* September 14, II, 617.
83. *RFC* September 14, II, 618. The rejection of a broader bill of rights would soon haunt the battle for ratification. Sherman, certainly a strong republican, may have wanted to ensure that citizens would continue to focus on the state governments; certainly some delegates calculated that the inclusion of a bill of rights would make the new government appear even stronger, more in need of constraints, and therefore even more objectionable to citizens. In the waning days of the Convention, in which the length of the proceedings had long been criticized, the delegates likely preferred to err on the side of avoiding additional protracted debates.
84. On the Supreme Court and the judicial branch, see Lawrence Baum, "Supreme Court Activism and the Constitution," in *The Constitution and American Political Development: An Institutional Perspective*, ed. Peter F. Nardulli (Urbana: University of Illinois Press, 1992), 150–79; Keith E. Whittington, *The Political Foundations of Judicial Supremacy: The Presidency, the Supreme Court, and Constitutional Leadership in U.S. History* (Princeton, NJ: Princeton University Press, 2007); David M. O'Brien, *Storm Center: The Supreme Court in*

American Politics, 8th ed. (New York: W. W. Norton, 2008); Kermit L. Hall and Kevin T. McGuire, eds., *The Judicial Branch* (Oxford and New York: Oxford University Press, 2006).

85. "Brutus," Number 14, February 28 and March 6, 1788, in Herbert J. Storing, ed., *The Complete Anti-Federalist* (Chicago: University of Chicago, 1981) 2,168–185.

86. *Marbury v. Madison*, 5 U.S. (1 Cranch) 137 (1803). See William E. Nelson, *Marbury v. Madison: The Origins and Legacy of Judicial Review* (Lawrence: University Press of Kansas, 2000); Larry D. Kramer, *The People Themselves: Popular Constitutionalism and Judicial Review* (Oxford and New York: Oxford University Press, 2004).

87. *Dred Scott v. Sandford*, 60 U.S. 393 (1857).

88. Kermit L. Hall, "Judicial Independence and the Majoritarian Difficulty," in *The Judicial Branch*, ed. Kermit L. Hall and Kevin T. McGuire (Oxford and New York: Oxford University Press, 2004), 69.

89. Richard Franklin Bensel, *The Political Economy of American Industrialization, 1877–1900* (Cambridge and New York: Cambridge University Press, 2001), 321–49.

90. Congressional Research Service, "Analysis and Interpretation of the Constitution Annotations of Cases Decided by the Supreme Court of the United States, 2008 Supplement to the 2002 Edition" Senate Document 110-17 (Washington: GPO, 2008), 164, 167, http://www.gpo.gov/fdsys/pkg/GPO-CONAN-2008/pdf/GPO-CONAN-2008.pdf (accessed July 3, 2012). On judicial review, see Keith E. Whittington, ""Interpose Your Friendly Hand": Political Supports for the Exercise of Judicial Review by the United States Supreme Court," *American Political Science Review* 99:4 (November 2005): 583–96; Christopher Wolfe, *The Rise of Modern Judicial Review: From Constitutional Interpretation to Judge-Made Law*, rev. ed. (Lanham, MD: Rowman & Littlefield, 1994).

91. Keith E. Whittington, *Political Foundations of Judicial Supremacy: The Presidency, the Supreme Court, and Constitutional Leadership in U.S. History* (Princeton, NJ: Princeton University Press, 2007).

92. Henry M. Hart Jr., "The Power of Congress to Limit the Jurisdiction of Federal Courts: An Exercise in Dialectic," *Harvard Law Review* 66:8 (June 1953): 1364. Alexander Hamilton implied that Congress could correct an overreaching federal judiciary in *The Federalist*; Alexander Hamilton, James Madison, and John Jay, *The Federalist*, ed. Jacob E. Cooke (Middletown, CT: Wesleyan University Press, 1961), Number 80, 541.

93. Patrick T. Conley and John P. Kaminski, eds., *The Constitution and the States: The Role of the Original Thirteen in the Framing and Adoption of the Federal Constitution* (Madison, WI: Madison House, 1988); David J. Siemers, *Ratifying the Republic: Antifederalists and Federalists in Constitutional Time* (Stanford, CA: Stanford University Press, 2002), 25–73.

94. PJM 12, 123; *Documentary History of the First Federal Congress of the United States of America*, Vol. 11, *Debates in the House of Representatives, First Session, June-September 1789*, ed. Charlene Bangs Bickford, Kenneth R. Bowling, and Helen E. Veit (Baltimore, MD: Johns Hopkins University Press, 1992), August 13, 1789: 1208–1209; August 19, 1789: 1308. The Bill of Rights was ratified in December 1791; Richard Labunski, *James Madison and the Struggle for the Bill of Rights* (Oxford and New York: Oxford University Press, 2006), 178–255.

95. Michael Kent Curtis, *No State Shall Abridge: The Fourteenth Amendment and the Bill of Rights* (Durham, NC: Duke University Press, 1986).

96. Michael J. Perry, *We the People: The Fourteenth Amendment and the Supreme Court* (Oxford and New York: Oxford University Press, 1999); Henry A. Abraham and Barbara A. Perry, *Freedom and the Court: Civil Rights and Liberties in the United States*, 8th ed. (Lawrence: University Press of Kansas, 2003).

Chapter 13

1. RFC May 30, I, 33.
2. RFC May 30, I, 33.
3. RFC May 30, I, 33; McHenry Notes, RFC May 30, I, 42.
4. RFC May 30, I, 34.
5. McHenry Notes, RFC May 30, I, 43.
6. RFC May 30, I, 34.

7. *RFC* May 30 I, 34–35.

8. *RFC* May 31, I, 53.

9. *RFC* May 31, I, 53.

10. *RFC* May 31, I, 53.

11. Pierce notes, *RFC* May 31, I, 60.

12. *RFC* May 31, I, 53.

13. Pierce notes, *RFC* May 31, I, 59–60.

14. *RFC* May 31, I, 54.

15. *RFC* June 11, I, 203–204.

16. Pierce notes, *RFC* May 31, I, 59–60.

17. *RFC* May 31, I, 54.

18. *RFC* May 31, I, 54.

19. *RFC* June 8, I, 164.

20. *RFC* June 8, I, 164–65.

21. *RFC* June 8, I, 166–67.

22. *RFC* June 8, I, 167.

23. *RFC* June 8, I, 165. In 1787, the term "police" did not refer narrowly to uniformed law enforcement. It had much broader application and can be best understood as public policy administration of state laws and rules in a wide range of areas, including economic regulation, safety, and morals. See Paul Kens, "The Source of a Myth: Police Powers of the States and Laissez Faire Constitutionalism, 1900–1937," *The American Journal of Legal History* 35:1 (January 1991): 70–98.

24. *RFC* June 8, I, 168.

25. *RFC* June 8, I, 165; King notes, June 8, I, 171–72.

26. *RFC* June 8, I, 167–68.

27. *RFC* June 8, I, 166.

28. Madison and Hamilton already had joined in a 1782 Congressional report stating, "The truth is, that no Federal constitution can exist without powers, that in their exercise affect the internal police of the component members." Report of a committee consisting of Hamilton, Madison, and Thomas Fitzsimmons, addressing Rhode Island's refusal to endorse a tariff power for Congress *JCC*, December 16, 1782, 801, http://memory.loc.gov/cgi-bin/query/D?hlaw:5:./temp/~ammem_Gipb:: (accessed March 15, 2012).

29. *RFC* June 8, I, 168.

30. *RFC* June 8, I, 168.

31. *RFC* June 16, I, 250; June 20, I, 337.

32. *RFC* July 17, II, 27.

33. *RFC* July 17, II, 27.

34. *RFC* July 17, II, 27.

35. *RFC* July 17, II, 27–28.

36. *RFC* July 17, II, 28.

37. *RFC* July 17, II, 28.

38. *RFC* July 17, II, 28.

39. *RFC* July 17, II, 28–29.

40. *RFC* July 17, II, 28–29.

41. *RFC* August 23, II, 390.

42. *RFC* August 23, II, 391.

43. *RFC* August 23, II, 390.

44. *RFC* August 23, II, 390.

45. *RFC* August 23, II, 391.

46. *RFC* August 23, II, 391.

47. *RFC* August 23, II, 390.

48. *RFC* September 12, II, 589; *PJM* 10, 163–64, 209–14.

49. Gordon S. Wood, *The Creation of the American Republic, 1776–1787* (Chapel Hill: University of North Carolina Press, 1969), 527–28; Jack N. Rakove, *Original Meanings: Politics and Ideas in the Making of the Constitution* (New York: Alfred A. Knopf, 1996), 182–84, 188–89.

50. King notes, *RFC* June 8, I, 172.

51. *RFC* May 30, I, 34; McHenry Notes, *RFC* May 30, I, 43.
52. *RFC* June 6, I, 136.
53. *RFC* June 6, I, 133.
54. *RFC* June 6, I, 134.
55. *RFC* June 16, I, 251.
56. *RFC* June 20, I, 339–40.
57. King notes, *RFC* June 20, I, 349.
58. *RFC* June 19, I, 323.
59. *RFC* June 18, I, 287.
60. *RFC* June 18, I, 287.
61. *RFC* June 19, I, 323.
62. *RFC* June 19, I, 324.
63. *RFC* June 29, I, 467.
64. *RFC* June 19, I, 324.
65. *RFC* June 19, I, 322–24.
66. *RFC* June 20, I, 344.
67. *RFC* June 21, I, 355.
68. *RFC* June 29, I, 468. Madison adopted this phrase in *The Federalist*; Alexander Hamilton, James Madison, and John Jay, *The Federalist*, ed. Jacob E. Cooke (Middletown, CT: Wesleyan University Press, 1961), Number 39, 257.
69. King notes, *RFC* June 25, I, 416.
70. King notes, *RFC* June 27, I, 442.
71. *RFC* July 6, I, 551.
72. *RFC* July 17, II, 25.
73. *RFC* July 16, II, 17.
74. *RFC* July 17, II, 25.
75. *RFC* July 17, II, 26.
76. *RFC* July 17, II, 26.
77. *RFC* July 17, II, 26.
78. *RFC* August 6, II, 181–83, 187. The word "necessary" was used five times in the Articles of Confederation, and the word "proper" appeared twice. Both are used to describe a specific power, such as the Confederation Congress's power to establish forts or maintain naval vessels. The Articles did not include a more general "necessary and proper" clause.
79. *RFC* August 8, II, 220.
80. *RFC* August 20, II, 345.
81. *RFC* August 22, II, 367.
82. Compare *RFC* II, 569 and II, 594. The preamble is at II, 590. The Committee on Style altered the punctuation in Article 1, Section 8 in a way that opponents thought broadened national powers. The Convention sent to the Committee on Style the following phrasing: "The Legislature shall have the power to lay and collect taxes, duties, imposts and excises, to pay the debts and provide for the common defense and general welfare of the United States." The Committee on Style changed the punctuation as follows: "To lay and collect taxes, duties, imposts and excises; to pay the debts and provide for the common defense and general welfare of the United States" (compare *RFC* II, 569 and September 12, II, 594). Luther Martin later claimed that he noticed the final wording in Section 8 and complained that "the grammatical construction is a general grant of power"; *Observations*, June 3, 1788, in *RFC 1987 Supplement*, 292.
83. *RFC* August 20, II, 345.
84. *RFC* August 20, II, 345–46.
85. *RFC* August 20, II, 345.
86. *RFC* August 20, II, 346.
87. *RFC* August 20, II, 346.
88. *RFC* August 20, II, 347.
89. *RFC* August 20, II, 347.
90. *RFC* August 20, II, 347.
91. *RFC* August 20, II, 347–48.

92. *RFC* August 20, II, 348–49.
93. *RFC* August 20, II, 349.
94. *RFC* August 20, II, 349.
95. *RFC* August 20, II, 349.
96. *The Federalist*, Number 51, 351–52. Before the Constitutional Convention, the word "federal" had been used to describe confederations like the United States under the Articles of Confederation, in which national government was very weak.
97. *RFC* August 13, II, 270–71.
98. *RFC* September 15, II, 630–31.
99. Ronald P. Formisano, "State Development in the Early Republic: Substance and Structure, 1780–1840," in *Contesting Democracy: Substance and Structure in American Political History*, ed. Byron E. Shafer and Anthony Badger (Lawrence: University Press of Kansas, 2001), 11. See also Samuel Beer, *To Make a Nation: The Rediscovery of American Federalism* (Cambridge, MA: Belknap Press, 1993), 23–25.
100. *The Federalist*, Number 51, 350–51.
101. Rakove, *Original Meanings*, 181–88.
102. James Madison, *The Federalist* Number 40 and Number 45, 261, 311.
103. Madison, *The Federalist* Number 45, 313.
104. U.S. House of Representatives, Debates on Amendments to the Constitution, in *The Founders' Constitution*, Vol. 5, Bill of Rights, Document 11, http://press-pubs.uchicago.edu/founders/documents/bill_of_rightss11.html (accessed December 15, 2009).
105. *Hans v. Louisiana*, 134 U.S. 1 (1890); *Seminole Tribe of Florida v. Florida*, 517 U.S. 44 (1996); *Alden v. Maine*, 527 U.S. 706 (1999).
106. *PJM* February 24, 1790, 13, 61; Madison to Edmund Pendleton, April 4, 1790, *PJM* 13, 138; editorial note, 13, 191.
107. Madison in the House of Representatives, February 2, 1791, in *PJM* 13, 373–75, and February 8, 1791, *PJM* 13, 387. See also Jack N. Rakove, *Original Meanings: Politics and Ideas in the Making of the Constitution* (New York: Alfred A. Knopf, 1996), 350–55.
108. J. H. Leek, "Treason and the Constitution," *Journal of Politics* 13:4 (November 1951): 607.
109. U.S. Census Bureau, "State and Local Government Spending Increases by 6.5 Percent in 2008, Census Bureau Reports," July 14, 2010, http://www.census.gov/newsroom/releases/archives/governments/cb10-108.html (accessed November 23, 2010); U.S. Office of Management and Budget, *Budget of the United States Government: Historical Tables Fiscal Year 2011*, http://www.gpoaccess.gov/usbudget/fy11/hist.html, (accessed November 23, 2010).
110. Paul Teske, *Regulation in the States* (Washington, DC: Brookings Institution, 2004), 9.

Chapter 14

1. Paul Finkelman, *Slavery and the Founders: Race and Liberty in the Age of Jefferson*, 2nd ed. (Armonk, NY: M. E. Sharpe, 2001).
2. Debate between Stephen Douglas and Abraham Lincoln at Galesburg, Illinois, October 7, 1858, at U.S. National Park Service, Lincoln home site, http://www.nps.gov/liho/historyculture/debate6.htm (accessed March 26, 2012).
3. *RFC* May 30, I, 35–36.
4. King notes, *RFC* June 6, I, 144.
5. *RFC* May 30, I, 36.
6. Joseph L. Davis, *Sectionalism in American Politics, 1774–1787* (Madison: University of Wisconsin Press, 1977), 49.
7. *RFC* June 11, I, 201.
8. *RFC* June 11, I, 201.
9. *RFC* June 11, I, 201. The two no votes were cast by Delaware and New Jersey, the two smallest of the non-Southern states that were attending the Convention. The three-fifths rule provided a reasonable point of compromise for the large and the slave states, but offered little to small states with a relatively small proportion of slaves.
10. *RFC* July 9, I, 562.

11. *RFC* July 9, I, 561.
12. *RFC* July 5, I, 542.
13. *RFC* July 9, I, 562.
14. *RFC* July 10, I, 567.
15. *RFC* July 10, I, 567.
16. *RFC* July 11, I, 580.
17. *RFC* July 11, I, 580–81.
18. *RFC* July 12, I, 596.
19. *RFC* July 11, I, 580.
20. *RFC* July 11, I, 580.
21. *RFC* July 11, I, 581.
22. *RFC* July 11, I, 581.
23. *RFC* July 11, I, 581–83.
24. *RFC* July 11, I, 582.
25. *RFC* July 11, I, 582.
26. *RFC* July 11, I, 583.
27. *RFC* July 11, I, 582.
28. *RFC* July 11, I, 587–88.
29. *RFC* July 11, I, 588.
30. *RFC* July 12, I, 591–92. John Dickinson had suggested representation based on contributions to the national treasury as early as June 2 (*RFC* I, 87).
31. *RFC* July 24, II, 106.
32. *RFC* July 12, I, 593–94.
33. *RFC* July 12, I, 592.
34. *RFC* July 12, I, 593.
35. *RFC* July 12, I, 593.
36. *RFC* July 12, I, 594.
37. *RFC* July 12, I, 595.
38. *RFC* July 13, I, 600–601.
39. *RFC* July 13, I, 601–602.
40. *RFC* July 13, I, 602.
41. *RFC* July 12, I, 595–96.
42. *RFC* July 13, I, 604–605.
43. *RFC* July 13, I, 605.
44. *RFC* July 12, I, 596.
45. *RFC* August 8, II, 220.
46. *RFC* August 8, II, 221–23.
47. *RFC* August 8, II, 223.
48. *RFC* August 8, II, 223.
49. *RFC* August 8, II, 223.
50. *RFC* August 20, II, 350.
51. *RFC* September 13, I, 607–608.
52. *RFC* August 6, II, 183.
53. *RFC* August 8, II, 220.
54. *RFC* August 8, II, 220–21.
55. *RFC* August 21, II, 364.
56. *RFC* August 22, II, 370.
57. *RFC* August 22, II, 372–73.
58. *RFC* August 22, II, 374.
59. *RFC* August 22, II, 373.
60. *RFC* August 22, II, 372.
61. *RFC* August 22, II, 373.
62. *RFC* August 21, II, 364.
63. *RFC* August 22, II, 373.
64. *RFC* August 22, II, 371.
65. *RFC* August 22, II, 373.

66. *RFC* August 22, II, 372.
67. *RFC* August 22, II, 371–72.
68. *RFC* August 22, II, 369–70.
69. *RFC* August 21, II, 364.
70. *RFC* August 22, II, 370–71.
71. *RFC* August 22, II, 371.
72. *RFC* August 22, II, 374.
73. *RFC* August 22, II, 374.
74. *RFC* August 22, II, 374.
75. *RFC* August 24, II, 400.
76. *RFC* August 25, II, 415.
77. *RFC* August 25, II, 415.
78. *RFC* August 25, II, 415.
79. *RFC* August 25, II, 415.
80. *RFC* August 25, II, 415–16.
81. *RFC* August 25, II, 416.
82. *RFC* August 25, II, 417.
83. *RFC* August 25, II, 416.
84. *RFC* August 25, II, 416.
85. *RFC* September 10, II, 559.
86. *RFC* August 28, II, 443.
87. *RFC* August 28, II, 443.
88. *RFC* August 28, II, 443.
89. *RFC* August 29, II, 453–54.
90. *RFC* September 12, II, 601–602. The Committee had reworked the language it had received from the Convention. As originally received by the Committee on Style, the fugitive slave clause had read: "If any Person bound to service or labor in any of the United States shall escape into another State, He or She shall not be discharged from such service or labor in consequence of any regulations subsisting in the State to which they escape; but shall be delivered up to the person justly claiming their service or labor." *RFC* II, 577.
91. *RFC* September 15, II, 628.
92. *RFC* June 19, I, 318.
93. Debate between Stephen Douglas and Abraham Lincoln at Quincy, Illinois, October 13, 1858, U.S. National Park Service, Lincoln home site, http://www.nps.gov/liho/historyculture/debate6.htm (accessed March 26, 2012).
94. Gunnar Myrdal, *An American Dilemma: The Negro Problem and Modern Democracy* (New York: Harper & Bros., 1944); Joseph Lowndes, Julie Novkov, Dorian T. Warren, eds., "Race and American Political Development" in *Race and American Political Development* (New York: Routledge, 2008), 1–30.
95. Eric Foner, *Reconstruction: America's Unfinished Revolution, 1863–1877* (New York: Harper and Row, 1988); Richard M. Valelly, *The Two Reconstructions: The Struggle for Black Enfranchisement* (Chicago: University of Chicago Press, 2004), 23–45, 99–109; Michael Vorenberg, *Final Freedom: The Civil War, the Abolition of Slavery, and the Thirteenth Amendment* (Cambridge and New York: Cambridge University Press, 2001); Garrett Epps, *Democracy Reborn: The Fourteenth Amendment and the Fight for Equal Rights in Post-Civil War America* (New York: Henry Holt, 2006); William Gillette, *The Right to Vote: Politics and the Passage of the Fifteenth Amendment* (Baltimore, MD: Johns Hopkins University Press, 1969).
96. *The Civil Rights Cases*, 109 U.S. 3 (1883).
97. C. Van Woodward, *The Strange Career of Jim Crow*, commemorative ed. (Oxford and New York: Oxford University Press, 2001), 97–102.
98. Alexander Keyssar, *The Right to Vote: The Contested History of Democracy in the United States* (New York: Basic Books, 2000), 117–62.
99. Mark V. Tushnet, *The NAACP's Legal Strategy Against Segregated Education, 1925–1950*, 2nd ed. (Chapel Hill: University of North Carolina Press, 2005).
100. Richard Kluger, *Simple Justice: The History of Brown v. Board of Education and Black America's Struggle for Equality* (New York: Knopf, 1976); Harrell R. Rodgers Jr. and Charles

S. Bullock III, *Law and Social Change: Civil Rights Laws and Their Consequences* (New York: McGraw-Hill, 1972), 70–71.
101. Valelly, *The Two Reconstructions*, 199–224.

Chapter 15

1. *RFC* August 13, II, 275.
2. Lansing notes, June 11, *RFC 1987 Supplement*, June 11, 69.
3. *RFC* June 2, I, 83.
4. *RFC* June 11, I, 197; Paterson notes, *RFC* June 11, I, 208.
5. *RFC* June 18, I, 286.
6. *RFC* July 17, II, 26.
7. *RFC* July 14, II, 11; July 17, II, 26.
8. *RFC* August 20, II, 359.
9. *RFC* August 6, I, 181; August 16, II, 308.
10. *RFC* August 18, II, 332.
11. *RFC* August 20, II, 344; September 13, II, 606.
12. *RFC* August 20, II, 344.
13. *RFC* August 18, II, 326–27.
14. *RFC* August 21, II, 355–56; August 22, II, 366–67.
15. *RFC* August 25, II, 414.
16. *RFC* September 13, II, 607–608.
17. *RFC* August 20, II, 350; August 21, II, 357–58.
18. *RFC* September 15, II, 625.
19. *RFC* August 20, II, 350.
20. *RFC* July 24, II, 106.
21. *RFC* July 24, II, 106.
22. *RFC* September 14, II, 618.
23. *RFC* August 21, II, 360.
24. *RFC* August 16, II, 305–306; August 21, II, 362–63.
25. *RFC* August 21, II, 360.
26. *RFC* August 16, II, 306–7; August 21, II, 361.
27. *RFC* August 16, II, 306–307.
28. *RFC* August 21, II, 363–64.
29. *RFC* August 28, II, 442.
30. *RFC* August 28, II, 442.
31. *RFC* August 16, II, 308.
32. McHenry Notes, *RFC* August 7, II, 211.
33. *RFC* July 10, I, 567–68; August 6, II, 183.
34. *RFC* August 22, II, 374.
35. *RFC* August 29, II, 449n.
36. *RFC* August 22, II, 375.
37. *RFC* August 29, II, 449.
38. *RFC* August 29, II, 450–51.
39. *RFC* August 29, II, 451.
40. *RFC* August 29, II, 452–53.
41. *RFC* August 29, II, 450.
42. *RFC* August 29, II, 450.
43. *RFC* August 29, II, 452.
44. *RFC* August 29, II, 450.
45. *RFC* August 29, II, 452.
46. *RFC* August 29, II, 451.
47. *RFC* August 29, II, 453.
48. *RFC* September 15, II, 631.
49. *RFC* August 25, II, 417.
50. *RFC* August 28, II, 437–38.

51. *RFC* August 31, II, 480–81.
52. *RFC* August 31, II, 481.
53. *RFC* August 6, II, 181, 187.
54. *RFC* August 21, II, 361.
55. *RFC* September 15, II, 625.
56. *RFC* August 28, II, 440–41.
57. *RFC* August 6, II, 182.
58. *RFC* August 16, II, 308.
59. *RFC* August 16, II, 308–309.
60. *RFC* August 16, II, 309–10.
61. *RFC* August 16, II, 310. The "Sign of the Beast" in the New Testament Book of Revelations most commonly is considered a reference to the Antichrist.
62. *RFC* August 16, II, 309.
63. *RFC* August 16, II, 309–10.
64. *RFC* August 28, II, 439.
65. *RFC* August 28, II, 439.
66. *RFC* August 28, II, 439.
67. *RFC* August 28, II, 439.
68. *RFC* August 28, II, 440.
69. *RFC* September 12, II, 597.
70. *RFC* September 14, II, 618.
71. *RFC* August 25, II, 414.
72. *RFC* September 4, II, 497.
73. *RFC* August 18, II, 327.
74. *RFC* August 18, II, 327.
75. *RFC* August 18, II, 327.
76. *RFC* August 23, II, 392.
77. *RFC* August 23, II, 392.
78. *RFC* August 25, II, 412–13.
79. *RFC* August 25, II, 414.
80. *RFC* August 29, II, 448.
81. *RFC* September 1, II, 484; September 3, II, 489.
82. *RFC* September 1, II, 485.
83. *RFC* June 25, I, 405.
84. *RFC* August 29, II, 454.
85. *RFC* August 29, II, 454.
86. *RFC* August 29, II, 456.
87. *RFC* August 18, II, 328.
88. *RFC* August 29, II, 456; August 30, II, 462.
89. *RFC* August 29, II, 454.
90. *RFC* August 30, II, 463–64.
91. *RFC* August 30, II, 464–65.
92. *RFC* August 30, II, 465.
93. *RFC* August 30, II, 466.
94. *RFC* July 26, II, 127–28; August 11, II, 261; August 30, II, 463; September 5, II, 510.
95. *RFC* August 16, II, 308.
96. *RFC* August 18, II, 325.
97. *RFC* September 5, II, 509.
98. *RFC* September 14, II, 615.
99. *RFC* September 14, II, 615.
100. *RFC* September 14, II, 615.
101. *RFC* September 14, II, 615.
102. *RFC* September 14, II, 616.
103. *RFC* September 14, II, 616.
104. *RFC* September 14, II, 616.
105. *RFC* September 14, II, 616.

106. *RFC* September 14, II, 616.

107. *RFC* August 7, II, 198.

108. Madison to Hamilton, November 19, 1789, in *PJM* 12, 450. Hamilton requested this advice in Hamilton to Madison, October 12, 1789, *PJM* 12, 435. Virginia had used land taxes in the 1780s; Jackson Turner Main, *Political Parties Before the Constitution* (Chapel Hill: University of North Carolina Press, 1973), 250–51.

109. Gary M. Walton and Hugh Rockoff, *A History of the American Economy*, 8th ed., (Fort Worth, TX: Dryden Press, 1998), 176–77, 281, 292–95.

110. Daniel Okrent, *Last Call: The Rise and Fall of Prohibition* (New York: Scribner, 2011).

111. Brian Balogh, *A Government Out of Sight: The Mystery of National Authority in Nineteenth-Century America* (Cambridge and New York: Cambridge University Press, 2009); Richard Franklin Bensel, *The Political Economy of American Industrialization, 1877–1900* (Cambridge and New York: Cambridge University Press, 2000), 205–527.

112. *N.L.R.B. v. Jones & Laughlin Steel Corp.*, 301 U.S. 1 (1937); *Wickard v. Filburn*, 317 U.S. 111 (1942).

113. David Brian Robertson, *Federalism and the Making of America* (Abingdon, UK, and New York: Routledge, 2011), 83–91.

114. *National Federation of Independent Business et al. v. Sibelius* (June 28, 2012); James B. Stewart, "In Obama's Victory, a Loss for Congress," *New York Times*, June 29, 2012, 1.

Chapter 16

1. *RFC* August 8, II, 220. On the framers' approach to national security, see Max M. Edling, *A Revolution in Favor of Government: Origins of the U.S. Constitution and the Making of the American State* (Oxford and New York: Oxford University Press, 2003), 73–128.

2. *RFC* June 29, I, 467.

3. *RFC* August 18, II, 329.

4. *RFC* August 18, II, 330; *RFC 1987 Supplement*, August 18, 229.

5. *RFC* August 18, II, 330.

6. *RFC* August 18, II, 330.

7. *RFC* August 18, II, 326; August 28, II, 442–43; September 5, II, 508–509.

8. *RFC* September 5, II, 508.

9. *RFC* September 5, II, 509.

10. *RFC* September 5, II, 509.

11. *RFC* September 14, II, 616–17.

12. *RFC* June 29, I, 465; September 14, II, 617. Madison's earlier statement is quoted in chapter 2.

13. *RFC* September 14, II, 616.

14. *RFC* August 17, II, 315–16.

15. *RFC* August 23, II, 387.

16. *RFC* July 18, II, 47.

17. *RFC* July 18, II, 47.

18. *RFC* July 18, II, 48.

19. *RFC* July 18, II, 48.

20. *RFC* July 18, II, 48.

21. *RFC* August 17, II, 316–17.

22. *RFC* August 17, II, 317.

23. *RFC* August 17, II, 317.

24. *RFC* August 17, II, 317.

25. *RFC* August 17, II, 317.

26. *RFC* August 17, II, 317.

27. *RFC* August 23, II, 390.

28. *RFC* August 30, II, 466–67.

29. *RFC* August 6, II, 182, 185.

30. *RFC* August 18, II, 326.

31. *RFC* August 23, II, 387.
32. *RFC* August 18, II, 331–32.
33. *RFC* August 18, II, 332.
34. *RFC* August 18, II, 331.
35. *RFC* August 18, II, 332.
36. *RFC* August 18, II, 331.
37. *RFC* August 18, II, 332.
38. *RFC* August 18, II, 332.
39. *RFC* August 21, II, 355–56.
40. *RFC* August 23, II, 385.
41. *RFC* August 23, II, 385.
42. *RFC* August 23, II, 385.
43. *RFC* August 23, II, 386.
44. *RFC* August 23, II, 386.
45. *RFC* August 23, II, 386.
46. *RFC* August 23, II, 386–87.
47. *RFC* August 23, II, 388.
48. *RFC* August 23, II, 389.
49. *RFC* August 27, II, 426–27.
50. *RFC* August 15, II, 297.
51. *RFC* August 23, II, 393.
52. *RFC* August 23, II, 392.
53. *RFC* August 6, II, 182–83.
54. *RFC* August 17, II, 318.
55. *RFC* August 17, II, 318.
56. *RFC* August 17, II, 318.
57. *RFC* August 17, II, 318.
58. *RFC* August 17, II, 319.
59. *RFC* August 17, II, 319.
60. *RFC* August 17, II, 319.
61. *RFC* August 23, II, 392.
62. *RFC* August 23, II, 392.
63. *RFC* August 23, II, 392.
64. *RFC* August 23, II, 392–93.
65. *RFC* August 23, II, 393.
66. *RFC* August 23, II, 393.
67. *RFC* September 7, II, 538.
68. *RFC* September 7, II, 538.
69. *RFC* September 7, II, 538.
70. *RFC* September 7, II, 540.
71. *RFC* September 7, II, 540.
72. *RFC* September 7, II, 540.
73. *RFC* September 7, II, 541.
74. *RFC* September 7, II, 540.
75. *RFC* September 7, II, 540–41.
76. *RFC* September 7, II, 541.
77. *RFC* September 8, II, 548.
78. *RFC* September 8, II, 548.
79. *RFC* September 8, II, 548.
80. *RFC* September 8, II, 548–49.
81. *RFC* September 8, II, 549.
82. *RFC* August 18, II, 324; August 22, II, 367; September 4, II, 497, 499.
83. *The Federalist*, Number 26, 165–65, 170, and Number 41, 270–73.
84. Helvidius, Essays Number 1 and 2, at TeachingAmericanHistory.org, http://www.teachingamericanhistory.org/library/index.asp?documentprint=429, (accessed March 26, 2012).

85. See Louis Henkin, *Foreign Affairs and the United States Constitution*, 2nd ed. (Oxford and New York: Oxford University Press, 1997); Ira Katznelson and Martin Shefter, eds. *Shaped by War and Trade: International Influences on American Political Development* (Princeton, NJ: Princeton University Press, 2002); Louis Fisher, *Presidential War Power* 2nd ed., rev. (Lawrence: University Press of Kansas, 2004).
86. Iver Bernstein, *The New York City Draft Riots: Their Significance for American Society and Politics in the Age of the Civil War* (Oxford and New York: Oxford University Press, 1990). President James Madison unsuccessfully called for a draft in 1814, during the war with Great Britain.
87. Richard F. Grimmett, "Instances of Use of United States Armed Forces Abroad, 1798–2010," Congressional Research Service Report R41677 (March 10, 2011).
88. Charlie Savage, "U.S. Law May Allow Killings, Holder Says," *New York Times*, March 5, 2012.
89. Congressional Research Service, *Treaties and Other International Agreements: The Role of the United States Senate*, U.S. Senate Report 106-71, http://www.gpo.gov/fdsys/pkg/CPRT-106SPRT66922/pdf/CPRT-106SPRT66922.pdf (accessed July 21, 2011). There are over 10,000 treaties in force between the United States and other nations; U.S. Department of State, *Treaties in Force: A List of Treaties and Other International Agreements of the United States in Force on January 1, 2011*, http://www.state.gov/documents/organization/169274.pdf (accessed July 3, 2012). Efforts to hem in executive orders (and to prevent international law from interfering with U.S. law) have not been very successful; see Philip A. Grant's analysis of such an effort during the Eisenhower administration in "The Bricker Amendment Controversy," Presidential Studies Quarterly 15:3 (Summer 1985): 572–82.

Chapter 17

1. Two of New York's delegates, John Lansing and Robert Yates, left the Convention in disgust in July, and Luther Martin and John Francis Mercer, two Maryland delegates, also left early. All four later opposed ratification of the Constitution.
2. *RFC* June 5, I, 122–23.
3. Pierce notes, *RFC* June 5, I, 128–29.
4. *RFC* June 5, I, 122–23n.
5. *RFC* June 5, I, 122.
6. *RFC* June 5, I, 123.
7. Pierce notes, *RFC* June 5, I, 129.
8. *RFC* June 16, I, 250.
9. *RFC* June 19, I, 314–15.
10. *RFC* June 20, I, 335.
11. *RFC* June 27, I, 437.
12. *RFC* July 23, II, 88.
13. *RFC* July 23, II, 90.
14. *RFC* July 23, II, 88–89.
15. *RFC* July 23, II, 89.
16. *RFC* July 23, II, 90.
17. *RFC* July 23, II, 92.
18. *RFC* July 23, II, 92.
19. *RFC* July 23, II, 92–93.
20. *RFC* July 23, II, 93–94.
21. *RFC* August 31, II, 475–76.
22. *RFC* August 31, II, 476–77.
23. *RFC* August 31, II, 476.
24. *RFC* August 30, II, 468.
25. *RFC* August 30, II, 469.
26. *RFC* August 30, II, 468–69.

27. *RFC* August 30, II, 468.
28. *RFC* August 30, II, 468–69.
29. *RFC* August 30, II, 469.
30. *RFC* August 31, II, 475.
31. *RFC* August 31, II, 475.
32. *RFC* August 31, II, 477.
33. *RFC* August 31, II, 477.
34. *RFC* August 30, II, 469.
35. *RFC* August 6, II, 189.
36. *RFC* August 31, II, 478.
37. *RFC* September 10, II, 559–61.
38. *RFC* September 10, II, 560.
39. *RFC* September 10, II, 562.
40. *RFC* September 10, II, 563.
41. *RFC* September 10, II, 561.
42. *RFC* September 10, II, 563; September 13, II, 608–609, 665–66.
43. King notes, *RFC* June 20, I, 349.
44. *RFC* June 5, I, 121.
45. *RFC* June 5, I, 122.
46. *RFC* June 11, I, 202.
47. *RFC* June 11, I, 202–203.
48. *RFC* June 11, I, 203; July 23, II, 87.
49. *RFC* August 6, II, 188.
50. *RFC* August 30, II, 468.
51. *RFC* September 10, II, 557–58.
52. *RFC* September 10, II, 558.
53. *RFC* September 10, II, 558.
54. *RFC* September 10, II, 558.
55. *RFC* September 10, II, 558–59.
56. *RFC* September 10, II, 559.
57. *RFC* September 15, II, 629.
58. *RFC* September 15, II, 630.
59. *RFC* September 15, II, 630.
60. *RFC* September 10, II, 559.
61. *RFC* September 15, II, 630–31.
62. *RFC* July 18, II, 46; August 6, II, 188.
63. *RFC* August 29, II, 454.
64. *RFC* August 29, II, 454.
65. *RFC* August 29, II, 454.
66. *RFC* August 29, II, 455.
67. *RFC* August 18, II, 324; August 30, II, 466.
68. *RFC* August 31, II, 479.
69. *RFC* August 31, II, 479.
70. *RFC* September 10, II, 560–61.
71. *RFC* September 15, II, 631.
72. *RFC* September 15, II, 632.
73. *RFC* September 15, II, 633.
74. *RFC* September 15, II, 637–40.
75. *RFC* September 10, II, 563–64; September 15, II, 632–33, 635–40.
76. George Washington to Henry Knox, August 19, 1787, in *RFC* III, 70.
77. *RFC* September 6, II, 524.
78. *RFC* September 15, II, 632.
79. *RFC* September 17, II, 645.
80. *RFC* August 31, II, 479.
81. *RFC* September 17, II, 645.

82. *RFC* September 17, II, 641–43.
83. McHenry notes, *RFC* September 17, II, 649–50; Nicholas Gilman to Joseph Gilman, September 18, 1787, *RFC* III, 82; William Pierce to St. George Tucker, September 28, 1787, *RFC* III, 100–101; *RFC 1987 Supplement*, September 15, 273.
84. *RFC* September 17, II, 643.
85. *RFC* September 17, II, 643, 647.
86. *RFC* September 17, II, 647.
87. *RFC* September 17, II, 644–47.
88. John Dickinson to George Read, September 15, 1787, *RFC* III, 81.
89. *RFC* September 17, II, 648.
90. *RFC* September 17, II, 666–67. An earlier draft of this letter in Gouverneur Morris's handwriting is reproduced in *RFC* September 12, II, 583–84.
91. James McHenry: "Anecdotes" (no date), *RFC* III, 85.
92. On the emerging Antifederalism at the Convention, see David J. Siemers, *The Antifederalists: Men of Great Faith and Forbearance* (Lanham, MD: Rowman & Littlefield, 2003), 39–72.
93. *RFC* June 23, I, 387.
94. *RFC* July 24, II, 100; July 25, II, 112.
95. *RFC* August 14, II, 291.
96. James Madison to Thomas Jefferson, September 6, 1787, *RFC* III, 77–78.
97. William Blount to John Gray Blount, July 19, 1787, in *RFC 1987 Supplement*, 175.
98. *RFC* August 8, II, 221.
99. *RFC* August 8, II, 221.
100. Pauline Maier, *Ratification: The People Debate the Constitution, 1787–1788* (New York: Simon and Schuster, 2010), 92.
101. Herbert J. Storing, ed., *The Complete Anti-Federalist* (Chicago: University of Chicago, 1981); Siemers, *The Antifederalists*.
102. Maier, *Ratification*; Patrick T. Conley and John P. Kaminski, eds., *The Constitution and the States: The Role of the Original Thirteen in the Framing and Adoption of the Federal Constitution* (Madison, WI: Madison House, 1988); David J. Siemers, *Ratifying the Republic: Antifederalists and Federalists in Constitutional Time* (Stanford, CA: Stanford University Press, 2002), 25–73.
103. U.S. House of Representatives, "Constitutional Amendments Not Ratified," http://www.house.gov/house/Amendnotrat.shtml (accessed July 26, 2011).
104. Abraham Lincoln, "Inaugural Address," March 4, 1861, *The American Presidency Project*, ed. John T. Woolley and Gerhard Peters, http://www.presidency.ucsb.edu/ws/?pid=25818 (accessed March 26, 2012).
105. Peter Radan, "Lincoln, the Constitution, and Secession," in *Secession as an International Phenomenon: From America's Civil War to Contemporary Separatist Movements* (Athens: University of Georgia Press, 2010), 56–75.

Chapter 18

1. *RFC* September 17, II, 648.
2. Benjamin Franklin To Mrs. Jane Mecom, September 20, 1787, *RFC* III, 98.
3. James McHenry, "Anecdotes" (no date), *RFC* III, 85.
4. *RFC* July 14, II, 11.
5. See remarks by Ellsworth, *RFC* July 19, II, 59; Morris, *RFC* July 24, II, 103–104; Charles Pinckney, *RFC* August 15, II, 298; Wilson and Madison, *RFC* June 2, II, 86; *RFC* August 18, II, 327; September 14, II, 616; Nathaniel Gorham, *RFC* August 28, II, 439.
6. Richard E. Neustadt, *Presidential Power and the Modern Presidents: The Politics of Leadership from Roosevelt to Reagan* (New York: Simon and Schuster, 1990), 29.
7. *RFC* August 17, II, 317.
8. Alexander Hamilton, James Madison, and John Jay, *The Federalist*, ed. Jacob E. Cooke (Middletown, CT: Wesleyan University Press, 1961), Number 51, 348–49.

9. George Athan Billias, *American Constitutionalism Heard Round the World, 1776–1989: A Global History* (New York: New York University Press, 2009). On the declining influence of the Constitution, see David S. Law and Mila Versteeg, "The Declining Influence of the United States Constitution," *New York University Law Review* 87:3 (June 2012): 762–858.
10. David Brian Robertson, *Federalism and the Making of America* (Abingdon, UK, and New York: Routledge, 2011), 169–71.

INDEX

Adair, Douglass, 13
Adams, John, 6, 32, 131, 146
Affordable Care Act (2010), 205
African-Americans, 119, 178–91, 235
agency, 81–83, 96, 116, 121, 123
agriculture. *See* farms, farmers and agriculture
Al Qaeda, 215
ambition, 13, 18, 26, 28, 49, 52, 55–56, 69, 73, 76,
    101, 110–11, 114, 132, 167, 206, 230, 232,
    234, 269n68
amendment, process of in the Constitution, 65,
    221–23
amendments to the Constitution, *See*
    Constitution, U.S., amendments
American Revolution, 39, 41, 62, 68, 100, 167,
    200, 208, 214
Americans, nature of, 40–42, 53
Anderson, Thornton, 12
Annapolis Convention, 5, 57
Anti-Federalists, 11, 32, 70, 157, 175, 214, 227–28
appointments, executive and judicial, 3, 50–51, 99,
    106, 116, 124, 130, 139–40, 145, 209, 285n135
army, 206–9, 224
Arthur, Chester Alan, 147
Articles of Confederation, 19, 25, 27, 30, 36,
    40–41, 58, 61–63, 121, 150, 164, 173, 193,
    218, 220–21, 232
assembly, freedom of, 158
attainder, 155, 287n62
authority and power, national government,
    15–17, 19, 55, 57, 59–60, 64, 69, 73, 81, 164,
    176, 224, 232, 289n28
  ambiguous division of national and state
    authority, 163, 204, 206, 214, 224
  difficulty of using, 233–34
  economic, 192–205, 231
  elastic, 173–74
  enumerated powers, 163–64, 172–73, 176
  incremental reforms, 69, 71–72, 76, 99, 69,
    272n29

link to Congressional apportionment,
    60, 178
military, 206–14
  need to strengthen, 8, 63, 69, 74, 145, 178
  opportunity to strengthen, 36
  redistribution, constraints on, 194, 197–98
  regulation, expansion of, 205
  threat to small and economically vulnerable
    states, 68
  use of force against a state, 64–65, 72, 165,
    169, 209, 238
authority and power, state government, 163, 166,
    176, 190, 192, 206, 231–32
  ambiguous division of national and state,
    163, 171–73, 204, 206, 214,
    224, 232
  prohibited powers, 173, 194–95, 198–200
  states retain "numerous and indefinite"
    powers, 176

Bailyn, Bernard, 10, 13
Baldwin, Abraham
  authority and power, national, 98
  slave trade, 187
  stronger national government, 7
Baltimore, 198
Bank of the United States, 176, 204
bankruptcy, 192, 201
Barbary pirates, 27, 262n7
Beard, Charles A., 12–13
Beck, Glenn, 10
Bedford, Gunning Jr., 231
  authority and power, national, broad, 172
  Connecticut Compromise, 102–3
  delegates, motives of, 26
  national government, strengthening, 36
  presidential term, 134
  veto, executive, 142
  veto, national of state laws, 166–67
  Virginia Plan, motives behind, 101

Sherman, Roger (*continued*)
  slave, evading the use of the term, 188–89
  states as root of Confederation problems, 100
  states' rights, 86–87
  states' self-defense, 72, 76
  states, value of, 71
  taxes on slave imports, 189
  taxes, broad national power, 193
  taxing authority, proposes limiting scope of
    national, 194
  term limits, 55
  three-fifths compromise, 184
  treaty-making, 213–14
  veto, executive, 142–44
  veto, joint executive-judicial, 143
  veto, national of state laws, 167
  vice president, 139
  war power, 212
ships and shipping, 27, 29, 182, 187, 196–97, 207
Sinai agreements (1975), 216
slaves and slavery, 8, 11, 17, 29–30, 33, 47, 60, 89, 92,
    106, 163, 172, 178–91, 208, 229, 231, 233, 238
  and Congressional representation, 178–85
  compromise on slavery and trade, 188–89
  divides nation, 99–100
  evasion of using the word "slave", 180, 184–85,
    188–90, 236, 293n90
  fugitive slaves, 189–90, 293n90
  slave revolts, 188
  slave trade, 8, 10, 14, 25, 30, 180, 184–89,
    223–24
South (region), 8, 28–30, 89–92, 100, 122,
    125, 163, 166, 172, 178–80, 182–88, 190,
    194 –97, 204, 215, 228, 231
  conditional nationalists, 16, 60, 231
  conflict with New England, 29
South Carolina, 28, 30–31, 158, 186–89,
    197, 201, 208
  and Madison's expected coalition, 59–60
  delegation to Convention, 16, 24, 32, 172,
    185, 229
  ratification, 227
sovereignty, 164, 166, 192
  indivisible, 68, 71, 74, 168–69, 174
  shared state and national, 71–72, 163, 168–71,
    174–75, 233
  state, 61, 73, 75–78, 100, 170–71, 218
Spaight, Richard Dobbs
  president, selection, 130
  presidential term, proposes extending, 136
  president, selection by Congress, 126
  Senate, selection by state legislatures, 95
  Senators, terms, 113
Spain, 27, 31, 183, 211
speculators, 200
speech, freedom of, 158
spending, government, 26, 118, 205, 207

state authority and power, *See* authority and
  power, state government
state governments, 6, 26–27, 38–39, 41, 44, 59,
    61–62, 75, 111, 116, 159, 169–70, 172, 177, 192
  as checks on national government, 96
  as root of Confederation problems, 61–63, 100
  as threat to nation, 68–69
  authority and prerogatives, 70
  authority, encroachment on national,
    62, 71, 74, 77
  commerical authority, 27–28, 198
  constitutions, 44, 62, 109, 156–57, 172, 219, 222
  courts, 23, 70, 72, 149, 154, 167–68, 225
  criticisms of, 28–29, 59, 68–70, 99–100
  governors and executive branch, 23, 113, 124,
    189, 209, 225
  ineffectiveness of governments in
    large states, 70–71
  legislatures, 6–7, 23, 48, 94, 96, 111–13, 116,
    131, 171, 179–80, 209, 217–20, 222, 224–25
  military, 28
  opposition to Constitution, 71
  insurrection and domestic violence, states
    request national assistance in, 208–9
  Senate, U.S., defensive power for states in 97,
    103–4
  senates, state, 62–63
  tax authority, 193
  threats from Virginia Plan, 69
  value of strong, 71
  See also authority and power, state
    government; federalism
states
  admission of new, 65, 72, 86, 90–92, 202, 224,
    228
  conflicting interests, 8, 25–26, 28–32
  interstate conflict, 150, 169
  rights and value, 69–71, 86–87, 96, 176
  self-defense, 98
  sovereignty, 100
  large, 58–59, 87, 101, 124, 166, 169
  large, coalition of, 76–78, 86–87, 89, 98–99,
    166–67, 196
  large versus small, 29–30, 84–85, 98, 102, 196,
    202, 267n35
  small and economically vulnerable, 16–17, 26,
    30, 58, 67–69, 86, 101, 238
Strong, Caleb
  complexity of the Constitutional system, 226
  House origination of spending and revenue
    bills, 109
  presidential electors, compexity, 126
  Senate, apportionment of seats, 104
successive filtrations, 7–8, 41–42, 83
suffrage, 53, 119
  African-Americans, 190
  restricted to property owners, 49